Ron Churchill

THE PARIS INTERVIEW

AVENUE A PRESS
New York
1995

In memory of Jerry Garcia

Thanks for being there,
When we didn't know what's where;
Thanks for taking us along,
When we were still fearless and strong;
Thinking of you, Jerry, as we gather here tonight,
Counting shows by candlelight.

Manufactured in the United States of America
A B C D E

Library of Congress Catalog card number: 95-60622

ISBN: 0-964-24550-7 — ISBN: 0-964-24558-2 (preview)

AVENUE A PRESS
147 Avenue A
New York, NY 10009

AveAnyc@aol.com

A great many of us wish to die in our sleep; or, if on a battlefield, to die as if we 'never knew what hit us.' I, however, prefer to meet my end in a not so instantaneous fashion—At least a split second of warning, I ask—So that I might experience it... feel it...look at it...and possibly even escape it!

Le Comte de la Chapelle de Saint-Martin

(A May morning in Paris)

MARK *A Million Words*—Is that an appropriate title for a book? I mean, you *do* want people to read it. Voulez-vous avoir des lecteurs?

CHARLES Pourquoi croyez-vous que je l'ai reduit mon livre à un million de mots?

MARK The reason you are cutting it down to a million? I don't know; perhaps you are no longer being paid by the word, especially if it's *not* a happy ending?

CHARLES A *happy* ending. Isn't that a contradiction in terms?

MARK Not according to Hollywood, sir. And Hollywood is *never* out of touch with reality. No understatements like *A Million Words*; only overflows and overloads.

CHARLES And...over there! What time is your flight back to New York, my boy?

MARK Noon-ish.

CHARLES I would like you to promise me something before you go: if anything should happen to me, I shall need you to come back to Paris to destroy the notes!

ONE

WHY—So simple a word, yet so complex in its meaning. Uncle Charles told me it is the single most important quest of mankind—the foundation upon which all humanity is built! Then why do I throw my arms in the air when I add a pronoun to it, as in *Why Me?*

From time to time through the dimensions of time, the unexpected happens. At least I didn't expect it. I mean, had I any inkling of the predicament I'm in now, that weekend in Paris would *not* have been so casually spent; so *aimlessly* spent. Damn that Charles! Either he was the finest actor that ever lived, or the most decisive man on the face of the earth—or was it impulsive? I don't know. Sometimes, I even think I had unknowingly contributed to such an end, by simply walking into something that was impossible to walk out of.

It's been ten minutes since my plane took off from the London City Airport. Any minute now we'll be hitting the turbulence of the English Channel. It wasn't so long ago, timewise, that I found myself on a decidedly different airplane to Paris—the Concorde from New York, to be more exact. No, I didn't pay for the ticket, nor could I have afforded to. It was sort of a graduation present, albeit a sudden one, from a man whom I've always known as Charles Martin. Or, in retrospect, a man I still know so little about.

Uncle Charles is not a real uncle but an old friend of my late grandfather's. Last March, Charles gave me an invitation to visit him in Paris, though it was supposed to have been for the Fourth-of-July weekend instead of May-morial Day. See, I had been flirting with the idea of broadening the scope of my research project on economic forecasting into a thesis on forecasting in general. The goal was to combine all the elements—the quantitative, the qualitative, and the speculative—into a possible unifying theory. And Charles was supposed to give me some guidance.

Everyone is familiar with forecasting to some extent. We do it everyday, and accurately too, when it's based on our own routines. But things get trickier, and more subjective, when we try to predict the actions of others—will she or will she not bring fruitcakes again for the holidays? Just as tricky, too, is predicting the financial markets. The forecasting methods used to that end are much too quantitative—resulting in conclusions that are, at times, even farther from reality.

Is there any way to bridge the gap, I often wondered—to inject scientific methods into the fortune-teller and psychic methods into the computer—even just for my sanity's sake. I mean, everyday, I find myself torn between the intuitive and the analytical. Take my views on baseball: at times I'm so dead set on such and such a player being a total stiff that, even if he hit 40 home runs in a season, I still wouldn't use him in the clutch. Of course there'd be other occasions where I feel I can manage a whole team from just the statistics alone. I don't even have to meet the players, or be on planet earth, for that matter.

To my surprise, Charles was unusually receptive to my chasing after the flyball-in-the-sky when we last met in New York. Besides enlightening me academically, he offered some emotional support as well: "Be angry," he told me. "But never execute such anger, and never execute *on* anger." Words of wisdom from Dr. Charles—the calmest, most composed man I know. The most old-worldly, too. Biased as it may sound, Uncle Charles is as sophisticated and scholarly as they come—eminently qualified to teach anybody a thing or two. But what's particularly impressive about his career, the thing that made him stand out from the rest, was his training in a variety of disciplines. He studied science and mathematics at the École Normale in Paris, studied and taught classics and history at Oxford, and was supposedly an ultra-radical philosophy professor at the Sorbonne until the 1968 student uprising. Then, from the end of the 1960s until his retirement a few years ago, he was a private banker in Geneva—and a very secretive one at that. I didn't even know about it until my sophomore year in college, the year Grandpa passed away; and Charles, as a favor to him, made a trip to New York to help me out with some legal and personal matters. We had since become closer, Charles and I, but that only meant that he had become even more a man of surprises. In fact, the way I was summoned to Paris that weekend was through a call from my travel agent. I didn't even know he *knew* my travel agent.

Before Charles had contacted me, I had already agreed to help my friend Edwin sail the *Slipknot!*, his big old sloop. Actually it'd be more like slaving. What usually happens is that Edwin, trying to act like some big-shot commodore, would go around and scream out a bunch of commands at everyone. But it rarely works. I dismiss his orders with the ease I dismiss my home-work assignments. Only thing is, sooner or later, I would end up going about doing what I've been told—less out of obedience than necessity—for if I don't do it, nobody would. Like all those times when nobody else on board wanted to operate the radio; or those other occasions when I just couldn't allow our spinnaker to get ripped up into early retirement as a giant, unscented tie-dyed shirt.

Edwin's boat was moored off City Island, just north of Manhattan. That Memorial weekend we were hoping to sail out to Block Island, way on the other end of Long Island Sound past Montauk. It was to be our first major cruise of the year. The spring sailing season had been a total washout. God, the rain we had had. Whatever happened to the Greenhouse Effect? Or was that merely another phase of it—monsoon one spring and drought the next! But the forecast for that weekend was supposed to have been excellent, so I was kind of excited about hitting the waves.

Unlike people watching or window shopping, sailing isn't very accessible to most New Yorkers, especially to those who have to work and go to school. That was the reason I felt I needed a sailing fix, and why when I first got my Concorde ticket to Paris from Uncle Charles, I wasn't nearly as excited as I otherwise might have been. But, what the hell, it had been a while since I was last in Europe, and a weekend on the boat isn't *too* different from a weekend at home in Manhattan; the difference being that when you really feel like throwing up on a boat, you simply stick your head out overboard—just like that kid in *Captains Courageous*—provided that you at least be sober enough to know which side of the boat to go to, so the wind won't slam the puke right back in your face.

My flight to Paris was on a Thursday afternoon, but it wasn't much of a problem skipping half a day's work as I was already granted that Friday off. My boss was out of town, too, in Connecticut. Then he was going to his house on Nantucket. He claimed it was going to be a working vacation. *Every* vacation of his is a working vacation; and every vacation I take is a complete waste of time. Now, I don't want to give people the wrong idea and have them rush to the airport for the next flight to New York—a place of four-day work weeks and eight days of pay. No way! People work their asses off in this city. Even me.

It had been only a week since I got my MBA in Finance, two weeks since my last final, so things had been pretty hectic. Just picture yourself putting in full days at the office, then dragging your ass to class for a few more hours of trance; and finally, cramming like hell in May to prepare for the whoops-I-missed-the-midterm-so-it's-100 percent-of-the-grade finals.

All right, enough complaining for now.

I woke up real early that Thursday morning, so early I even beat the shock jocks to the air. Rare it was for my sleep to be sandwiched between the last grimaces of Letterman and the first rantings of Howard and the I-Man. But that night was an exception since I already knew the next day was going to be a short one—Paris being six hours ahead, and therefore, less need for my regular seven hours.

To get to work everyday I normally walk: from an old walk-up on Seventy-eighth off Madison to a modern high-rise on Sixth Avenue in the Fifties—half-an-hour tops. That morning, since I was carrying my garment bag, I took a cab. It wasn't so tough flagging one down as it was still quite early. But in mid-town at rush hour, it's looksy but no tooksy!

I was working in the New York office of the Alpha Group, a management consulting firm. I had been with them for over three years: first as a research analyst, then working almost exclusively for Warren Rhoades, one of the firm's founders. Besides consulting, Warren was also involved in many outside projects, sometimes as a critic of corporate America, other times as a lobbyist—spokesman is a better word. My duty, if it can be pinpointed, was to help him work at peak efficiency—from number crunching on the toilet seat in our men's room, to clipboard-and-pencil fact-findings on the assembly line. Occasionally, I even attended presentations in the corporate boardrooms. It was interesting work, my job. The money was good, too; but not outrageous. Hell, you can be a junior associate on Wall Street, or better yet, a junior asshole's here, and make more money Xeroxing prospectuses; or, you can do what some of the other people I had gone to school with are doing: sitting at their computer terminals and trading their currencies, bonds, or cow dung.

Anyone who thinks that half-days at the office are like summer-hours at an ad agency is in for a surprise. It is rush, rush, rush as I rush to fix and polish up my portion of a presentation where Warren had already made his comments and corrections. In fact, I was sitting in my office with a new draft of "Growth Planning Strategies for the 1990s, XYZ, Inc." when Connie, our secretary, walked in with some bad news.

"Mark, Anthea Benson is on Warren's line. She might have to cancel Washington next week—emergency board meeting in San Francisco."

"Bummer! Did you ask her about her backup?"

"No, you talk to her! You are the one working on the Trade Advisory Committee."

"Good morning, Dr. Benson. It's Mark Vermont, how are you? Um, what of Jerry Warfield?... Oh good, because if Warfield can't make it, then it would look real awkward.... Also, just a reminder from Warren, the speeches are to be in lay person's language, and all speakers should refrain from pushing their own ideas too hard.... That's right, Warren's got the other rim; the other ocean, rather. And he's got a whole weekend to stare into the Atlantic for an opening line.... Hahaha, I'll tell him you said that.... Yeah, best of luck to you, too. And say hello to the foggy Golden Gate for me.... Whew, tragedy narrowly averted!"

"That was cute, Mark: say hello to the Golden Gate for me, say hello to the cable cars."

"Oh, be quiet, you. Just leave me in peace, please."

"Not so fast. Here, say hello to more mail for you, too."

"Rats!"

"FYI, Mark, there *is* such a thing called the letter opener."

"I prefer ripping—faster that way."

"Showing your frustrations again? Sexually frustrated lately?"

"Listen, when I need an analyst, I'll pay for one!"

"Mark?"

"What now, Stanzee?"

"I can't find the spread sheet tables that I'm supposed to merge on to your Industry Trends report."

"Jesus, what am I gonna do with you, Connie?" Now it was my turn to bust *her* chops a little: "The other day, you couldn't find charts from the dBase; today, you forget how to import Lotus tables; and tomorrow, you are gonna walk in here and tell me you can't find the files on all your boyfriends. Whata'ya gonna do, Constance, just relegate yourself to doing Warren's itineraries and expense reports for the rest of your life?"

"Ouuuu, viciooooous!" She liked to say that about twice a day, usually to keep me in line. "Just for that, Mark, I'm not going to order you any plants next week!"

"Whoopee! See if I care...What were you thinking of getting me?"

"Let's see, I was going to be nice and get you an areca palm and a phoenix palm. But seeing how mean you are to me, you'll be lucky if you even get any desktop aglaoema or anthurium."

"Yuuuck! Sounds horrible. Please don't give me any of those awful aneurysms. Whata'ya getting Warren, by the way, Miss Whore-of-Culture?"

"Two huge specimen bamboo palms with ivy, and a Ming aralia."

"All right, Stanzee, let's make a deal. Give me back the palms and I'll help you with the database. *Unless,* that is, if you want me to get Ulysses to help ya?"

"Mark, please. *I* was helping Ulysses with *his* homework this morning."

"Oh, so that's why he came knocking on *my* door right afterwards. Hey, Ulysses, come in here for a sec." Ulysses was one of the students in our co-op program. Hard working but very high strung; even more hyper than I was at his age. At least I took mellowness breaks. But not Ulysses. Take his feet: they never stop moving.

"Hey, what's with you, Marco. Now you wanta see me, now you don't."

"My apologies, Ulysses. I was in the middle of making an important check list when you knocked. What seems to be the trouble?"

"No trouble. Just Connie trying to confuse the hell out of me."

"Liar!"

"Hey, all I did was to ask her about a word problem. Then she started going off on things like 'of' means multiplying and 'ratio' means quotient and 'what' means 'x' and...give it a rest, girl!"

"You forgot product," Connie pointed at him. "*And* difference!"

"What is the difference?" Ulysses threw up his hands. "Or according to you: x=minus!"

"He's got you there, Connie," I laughed.

"Spare me, Mark," she snapped back.

"Spare me a little, too, why don't you," Ulysses said to Connie. "Hell, the only product *I* know is that I'm a product of the Bronx. It's a war zone up there, man. How many other places *you* know have names like Fort Apache, Gun Hill Road and Cannon Lane?"

"You forgot the Bronx Bombers," I added.

"There you go, bro. Look, if I want people to mess with me, I can just go walk around in my neighb'hood. Take last night, this stupid ass from the Diamonds, he tried to goof on my office clothes again. If he was alone I would've smacked him. That fool makes me sick, man. He struts around all day trying to act cool. Every time I see him, he's got his arms out and back arched and is uttering shit like, 'Yo, you know what I'm *sa*-ying.' No, I guess I don't, knucklehead!"

"Now, don't get agitated, Yul," I said, shaking my head. "Just calm down, pull up a chair, and I'll give you a word problem or two that we can work on. You want to be a Navy SEAL, right?"

"Yeah, they're the best!"

"Okay. Say a couple of SEALs from the βeta detachment are on a clandestine reconnaissance mission behind enemy lines...." I took a little coffee break and made up a problem dealing with distance, rate and time, and ways to solve for each. Ulysses grasped it pretty well. Interest, sometimes, is more than half the battle.

My Concorde was scheduled to leave at 1 P.M. from Kennedy. It being an international flight, passengers were advised to check in two hours before departure. So I gave myself a reasonable start... forty-five minutes. Just kidding; though I have made it to LaGuardia in half that time. No, I actually left the office at around 11:30, after putting in some quality time in one of our conference rooms organizing documents. Our main conference room, I tell you, our once immaculate state-of-the-art communication center of a conference room had now so many boxes of documents in there that it could have easily passed for a storage room. It was certainly dark enough, with papers piled so high up the window sill that it was blocking out all the sunlight. Whatever happened to the computer age?

So anyway, I was pretty happy to have charged almost four hours of work that morning. Employee utilization rate—very important in consulting. That's how we make money. Allow me to talk about consulting for a bit, or at least what I know of it.

Management consulting is a growing industry, one which the Americans still dominate, and are likely to continue to reign supreme for years to come. This is partly due to the tremendous growth in Information consulting by the big international accounting firms. Our firm belongs more to the old school: we tackle mainly strategic and organizational issues—the big picture, so to speak.

Unlike Wall Street, which is perceived as Greed Center, USA; the consultants actually thrive on intellectual challenge and stimulation. At our best, we act like a rapid deployment force—compressing what normally would be months of corporate planning into weeks, even days. But in most cases, we are sort of like high-level temps. The management hires us, gives us a period of time to look into a situation, we deliver, and then we're out of there, until next time, hopefully. The innovations we have set up for many of our clients have been noteworthy; even more impressive, I think, are some of the recommendations our clients have declined to implement. Too big a shock to the system, they say.

When the consultants are good, they are a combination of doctor-lawyer-accountant all rolled into one. Frequently, after a long assignment, the consultants would know more about a company than many of the company's own managers, even the CEO. Warren, my boss, is such a person. He can take a complicated matter, say R&D accountability, comb away its layers of misconceptions, and arrive at a revealing solution. Quite often, the problems he has been asked to solve have turned out to be consequences of weaknesses and foul-ups elsewhere in the organization. (The problem, my dear Ike, lies not in the penicillin or rubber but in its host!)

That Thursday morning, and on and off since April, I had been involved in an assignment for a conglomerate based in Connecticut. The Alpha Group was asked to formulate a growth strategy for the 1990s for that company. There were about ten consultants on the engagement, which was a sizable undertaking. Besides a formal presentation at the end, we also give periodic progress reports to the client in a series of joint review sessions. That following week was supposed to be one of them. So we'd been pretty busy. Generally speaking, we believe the best results are achieved when the client side is working with us. However, it's not always possible. Frequently the outside consultants are met with resistance and hostility—from managers and employees alike. To many of them, seeing consultants today means losing their jobs tomorrow.

Citylink, our radio car service, was right on time. I had called them earlier that morning and ordered a car using our account number. It was easier and surer than hailing a taxi: an air-conditioned Town Car arrives and waits in front of your building. You simply sign the voucher and go. Warren might even pay for it. He knows that on the many nights I've worked late, I've never taken our car service home. So the firm is still way ahead. Which reminds me: Mitch, a poker buddy of mine, is a young sales executive. He travels a lot, but always takes buses and cabs to and from airports because he's not wasteful. Then one day, a colleague came up to him and said: Mitch, your car expense is way below budget. If it remains at this level, they are going to cut into your budgeted amount in the future. So for the remainder of the year, Mitch ordered expensive stretch limousines to bring his cost back up to budget. Corporate America is a strange a place.

The drive to the airport was reasonably smooth. The Long Island Expressway, or LIE, or the Distressway, as we some times call it, was better than I had imagined. Of course, it was still Thursday. Just wait till Friday afternoon, when the summer house crowd would start their Hamptons pilgrimage. If the coming summer was going to be anywhere near the humidity of last year, then the LIE would absolutely solidify its reputation as the world's longest parking lot.

I got to Kennedy Airport surprisingly quick. Mid-day is a good time to catch a flight there. But no airport is slower during the late afternoon-early evening rush, when the just arrived international passengers mingle with the ones about to depart. Man, the hours I've sat in the damn traffic and sweated it out.

"Welcome to Air France, Mr. Vermont..." The check-in was such a breeze that I even allowed them to check my bag. Maybe I had wanted to act like a gentleman, or at least not wanting to be seen as an uncooperative Yankee troublemaker. Still, business flyers know this: always take your baggage with you whenever possible. Keep hounding them even if they don't at first let you; ask them to check the capacity. Not only do you save time upon arrival, but it also saves you from the nightmare of being trapped in your hotel room in Akron while your baggage is on its way to Peoria.

Ascending the elevator to the Concorde lounge, an elegant receptionist greeted me and pointed me toward the bar at the other end of the room. The waiting lounge was luxurious and welcoming. Perhaps it was due to a higher concentration of people present. There was leather sofas and chairs neatly arranged around some coffee tables, sort of like the lobby of the Hilton near my office, except there were magazines all over the place. There were more magazines in that room than in all the shrink joints in all the world.

When I spotted some trays of canapés in front of the mirrored bar, it struck me that, save half a bagel, I hadn't eaten a thing all day, which was also the reason that I declined any alcohol from the hostess. While munching on some shrimp, I told her I was kind of surprised at how casual some of the passengers looked, that I figured there'd be more business folks on these flights.

"Most of our flyers are business people," she said. "Many of them have already boarded."

"I guess what's left are rich cowboys and amateurs like myself."

"Is this your first Concorde flight?"

"Yeah, *la première fois*," I admitted reluctantly.

"Hope you enjoy it then."

"Thanks." I walked over to a small window and took a quick peek at the plane. I was amazed at how long it was, with a row of tiny windows that became mere dots toward the tail end. The wings of the Concorde resembled that of a jet fighter more than a Boeing 747. The wings were triangle-shaped with engines way in the back—sort of like the type of wings you fold for your paper airplanes. In fact, the Concorde could almost be seen as a long and skinny white bird with a threatening needle-like beak. It was tilted slightly downward from just beyond the window glass, as if to be possibly seeking me out for lunch.

Moments later, when I turned around, I saw a few executive types whisking by: not looking anywhere, not stopping for a cocktail, not smiling, nothing. One of them, a field marshall looking fella, almost ran me over while reading a report he was carrying. So they were the regular Concordians. And my driver thought *I* was late.

My first impression of the Concorde's interior was a disappointment. The seats were mostly occupied, so I didn't get a whole side to myself. I also could do without the seat-color being so red, but my biggest complaint was the narrowness of the aisle—it was a tight squeeze—a pain in the ass when others wanted to get by. Yes, the only difference between the rush hour commutes on the LaGuardia Air Shuttle and the Concorde was the ticket price.

I sat down toward the back of the compartment on an aisle seat, next to a man of thirty-something. The lounge hostess was right: most passengers *were* business people. And wouldn't you know it, that graying, field marshall type who I had almost collided with back in the lounge was hogging the two seats diagonally across the aisle.

The takeoff is always the highlight of a flight, and, let me tell you, I've never heard a more thunderous thrust of engines than that Concorde moments before it took off. The acceleration was unbelievable, as if I hitched a ride with Mario Andretti on the Indianapolis Speedway.

"What a blast off!" I said to the guy next to me, my earlier gripes somewhat diminishing.

"We're going to make a sharp turn then reduce speed," he said.

"Wouldn't it be dangerous to slow down this early?"

"No, you'll just feel a slight braking sensation. This is the only airplane in the world that could gain altitude on just two of its four engines working; it just climbs at a less steep angle. The speed reduction is to comply with the noise complaints of local residents."

"Yeah, come to think of it, there was a major fuss over the Concorde's noise pollution when it all began." Although I grew up in Port Washington, on the less affected North Shore of Long Island, I did remember how the Port Authority, at first, wouldn't allow the Concorde to land, till finally the Court stepped in.

"The slow-down only lasts a few minutes," the guy reassured me. "When we pass the Long Island shores, the noise and speed will pick up again; and as we approach the Atlantic, we'll be supersonic."

"I feel like I'm in the starship Enterprise," I said. "Warp Factor 10, Scotty!"

We joked around a bit as I learned of some engineering feats that enabled the Concorde to fly like an ego. There was the advanced heating system that could process the extremely cold air from the atmosphere and bring it up to cabin temperature. There was the so-called body frame inside the main frame which prevented the plane from splitting apart at high speeds. And last but not least, there was the rotating nose: it must be monitored meticulously, since it only takes a few degrees to change a normal descent into a total, almost uncontrollable nose-dive.

As for the ride itself, the Concorde's high flying altitude, ten miles up from the sea, helps to eliminate most of the turbulence. Also, it is pressurized at about five thousand feet—as compared to seven thousand feet for regular jets. The lower the pressure, the more comfort and less fatigued you'd feel. How do you think the Denver Broncos win their home games at Mile High Stadium?

So anyway, Luke was the name of the fella sitting next to me—a computer guy from Massachusetts. Yet with his yellow tinted glasses and his low pony-tail, he looked more like a record executive. Luke had a company that specialized in developing scientific application softwares, for workstations and stuff. He was going to spend a day in Paris meeting with some software graphics people before proceeding down to Nice. While Nice, being in the South of France, is noted for its glamour; on its outskirts is a place called Sophia, a high-tech area that's sort of the French Silicon Valley. Luke was going to meet up there with his new partner, who had been attending the Cannes Film Festival. His partner, another programming whiz, had just retired from a computer company before reaching middle age, "cashing in on his $30 million worth of stocks along the way." He and Luke were about to combine resources to work on programs related to artificial intelligence—very frontier stuff!

I don't know that much about computers, just some of the basics, such as Lotus, dBase, and word-processing. I'd like to know more, but it's changing too fast: the interactive operating systems, the new generation of chips—hell, not only do you need managers of technology, but managers to constantly inform those managers. "Luke, to be honest, lots of people view computers as a necessary evil. Once they're used to a particular system, they hate to try something new, even if it's better. There is a tremendous fear of things going wrong, of losing all the data; not everyone is like you."

But Luke was pretty humble about his computer know-how. "What are the three most important things in real estate?" he asked.

"Location...price, um—"

"Location, location, location," he cut in. Then he asked: "What are the three most important things in computing?"

"Bill Gates, Bill Gates, Bill Gates?"

"No, it's backup! Backup!! Backup!!! Nothing is more important than backing up!"

I laughed, but nodded in total agreement. I told Luke I wished I had said that to Connie back at the office. Boy, did I wish I could have said that to her that morning. Partly due to her naggings and manipulations, I was getting as confused as she was on mail merges and graphic links.

What Luke just said, of course, was absolutely true. Storing the content of your data and programs onto a backup memory source should become almost automatic, even if you have loss retrieval software. It made me feel better that Luke had also learned the hard way: "All those times at MIT when I just sat there in uncontrollable tears after losing chunks of my programs. Even a million dollars couldn't cheer me up. It was as if somebody had died, only it was ten times worse." Luke was not joking; there was a look of deep sadness on his face. Like inadvertently throwing away a winning lottery ticket, you get a little pissed off every time you think about it. Though fortunately for Luke, the adversities turned into blessings: "Each time I got wiped out, I found ways to creatively improve upon the original. Perhaps it was those character-building setbacks that are now paying for this plane ticket to France."

In a strange way, despite the Concorde's outrageous ticket price, everyone on board seemed to be equally treated: the same service, the same designer souvenirs and so on. No first class movie moguls looking down at business class managers, no standby airline folks maneuvering their way into first class. Everything was professional, refined, and civilized. The attentive flight attendants, despite knowing many passengers by name, were extremely courteous to everyone.

I was also starting to appreciate the aircraft itself. Perhaps it was due to the things I had learned from Luke, or simply the thrill of something far out, like observing the Mach Meter at the front of the compartment that showed how fast the plane was flying. The top reading was Mach 2.2—more than twice the speed of sound. Yet except for the window glass being slightly warm to the touch, due to the heat being generated at such high speeds, traveling at twice the speed of sound was as easy as getting a sunburn.

My seatmate Luke, however, seemed to be pre-occupied with other thoughts. It was almost like a religious experience to him: "When I look up into the sky, I can see a hint of dark space—dark infinite space—the area only traveled by astronauts and Superman." I turned my head toward him in amusement. Then he said, "When I look down, I can visualize the curvatures of our planet Earth."

"Wait, this I've got to see." I peered outside the window. It got darker all right. But even in total brightness I would have found it hard to see any globe-like curves. I mean, you can certainly say the earth is round, and you are not wrong to say that the sky outside the window looks dark blue enough, purple enough, to be almost at the upper reaches of the stratosphere, which is about where space begins.

"Well, whatever you say, Luke Skywatcher. Sure you're not a California angel cake?" Boy, them spaced out silicon junkies, next thing you know, he's going to tell me he can hear the sonic boom, which can only be heard from the ground. Or better yet, he's going to tell me that he had just sighted the Great Wall of China, the only man-made structure claimed to be visible from the moon. It was a good thing he didn't say that, for I would have quickly downgraded his multi-million dollar company and sold his stocks short. Any twelve-year-old can tell you that China is on the other side of the Atlantic, and there is no way in hell you can see it from where we were.

It wasn't too long after takeoff that the attendants began working the aisles. Lunch, or *déjeuner*, was served on a table setting of thin-to-the-bone china with white-as-cloud linens. I ate some smoked salmon, followed by a very fresh cold lobster in a light white sauce, and finished with a fruit salad and some chocolate covered strawberries. The key to airplane food is to make the presentation look like the pictures you see on those gourmet frozen dinner boxes; yet, to have them taste fresh as hell—like Luke's courses of foie gras, lamb with chanterelles, and a Grand Marnier cake. There was to be no seafood for him. "I find it very hard to be eating fish at 75,000 feet over the Atlantic," he said. Yeah, like baby lambs can fly!

After lunch, I flipped through the glossy Air France *Atlas* and filled out the *Carte de Suggestion.* I had only good things to say about the aircraft and service. The narrow aisle was a necessary evil: it left the interior with more space for seating. Although my seat was not even the size of business class, it was well-contoured and comfortable, with ample leg room to stretch out. In all honesty, if you really want to live like those rich and famous champagne-dreams celebrities, you would definitely be more at home in a sleeperette seat aboard a jumbo jet, with an exotic flight crew to pamper to your every whim. Not to mention the extra hours of flying time for your filet mignons and Dom Pérignons.

Time flies when you're having fun, and time flies supersonically when you add a little rum. For about the time a regular jet takes to reach the Mississippi, we were already approaching Europe. The landing was less thrilling: one, I was already in the plane for three-and-a-half hours; and two, it was night time so there wasn't a hell of a lot to see out there. We did not fly over the lights of Paris.

As we were about to get off the plane, a male attendant appeared from the back cabin and had a quick chat with that field marshall looking guy from across the aisle. Apparently, that passenger was a regular. "The States is no place to get any work done during the Memorial Day Weekend," he said. "Every city is closed. It's four days down the drain!" Well, there are certainly enough countries in Europe for you to pick from, Herr Über Achiever. One of them is bound *not* to be on holiday. Perhaps Mr. Type-A was one of those high priced international lawyers, who wanted to show his clients that the thousands of dollars he would bill them over the holiday weekend was absolutely legitimate.

As excited as I was to be in Paris, I also felt some uneasiness; kind of unusual considering I had visited Paris on two previous occasions and was reasonably familiar with the city. Perhaps it was the emptiness and the coldness of the ultra-modern terminal that gave me a sense of foreboding, a sense of not knowing exactly what awaits in a foreign-languaged land.

"Mark, old boy! How kind of you to come on such short notice." It was the voice of Uncle Charles, in that distinguished English gentleman's accent of his. To my surprise, he had come to pick me up. When we had spoken two days earlier, he had told me to give him a ring from the airport. Instead, he was standing right in front of me with open arms.

"Nice to see you again, sir," I gave him a hug.

"I trust you had a pleasant flight?"

"What flight?" I deadpanned. "Oh, that! Not much longer than from City Island to Coney Island—with a light little lunch to boot."

"Yes, the food has indeed gotten lighter over the years. In the earlier days of the Concorde, we used to call it the 'World's most expensive three-martini lunch.'"

Uncle Charles, cracking me up right off the bat. We stood in the middle of a crowd and chatted a little. He told me that I had never looked more grown up. Blame it on the suit, I replied. For a man bordering on seventy, Charles was noticeably vibrant. His full head of whitish hair combed neatly back, his warm face tanned just enough to mask some of the wrinkles that I'd come to expect; but most assuring was his relaxed demeanor: sporting an old tweed jacket and a shirt with fray collar, he seemed completely at ease with himself. He *even* tried to help me with my bag.

Before we got going, I went to say good-bye to Luke. It turned out that Luke was about to take a taxi into the city, his request for a chauffeur had been made too late. But Charles insisted that Luke should come with us, that our car was just out the door.

A dark Saab convertible was on the ramp waiting for us. In the driver's seat, and playing a very loud stereo, was a girl flipping through a textbook. For some reason, whatever apprehensions I had felt earlier was lifted. It was no longer your parents picking you up from the airport at Thanksgiving.

"Luke, Mark, this is Alexandra Lachapelle."

"Hello, how do you do," she said, bouncing her head a little. She and Charles then exchanged a few words in French. I couldn't quite hear it over the loud music, but it was something about making two stops. Alexandra at first seemed a little upset. Then she said: "*Bon, on y va!*" and stepped on it.

Paris wasted no time in proclaiming itself the City of Light. The airport's disc-shaped International Terminal was lit up like a spaceship, appearing as if floating above ground. We quickly got onto the A1, the highway that leads into the city. Charles and Luke did most of the talking, mainly about aeronautics. The only time I made a comment was when they were talking about the Concorde's shifting center of gravity. I said that weight distribution is a concern in sailing as well. Like when you need people to sit on the higher side of the boat to counter the effects of heeling. But sometimes, when all the girls refuse to budge from the sunny and tanning side, you have no choice but to reduce sail. "Sexist!" Alexandra suddenly blurted out. Well, at least she knew some *important* words in English.

Charles then told us of the time when he and an American investor had a breakfast meeting in Paris. Then they hopped onto the Concorde for New York, got to Kennedy before 9 A.M. Eastern time, choppered up to the Pan Am building for three final hours of negotiations, and before the champagne was dry, Charles flew back to Paris that same day on the same Concorde flight we were just on—not to go to sleep in his own bed, but to appear at an important evening function. Uncle Charles, truly a member of the Supersonic Set! But for how long? That is the billion dollar question. "At this rate," Charles said, "the Concorde aeroplanes will be retired soon after the year 2000. Yet, as we speak, there is nothing on the drawing board that can replace them on time. If they don't start soon, the world may be forced to fly its passengers *subsonically* for years to come."

"That's outrageous!" I said. "How can we go back on progress like that, especially in the era of an international economy? Hell, the Concorde, not to take anything away from it, is pretty much decades-old technology. What about that space-shuttlish Tokyo Express?"

"It's not going to be built on time," Luke added. "It'll take years just to perfect the prototype."

I was furious on hearing that. Okay, if we don't make progress, then at least remain where we are. It's embarrassing to go backwards! Granted, I'm not speaking for my student-loan-loaded self, nor even for 99.44 percent of the population, but on a symbolic level, and for people who regularly use the Concorde, it's truly an outrage.

While we were bullshitting away, Alexandra had been driving at a torrid pace. I was sitting diagonally behind her so I was looking her way. She had dark blonde hair tied back with a red band, and wore a stripped jersey with a denim jacket over it. And, looking like a real Parisian, she had a polka-dot scarf tied loosely around her neck. Although I'm far more a New York City foot soldier than a car carrying liberal American, I've always been interested in people behind the wheel. That is, to see if they are the real safety conscious types, with head leaning forward and hands on the wheel at 11 and 2 o'clock; or, if they try to be real cool by putting one hand on the wheel and an elbow out the window. Or finally, whether they drive like lazy old me—leaning back nice and easy with a couple of fingers at the bottom of the steering wheel. Alexandra's style was intense but not overpowering; fast but not reckless. If there was a wide gap between her and the next car up, she'd narrow it rapidly, but she'd always slow down before she got too close. I liked that because there is nothing I hate more than tailgators, especially when I'm going at 70 mph myself. I also liked the way she passed: lightening quick, yet inoffensive. The cars, or rather, the drivers on the road whom I loathe, are the ones who take their sweet-ass time in passing me, long enough for us to make eye contact; then they cut sharply into my lane to aggravate the hell out of me. When Alexandra passes people, she zips them by.

"So, Luke, I'm delighted you'll be staying at L'Ostrib," Charles said, "a very stylish place."

"A change of pace from the Bristol, so my contact tells me."

Charles then told Luke of some of the famous people who had lived and died at L'Ostrib. Although I was unfamiliar with those Left Bank "in" spots, I did know of the Bristol: they send Warren the prettiest Christmas Cards every year.

As for a pretty site, Charles suggested the Place Dauphine, on the Ile de la Cité and minutes from Luke's hotel. "Thousands walk over the Pont Neuf everyday, but only a few know of the unhurried seclusion mere steps away," Charles said, lowering the volume on the stereo while at it. Alexandra then gave him a little look and drove even faster.

We got to Paris in no time at all but began to see traffic as we drove by the two railway stations—*Gare du Nord* and *Gare de l'Est*. Why the hell the French built the North station and East station a few blocks apart, I'm not sure; though it probably isn't as catastrophic as if they built the new Comiskey Park right next to Wrigley Field. One thing you ought to know about the French: they have an excuse for everything.

What fond memories I have of Paris train stations. When some friends and I were touring Europe one summer, we sometimes took overnight trains to Paris just for the hell of it. Quite often, before finding a hotel, we'd shower and shave at the train station. One time we took this all-nighter from Amsterdam, and, sitting in the same compartment with us was this incredibly beautiful girl in a short skirt traveling with—of all people—her mother! That girl was sitting directly across from us and, boy, did she work us up. That morning, my shower stall was not merely for the sole purpose of that hot, eye-opening *douche*; and the shower head was not the only *head* that was pulsating with hot, explosive streams—if you catch my drip.

"A droite au quai Augustin?" Alexandra asked.

"Yes. Then turn left when you see the Institute, then a sharp right will take us to the hotel."

We had already crossed the bridge to Rive Gauche, the Left Bank of the Seine, with the Notre Dame glowing toweringly behind us. Hard to believe that monster of a cathedral was eight-hundred-years old.

I wished Luke a successful trip. He said he might be in New York again to meet up with some venture capitalists, so I told him to feel free to look me up. I'm the only Mark Vermont in the phone book.

Before I had a chance to ask how far we were from Charles's house, we had already arrived. Luke's little hotel was in the Sixth Arrondissement; so is Rue Jacob, where my grandfather used to live. Charles's house, though, is in the Seventh. There aren't any visible barriers in between, as far as I know. New York is sort of the same way. Where I live on Seventy-eighth Street, the post code is 10021. But two blocks up on Eightieth, it's a different number. I know it because I'm pretty keen on borders; but to most New Yorkers, zip code boundaries are more like trivia questions.

The Parisians, however, are well aware of the boundaries to their Arrondissement. One reason is that each of the twenty-one districts has its own mayor. Another reason might be to serve as a point of reference, as it's no easy task to keep track of the hundreds of little street names that they've got. I doubted even Charles knew them all.

"Finalement, treize Rue de Capet!" Alexandra said with a sigh of relief. Then quickly she made a turn, stopped the car inches from the gate, dropped us off, waved, and drove on.

"Made it in good time," Charles said. "And Mark, my dear boy, the night is still young."

TWO

Viewed from the street Charles's house seemed—well, about the only thing you could see was a wall that ran along the sidewalk. In the center of the wall was an arched stone portal closed with massive wooden doors. The doors hung crookedly, probably due more to old age than to a bad fit. It had carvings on the panels for decoration and rusty metal handles that were perhaps used in the bygone days to allow passages for horse and carriages and stuff.

A dimly lit cobblestone courtyard separated the street from the house. It was empty except for a car wrapped in a cover. From a distance, the house was a good three townhouses wide. The main residence, two stories high, had seven tall windows on the ground floor facade: two on each side and three in the middle that also served as the entrance. As I followed Charles toward the steps leading up to the entry, I had a feeling of moving away from a Paris which existed only minutes ago. The utter silence of the courtyard was unnerving, as if I was being transported back in time.

Back in time was indeed my initial impression of the entrance hall. The French call it the *vestibule*. It was altogether very grand and very old. The floor was a pattern of diagonal blocks of black and white; the walls were blue-veined marble, with archways connecting to other rooms. Placed between the two archways in the back was an antique bureau and a chair, and flanking them both was a pair of extra-large suits of armor. On the right wall of the room, between the two side arches, hung a full-length picture of a man on his white horse. Under the painting was a long and narrow table with a marble top sitting on heavily carved legs.

"You expect me to actually sleep in this museum?" I said to Charles, who was standing under a ballroom sized chandelier in the center of the vestibule.

"I can always book you into the Hilton if you'd prefer," Charles replied. "Come along, old boy, let me show you to your room first, and you can have the grand tour later." Charles started heading up the stairs on the left and I followed along.

It was probably the longest climb I've ever had in a private residence—partly it was due to the vestibule's high ceilings; partly it was due to the steps being extremely shallow. Although the center of the stairs was covered with carpeting, the uncovered area was white marble. The greatest feeling of space I felt was at a point midway up the stairs, where the dimensions of both the first and second floors converged in full view. I felt a sense of possession standing there as I looked all around: behind me was a painting of an old man in an ornate costume; above me, on the wall of the second-floor foyer, was a life-sized painting of a lady; and down below, slightly obstructed by the sparkling chandelier, was that painting of the horseman. The sensation of height and of the art around me was vast and overwhelming.

As I continued up the stairs, I noticed the wrought iron handrail that curved up along the left side of the staircase. It was intricately twisted and trimmed with gold. When I arrived on the second floor, I turned around and looked down along the handrail's curving lines, and leaned my body hard toward the railings to test its strength. It was rock solid. Credit must go to the master ironsmith who actually bent the thing into shape hundreds of years ago. I ought to know, having barely passed metalwork class in eighth grade when I bent out a rocking, and terribly uneven bookstand. Man, those sparks on the spinning grinder I saw as I tried to smooth out the metal's edges, and all those vibrations and shockwaves that went through my hands each time I didn't grind properly. It made me cringe just thinking about it.

"Mr. Vermont!" Charles was calling me again, in front of a door to one of the rooms this time, "Your bedroom is straight through here."

"Okay, thanks." I walked from the upstairs foyer into a large sitting room, then through a double door and into the guest bedroom.

The oddest thing about the bedroom was the bed: it was built into an alcove, one much smaller than those in typical Manhattan apartments. It only had room for the bed and curtain, that was it. However, on both sides of the bed alcove were small doors that opened into closets. I thought it was a pretty cool design; functional, too. Combine that with the calming effect of wallcoverings in the style of a blue and white Ming vase, peace and quiet seemed to be assured.

I went on and unpacked some of my stuff—nothing fancy, comfortable clothes, mostly. I got out of my suit and tie and hung them in the closet, took out my sportcoat, went into the adjoining bathroom to wash up a bit, and before you knew it, I was back down those marble stairs and out the door, ready to face Paris. As I walked out with Charles, I reassured him that I felt great, much better than if I had taken a regularly scheduled red-eye flight, as virtually all other flights to Europe were. That's the one negative thing about the first day in Europe: if you can't sleep on the plane, the day can get mighty long and rough—especially if you have a full day of meetings ahead.

Down the road from the hustle and bustle of Saint-Germain's café society was the Brasserie Berthe. Tucked into the middle of a dead end alley, it appeared at first to be a sedate watering hole; once inside, however, it felt as lively as any. Immediately to the right of the entrance was a table full of boisterous smart Parisians. One in particular, a man with a Kojak head, thick brows, and leather pants, had thoughts of getting up to shake Charles's hand, but he couldn't. He forgot he had a real fox of a lady sitting on his lap. So after a quick wave of hand, he turned back to his audience to continue to thrill them with his rhyme and *raison d'etre*.

"*Monsieur Martin, comment ça va*? I was not expecting you until Sunday night." A big man with a large mustache walked up to the front and gave Charles a warm greeting.

Charles then told him that I had just flown in from New York and was positively starving, which was not entirely true.

We were given a banquette near the cash register, along an old beat up leather bench. Except for the entrance area, most of the dining room was long and narrow, with mirrors extending all the way to the back. The room looked a little like an expanded dining car on one of those Orient Express-ish trains, except the squarish banquette were combined in various odd formations, to suit the size and preferences of diners and partiers alike.

A waiter, in a tiny bow tie and a huge white apron that nearly touched the floor, came around and took our drink orders. Two *géants*, Charles told him; two large beers.

"Is this your regular hangout, Uncle Charles?"

"Not so much anymore. I now alternate between here and a fish restaurant that is even closer to the house. Closer but already closed."

The beers arrived quickly, and they were giants all right, in mugs that equaled two Budweiser tall boys. I smiled at Charles and said, "I should have known!" Although Charles would deny to be a beer drinker, he could surprise you. The last time I saw him was in New York, when he came to attend a Franco-American social function. It was also the NCAA Final Four weekend, and therefore, a party at my place. It was mostly my roommate's friends, whom I like except when their ACC teams play the Big East. So anyway, we ordered some party platters from our grocer, some white wine for the girls, and had a decent party. But it was Charles who stole the show. At first, I thought maybe he might be uncomfortable and feel out of place—it wasn't exactly a sit down dinner for twenty-four at a Park Avenue maisonette, but a bunch of foul-mouthed kids with hundreds of dollars on the outcome of the game. Plus the fact that I didn't think Charles knew a damn thing about college basketball. But I invited him anyhow. It was me, my place, the way I lived, and he knew me well enough to realize that I was no boy scout. True, if His Holiness the Pope had shown up that night, then perhaps I might have restrained myself from the cursing and the prancing, especially when I get pissed off at the referees. But with Charles, I didn't have to worry.

As it turned out, Charles was not only at ease, but utterly charming as well, particularly with the young ladies. You should have seen them practicing their French on him. Some of those girls can be a little snotty at times, especially my roommate Edwin's friends. But Charles was great. After going out to dinner with me, he went back to his suite at the Carlyle and picked up several bags of party gifts that he had received from the Colbert Foundation party that he was in New York for. How Charles had managed to get more than one bag I did not ask. But it was supposedly a hell of a charity event: musicians and three star chefs were flown in from France just for the occasion.

For those of you who have gone to benefits, you'd be familiar with the cheap party favors that the sponsors give out at the end as you're on your way out. But the gifts from the Colbert party were first-class, and worth a pretty penny. The members of the Foundation, consisting of some of the best known luxury goods names in France, had donated miniatures of their cognacs, crystals, perfumes and cosmetics, and much much more. And there was Charles—giving them all away! The girls were ecstatic. Hell with basketball stars for them as they sat around Charles and asked about the other game in town. What did Catherine Deneuve wear at the party? How was Regine's new toy-boy husband? Which New York glamourite was sitting next to whom and so on. Charles was entertaining and amusing, too; all the beers he had drunk along with the drinks he'd had at dinner didn't appear to affect him in the least. He seemed so at home that, after the Big East lost the game and I lost a bundle, I went back to my room to sulk without thinking I had left him alone in the living room. I did steal a few Lenôtre chocolates before they disappeared, though. They were soooo good.

So good of the waiter to come by to tell us the specials, too. There was a *gigot*, an *entrecôte*, and a fresh fish. Charles wasn't interested in any of it. Instead, he ordered a *choucroute*, a house specialty, for us both. The waiter couldn't even sell him a pickled herring salad.

The word *brasserie* means a brewery. They had originated in Alsace but are now popular everywhere. According to Charles, many Alsatians came as refuges after the Franco-Prussian War to Paris, where they opened brasseries and stayed. The dish we were having, the *choucroute garni*, was a haute cuisine version of hot dogs and sauerkraut: served in a large deep dish, it contained several different kinds of sausages and meats, all carefully seasoned and spiced and sliced up real nice and laid on top of a bed of sauerkraut. The sausages were unbelievable, especially the sweet ones with just a hint of fat and a mellow, smoky flavor.

"You know Uncle Charles, leave it to the French to do up a better sausage than the Germans."

"And almost as good a beer."

"What do you think of American beer?"

Charles thought about it for a moment: "It goes rather well with American food, does it not?" He was trying to be funny. "Actually, that American restaurant you took me to a couple of months ago, what was it, on Lexington and Seventy-ninth?"

"The Lenox Grill."

"A superb establishment. Not too new, not too old, no nonsense food, and a most vibrant atmosphere. Their Maryland crab cakes are as good as they can be."

"I'm glad you liked 'em," I said. "This sauerkraut is as good as they come as well—if not the best. Why, there's not even a need for a hot dog roll." Like most people, I don't eat sauerkraut unless if it's with hot dogs or on a reuben. Yet this kraut was unlike any I'd had. It wasn't watery and bland, but was flavored with wine and spices and had a fried, crunchy, peppery taste. "It is an unusual preparation," Charles said. Unusual but I loved it; especially chasing it all down with lots of beer.

"So how does it feel to be in Par's in three'n hahf r's?" Charles elocuted in his Masterpiece Theater-ish English.

"All the more reasons why I needn't ever bother with California."

"Good lord, we might make you a European yet!"

"And you, sir, an American!"

"I believe I've just been insulted."

"It was meant as a compliment," I said. "You do like America, don't you?"

No answer.

"You have made tons of money in America, have you not?"

Still no answer, though he did lower his chin a little, somewhat bewildered.

"You know what I was thinking about on the flight over? Mobility. That perhaps one day we could give the Concorde enough fuel capacity to fly around the world in one shot—wouldn't that be something?"

Still no answer.

"Wait a minute, I have to correct myself. It is not practical to carry so much fuel. The shortest distance between two points is *not* a straight line in the other direction. But still, aren't we modern beings the envy of history? Just think, Uncle Charles: it took Jules Vernes eighty days to go around the world. If someone were to be as obsessed with circling the globe today, then he could, theoretically, accomplish the task in a single day. And if orbiting were all he ever wanted to do in life, as in 'he who dies with the most mileage in his bank wins,' then today's road warriors could implicitly live a life that is eighty times longer than his ancestors—thanks to the Wright Brothers—Americans both!"

"Tell me, my boy," Charles finally spoke. "Do you think man would still have progressed toward flight had the earth been completely devoid of birds and insects?"

That was the first glimpse I had that weekend of Charles the thinker. There I was, talking up a storm, only to be thrown back to the ropes by a single decisive blow. Suddenly, I was the one without a mouthpiece.

"It's a good question," I said, trying to buy some time as I scrambled to put together a coherent reply. I thought about leaves, but leaves fall. "It's a toss up," I said. "While I believe the engine is the soul that propels a flight—meaning, that it's irrelevant whether birds existed or not—I still can't help but feel that we might not have done it without the inspirations from seeing actual wings flapping in the air. Not in so short a time, anyway."

I was relieved to find Charles more or less in agreement. "So it all comes down to the way we perceive scientific breakthroughs: what portion of it is originality and inspiration, what portion of it is knowledge and logic."

"Certainly a combination of both is essential," I said.

"As is luck and good timing," Charles added. "Newton, Maxwell, Pasteur, Einstein and Bohr—not only did they pose the right questions, but posed it so at the right time."

"Are you saying that if one or two ingredients had not been in place, say if the apple had missed Sir Issac, we wouldn't be where we are today?"

"No. If Newton had missed out on gravity, another mathematician would have seen it later on—and did, for that matter. Similar to Adam Smith's invisible hand of competition, science is rather more who will discover it first than if it will be discovered at all."

"On the other invisible hand, sir, we could've also discovered gravity sooner. Perhaps someone had thought like Newton, but lacked an environment to solidify his Principia."

"Very true, indeed. Good to see you thinking, my boy. Remind me to show you a section of the Guttenberg Bible when we get home. That Bible was the first product of the printing press. But did you know that the technology, or rather, the material and craftsmanship necessary to make such a printing press had already been in existence for hundreds of years prior?"

"Really?" I was astounded. "So it's conceivable that we are hundreds of years behind our history making potential." Being a reasonable student of historical facts, I knew what a catalyst for change that printing press was.

"As terribly little progress was made in the Dark Ages," Charles followed, "it is conceivable indeed, with the correct circumstance, for us to be hundreds of years into our future." The usually mild-mannered Charles gave off an expression that revealed immense puissance and passion. His eyes wide and unblinking, face set and still. It was the first of several occasions that I would find him in such a state.

"Wow! Wouldn't that be something, to be hundreds of years ahead of our time. But, as Lady Macbeth says: 'What's done is done.' Or, rather, what was not done cannot be undone."

"I beg to differ; Mark, old chap."

"But, sir, what's done is done. You can't change the past!"

"There might be a way."

"What?" That Charles was even crazier than I thought.

"First we start with the definition of change," he said.

"Well, change means 'to bring about a different end.' We got kicked out of Vietnam with fifty thousand lives lost, and billions of dollars drained. How are we going to undo that? The war altered the future of American history immeasurably."

"My dear boy, I'm not saying it is easy to change the past; rather it is impossible to change the future with your definition."

"Of course, it's possible. I have tickets to some Grateful Dead shows this summer. But if I have to go away on assignment, then I have effectively changed the future."

"That is not changing the future; it is changing your plans for the future."

"Well, what the hell…what's the difference? That's just a technicality, a question of semantics."

"The difference is absolute certainty," Charles said. "We cannot change something in the future unless it's outcome is absolutely certain. And, the *only* way to create certainty is…well, after having done it or witnessed it. A sort of a paradox, is it not?"

"Waaait a minute, wait just one minute. I understand it and I don't understand it, and that *ain't* no paradox. All right let me see, you're saying that the future can't be changed because, as reasonable and efficient beings, we tend not to do something just so we can undo it later on; POW tunnel diggers not included."

"Amusing," Charles said sarcastically.

"Well, there's just one problem, sir. Say I have plans to pick up a couple of shirts at Shirt Basement next week. However, if I end up getting some shirts in Paris, then the Basement would lose out. Which is fine. But here's the twist: what if the shirts I bought in Paris turn out to be horrible? Yet the damage had already been done?"

"If one subsequently discovers a previous act to be a mistake, then one moves to correct it. The correction process, though, is merely an effort to change one's past thinking and habits; to make one realize that if ever a next time one were to be given a choice of expensive Charvet shirts or bargain Basement, think again. So, in a sense, what's done *can* be undone. But what's not done *can't* be changed. How does one possibly change the outcome of something that hasn't even been done?" Charles raised his voice a notch.

"Simple—because I full well plan to do it."

"Nonetheless, your decision is based on an incomplete knowledge of all the facts. Take the rock concerts and the business trip: just because you weren't aware of going away at the time you made commitments to the concerts, it doesn't necessarily mean that your boss, or your client didn't know. Perhaps they forgot to mention it to you early enough."

"So you're saying that there is only one way to change the future, and that is to change the past. Like, if I were to simply go see another concert to make up for the one I originally missed, thereby fulfilling a past wish."

"Partial fulfillment, at least."

"But what about your printing press example? You just said earlier that we might have wasted several hundred years, and we can't get it back. So what's done *is* done."

"Look here, my dear fellow. I never said that it would be easy to change the past. Nonetheless, if we realize the loss, we can perhaps work faster and harder to make up for lost time. Observe Japan and Germany after the war. Their recovery could very well be seen as changing the past, changing an old defeat into a subsequent victory."

"Hmmm..." It was the first time I came to realize that Charles might have a point there. But I wasn't about to give up yet. "What about the scientists you mentioned earlier, Newton, Niels Bohr and the rest, who changed forever the way we look at things?"

"They changed our views because our views were, in the main, wrong. Once again, they were simply undoing our past mistakes. The earth did not change its trajectory from being the center of the universe two thousand years ago to being merely one of the planets today. The earth has been a planet going around the sun for billions of years...."

"Hmmm... I think it's starting to make some sense." I found myself slowly shaking my head, almost ready to give up. "But what about Karl Marx, he changed the world. Oh, right, we also touched on that. The situation was so ripe that if Marx didn't invent communism, someone else would have stepped in and nailed the hammer to the sickle."

It was at that time when I suddenly experienced a brilliant moment. Perhaps it was due to something in my subconscious, or just the gambler's mentality in me that's always seeking out certainty. Looking back, it was hardly so big a deal; but at that moment, it gave me great confidence. "Uncle Charles," I said. "Let's say you are right. That if we can't change the future, it means that there are lots of fixed elements in it, that much of it is all laid out."

"Correct."

"So say the future is fixed, then we can make predictions about it. I mean, if what you say is true, then people won't be able to intentionally change the future no matter how hard they try."

"Correct, in the sense that their actions are already partially incorporated into the future."

"Wow! That means there is a certain logic to the way in which the future is laid out—perhaps a built-in discount mechanism with future indecisions and probabilities of various scenarios factored in. Almost like a flowing equation that translates chaos into order. And, god, if you can forecast the future better than your neighbor, then you'll be way ahead in the game." I felt an injection of power with that realization. It was as if a voice from heaven had just told me: yes, there is a way!

I knew my vision was different from the notion of fate, which involves resignation, of not being able to control things, of simply letting things happen. On the other hand, if you can predict the future, then you can also take advantage of it. Not really to change it, but to work with it, to be ready for it. It might take us a million years to perfect that equation, I told Charles, but the odds are still better than me finding the right shirt to go with my jacket and tie.

Charles laughed. "Twenty-six birthdays and a MBA later, you remain bloody useless!"

"Yeah, as bloody as the tie on my birthday suit. Sorry to have disappointed you."

"On the contrary, my boy. You've done some good work over the years. Have you decided on your next step, Mr. Color Coordination?"

"Well, Warren, my boss, was pleased to hear that I'm going to stick with him. He has also indicated that, after this summer, he's going to make me an associate. But nothing is final. This project we are doing now, for a conglomerate, could be the key. I'm really trying to do a good job on it. You know what's amazing about it? Sometimes, I feel I know that company so well that I can actually advise them, with confidence; but other times, I don't know what the hell is going on."

"Are you referring to the technical nature of certain businesses or operations in general?"

"Even concerning the general operational structure. For instance, besides our primary recommendation of streamlining or even the dismantling of unprodcutive assets, Warren wants to offer the company management yet another alternative—a way to keep the spirit of the conglomerate alive should they wish to do so, by re-organizing and possibly even branching off the numerous divisions according to their profit and growth potentials."

"Interesting concept," Charles said. "Like having a bunch of little conglomerates operating inside a giant corporate umbrella."

"Oh, it's a bold move—new and untested thinking—quite a departure from the normal practice of grouping divisions in line with related businesses. Nevertheless, the new approach would prevent the poor performers from dragging down the prosperous divisions. Moreover, by putting all the deadwood into one division, you could, if need be, spin it off or sell it all in one bold stroke."

"Yes. Synergy, if one believes in its existence, could best be achieved with subsidiaries that are in similar operational health; otherwise, it is cross-subsidization."

"In addition, sir, Warren hopes that the grouping together of the unprofitable divisions could unleash a competitive, entrepreneurial spirit that just might be what it takes to nurse the sick back to health."

"Do you believe that it will happen?"

"I'm going to be as diplomatic as the State Department and say I'm cautiously optimistic. I told Warren that it was sort of like at an AA meeting, where misery loves company."

It was at that time that Charles made me a job offer; sort of. "If you should decide in the months ahead that you might like to investigate other options, I want you to come to me. There is tremendous activity in Europe right now, as we are all trying to position ourselves in preparation for the eventual single market."

"I'll certainly keep that in mind, sir. Sounds like a great opportunity." Yeah, if I can only see myself leaving my beloved New York City. Not unlike fellow AA members, we hard-core New Yorkers also love the misery of abusive company.

After getting back to the house, I lingered in the sitting room for a while, snapping on the television and flipping through some magazines. Reading with the television on relaxes me, even better than going straight to bed. The sitting room, despite being connected to my bedroom, had a character all to its own. It was also larger and more lavishly furnished. I was sitting on one of the two curvy-edged couches perpendicular to the center window. The couches, along with the big coffee table in the middle, sort of divided the room in two. The side near my bedroom had a lacquered six-panel Chinese screen. Next to that were two chaise longues with a half-height bookcase stuck in between. Then, down at the corner, stood a bed that was probably named after one of the Louises: it was wrapped in a veil and had a crown on top.

The other side of the room had a couple of pieces of furniture that were just as ornamental. One was the mahogany secretary. It had toy-sized drawers stacked on top and four sets of gold column-like legs as support, which made the piece look uncannily like a gigantic gold trophy. Another strange piece was that heavyweight commode—fat as a pig, and funny-looking, too—it had a marble top, carved legs, and a huge, protruding belly. Hell, with a room like that, who needs a room with a view. Certainly, you needn't be a damn furnishing expert to appreciate its fine decor. From the cherry-colored floral fabric which covered the walls to the small corner stands that round out the edges, every piece was arranged in a well balanced manner; even the television was in its own antique cabinet.

I must have dozed off for a while because all of a sudden I began hearing music, some footsteps, and what sounded like some very angry mutterings. Then the door, which I didn't fully close, was pushed wide open.

"Ooops, *pardon*!" It was Alexandra: shoulders up, hand over her mouth—visibly embarrassed at her intrusion. "I'm sorry, Mark," she said, "I was on my way down to the toilet but then I saw the lights on. I didn't know you were still awake."

"I didn't know, either," I said, feeling a little embarrassed myself that a girl had to barge in to turn off my lights. Then I lowered the volume on the TV, removed the magazine from my lap, and stood up, wobblingly.

"So, Mark," she said in a thick French accent, "owl was your evening?"

"Very nice, Ally. Hey Alexandra, mind if I call you Ally?"

"Ally, Alex, whatever you want. But Ally's good. I like it!"

"Great. Then Ally it is," I nodded. "So anyway, after you dropped us off, we went to the Brasserie Berthe for a little supper."

"Was it good?"

"It was great. We shared a deep dish of *choucroute*."

"Uh-huh, *choucroute*; it's too heavee for me."

"Did you ever go there?"

"No, never. It's one of those snobby places. If they don't know you, they don't want to know you."

"How did your evening go?"

"I had to meet some people from my school. We had some studying to do."

"Do you always study till this late at night?"

"This week, yes. For the past two days, I was studying for an exam which I took this afternoon; I o'so had some work for Monsieur Martin left over, then I had to pick you up at the airport. I said to myself: *Merde! C'est bien ma chance!*"

Shit, my lucky day, was what she said. There was true anger in the way she said "merde"—the most popular word in the French language—with a little twitch of the head, and a little frown of the face.

I'm sorry to have troubled you out to the airport," I said, "but it was a great thrill watching you drive. Lots of bravado!"

"Thanks," she smiled back. "Usually, I go alone. But Monsieur Martin had time yesterday night so he went with me. I have to pick up his guests at the aeroport *all* the time; it drives me crazy!"

"I bet you do...I mean, I bet he does," I corrected myself in time. "Charles still doesn't do much driving, aye?"

"A few times a week, tops! Even so, I can't just sit there and watch him drive; it puts me to sleep."

It was true what Ally said. I remember when Grandpa took me to France and Switzerland twelve years ago, when Charles still had his house on Cap Ferrat. The morning we were supposed to be taken to the Nice airport, Charles came down and said his valet had had too much to drink the night before, so he would take us there himself. I remember us getting into his clunky old Mercedes convertible and moving at a snail's pace.

After Ally had gone to the bathroom, she made a stop at the fridge and brought back some fruit juice. We went on and chatted some more. I told her that it was the first time I was staying with Charles in Paris. The year that Grandpa took me to Switzerland and Paris, Charles had already gone down to the Riviera—the Midi as the French call it. I also missed Charles again after college when I toured Europe with friends. That was because it was in July and August, when every Parisian was on vacation. "It was also the year that Charles relocated his summer residence to Corsica," I said. "And since my friends were more interested in Costa del Sol, where the girls were, I missed seeing Charles once again."

"Buttuh, there are girls on Corsica, too," Ally argued, "I was there one summer."

"Yeah, how was it? Did you go to Saint-Florent and Cap Corse?"

"Those places are boring. We went to the southern part of Corsica. It was great. We slept on the beach *à la belle étoile*, and we also did some camping." Ally then gave the big antique globe next to her an impulsive and animated spin. Camping, aye? Great fun indeed, just ask the Brady girls: one minute you're helping them plant their tent pole, next minute you're scaring them out of their tent.

How curious, I thought. Here was a French girl who, after ignoring everyone while driving back from the airport, had suddenly burst into the room and made herself completely at home. She was lounging on the sofa directly across from me. Her head on one end, feet the other, her faded jeans fitting nicely over her shapely legs. She was lying pretty all right, with one hand behind her head, the other one flicking the remote. We sat around and watched a few music videos. Rita something et les Sparks doing a bland French number; a funky tune by Julien Clerc, who looked a little like Bruce Springstein; and finally, two videos from Vanessa Paradis, a pouty French teen with somewhat of a shy voice.

"This girl is very popular in France," Ally said.

"Do you like her?"

"Not that much. But my little sister does."

"Oh, I get it; she's kinda like them bubble gum artists, The New Kids on the Block of France."

"But there is no *action* in this kid," Ally stressed. "The song talks about cutting sugar, yet she is just standing there in a dress, not doing anything."

Personally, I thought she was surprisingly seductive; but I didn't want to argue, so I changed the subject. "So, Ally, what were you studying earlier?"

"Eh, it was *Droit de Travail*, business law, a *pain* in the ass!"

"Labor law, sounds like an advanced subject?"

"Of course. I'm almost done with my studies for my degree."

"At the Sorbonne?"

"No, at Université Paris at Dauphine."

"Is that nearby?"

"No, it is not in le Quartier Latin; more near l'Arc de Triomphe"

"Wouldn't it be easier for you to go to the Sorbonne?"

"Right now, yes. But Dauphine is not far from where I used to live, with my parents. Plus, it's a better school. You need a high test score to get in there. Do you know Porte Dauphine? At the entrance to Bois de Boulogne."

"Oh, the bwah!" the park, I said, "Sure, I know the Bois, it's near the Arc."

"*Ouais*, from l'Arc de Triomphe, you go down Avenue Foch until it terminates—*et voilà, c'est Dauphine.*"

"Avenue Foch, that's a grand street; you used to live nearby?"

"Not very near."

"How about the Champs-Élysées? Or the avenue des something Armée?" I tried to show off the two other streets I knew.

"Ha ha ha!" she slapped her arm onto her lap and laughed.

"What's so funny?"

"Those streets all meet at l'Arc de Triomphe! I just told you I deedn't live around there!"

"Well, excuuuse meee!"

She liked the way I said it and repeated it right back at me. But I didn't mind. I kind of liked her French-accented English, with her voice getting higher and higher pitched as she approached the final syllable of a sentence.

"How about the Eiffel Tower, Ally? Did you live near the Eiffel Tower?" I was not about to give up on my inquiries just because she was laughing at my knowledge of Paris geography.

"Not too close;" she said. "Let's see, do you know Boulevard Suchet?"

"No."

"That is a long boulevard on the eastern edge of Bois de Boulogne. I grew up on a small street off Boulevard Suchet."

"Oh, you were homeless, too?"

"Com'on, I mean an apartment building on—"

"Only kidding, Ally. Still, will I be able to see your building from atop the Eiffel Tower?"

"I don't know," she shrugged. Then she hesitated for a moment and blurted, "I never went to the top."

"You have *never* even climbed the Eiffel Tower?" I was in shock when I heard that. "*Moi*, I've even done it—twice!" Though come to think of it, I've never been to the top of the Empire State Building, either; and only once the Statue of Liberty, when I was really tiny. But we're New Yorkers, we're not *supposed* to do those things. However, you would definitely expect them Parisians, who are extremely attached to their past, to be more passionate about their monuments. They probably are. Perhaps it was just Ally who was a little cuckoo.

"Hey, Ally, do your parents know that you've never gone up the Eiffel Tower?"

"I don't know. They don't care. Actually, I did have a chance once, when I was a student at *Couvent du Sacré Coeur*, but I took the opportunity to run away with a friend of mine: we lost the *bonne soeurs* completely, the nuns."

"You mean you cut classes; or rather, a field trip. What was so important?"

"Ehhh, we decided to go into the Bois de Boulogne to smoke cigarettes."

When I heard that, I had to seriously control myself from laughing too loud. Hell, I've cut my share of classes; but *never* field trips!

"Did the good sisters get worried?" I asked.

"Yes, they punished us."

"Do you know what we'd call you, Ally? A problem child, a bad girl."

She quickly defended herself: "But Mark, I did very well in school. I even skipped a year because I had already learned everything."

"You mean you actually made good grades in school?"

"Of course. How else can I be going to Dauphine. It was just those nuns I couldn't stand. They were such a pain in the *ahss*."

"Did you tell your parents that you didn't like the nuns at school?"

"I didn't have to. The nuns met with my parents often, until one day they decided to kick me out."

Jesus Christ, that had me laughing it up again, almost uncontrollably. And if that wasn't enough, Ally went on and said, with her hands up in the air: "It was not the end of the world; lots of girls got kicked out, some even before me."

How very beautiful she looked at that moment: there was a glisten to her eyes, her soft yet proud face bore no hint of regret, but rather an expression which hinted that perhaps it was all for the best. Boy, I wished I had a photograph of that moment—which reminded me—I did not bring a camera to Paris.

Ally and I continued talking for a while. I told her I was from New York and what I did and stuff, in a mixture of English and French. I was holding my own as well as to be expected, considering how superb Alexandra's French was. Yes, I know she's French, but that's not quite it. There was a sense of strength and confidence in her voice, something not everyone's got. And oh, how expressive she was, like when we were arguing about why she was playing her music so loudly, even after two o'clock in the morning. "I need music at a particular volume," she said. "My hearing does not improve just because it's late at night. If anything, the music should be even louder at night so people dancing in the clubs can stay awake into the morning, *n'est-ce pas*?"

How can you argue with those one-sided-logical-reasoning-statements that only the French can give, except to simply let a cute girl have her way. *"Oui, tu as tout à fait raison!"* Yes, entirely reasonable, I replied.

Then, when I was asking her about the merits of wearing a scarf around the neck all the time, even indoors; she said: "Well, it's really soft, it protects the skin—it's like clothing for your neck. Besides, it adds an ex-t-ra something to your look." Like she really needed an extra little something to her look. When I was in the car, I could not really see her body because she had a jacket on; but now, with her lounging right on the sofa, chest arched forward, legs stretched, bare feet resting on the other end, she was showing all the traits of a sister-at-arms at a nunnery.

It was getting late. Ally courteously asked if I needed anything, I said I've already checked out my bedroom, the chambre à coucher, and that everything was in working order. With that, I took her to the entrance of the sitting room, and closed the door behind her.

"Ciao, Ally, *dors bien*!"

"*A demain.* Sleep tight."

It didn't take me long to fall asleep, but long enough for me to lay in bed and think about Alexandra Lachapelle. What kind of a girl is stupid enough to have never gone up to the Eiffel Tower, yet smart enough to skip a year of school? Either way, she was quite a girl. Besides being cute as hell, she was quick, spontaneous, and natural; not to mention she'd made me laugh, as when she talked about her getting kicked out of her Catholic school.

I was once kicked out of—well, left before I was kicked—I had spent part of my ninth grade away at school. Then I escaped. It was shortly after my mother got remarried and moved to California. Due to the fact that I had flat-out refused to go to the West Coast, I was shipped off to Litchfield, a school way up in the Connecticut woods.

Looking back, there were some favorable memories, especially in view of my surprisingly lasting friendship with Edwin, my current roommate. But, boy, did he used to drive me crazy when he lived next door to me at the dormitory. You know, I don't want to swear to god, but I think god has made me remember more good times than bad as I look back. I mean, back in those days, I did not look forward to boarding school anywhere *near* the degree that most parents usually hope their kids will. In fact, I nearly hated it. I was more used to the freedom of Port Washington; and, on weekends, going to the city for sports and shows. Litchfield was pretty strict, with leanings to a more spiritual end of things; or at least it tried to anyway, in hopes of influencing first-year students. There were just too many stupid regulations. Plus the fact that the school was right in the middle of nowhere, with no town to walk to, and no entertainment to be had. I pretty much just studied. One reason was because I was forced to, after having been admitted as a special case; as sort of a volatile misfit. Secondly, lord knows I was no jock, nor was I much of a wannabe. Luckily I excelled there academically and proved everyone wrong, and eventually became friends with Edwin. ("Mark, enlighten us, if you would, on the Holy Trinity of our school?...No answer? How about you, Edwin?" "The chapel, the school house, and the playing field, sir." "Did you get that, Mr. Vermont?" "Umm...more an isoceles triangle to me, *sir*!")

Not too long after I enrolled at Litchfield, my grandmother got very sick. As I felt Grandpa could use some extra help, I suggested that perhaps I ought to move down to Manhattan instead. Eventually he agreed. He felt that was one way we could both spend more time visiting Grandma at the hospital.

So that was how I got out of my cellblock in the sticks and became a student at Lenox Hill, a school not far from where my grandparents lived; where I still live now. But I didn't stay long at Lenox Hill, either. Boy, was I ever on the run. Even though I absolutely adored New York City, after Grandma past away, it was decided that I would attend high school back on Long Island, where I would live with my childhood friend Stewart and his family, who, incidentally, were also relatives of my grandmother. Of course, I promised Grandpa that I would visit him often on weekends, to give him a hand with the store and stuff.

Jules, my grandfather, was a dealer in antique clocks, watches, and instruments and things. Occasionally he made them, too. Some of his family had been watchmakers in Paris, which was where he learned his craft. They had kept a store on Rue Jacob for many years, not far from Charles's house. But in the 1930s, Grandpa befriended a Yankee girl living in Paris—literally a girl living next door to the store—and eventually married her. Around the outbreak of World War II, my grandparents moved safely to New York, where Grandpa then opened a shop on Madison Avenue and made a living off of watches and clocks ever since.

Yeah, I certainly did some quick growing up in the late '70s, the years I was shuttling back and forth, up and down, and left and right. Sometimes as a basket case, other times as a special case. Many things happened, good and bad, not to mention my first trip to Europe. But I quickly became a teenager once again when I went back to my friends in Port Washington, where we definitely partied it up for the remaining years of high school. In a way, I never really left Long Island. Boarding school was all right, especially looking back, but I think I'm too free-spirited: I need room to roam, to do what I feel like doing rather than following some grand traditions of the past. At Litchfield, despite our thinking we were pretty cool for being away from home, we were never taken seriously by the big senior jocks at all. I know that because when I was a senior at Port Washington High, the incoming tenth-graders were looked down upon as strictly infantile. Yet the teachers were always trying to con us into thinking we were old enough to be the President of the United States or something. If you can remember your first day of school every year, you'll know what I'm talking about. Every single year, starting with the sixth grade, teachers would constantly remind us of how we were no longer kids anymore: "Next year you'll be in junior high," said one; then the following year, a new teacher would start hounding us with things like "You're in junior high now, not elementary school." And the year after that, we'd hear reminders of "Next year you'll be in high school," and so forth. Then when we finally got to high school, out comes speeches like "You're almost college students now, we will be expecting more from you—especially you, Vermont!—no more run-on sentences! No more 'yeahs' but 'yes'! And no more 'you knows' and 'stuff!'"

On and on and on this goes—even after we've gone to college. Every damn year, the teachers mercilessly remind us of what mature adults we were. Hell, by the time we are finally finished with our schooling, we feel like senior citizens already; but without social security—without any security. Because what the adults do next is called operation lock-out. Ready, willing and able college graduates are being turned away while the old boy's network hold on to their cushy salaries and bonuses and stock options and take all the credit. More than all the credit. If you could add up all the credit that all the executives felt they deserved—be it Fortune companies or Hollywood—the sum total would be many times the gross revenue. I'm not even a CPA and I know it's a mathematical impossibility. And now that I'm agitated, I'll go on record and say that when it comes time to take responsibility for stupidity, forget about it! "The zillions we lost last year was due to unforeseen circumstances." Unforeseen my *culo*! Fucking around with people's money like pennies from hell. Listen Mr. Big Shot, see that expensive computer that's been sitting on your desk collecting dust? Well, turn it on and learn something. Better yet, sit back and let the younger generation show you how it's done. They were already watching the Financial News Network at the age when you were still playing ball in Little League.

THREE

"Salut, Ally!"

"Mark-uh, you're up! How was your niii-ght?"

"I slept well, thank you. A little too well, even. And you?"

"I had a good sleep. Just got up a short time ago."

"Charles's already out the door, I take it?"

"Absolutelee. He's an early pair-son. Why don't you have a seat, care for some breakfast?"

"I'll just have a little juice, if you don't mind. I usually skip breakfast at home—no time."

"But you are in Paris, not going to your job. *Il faut que tu prennes un café au lait!*"

"Whatever you say, Ally. So how do feel this morning after a rather late night?"

"I feel ree-ly cooool," she said, dragging her "oo" a little.

"You look cool, too," I told her. She had on a sunny orange-colored T-shirt with a little pocket and white sweatpants that had shrunk to almost knee-high, enough to expose most of her calf. But instead of staring at her legs, I chose to focus on the kitchen. While it was connected to the dining room, the kitchen was not exactly part of the main house, but located in the service quarters, a long and narrow stretch of housing that connected the main house to the street front. There were windows on one side of the kitchen looking out onto the courtyard and white cabinetry along the wall in the shape of an L.

"This is a nice new *cuisine*," I said, as if the rest of the house was just used furniture. "I mean, it looks contemporary, the center island, the sleek fridge"

"I helped design it," she said proudly. "This and the bathroom next door are my favorite rooms; just redone last year, after I started working for Monsieur Martin. Do you really like it?"

"I like it a lot," I said. How could I not like her favorite room. "Yes, I especially like the display cabinets above the counter. The way the glass catches the brilliant reflections from the sunlight and redirecting it to the other parts of the room."

"You're full of sheet!" she said with a grin.

Perhaps I was. What I really felt like saying was how much I liked the way the sunlight played on her hair, her fresh and free-flowing hair, beautifully capturing the golden rays and redirecting it to the only other person in the room—me. But I was able to restrain myself from acting like a Beach Boy and only compliment the kitchen.

"So tell me, Ally, how did you end up working for Charles?"

"Eh, it was by an accident."

"What happened, did you get stuck with taking him home from Castel's one night? After he had too much to drink?"

"I don't think he goes anywhere anymore," she said mockingly. "Maybe a club or two once in a blue moon. No, we met when his car was in my way, and I drove into him."

"Ohhhh, a *car* accident." I thought she meant that they had met accidentally; but then again, people don't intentionally get into car accidents either—at least the drivers outside of New York and Paris don't.

Boy, you should've seen Ally's face at that moment. Her mouth closed, her eyes blank; angry as hell yet somewhat lovable—like the expressions of a child who got yelled at but still didn't give a shit. She proceeded to fill me in on some of the details: it happened the previous September, around Porte Maillot—one of those infamous traffic circles of Paris where cars rarely stop for pedestrians, let alone other vehicles.

"He was driving in circles in that slow old Mercedes…then he suddenly stopped, right where I had to accelerate to turn out…and *touché*! Then we had a big fight, and I made fun of his slow reflexes. His car's license plate was not even from Paris!"

I tried to picture what it was like that day: an old Frenchman and a young French girl, exchanging insults and yelling their heads off. Ally saying something like a country person should just drive around his chateau and stay away from Paris—similar to the way New Yorkers put down Jersey drivers, only worse. Then Charles would snap back at Ally, saying he had been driving in Paris long before her parents were even born. But Ally didn't seem to be the easily intimidated type. She had probably held her own pretty well; longer than most people her age. The only problem was, she was dealing with Charles Martin, not your typical Joe *prole* from some remote pig farm. And finally, as much as Ally thought she was in the right, her car did hit his, and suffered the most damage.

"Tout va mal!" I was in the dumps, she recalled with anger. "It could not have come at a worse time. I had been in a fight with my parents earlier that year and had moved out to my half-sister's in Neuilly. But she was soon to come back from a year in Ile Maurice so I had to find my own place. Then I damaged her car, which I was planning to buy as soon as I raised some money. Now, not only had I lost the car, I also had to pay the high city rent to go to school. And what's more, since I had been away all summer traveling in California, I had spent all my money so I was *completely* broke."

"Not only did it rain, but money, too, down the drain," I said, shaking my head. "What kind of car was it?"

"It was an old Volkswagen, but in *perfect* condition. It was already a collector's item."

A collector's item, that cracked me up. Nevertheless, from the way Ally sounded, I couldn't help but feel a little sorry for her. Apparently, she must have told Charles the same thing she had told me and had gotten some sympathy from him as well. When they finally worked it all out, Charles said he was willing to pick up the cost of expensive repairs if she was willing to work for him part-time to gradually pay him back. Charles was about to look for an assistant anyway and could even provide her with a room.

"But I almost did not take his offer when he told me he had a maid who was getting too old. I said I can help you manage her, but I'm not going to clean your house for you."

"You drive a tough bargain," I said.

"Naturellement!"

It turned out that Ally was also a good assistant. Besides secretarial work, she also helped out when Charles entertained. Since

Charles no longer had a valet nor a chef, he left it to Ally to oversee the not-so-entertaining details.

As she told it, she was a natural. With her no-nonsense manner, I didn't doubt her for a moment. Ally was so good at her job that she had begun to get on the old maid's nerves. "We were having more and more fights," Ally said. "She was too lazy, too senile, and if you asked me, definitely too much drinking."

"Did Charles agree with you?"

"Yes, but he felt responsibility for her."

"Noblesse oblige!"

"Whatever," she shrugged. "But he finally convinced her to go to his house in Corsica. It's warmer and more relaxing there, and—"

"And the gardener did it!" I said.

"Exactlee!" Ally aimed a finger at me, not exactly sure if I was making a joke.

"Then what?" I asked, already impressed at the lightning-quick speed she had consolidated her power. "Did you all then live happily ever after?"

"Not exactlee. I asked Charles Martin to pay me 5,000 francs a month, that's the minimum salary in France."

"Five thousand, that's about a couple of hundred dollars a week—seems reasonable."

"But he absolutelee refused at first. He said he paid in advance for the damage to my sister's car, plus he paid for the costs related to the repair of his own car, and he has given me room and board. He said if I wanted money, I had to do some extra work."

"Like what?"

"He said for me to be the driver and messenger—deliver and bring back things; drive him to train stations and airports; pick up his guests, etc."

"Ahhh, Charles is a shrewd dealer!"

Then Ally really turned it up a notch. "Maybe he is, but I'm better. I said to him, 'Dear Monsieur Martin, I don't mind driving, but you have to give me a better car than that old *teuf-teuf.*"

"So that's how you got that Saab parked out in the courtyard," I said, glancing out the window.

"Not exactlee, I recommended to him a smaller sports car, like a Volkswagen Cabriolet. But he didn't want that, he said it was too popular with all the young people. Get a Jaguar, then, I told him. 'No, no, that's too much money from me, and too much car for you.'"

"Huh, huh, huh...," I laughed.

"So he bought a Saab, a compromise. Wasn't that funny?"

"Yes, very." I said. Not only was the story funny, but also the way she told it—with lots of emotion and gusto. It was as if telling the facts were only part of the story. Far more important was the emphasis on how she brilliantly managed to come out of that ordeal unscathed, and possibly, even better than before.

"So that's Monsieur Martin's car parked in the courtyard. The commanding way you handled it last night, I wasn't sure."

"Of course, it's his; he owns it." She then waited for a moment, leaned toward me and said enthusiastically, "But I *drive* it!"

She was delighted. I was, too. There was something about her deviosity that I found extremely alluring. "So you got a pretty good deal here, Ally. A place to stay, a car to go—and now and then a pocket full of dough."

"But it's a lot of work," she said. "I keep records, I go to the market, I wait for service appointments, and many, many other *things*! Not to mention I speak English, which alone is worth 5,000 francs to him. My pay should be at least double what I get now."

I shook my head and sighed. Here was a college girl, getting free room and board, not in a little tenement flat, mind you; plus a little tax-free spending money to boot. Yet she thought she was overworked and underpaid. I mean, how many kilos of work was there in a one-person household? Perhaps she was just being childish. Yet sitting there listening to her, I truly believed she had overcome a crisis, and deserved every franc she got. I would've believed her even if she hadn't given me this whole spiel on how talented and indispensable she was. I really thought she was worth a lot more than minimum wage, even after taking into account the money Charles had prepaid for her. Even so, if she thought she could use *me* to persuade *Charles* into giving her a raise, she was out of luck. That, she had to do on her own. Like the crew on Star Trek, I, too, believe in non-interference. "So, Ally, are you going to ask Monsieur Martin for a raise soon?"

"Of course, I must ask. But he's really, really cheap so he is not going to give me the raise easily. I am waiting for the right moment. Maybe after he comes back to Paris in September."

"That's right. He goes away quite often. So there's another added bonus for you." I was sharp, too. How she *conveniently* managed to overlook that fact.

"Yep," she smiled again. "He goes away often. Still, he once had a big staff: including a butler, a chef, and a maid. Okay, so he had more parties back then. But his workers were constantly drunk, and always fighting, too. And you know what else," Ally then lowered her voice and said, "I heard that one of them died of SIDA."

No wonder Charles was able to put up with Ally, I thought. He's used to chaos in the household. He's just letting her slide—letting her have her way; or, knowing how shrewd Charles can be, to let her think she is having her way.

"But look, Ally: without M. Martin, you might still be living out in Neuilly and fighting with your half-sister."

"You are right, you are absolutelee right!" That said, she quickly changed back to her earlier state of that of a harmless child—of peaceful coexistence—without even the slightest agitation whatsoever. Some girl I had on my hands: mad as Ophelia one minute; calm as a monk the next. Calm as a manager of monks, actually. Ally had aspirations to be a successful businesswoman someday. She was a business student at Université Dauphine, her favorite courses were in marketing and advertising. Ally was hoping to eventually get her Master's degree from America. "With an MBA in marketing from a top American school, I can get a job in Paris just like that," she said, snapping her fingers.

I'm not much of a marketing person, but I work for a management consultant, and we're *supposed* to know things in all aspects of business. "Did you know, Ally, that while trade is an activity old as man, the concept of marketing as we understand it today is virtually an American invention. As a matter of fact, the word 'marketing' is totally international. All of Europe uses the word *as spelled* and many other countries use its phonetic equivalent."

"Well, since we in France invented capitalism, we will give you one for marketing."

Girl's got an attitude, all right. But my burst of flag-waving didn't stop there. "Moreover, America's influence in marketing is so dominant that most of our accessory terminologies relating to product characteristics are also widely used."

"I know, I know. Let me see, there is product mix, product line, product life-cycle, product this, product that."

That was my problem with product analysis, I told Ally, and marketing as a whole: lots of things they teach you are just plain old common sense. But those experts, by glamorizing the basic concepts into fancy words, have made it all the more confusing. Students come out of the classroom knowing how to recite the five P's, three E's and twelve I's and think they know it all."

"But, Mark-uh, you have to know all the terms to communicate exactly what you mean."

"Ally, if you like terms, you'll love going to a graduate business program in America. The MBA's probably have the highest buzzword to English ratio of any one around. They can chop up the English language with abbreviations and terms the likes of which you have never seen, especially the consultants."

"I, too, like to chop up the English language," she said. "But I'm sorry, Mark, I have to defend marketing. It is something that keeps the products staying on top. Coca-cola, Walt Disney, McDonald's—they spend many millions marketing their name."

"I'm not disputing that. I just think marketing is something instinctive; that you can't really teach it like you can teach accounting, though I'm sure Proctor & Gamble will be the first to disagree with me."

"And me, second. I have been learning so much in my marketing and advertising classes. Have you read any of David Oglivy's books on advertising?"

"Nope. I know nothing about advertising; just common sense, like understanding consumer psychology. I'm a tough man to market to. I still have my Pioneer stereo system from the high school days—the type with them big rotating dials. And it works great. Not to mention my tapes are still dubbed the old fashioned way, from one cassette deck to another. What's a laser disc?"

"It is the best. It is today...and tomorrow!"

"But my stereo suits my purposes just fine, and I'm attached to it. It's almost like a friend to me; and once you reach the friendship level with a product, you become hard to market to."

"I disagree. Marketing is not only getting people to buy the newest, but finding ways to hold on to loyal customers."

"But Ally, I don't want to buy!"

"That's where you are wrong. We can find ways to market to sentimental people like you. How about a stereo new in technology but old in design."

"Huh!" Even though I was laughing, I could tell Ally was pretty sharp.

"It's just like my old jeans," she said. "They are my friends, too. But I still buy new ones—of the same brand, of course."

"Oh, me too. I'm very brand loyal: Ivory soap, LL Bean, Fritos, even intangibles like Chase Manhattan, AT&T and AAdvantage. What's more, I don't need constant advertising to keep me brand-loyal, either. Look Ally, I'm not saying I yearn to be some hick who is totally oblivious to the material world; you can't help but absorb name brands if you live in New York. I'm just saying that most of the loyal customers don't need pampering. Just deliver the goods and charge a fair price. In fact, I'll bet that if you do a study, you'll find many people suggesting that the best way to keep them as customers is to *not* market the products too hard."

"But we have to advertise so people won't forget the brands; and to attract new customers."

"Ally, I've walked up and down Madison Avenue enough times to be subconsciously aware of many of the famous names, but to get me to make a purchase through advertising, *ça c'est une autre histoire"*

"Alors, comment choisis-tu un nouveaux produit?" How do you buy a new product then, she asked.

"Not through advertising; nope. I like the joy of bumping into something myself, or perhaps through word of mouth."

"Eh, you are very old-fashioned for a young person. But what if *my* word of mouth tells you that I love things by Ralph Lauren, will you like them, too?"

Boy, could she really stick it to you—playing with your emotions. I almost felt like saying that I'd go out and by some Polo shirts in fancy colors just for her, despite my having never personally paid for one in my life. "Well, yes, Ally, if you like ol' Ralphy boy, I'll like him, too. Though I would hope that you'd like Chanel just as much. It's more French."

"I love Chanel!"

"Good, then that settles it." I was anxious for a cease fire. Perhaps I was still under some economic forecasting delusion that demand precedes supply. Yet the tide of brand marketing is universal and unstoppable. In fact, you can no longer be *au courant* these days without knowledge of designer names. It's not even all materialism or commercialism anymore, I don't think; but a new and even accepted form of using language. Confucius hit it on the nose thousands of years ago when he said that "A picture is worth a thousand words." But there weren't any brand names back then. Because today, the right brand name can be worth a *thousand* pictures. Take the simple phrase "Just like something out of a Ralph Lauren ad"—it conjures up more images of a particular American lifestyle than many photojournalists could ever hope to depict in a lifetime of picture-taking.

Ally and I continued talking about marketing for a while. I was very impressed with her—a young, quick-minded French girl who could not only feel the pulses of the marketplace, but also aspired to make an impact. Who knows, I thought, she could very well be a natural.

Ally was also a natural hostess. Getting me a refill on my café au lait. She was pretty observant as well: she noticed, as I was sipping my coffee, that I hadn't adjusted the time on my watch yet. "Your watch is still on New York time," she said.

"Yeah, I'm always too lazy to adjust my watch. Besides, it isn't bad to think of the time as being very early in the morning instead of almost noon."

"How come, so you can still make it to your office on time?"

"Ha!" I was cracking up again. "Absolutely not, Ally. One thing you try not to think about when you get up in the morning is the prospect of going to work."

"Then you don't like your job. If you liked what you do, you would look forward to it."

"Well, I do look forward to some of it, like getting high on taxi fumes during my lunch break." She didn't laugh at that one, so I changed the subject. "Actually, if I hadn't come to Paris, I wouldn't have gone to work anyhow. I'd just about be ready to go sailing around this time."

"Oh, really," she said, "Where would you go, the Atlantic?"

"Eventually, yes, we had plans to get pretty close to it. Do you know Cape Cod, the part that sticks out near Boston?"

"I think so, but I definitely know where Boston is so it's okay."

"Well, we were going to sail out to Block Island, that's about fifty miles southwest of Cape Cod."

"Oh, I love to go sailing, too!" she said enthusiastically.

"Yeah, you sail?"

"I learned how to wind surf."

"That's pretty good. Just learn to tie a few more knots and you can already be of help on a boat; and after you've learned navigation, you'll be able to start looking for the lost city of Atlantis. Or at least get lost in the process."

"Have you ever gotten lost in the open seas?"

"Of course. But sailors prefer to call it '*off* course.'"

It took a little while for Ally to get that one. "That's one reason I prefer to be near the coastline," I said. "However, my roommate Edwin likes to get out into the open, like the Newport-to-Bermuda race he sails every other year. But me, I'd rather see some land now and then instead of days on end in what seems like a washing machine."

"Haw haw haw..." Ally let out a hearty laugh. "Which cycle?" she played along.

"Even on gentle" I shook my head, "but god forbid it be on spin." Boy, that Ally, she's almost as bad as me. In all seriousness, though, the most spiritually rewarding part of sailing, for me, is to follow that fine line between land and sea. Whenever I'm close to shore, I get this urge to escape it—to share my solitude with Neptune and Moby Dick. Yet once out in the deep, a yearning for the slightest hint of landfall inevitably returns. It really is the ultimate tease—that magnetic field known as land. You are constantly drawn to it; but at the same time, with practice, you can generate enough power from within to resist it. It's quite a powerful feeling to toy with nature, to be on the fringe, to traverse the tangent between soap and liquid soap.

Ally and I were still relaxing at the breakfast table when Charles came strolling in. "Oh, there you are, Vermont. Why in heavens are you still in your New York jogging clothes?"

"Homesick!"

"Already? Now kindly go and get dressed properly, you lazy chap; as we are nearly ready to go for lunch."

"Why, are we meeting St. Laurent or something?" That got a giggle out of Ally.

"No. But neither are we going to a Memorial Day barbecue in Highland Park."

"Jacket and tie, just like you?"

"Savile Row, just like you?" Ally asided from the sideline.

"Sorry Alexandra, my paycheck is already bespoken for."

"Then borrow a suit from Monsieur Martin," she said, still in a mocking tone.

"But then it wouldn't be *bespoken* anymore, would it?"

"The English language is so stupid!" Ally shook her head and turned away.

"Yeah? Well, at least I know it when I hear it," I countered. "Or, to paraphrase one of the Supreme Court justices: I'll know it when I wear it!"

"Wear something, Mr. Vermont," Charles said impatiently. The satirized had now managed to come out the peace-making diplomat. "The same suit you came with, if not too uncomfortable. And do be quick about it!"

When I came downstairs after getting dressed, I found Charles and Ally talking over some matters in the *salle à manger,* the dining room. It was located to the right of the entrance vestibule and connected at its other end to the kitchen wing.

The first thing I noticed about the dining room was that huge piece of tapestry on the far wall. It was a Renaissance work of a Roman garden. I guessed it Roman for its fountains and statues in the garden, and a girl in a red toga-like robe carrying a heavy object over her head. On the wall opposite the tapestry was a marble fireplace with a long mirror on top. Two tall windows facing the courtyard took up the third side of the room, and still-life paintings hung on the wall opposite the windows. There was a soothing simplicity about the room. Not many artifacts, only some silver centerpieces resting on a marble base directly below the still-lifes and a few more silver pieces on top of the sideboard just beneath the tapestry.

Charles was sitting at a dining table and sifting through some silverware. The dining table, or rather tables since there were two, were made from very dark wood, which, despite its age, still managed to give off a shiny glow. It was a bit odd that the two tables were placed on a diagonal; not to mention that each table was wide enough to fit two chairs on each side to seat a total of eight.

I took a seat near Charles at the table closer to the windows. He had been directing Ally to look for a certain type of china. But Ally couldn't find them in the storage closets at the corner of the room. Then she realized that perhaps they were stored somewhere inside the sideboard. Despite her earlier gripes, when it came time to work, Ally didn't slouch around.

So there I was, giving Ally a hand in bringing the china up onto the table. She was still sitting on the floor, both legs spread to one side and looking cute as hell. Her head was peeking into the dark sideboard as she counted all the different types of plates. It was a massive piece of furniture, that sideboard buffet; embellished with life-sized silver medallion heads that stuck to its doors like a hubcap to a tire. It was also an extremely long piece—long as the tapestry above it—and filled on the inside like the lower decks of a slow boat to China.

After I did the dishes, Charles had one last job for me: "Mark, be a good chap and fetch me a couple of champagne bottles from the kitchen."

"Look in the cabinet next to the Frigidaire." Ally added.

They were there all right. Did Ally know her shit or what? I brought the bottles out to Charles: "Here they are, sir... Veuve Clicquot 1926!"

"Ah, splendid. Now we are all set to go to lunch," Charles said. Then he told Ally something in French. No problem, she replied.

"A bientôt," I said to Ally on the way out. She was about to leave pretty soon too, for school. But she also said that she'd be back late in the afternoon, at which time we could then decide on what we'd do for the evening. Needless to say, it was something I was more than pleased to hear.

I was preoccupied with thinking about what I ought to do that night as I followed Charles out of the house. It wasn't until we stopped at a red light before a crosswalk that I realized we weren't taking the car. "I take it we are walking to the Right Bank?"

"I don't drive much anymore. Always preferred walking, actually. It is the highest form of exercise—a wonderful way to relax and reflect."

"Did'ya ever get jogger's high? Or in your case, a walker's high?"

"Not so much a high as maintaining a degree of level-headedness. Walking helps to get rid of the thoughts that one would like to forget, as well as to trigger other thoughts that one has already forgotten. Personally, if I don't at least walk an hour or two a day, I'd feel a bit claustrophobic. Besides, walking has the added benefit of absorbing the vibrations of the city. Cars simply don't allow for the same."

"But a convertible is okay, right? As it interacts directly with the surroundings."

"To a certain degree, yes. Now that you mention it, would you believe that I have never owned a hardtop motorcar in all my life? Even drove a jeep in the army."

"*Everybody* drove a jeep in the army," I cracked. "How's that jeep à *la* Mercedes doing, by the way?"

"It was shipped back to Corsica."

"Oh, I didn't know that. So whose car is it that's under the cover in the courtyard?"

"It belongs to a friend from London."

"How does it feel to get a new set of friends, after all these miles."

"Some thirty-thousand dollars poorer, I suppose," Charles said. "Actually, that old Benz of mine is not as old as it looks. Indeed, it was one of the last few built on the larger chassis—the same year they had begun production on the sleek two-seaters, which became a top seller." Charles then told me that he was among the earliest on board when the 200 series first came on the market in the early 60s, and how he completed the line's product life cycle by purchasing a newer version of it in the early 70s, when that particular chassis was on its final leg.

"Uncle Charles, I guess you are among the few people in the world who happened to have inadvertently skipped over the hardtop age, since convertibles are now considered fashionable again." Hard to believe those two cars back to back lasted twenty-six years, as long as my whole life. If Americans would have behaved as Charles did, General Motors might now be a much smaller company.

As we walked toward the Seine, Charles briefed me on the history of his neighborhood. The part of the Seventh Arrondissement we were in, he told me, was as central a location as can be. However, in the era of prince and kings, the district was often referred to as the outskirts, or *Faubourg*. Thus the name Faubourg Saint-Germain. As Charles explained it, the most fashionable place to live back in the 1600s was around the Place des Vosges, on the Right Bank. But when Louis XIV erected the Palace of Versailles, many courtiers began building grand houses, or hotel *particuliers,* on the Left Bank. It was closer to Versaille, and therefore, a more happening place to be. Unlike the English, the French nobility were more interested in being city dwellers than country squires. They liked the festive feasts and parties, and the minglings with philosophers and writers like Rouseau, Voltaire and Molière. "The provincial nobility," Charles said, "was never quite as chic."

The character of the Faubourg, though changed, still retained some visible vestiges of the past. The major streets were much narrower; the houses were mostly low-rise—many of them spread far apart—with walls and courtyards to keep their distance from the street front. The feeling of the neighborhood wasn't typical of what you'd come to expect from Paris: the door after door of *boulangeries, pâtissieres* and *charcuteries.*

Despite the fact that many of the old hotel *particuliers* still remain, most have been transformed into government ministries, foreign embassies, and historic museums; or, subdivided into smaller residences. Not many families have the rationale or the resources to keep up with the upkeeping of old family compounds. I mean, who the hell is going to clean all the windows of a fifty-room hotel *particulier*? Charles's house, on the other end, was much smaller in scale, and therefore, still managed to be privately kept. This is true of old New York mansions as well. The Frick and the Carnegie have long been transformed from residences into museums; while others have been razed to make room for ugly apartment buildings.

Although Paris wasn't as ruthless in the wrecking of all its old buildings, it did have its share of destructive streaks. In fact, after all those wars and upheavals and revolutions, it's hard to find any property that hasn't been vastly altered or confiscated—some several times—with much of the original treasures pillaged and plundered.

"The finest wood wainscotting from the best hotel *particuliers* were ripped away and sold as firewood—to be bought and burned later in the same fireplaces of the same hotels from which they were taken." Charles then turned a bit gloomy: "While we in France have left the books alone, we have certainly participated in the sport of burning!"

It was a delightful day in Paris. The temperature in the mid-60s and sunny—perfect jacket weather, though the breeze did pick up a bit as we hit the Seine. The Quai along the Seine is what gives Paris a sense of unity. Off hand, I don't think there is another city that better integrates the both sides of the riverbanks than Paris. As I stood in the middle of a bridge over the calm and untroubled Seine—with the riverscape of the Louvre and the Tuilleries on one flank, ministries and fine residences on the other—I had the sensation that I was personally holding up the Left and Right Banks together, with a little help from my fellow bridge-arches, that is. "Uncle Charles, it's a good thing that the German army didn't destroy the bridges when they left Paris."

"Yes. Unlike Florence, where all the historic bridges were blown up except for one, Paris met a kinder fate." Charles then told me about the Pont Neuf, the oldest bridge in Paris, and how an artist, in pursuit of creative expression, tried wrapping the bridge with ropes and plastic bags.

"What was the purpose of such in-Seine-nity, so he could microwave it?" Don't ask me why I said that; it just came out.

"It's as good an explanation as any," Charles said. "Critics have compared it to everything from the liberation of women to being a symbol of capitalism."

That cracked me up. The French, give them nonsense and they will formulate it back into reason. Give them real American know-how and they will dismiss it as nonsense. Charles was no exception. From the late 1950s up to the 1968 student unrest, he was a professor of philosophy at the Sorbonne as well the founding editor of a journal called *Réflexion.* One of my earliest exposures to Professor Charles was from an old magazine clipping that my grandparents had saved. It said that while Charles's classroom teaching was relatively orthodox, his voice among the intelligensia was that of an unrelenting rebel. Using *Réflexion* as the vehicle, he mounted assaults on anything and everything—be it Kierkegaard's "essence before awareness" or Sartre's "existence before essence"—no idea was so sacred as to be beyond reproach, and no person was so high and mighty as to be spared exposés. Even Charles himself was fair game. One time, he was denounced in his own journal as being nihilistic for a talk he had given at a gathering of mystics. In the speech, Charles introduced a theory called the "Reflection Principal of Reality." It states that we are fundamentally all invisible creatures of extreme likeness. Reality, or three dimensionality, is merely a reflective trick that the invisible beings devised to distinguish themselves from one another—as a way to keep score. It's as if things are at once similar and uniquely different. I wonder if Charles had ever taken LSD. It was, after all, the '60s; and be it Montmartre or Montery, something was definitely in the air.

It is said that some thinkers—Heidegger and Lacan, to name two—were misunderstood due to the difficulty of their material. Then there were others, such as Charles Martin, who were perhaps incomprehensible due to their intentional disregard for the comprehension *of* their material. One of the heights of misunderstanding was reached in 1968, when, to the astonishment of friends and foes, Charles suddenly withdrew from the arena of far-flung philosophical inquiries for the closer-to-the-chest games of capital accumulation—to become a managing partner of Bank LeMan, a private bank in Geneva. His only explanation—family obligations. So, with the virtually overnight 180 degree turn, Charles transformed himself from a radical outsider to the inner sanctum of capitalism, and remained there until his retirement.

After relinquishing much of his duties at the bank in the mid-80s, Charles began teaching again—part time at L'École Nationale d'Administration—in more policy-oriented fields such as international affairs and diplomacy. ENA is known as the school that runs the government. It has produced many of its future technocrats, bureaucrats and diplomats. Apparently, Charles had become more conservative and pro-establishment, perhaps for appearance's sake.

Then again, what's appearance to a man with so many faces. One of the stranger moments in my memory occurred a few years ago in New York. One evening, my telephone rang and it was Charles. He had flown in from the Cayman Islands earlier that day and was giving a reception at his hotel suite down the block. But what he wanted from me, strangely, was to see if I would avail to him my living room for half-an-hour. No problem, I said, just come on over. I then turned off my TV and stereo, shut the windows and pulled the curtains as he'd asked, and more or less had the place ready. Shortly after, a lady named Theresa walked in; very stylish and impeccably dressed. Had she been a little younger and more slutty looking, I might have mistaken her for a call-girl. But you know what? Charles ended up placing her on the couch anyways, for Dr. Charles had suddenly transformed into Dr. Freud. Christ, did that Theresa have problems: the guilt from all the money that her husband had left her; the lawsuits from other members of her husband's family, not to mention her ongoing battles with her own mother, who had very much disapproved of her tactics. But the best part of that session was when Theresa started going off on how she had begun to drool heavily in her sleep. I was in my room down the hall so everything was a bit sketchy; yet I believe what Charles was trying to do—incredible as it may sound—was to cure Theresa of her drooling. It was *really* bizarre. "You were upset, Theresa, and couple that with sadness, you have been crying loudly in your dreams... They were real tears, Theresa. But due to the body being virtually incapacitated as one dreams, and the tears being virtually dry as one is asleep, you have been resorting to the oral channel instead by way of drooling. Everything is fine, Tair-rai-za; you were merely expressing some desire to reconcile with your mother. The main obstacle here, so far as I gather, is your iron will and toughness. For what you really want, above all, is to force your mother to apologize *first*."

You know what, Charles might well have knocked some sense into her, and stabilized his own stake in her psychological well being in the process. I was so entranced by that whole episode that, soon as they left, I took out my old psychology textbook and tried to look up drooling. Zilch! Then I went to the library the next day; still zip! Lots and lots about sleep, but nobody had done any research on drooling. Clearly, the subject had its difficulties. Perhaps the secret was Charles's and Charles's alone. Or, to quote the parting line from him that night:

"The sincerity of the sorrow of a young widow,
at her billionaire husband's funeral."

4 / MARKET VALUE DE L'HOTEL D'AMBASSADEE D'UNE RÉPUBLIQUE BANANIÈRE

THE GDP OF SAID BANANA REPUBLIC

The restaurant Vignon was situated across from the Madeleine, a Greek-columned church at a busy intersection just beyond the Place de la Concorde—the *Red* Square of Paris. By the way, if you go to Paris, there is no need to go deliberately to that historic and bloody square. It is so centrally located that, sooner or later, even if you're not guillotining royalty or storming the American Embassy, you shall stumble upon it.

Inside the restaurant, Charles was greeted by the maitre d', a cordial, heavyset middle-aged man. Instead of going into the dining room, Charles opened the door to a narrow stairway leading upstairs and told me to wait in the foyer for a minute until he came back down.

While waiting for Charles, I took a look around. I was glad I was in coat and tie. Most men had suits on, though they did tend to favor checks and plaids; more colorful shirt selections, too—to compete with the red and purple outfits of the ladies present. The tone of the dining room was more sedate and formal: panels of dark wood alternated with panels of mirror; paintings were hung evenly between the mirrors, and chandeliers in the middle to soften the lighting. All in all, it was a stately setting. Far more hushed than that brasserie the night before, or any place I'd normally go to in New York.

When the consultants do lunch, they generally take the middle road. They don't stuff down sandwiches while cursing at their monitors as they do on Wall Street, nor do they entertain clients to the degree done on Madison Avenue. Because of a heavy workload, lunches are more often working sessions on location—ranging anywhere from elegant executive dining rooms to student union-like cafeterias.

My boss, being responsible for generating business, goes to those midtown power-nosh joints more regularly. Yet quite often on Fridays, if he isn't traveling, he'll try to take a bunch of us out. Sometimes, strictly me and his secretary Connie. It was my turn to pick out a restaurant the previous week, so I opted for a nice Indian place across from "21". Why bother with a burger at a *speakeasy*, I told Warren, when you can have three lunch buffets at a Bombay *palace* for nearly the same price. Connie got on me good for that one: she said I was trying to subliminally ask for a raise. Well, that's because she normally does the picking, and we'd always wind up in a trendy Italian place. Not that I mind. I mean, like most young people, I eat far more Italian fare than classic French. Perhaps it was because French is seen as a cuisine for the older crowd. A quick survey of the Vignon dining room had reflected that. And, looking at the menu, the price must've had something to do with it, as well. That's how restaurants pay their rents, I guess. Remember Calvin Coolidge, who said that the "business of America is business?" Well, it might also be said that the *business of the business lunch is the lunch business.*

Charles came down and we were led to a booth near the entrance. Our seats were of the sleek contoured variety. It felt closer to sitting in Ally's convertible than to those traditional upholstered chairs in the center of the dining room. Our table was formally set for lunch, with three crystal glasses on top, a bread-and-butter plate on the left and so on. The napkin rested on a large plate, folded to look like three pieces, and as starched and crisp as a consultant's shirt.

Instead of cocktails that kill the taste bud, a bottle of house champagne was brought to us and put in an ice bucket next to the table. According to Charles, Vignon's house champagne was better than most brands sold in stores. "Wonderful champagne," I said after a sip. "Not too sweet, not too dry."

"And very chilled." Charles added. "Nothing kills a champagne more than too warm a temperature."

Don't know much about champagnes, I'm afraid. To me, so long as it doesn't taste like a ginger ale with alcohol in it, it's good champagne.

"What would you like, Mr. Vermont? Clams and oysters, or will you be a little bold and tackle the *escargots*?"

"Will the S CAR go with the champagne?"

"It does not matter in the least. Everything goes well with a fine Champagne."

"Then *escargots*, definitely! Had them once in San Francisco's Chinatown; tasty but messy."

The French version, *Escargots de Bourgogne,* were much larger. Served on a metal plate with shallow cups on the bottom that held the shells in place. Even if you don't like the idea of eating those little mollusks, you ought to do it at least once just for the fun of it; and, as well, for the smell of that butter sauce. The way to properly eat the escargot is to use a metal holder to first pick up that slippery son-of-a-gun, then take a tiny fork to dig up the meat inside the shell. But whatever you do, don't touch the plate. The heat will take your fingers right out of action. And you need your fingers dexterous through out this whole affair. Also, don't think about using your mouth, either, to suck out the escargot in that amazing parsley butter sauce. Well, you can think about it—I sure did—but don't do it, for it will also burn you mad.

"Escargots must be starved for a while before being eaten," Charles said. "They often ingest poisons from plants that could make one ill."

"Kind of like that expensive fish them Japanese eat," I said.

"Only the *fugu* could kill."

"Ever tried 'em?"

"Only in Japan. And only with an acclaimed chef."

"Been to Japan lately? What do you think about the Japanese?"

"They love the French more than anybody, in spite of our tough trade policy toward them. See any Toyotas on the road this morning?"

"No, but the Japanese are certainly making big inroads in New York, buying up everything around us in Midtown."

"In Paris as well, particularly around the Arc de Triomphe. I must say, however, that buying real assets is different from dumping automobiles. When they buy, some Frenchman or previous owner gets the money from the sale—quite a bit of money, for that matter. Not to mention the fact that the buildings still remain where they were. Surely, they are not being moved to Japan."

"I don't know, sir. What if they buy up the whole of Paris."

"Well, if the French wish to do so, they may use the proceeds to buy up a piece of Tokyo, albeit a tiny one. With the property price on the Ginza at millions of francs a square meter, can you blame the Japanese for looking abroad for opportunities?"

"So you are not so alarmed by the Japanese threat."

"What threat? The problem with you Americans is that you're so used to buying out everyone else on the cheap that when someone wants a piece of you, you get nervous; as if an invasion is coming—the beginning of the end!"

"I'm not nervous; not nervous at all."

"You shouldn't be. As a matter of fact, I even feel a degree of sympathy for them."

"Huh?"

"Truth be known, the Japanese have been paying too high a price. When the wealthy Americans began their European shopping sprees a hundred years ago, they bought our finest at giveaway prices. Yet look at what the Japanese are paying today. How are those poor souls ever going to build a great art museum if they have to fork out millions per painting."

"Who cares how much you pay for them. It's how much they'll be worth tomorrow."

"But how much *will* they be worth tomorrow? How much upside potential is there? Rare paintings aren't so bad due to their fixed supply. But what about office buildings and companies? The Japanese don't want to acknowledge it publicly, but they've lost billions on their foreign investments due to overpaying and currency loss. And they will continue to lose billions more in the future."

"I agree." I said. "They have to learn to acquire assets in a less costly manner. If the top five bids for a building were all Japanese, they would indeed be bidding against themselves." When the subject was business, Charles and I shared similar philosophies.

However, we did not see eye to eye with regard to America's mounting national debt. The trillions of dollars the government is currently in the hole, and the hundreds of billions that they continue to tack on by way of yearly deficits. I am outraged. So outraged I told Charles that I could even see myself in a tax rebellion if the politicians plan to dump all that debt on to the younger generation. Charles didn't empathize with my bitterness: "You are mixing up the issues here. Government debt and surplus, by themselves, are neither detrimental nor beneficial. The only thing that matters is how they use the revenue."

"Yeah, and they're throwing the money right out the window!"

"Oh, I'm sure somebody's got it. Let us suppose, shall we, that a god dressed in red, white and blue descends one day on to the White House lawn and offers you a trillion dollar loan at one percent. Would you take it?"

"Sure, I would. Be a fool not to."

"But wouldn't that have made your total debt a trillion dollars greater?"

"Yeah, but that's almost like getting money from a tree. Who's going to turn that down?" Though I realized as I was saying it that I had sort of repudiated my earlier statement. I tried to save myself: "Actually, what I'd do with the money is, I'd refinance the debt and save billions in the process."

"Second scenario: let us replace god's money with savings from millions of charitable Americans. Would you take the money from that type of tree?"

I hesitated. I felt like saying: yes, but...; then changed my mind. "No. It'd be just like a tax, wouldn't it? I mean, as much as I want the money, if the market rate is 6% and the people are only getting 1%, then it's merely another form of taxation. And if there is one thing I hate more than taxes, it's taxes in disguise. However, if the Japanese wanted to lend it to me at one percent, then by all means! I might even give them each a Congressional Medal of Honor for doing it."

I thought that was pretty funny but Charles was in a serious mood. "Supposing your advisors tell you of yet another way to lessen the debt load: through inflation. Would you do it then?"

"Hmm. A streak of double digit inflation would certainly reduce the burden on the government, especially if they could lock in the rate before they inflate. But again, it's still a tax in disguise: good for debt holders but bad for fixed income folks and young people without much debt."

"Your analysis is largely correct. Indeed, it was not so much Reaganomics, but the spiraling inflation of the 70s, that got your country into its present budgetary mess. It was during the Jimmy Carter years that America had the biggest tax hikes in its history.

How, you say? By pushing up everyone's tax bracket but not their underlying purchase power."

"Yeah, 70% top marginal rate in the 70s. So that was why there wasn't much deficit in the Carter years: the tax dollars were rolling in as nominal income shot up, but living standards actually went down as larger and larger chunks of a family's income went into the paying of taxes." Leave it to Charles to elucidate me on the finer prints of American history. "So what would you suggest to Uncle Sam, Uncle Charles? Just keep the debt mounting until the folks finally decide they are not going to take it anymore?"

"If that is the only way for everyone to learn, so be it."

"Even so, I don't want to be the one getting screwed. Actually, I wouldn't even mind so much had the tax money been going toward projects that promote future growth. That way, at least I know that people my age can stand to benefit. I mean, in a sense, I'd rather see us billions in debt yet having productive projects in progress, than billions in surplus with the government acting merely as a transfer agent, moving money from one group to another."

Charles began grinning all of a sudden: "I think I have a selfish Marxist on my hands, one who believes in government spending, but only if he were part of the beneficiary."

"No, no. I still believe in the private sector. However, if the government demands to have its hands wet, then let them dip it in pork barrels. That's one thing I admire about France and Europe—vast train-sportation networks and grand Mitterrand-esque monuments. They benefit everybody. Costly to build but beneficial.

"Not to worry, my boy," Charles said earnestly. "America remains a place of vast wealth. Your country has plenty to spare—natural and otherwise—far more than Europe. You did, however, touch on a good point earlier: the important thing is *how* the government spends the money. Whether it is borrowed or derived from taxes is irrelevant, though I might even argue that at times it would be more shrewd to borrow as it lessens the burden on taxpayers and increases financing from abroad."

"Good, then let's really re-inflate," I said. "All kidding aside, since the government is not a corporation trying to make a buck, the projects it accepts or rejects ought to depend more on how much each will increase the net worth of the country as a whole."

"Yes. If fiscal expenditures would target less toward transfer payments and subsidies, and more toward the building of roads, schools, bridges, and housing; then the country as a whole would be far more productive. Not to mention that the future generations will benefit, as well. As a matter of fact, not only will the future citizens benefit, but so will the future governments, for they will have become recipients of gifts that are worth far more in replacement value than their initial cost to the donor."

"Kinda like handing down a 40-million-dollar Van Gogh that had only cost you a hundred thousand way back when."

"More so than the art market, which goes through booms and busts, the cost of building the infrastructure is constantly going up; and quickly. Have you any idea of the replacement cost of Hitler's Autobahns if they had to be built at today's prices?"

"I can't begin to imagine," I said. "Or conversely, the billions in savings that might have been achieved if the Channel Tunnel were built in the Autobahn days."

"Quite. Only we'd be speaking German now."

I laughed. One thing about Charles: age does not wither, at least not his quick and razor sharp mind.

After the escargot came the fish course. And it was extraordinary. I was all set to order a *Truite Farcie* when my eyes caught a plate of turnover-like pies passing by. The waiter said it was the *Vol-en-Vent d'Écrevisse à la Nantua*, a crayfish pie. Looks like the stuffed trout will have to wait, I told myself; though I made sure it was all right with Charles that I would not be exactly eating fish.

"It is fine as long as you save some appetite for the roast."

"Guaranteed!"

From escargots to crayfish pie is like going from beef jerky to beef Wellington. Each distinctive in its own way. The crayfish looks sort of like a giant shrimp, but its meat is more moist and delicate. And, as its best part is from around the tail, it is also a bit lobster-like. Boy, did that thing ever taste good. See, in addition to having the sauce on the side of the plate, the chef also stuck some of it inside the pastry around the meat. The Nantua sauce was a yellowish cream sauce with crayfish butter mixed in. Although there were only two pies, a single serving, the chef was not stingy with the sauce. And it was a good thing that he wasn't, for as much as I tried not to take as big a bite as I would have an Italian sub, this being a posh bastion of gastronomy and all, I still managed to dip the pies in the sauce and wolf them down long before Charles was done with his fish. Maybe I rushed it a wee bit. But, my rule is, the pie, being finger food, need not be eaten in too genteel and orderly a manner as say, Charles's *Sole à la Normande*.

"How is your sole, sir?"

"Superb. Though probably not as good as your *vol-en-vent*." Charles smiled. "Dover sole is famous the world over," he said. "The ones you get in America just aren't quite the equal of those that come out of the English Channel."

"Thanks for telling me that, sir. I'll try to stick with fishing for blues from now on."

"Oddly, one of the most memorable Dover soles I've had was at a restaurant in New York. Remember the old Le Pavilion?"

"Remember? Never even heard of it!"

"Well, it was a while back, in the early sixties. In any case, Le Pavilion was the first and only French Restaurant in New York that was getting regular air shipments of fish from France. I had the good fortune to be on hand as one of the very first to taste their Dover sole. Those were the days before the jumbo jet so one could imagine the cost. Nonetheless, the sole I had that particular day was absolute perfection. Only hours old, and as firm and flaky as any in France."

"Was it a sauce *Normande*?"

"Oh, I don't remember."

"Maybe that's why there is no more Le Pavilion," I said. "It eventually went broke after paying all those 'same day air' charges from *La Manche*."

Our next course was the *Poulet de Bresse Vignon*, the house roast chicken. It sounded so basic, yet it was such an overwhelming dining experience that I'm finding it difficult to explain things in order. First of all, it was Bresse chicken, arguably the best chicken in the world. "These are free-range chickens that roam in unhurried little farms," Charles said. "Although one could invariably raise free range-chickens in Texas, it is the environment of the Bresse region that really set them apart. With the rich soil, the worms are juicier, insects more plentiful. And the chickens wash it all down with pure stream water melting from the neighboring snowy peaks."

"Sounds like the chickens have a better time eating than we do," I said.

"It gets better. After a few months, the chickens spend two weeks on the farm being fed on only milk and corn—just before the kill. This makes their meat plump yet fat-free."

"Have you ever seen 'em in action, before they bought the farm?"

"Ah, they are beautiful creatures. They all possess those unique bluish legs that cut down on counterfeits." That's the great thing about Charles: I could ask him anything, and odds are, he would know about it.

It was the maitre d' who carved the chicken for us. And, boy, was he impressive at it. Armed with a giant fork, he first stabbed the chicken in the thigh and lifted it onto the carving table. In seconds, he had cut into the thigh and twisted off the leg. After that, he struck into the other side of the chicken and removed the other thigh. He then popped off the wings with just his fork alone and placed the chicken breast up, to be cut into slices and served onto our plates. The complete operation was done with such speed and precision that he sort of reminded me of a surgeon.

The sauce that accompanied the Bresse chicken was made mostly from combining its dark juice, Madeira, some burgundy, mushrooms, and, of course, butter. The French eat less meat than the Americans but they sure use enough butter to make up for it!

Just before the maitre d' served the sauce, he looked at Charles and asked, "Champagne?"

"*Bien sûr,*" Charles said.

The maitre d' then quickly took our bottle of champagne and poured some of it on to the sauce as it was still being reduced, "To give the sauce that supreme lift!"

Unorthodox? Perhaps. But *that* was what many people go to France to experience—a mixture of style and substance—the traditional art form of haute cuisine practiced with a dash of spontaneity. Of course, I barely tasted the champagne. But knowing it was in there, knowing the way the whole dish was served, knowing a little background on the *Poulet de Bresse*—all of these things and more—had made that dish a complete culinary experience.

"Is it the maitre d' or the chef that makes a restaurant go?"

"Both. And, a passionate owner, who is working upstairs today. If the maitre d' is lacking in strength and skills, the best of dishes cannot taste as good. Some maitre d's are so well trained that they could cut a whole bird in the air, and then there are others that are so slow it takes them longer to carve a pot-au-feu than it takes for me to eat one. See the maitre d' standing out there near the wooden screens? See how alert he is? No detail escapes him, yet he fools everyone. Look at him, is his mouth moving?"

"Don't think so."

"But he's eating. He's constantly eating!"

"Pretty funny: weird scenes inside a French restaurant. How old is this establishment, by the way?"

"After the turn of the century. It was a late-comer. Shortly after Baron Haussmann built the *grands boulevards* over a hundred years ago, many restaurants opened for business in this quarter, from the Madeleine to the Opera, then continuing along on the Boulevard des Italiens. Heavens, I used to hear stories of feasts at the Maison d'Orée and Café Riche that were out of this world." There was a thirst for nostalgia in Charles's voice. Kind of like the thirst I get when I'm wondering about those 1960s Woodstock years—wishing I was there!

To quench our thirst that afternoon, the sommelier handed us the wine list. I almost couldn't believe my eyes: it looked more like a book than a list—thick as a beefsteak from Peter Luger's. Certainly I felt intimidated. Why, just the sommelier's appearance alone might have made some Americans wish that if only they hadn't been brought up on jug wines from, well...California. On his uniform, the sommelier had, among other things, a huge piece of fancy gold medallion hung in front of his heart on some really colorful ribbon. The man was more decorated than a dictator from Africa.

Having been brought up on beer and vodka in high school, and Italian Soaves in college, my experience with real wines was only at the recognition stage. I've tried a few Bordeaux and Burgundies here and there, and could probably name a handful of great French Châteaux, but ask me the difference between a St.-Julien and a St.-Emilion, and I'll tell you they are named after different Saints.

"Uncle Charles, Bordeaux or Burgundy?"

"When in doubt, it is best to select a Bordeaux."

"But the chicken is from Burgundy, right? So isn't it better to stay local?"

"The problem is: the Bordeaux region produces ten times the wine of Burgundy, yet it is not particularly renowned for its food. So how does one reconcile with such an imbalance."

"I don't know. But isn't there an order imbalance, too, in the traditional way of meat with red and fish with white, due to the perception that the public is generally eating lighter, and yet, there is still all that red wine flowing around. How are they ever going to drink up all that Bordeaux, or does nothing matter anymore?"

"Things matter differently to different people. While growing up in France and during my years in England, I had seen students drink Bordeaux with everything. When one's been given watered-down old clarets since childhood, it then becomes a lifetime habit. But the English generally drink wines that are much too old, often past their prime. Sometimes I get the impression that they are drinking more for nostalgia. The American connoisseurs, meanwhile, have to learn to relax. They are too careful in choosing their wines, making sure it is the perfect age, with the perfect food compliment and so on."

"And the French don't?"

"The French are the most careless wine drinkers in the world. Personally, I love collecting old wines, but prefer to drink the great ones as soon as they are ready."

"But too early make those wines less great."

"Possibly; but less costly, as well. Indeed, as the best Romanée-Contis begin to age, one sees them increase in value with each passing day. By the time they are aged to perfection, one can't afford to drink them anymore. What good is that going to do anyone? When the Americans were stocking up on the '82 Bordeaux, I was already drinking them."

"Le Grand Cru nouveau est arrivé!" I laughed. Casual drinker, Charles? Not always; certainly not due to his lack of knowledge on grapes. Ask him what the rainfall level in Bordeaux was in 1964, and he'll be able to tell you. We saw it first hand when Grandpa and I visited Charles at his villa in the South of France twelve years ago. It was at a dinner in his garden with some other guests. At one point, Charles carried on a mild debate with a bon vivant regarding the merits of a 1964 St.-Emilion that was being served. This guest was insisting that 1964 was a bad year due to the torrential rains, but Charles told him that the Cheval Blanc had already been picked before the rains came and was thus exceptional. Now, supposedly, the reasoning is, that since the Cheval Blanc is composed mostly of Merlot grapes, which mature sooner and are consequently picked earlier than the Cabernet Sauvignons, they were saved from disaster.

"Uncle Charles, how do you remember all those rainfall levels?" I said with awe and admiration.

"It's not much to remember, really. Just know the Burgundies and the Bordeaux. One does not need to be overly concerned with California nor Italy as their climates are rather consistent."

"How are the current crops looking so far?"

"They are doing quite well. The weather is good; no damaging rainfalls, at least not yet. Indeed the 1980s, overall, has been a resounding success. Its wines should supply ample fine drinking for the next decade."

"Does this mean that the prices should also be coming down, since there is an abundance of quality?"

"Not for the first growths, *les premiers crus*, which many people collect. Those prices are already up. But go down a notch or two and the values shall be excellent." Charles then handed me the wine list and asked me to go ahead and pick out a wine.

Incredibly, I wasn't that nervous. I decided that it would be either an 1985, or an 1986. Then I remembered the great weather in France that summer we toured Europe. "Since I passed through Bordeaux in 1985 on the way to Pamplona, let's go with a second growth Haut Brion, to find out what I had missed."

"Fine choice!"

The moment arrived. The sommelier opened the bottle and handed me the cork. As I was about to sniff it, Charles stopped me: "Just check the year on the bottom and throw it in the ash tray." The sommelier then gave Charles a look as he poured a little wine into my glass from his wine basket. Now it was my turn: I grabbed the stem with three fingers, brought the wine up near me, swirled it around a bit to check out the leg, and took a tiny sip. "It's fine," I concluded rather impulsively.

Next thing I know, the sommelier began pouring some wine into Charles's glass. Charles then broke off a piece of breadstick and put it in his mouth; then he picked up his wine glass and brought it over to the edge of the table, carefully checking the wine's color against the white table linen; then, finally, he placed his nose above the rim of the glass to smell the bouquet. Shit! That was what I forgot to do. *Dammit, Mark, how the hell could you forget to take a big whiff at that sucker.* When I was stopped from sniffing the cork, I must have overlooked sniffing altogether. *Damn!* I was shaking my head in embarrassment. No wonder the sommelier poured some wine for Charles: an amateur's verdict needed a second opinion.

Charles then tasted the wine with the most intense look on his face. He seemed to be silently chewing it and looking very disturbed. Oh god, was I hoping for that wine to be okay. I dearly hoped that there was not going to be a scene. Charles could get very finicky in situations like this. And the way that sommelier was looking at him, his towering body slouched toward Charles, with the biggest goddamn stare on his face, was scary and intimidating indeed. He reminded me of that guy on television that used to do them Nacho Cheeze commercials. Every time he takes a big bite at his chips, everything around him begins to shake and quake.

Finally, Charles swallowed the wine, then waited, and waited till he slowly opened his eyes. "*Excellent!*" he said to the sommelier. "*C'est excellent!*" Finer words were never spoken, boy! What a deep sense of relief I felt. But it was *major* slow motion for a while, the way those final seconds had elapsed. Holy shit was I nervous. I thought I had picked a spoilt wine.

This was the kind of crisis amateurs like me faced. Although I liked the wine after my first sip, I didn't have enough confidence to know why. Looking back, I realized it was unlikely that the wine was spoiled. Charles was probably just playing games with the sommelier, I concluded. That's another reason to order younger wines. They are much safer.

"It is vitally important to use one's sense of smell," Charles said. "The bouquet, more so than the taste, is that which gives each bottle its distinctive personality."

At last, I gave that Haut Brion a solid sniff. There was a rush of intense fragrance filling into my nostrils—herbs and spices mixed with wood. When finally I drank down a mouthful, it was like drinking flowers, with a deep lingering after-taste.

We talked some more about the Bordeaux. I learned from Charles that it is actually the bad soil that is most responsible for a chateau's greatness. Charles called it the sun-to-grape ratio. All it means is that when the soil is too rich, too many grapes get produced, resulting in each individual grape not getting as large a share of sunlight as it otherwise might. Therefore, it is the chateaux with the poorest soil—the ones that yield the fewest grapes per square foot—that also produce the best quality grapes. So the next time you open up a bottle of Margaux, admire the chateau's splendid architecture, not its soil.

On the subject of how best to enjoy the finest Châteaux, Charles was less tour guide and more guidance counselor: "Wine ought to reflect a purpose, an inner philosophy, however a flexible one. Although there are no hard and fast rules, neither should there be total ignorance."

I told him it's sort of like some people's approach to fashion. As long as they can reasonably justify what they're wearing, they are making a fashion statement.

As to the way to become a fashionable oenophilist, Charles recommended slow absorption over total immersion. One key point he mentioned was to set yourself a target, and stay with it. For example, spend some time drinking different years of the same Château, then drink a variety of Châteaux of the same vintage. Those vertical and horizontal integrations are some of the best ways to recognize and remember. Another thing Charles suggested was to not be afraid to challenge yourself. "The general rule is, strong wine, strong food. Should you be in the mood, however, do try a Zinfindel with fish. Find out why it's improper, if at all. Many who decry such a mix have never even tried it."

"So what you're implying, sir, is that the difference between a light white and a strong red is far less than say…um, a Coke and a beer; yet, we wouldn't think twice about ordering either with our hamburgers—*I* wouldn't've thought twice."

"Well put."

"You know, Uncle Charles, there is this bookkeeper at work, an older woman, but a very free-spirit, who, during the summer months, would take Wednesdays off to go to Sandy Hook, New Jersey, where there is a nude beach colony. And for lunch, she'd have baloney and cheese sandwiches with a bottle of good wine."

I got a laugh out of Charles with that one. "Wine is a cook's best friend—a bad cook's, in particular. The worst of foods taste better with wine. But, to be frank about it, your bookkeeper is just as big a wine snob as a Chevalier du Taste-vins. There is no one way of drinking wine, just as there is no one way to make money. Indeed, the appreciation of wine can be quite personal and most inwardly directed. Sometimes, one is in a mood for confrontation. The wine thus becomes a person, a rival, so much so that if one doesn't give it the proper respect, it will come back and punish one. In such a case, one would allow a strong wine and a strong stew to slug it out. On the other hand, occasions would arise where one feels compelled to toy around a bit, so one creates a little mystery by having a red with pasta."

"A little mystery? This whole thing is more mysterious than the Bermuda Triangle."

"Then acknowledge the fact. It is perfectly all right to describe a wine as mysterious. Indeed, it is better to describe a wine as a personality than as a reaction to one's own taste buds."

"How do you mean?"

"When one develops an intense love for one's wines, one prefers to describe it in more precise terms than simply sweet, sour, bitter, or salty. If one ever finds oneself at a verbal impasse, describe a wine as one would with adjectives reserved for a beautiful woman—elegant, charming, spirited, tender, engaging, graceful...."

"Voluptuous, full-bodied, substantial, lots of leg," I had no trouble filling in the additional adjectives. Perhaps I was getting a little giddy from all the alcohol.

"Ehhh, if you please, Mr. Vermont; let us try to stick to the more *emotional* characteristics—"

"Of French women or American women?" I uttered. Charles apparently hadn't met any emotionally charged Harvard MBA's in their Brooks Taylors. They'd give Mr. Spock a run for his money.

Incidentally, a fair amount of Charles's expertise in wine was developed during his years at Oxford, where he enrolled after a stint with the British Intelligence during the war. There was great fondness as Charles recalled his dining experience at Oxford. "I was constantly under pressure from the Dons to name the wines at the great dinners," he said. "It was an impossible task. No one in the world could do well in blind taste tests. No one! Finally, I and a Russian history professor were able to bribe the butler into telling us about the wine being served with the promise that we'd guess imperfectly. As a result, we always guessed wrong; but never so embarrassingly as to claim a bottle to be a Petrus when in fact it had come from Chile."

Charles, ever prepared to act *un*prepared. "What was Oxford like, really? A place where twenty-year-olds act like they are two hundred, or the other way around?"

"A bit of both, actually—traditional, yet eccentric—unlike any other place in the world."

"Did you feel out of place there, being French and all?"

"My dear boy, I've been out of place *all* my life," Charles said, half seriously. "My years at Christ Church were rather agreeable, though at first I was a bit upset at not being able to join my friends who lived at the Tom Quad. I was instead relegated to the housing near the Meadows, where most of the international students were housed. That was not a problem; the cast of characters were just as colorful, and so were the views."

"Did you have to study a lot? I mean, how was your English back then?"

"I was partly a Classics student; working with Latin and Greek."

"But you still had to translate it into English, not French?"

"I had my tutor to thank. I would never have passed the Classical Honours Greats without his help."

Charles was just being humble. He did his program in record time. He was, even back then, a superbly educated man. Honours Greats in Classics was as tough a program as you could take up at Oxford. Some of the greatest British leaders had gone through it. But it was true that his tutor had a big effect on him. Oxford, the great institution that it is, has been just as well known for its chaotic, non-systematic way of learning. "You had august Dons that didn't give exams, privileged students that drank, gambled and misbehaved, and no one telling anyone what was going on. A far cry from my well structured program at the École Normale in Paris before the war."

Besides teaching, his tutor also introduced Charles to Lady Fiona, a family friend and a student at Sommerville, who eventually became Charles's wife. It was partly for that reason that Charles had such lasting impressions of his Oxford years. As much as he tried to control his emotions, Charles's eyes gave away just enough for me to realize that those were perhaps some of the happiest years of his life.

"It had always been my tutor's contention—not necessarily mine—that Lady Fiona was too brilliant for those room-wrecking Christ Church drunks."

"Yeah, as if a gentleman-drunk is any better," I cracked. "Was he right, though?"

"Well, one must admit that a great many of the old English families didn't value education as much as the French, not least education for women. So to see a girl with a hunger for learning and knowledge was indeed quite a thrill. When I entered graduate studies at All Souls, Lady Fiona and I used to spend the afternoons at the cinema and evenings at the All Souls Quad—watching the sunset between St. Mary's and the Bodleian while discussing everything from Stalin to tyranny in the fourth-century."

"Sounds very romantic," I said. "What a shame she had to die so young. It must've been an awful ordeal for you, the time of her sickness."

"Such is the nature of cancer," Charles said in a resigned tone. "It can strike at any age. And in those days, with devastating speed."

"With my grandmother, too," I said. "Though she was much older when she died."

"Audrey was a brave woman," Charles said. "Not trying to make light of our tragedies, but one of the last things your grandmother said to me was, 'Charles, darling, could you ever forgive me for eating so much out of a tin?'"

I shut my eyes for a very long second and smiled. When I opened them, I had to use the napkin to blow my nose, and, to wipe my eyes of a thin coat of glaze.

Just then the dessert arrived; always the strong point of all my meals, but unfortunately a course too frequently skipped over. I had the *Soufflé aux Framboises*. It had powdered sugar on the outside, and raspberries and liqueur blended in. "Uncle Charles, alcoholic mixtures do have a way of sneaking into French food, do they not?"

"Yes—the best of both worlds—the flavor of the liqueur with the alcohol flamed away."

The raspberry soufflé was served in a cup hot from the oven—so flambeedingly hot that the batter expanded quite a way over its rim as to form a little hat. It was so light and puffy at the top that, when I touched the raspberry with my spoon, it began vacillating back and forth, shaking like a certain part of a girl during a wet T-shirt contest.

Charles the grown-up passed on having a sweet dessert. He took a piece of Roquefort from the cheese cart instead. Roquefort, one of the great cheeses of France, is made down in the remote, mountainous region of Languedoc. "A good Roquefort shall be hand-made from unpasteurized milk," Charles said, "never manufactured. They are aged in extremely humid caves to develop that blue-green mold. Here, sample it."

"It tastes like a strong blue cheese," I said after a bite. "Though the moldy parts might take a novice some time to get used to."

"Not too long, I hope. I've seen six-year-old French children battling it out to see who is to get the moldiest piece."

When I was around six, I was wondering how a bicycle could possibly move on two narrow wheels. Till this day, I don't have the perfect explanation. Horizontal gravity, possibly?"

"Twenty years and a MBA later, you remain bloody useless!"

"So it's down to twenty years now. Last night it was twenty-six years of uselessness. An improvement, I presume?"

"You do have a remarkable ability to recall useless numbers," Charles said. "A skill I hope you can put to some good use."

"Card counting in Vegas, you and me?"

"I meant here in Europe, my boy." Then Charles abruptly asked: "Can you stay a few extra days?"

"Sorry, not next week, no," I regretfully said. "Why, what's up?"

"I've got some business in Switzerland, and thought you might like to come along."

"Thanks for the invite, though. You *know* how much I love to play your set up man. Who are we stealing from this time?"

"Stealing? Perhaps *after* I bring together some old enemies."

"You and Kissinger both! Or, to borrow a line from *Henri*: there better not be any crisis next week as my schedule is all booked up!"

5 / MONEY IS NO OBJECT IF THE PRICE IS RIGHT

I lay down for a little nap after we got back from lunch. Both my head and digestive system demanded it. Although no longer a kid, I still remained a terrific napper. Sure had gotten plenty of practice through all those boring classes in school, boy. The cycle usually went like this: for the beginning portion of each class, I tended to be fairly open-minded, at least insofar as to give the professor a fair chance to captivate me. But when they had fallen short of expectations, the natural tendency would have been to lose concentration and doze off. Now, if you were in the back row of a large lecture, it wasn't disastrous; however, this even happened to me in the smallest classes, which was pretty embarrassing.

Fortunately, the thing that continuously saved me from being an academic dropout was my knack for waking up on time—with a surge of renewed attentiveness, I might add—especially during the final stretch. Man, I could be found hassling my neighbors and even shamelessly asking questions in a desperate scramble to recoup what I had missed. It's really amazing how much information your brain can absorb if you just heighten your senses a bit and give your head a quick burst of nervous energy.

Another reason I hadn't flunked out of any classes, despite my penchant for cat-naps, was due to my being a slightly unorthodox student. See, I hadn't been seriously taking notes since I began high school. Up until then, I had been a thorough note-taker. What did me in was that European History class I took at Port Washington High. I had an extremely hard teacher, and our textbook was the thickest ever. For a while in that class, I wrote down everything, almost paraphrased all the chapters. But when it came time to look over my notes to study for an upcoming test, I found I had a serious problem reading my own handwriting. My penmanship was more confusing than King Tutankhamen's hieroglyphics, worse than that of a Mesopotamian tablet carver (or was it a Macedonian). See what I mean? It really scared the hell out of me, all those precious hours of note-taking wasted away.

Then one day, a Newtonian apple dropped on me when I saw, resting on the window sill of my history classroom, a perfectly harmless copy of the same textbook, just begging to be taken. Perhaps someone had dropped out and returned his book or something. Well, I certainly wasn't about to find out by asking the teacher. I was like—finders keepers!—and literally became a new student overnight: highlighting and jotting down choppy sentences in the text was suddenly all the rage. What extra writing I had to do was done on the back of those mimeographed handouts. Why should I walk around with heavy notebooks of mostly blank pages? So, from then on, the days of carrying a heavy load of books home from school were history, as there was always an extra set of books back at the house should I need to refer to them.

Looking back, I think that solving the textbook problem had had a major effect on my learning. I mean, every September, my eyes would be hawking around for sitting-duck textbooks. If I couldn't find an extra copy, which was rare, then I would draw and scribble notes on the only copy I had and paid whatever the fines levied at the end of the term. It was worth every penny in both the time saved and aggravations averted.

Slowly, with the passing of each school year, my recall of specific parts of the printed text vastly improved—call it the photo-of-text memory, if you will, for my tendency to rely on my brain to pull out a particular section of a book to answer a question. But my brain couldn't photograph my own hand-written notes for beans, especially if what I had written was just another version of the printed material. I think it had something to do with my brain cells being confused as to which file to pull up, the hand written or the printed; and in the confusion, the completeness of the recall had been far less than the total recall had it come strictly from a single source—the printed text alone. I had never had a chance to ask around to see if there were others like me. Everybody *else* seemed to have the grandest old time taking notes, often asking the teachers to repeat things over and over, then copy them down word for word. That was just the worst. I could never do that.

Perhaps it was due to this carelessness that I hadn't gotten many A's in school—wasn't even among the top ten percent. My laziness and my tendency to find ways around the conventional had made me an underachieving student. I was ambivalent: I wanted to do well in school, but I hated even more to invest overtime to do it. The worst classes for me had been the ones where a big chunk of the grade were homeworks and pop quizzes. But you know, one thing I had done that I remain very proud of: I frequently took the hardest level courses, like the A.P.s, and took them as soon as I was eligible to take them, too. In fact, I had done surprisingly well enough in those college advanced placement tests that, when I graduated from high school, I had already had college credits in History, Calculus, and French under my pelt. Not a bad deal considering the thousands they would charge you in college just to take those courses over again. So while not a great student, I made up for it in selectivity: spending five minutes whipping up a stupid essay for English composition, and spending the rest of the time reading up on the Treaty of Ghent. Another thing that was screwy was, I could take some of the hardest courses and walk off with a B; yet, I couldn't even get an A in American Government. Everybody got an A in American Government—it was taught by the easiest teacher in our high school; though I think part of the reason I didn't get an A was that there weren't any textbooks, which killed me because I then had to resort to borrowing notes from people to study for tests and stuff. I was such an idiot at times.

So anyway, from those textbook days on, I have grown to be very critical of teachers. It was no longer learning by verbatim. Before I would waste any calories from my finger muscles to take notes, I opted for a few seconds of brain waves by asking if I truly had to write that stuff down or not—especially if those instructors were graduate students from abroad. So when my classmates were busy asking the instructor, who didn't speak understandable English in the first place, to repeat the definition of *pareto-efficiency*, I simply circled the part in the book that he had been trying to make more confusing. How could all my fellow students go to class without bringing their textbooks along was just beyond me. Beyond me! If I didn't have my textbooks next to me, I'd be as nervous as a deprived nicotine addict.

In retrospect, now that my schooling is finally over, now that I'm less of a devil, I'm quite a lot embarrassed at how willful I had been. Although my college textbooks have long been sold, a number of my high school texts still remain. I think after I get my tax refund back this year, I'll send a big check to the Port Washington High School, as a small step toward alleviating my guilty conscience.

On the way down the stairs after my nap, I noticed through the glass doors a big old car in the courtyard. After hearing voices from the direction of the *salon*, I knew we had a visitor.

The *salon*, or drawing room, was straight back from the vestibule. After you walk down the marble stairs, you turn left and go through a columned doorway. The French are really into doors. Every damn room in the house had more than one set of connecting doors, with decorative reliefs over each doorway and gold carvings and cornices along the edge of the ceiling

The salon, either by design or through time, was filled entirely with formal, period furnishings. Well, not *too* filled as the middle part was kept rather free-flowing. The room itself was rectangular, lined with arched pallandian windows on the longer side to bring in the light, and an off-white color scheme along its walls to give it an impression of opulence and tranquillity. I think the tranquil feeling had also something to do with the ceiling being bright and simple, absent of any wild and fancy artwork that are found on the ceilings of newer and more elaborate European homes.

There was, however, no shortage of fine art in the salon. To begin with, covering an entire side wall was the largest piece of tapestry I'd ever seen, even larger than the one in the dining room. While the piece in the dining room depicted a Roman feast, this tapestry showed a more exotic, more fantasy oriented landscape—lots of water, sky and trees, all mingling along with animals, people and flying angels. It was the type of picture that you could look at off and on for a year and still find details you hadn't noticed before. I'm not even going to speculate on how many man-hours it took to thread that damn thing up.

Across the room from the tapestry was the fireplace. Placed around it were sofas and armchairs—gilded, of course—and upholstered in a silk fabric. To make that part of the room more distinct, an additional smaller rug was laid on top of the main one, just covering the area taken up by the sofas.

As for the fireplace, it looked cold. No knic-knacs on top of the mantelpiece to warm it up. The only item on top of that chunk of grayish-white marble was an antique jeweled clock, in a gold casing with movements signed by Thomire.

Set atop the mantelpiece, and extending all the way up the ceiling, was a gold-trimmed mirror reflecting squarely the tapestry on the opposite side. The gilded feeling was truly everywhere—walls, desks, and chairs—everything had hints of gold on it, including paintings, of which there were many.

One area with a heavy concentration of paintings was around the mirror of the fireplace. They were mostly works in oil depicting the lives of the happy and the content in their costumes. The paintings didn't look to be the works of Impressionists. I've seen enough of them on calenders and postcards to pick them out. Charles's paintings were too detailed, though they didn't appear to be that of the Old Masters variety either, as they lacked that solemn and darkly lit somberness of Rembrandt et al. Well, one way to find out for sure is to go into the next room and get it straight from the owner.

Entering the library, I smelled cigar smoke right away. Charles and his guest were sitting down on leather armchairs next to a coffee table and having drinks.

"Good afternoon, Uncle Charles!"

"Oh, hello there, Mark. I was just about to call you," Charles said. "Allow me to present the—"

"Thomas Mellery, an old friend of your uncle's; and if I may add, the only friend he has left."

"Mr. Mellery is too kind," Charles smiled. "And this is Mark Vermont, an open-minded and free-thinking young man from America."

"Aw, shucks," I said in a real American tone. "I'm only open-minded as long as I haven't made up my mind yet!" And I might've also added that as for free-thinking, that's when I wake up in the morning with a hangover, and my mind is totally free of any inkling from the night before.

Mr. Mellery and I shook hands. He was taller and heavier than Charles, with a rather firm handshake. When I said I was from New York, he gave me one of the best lines I've heard about my city: "New York is a city that can only exist in America; yet, it is nothing at all like America: it has the best of Europe and the worst of America all rolled up in one." How true, how true.

"I was just admiring the paintings in the salon," I said to Charles. "All those flying children, dancing courtesans, and nude ladies in storybook landscapes."

"The term is *fêtes galantes.* It refers to the sensual and pastoral themes of Watteau, Boucher, and Fragonard."

"Fragonard and Boucher, which period were they?"

"They were eighteenth-century," said Mellery. "Eighteenth-century Rococo—known for its wanton frivolity and gay intrigue."

"Ornamental, superficial and escapist—I have heard them all!" Charles responded. "Yet Mellery the *art critic* ought to be aware that those paintings in the salon are part of the house and *not* for sale."

"What of the Lancrets and Guiards here in the study?" Mellery went on. "And that Chardin in the dining room?"

"Only if you bring them up to investment grade!" Charles said with a little smile.

"That still-life is a Chardin, sir? I thought it was by an Impressionist."

"A case can be made to credit Chardin as a preamble to the Modernists. He was a master of colors, shapes and textures. All the *Rubénistes* were, actually; and, thus, were immensely influential to the Impressionist movement a hundred years on. Should Mellery have further doubts, I advise him to look at *Embarquement pour Cythère* by Watteau, then *Le Déjeuner sur l'herbe* by Monet."

My favorite painter—with all due respect to Charles, his Watteaus, and the way Watteau painted water—is the English water and landscapist J. M. Turner. Can he do up a boat in troubled waters or what? In order to accurately capture the rough and tumble of the raging seas, Turner would ask to be leashed to the mast of his ship as it goes through a storm, so that he could observe the sea without getting blown away. Talk about guts and determination.

This brings me up to the scary part of sailing. In foul weather, the seas could get downright treacherous, with waves so high that they appear to be waterfalls about to crash over. Having your boat airborne and taking thirty-foot dips between waves will not only make you feel that the earth is indeed round, but that it could also seriously make you ask yourself if you still want to keep sailing. Yet there is no thrill quite like a total wipeout narrowly averted. One of my dreams, and perhaps of many other sailing fanatics as well, is to one day sail through both the Atlantic and Pacific by way of rounding Cape Horn—down at the tip of South America—where the wind easily blows at thirty-five knots and frequently doubles up to seventy. It could get so gusty down there that when you move around, you need to lean your head tightly against a flat surface on the boat in order to prevent your head from getting smacked around by the tremendous force of the gust. In fact, if you look at a globe, you'll notice how void of land mass the South Seas are. There is no continent down there, so wind just goes round and round above the Antarctic nonstop, with the seas as high as a hundred feet. On the reassuring side, if you do have a solidly built boat, you just seal it, go underneath the deck, close the hatch, and hang on for your life when a storm comes. The boat will take care of itself. Even when the boat does go bottom up, it will keel back. Just hold onto something and count to fifteen, though it might seem more like fifteen years and counting. See, a sailboat is sort of like a condom with a cork in it—and sailors genitals in a bottle—it'll just float along till things clear up; or, till you slam onto Gilligan's Island or something. I see my mind is getting carried away again. Back to the library.

Unlike the other rooms of the house, the color of gold was conspicuously absent from the library. Instead, dark mahogany paneling with built-in bookcases surrounded the room, and desks and lamps of all sizes filled up the remaining spaces. The most noticeable desk was an old double-ended type that stood between the two windows, I think it's called a partners desk. It was topped with leather and decorated with fancy feathered-pen stands. Another oddity about the library was the absence of a room-sized rug—just a couple of smaller ones scattered about. Ironically, if anything, the library's wooden floor was the one that could have used some serious covering. The squeaking sound it made as I walked around was even worse than the squeaky hallway of my apartment.

"Mr. Vermont, would you care for a cigar?" Mellery asked.

"Thank you, no."

"In that case could I interest you in a Sherry?"

"Sherry'd be nice, thank you." I liked sherry. A philosophy professor at Penn used to pass it around in class sometimes. Sweet, cheap sherry, that is.

I went and sat down on one of the old chairs in front of the book-cases. They were just burgundy armchairs nailed down with brass stitchings, nothing special. In fact, the leather had so many crack lines that the seating surface didn't even look burgundy any longer. Moreover, my seat cushion was so bloated out of proportion that, as I sat on it, I heard this big puff of air being released as my rear-end nearly dropped into a free-fall. Good thing I didn't lose my balance and spill the Sherry.

Like me, Mellery was also in Paris for just a few days. His merchant bank in London, one which Charles had a stake in. had recently bought into a brokerage firm in Paris. Even more so than New York to America, London is hands down the financial capital of Europe. According to Mellery, France has powerful banks, but its domestic capital market remains small; thus, London leads the way through sheer volume. Before the Paris Bourse had begun its modernization, far more French stocks changed hands in London than in Paris.

I didn't go to London when I toured Europe a few years back. Not because I didn't want to go to Europe to hear English spoken; but because those luvely, luvely Brits—those jolly good fellows to Americans but tight-assed isolationists to Europeans—wouldn't let us roll our Eurorail Passes down their crummy ol' railroad tracks. Well, it's their loss! I could have given a badly needed boost to the dwindling intakes of those bookies and card sharks up there. Then again, I might've not.

Speaking of odds, Mellery was quite a gambler in his own right, though he masked it somewhat by touting his bottomless devotion for his thoroughbreds instead—two of which were to be running at the upcoming Derby week in England. "We are quietly confidant with the long striding Song and Dance; while Vagabond, our explosive two-year-old, has a tendency to move too early. Just how good a finisher he is remains to be seen."

"How long is the course?"

"One and a half miles, with the last two furlongs mostly downhill. It's the perfect race to test Vagabond's staying power."

"Sounds very exciting, Mr. Mellery."

"Very exciting, indeed. The joy one gets from seeing one's horse win a great stakes race is out of this world."

"A nice fat purse doesn't hurt either, wouldn't you say?"

"Perhaps. But I should emphasize, Mark, that this is above all a labor of love; of chasing a dream; of competing against great odds to fulfill such a dream—occasionally against the better judgment of one's peers; just ask Monsieur Martin how many times he has tried to discourage me."

It was now Charles's turn to make fun of Mellery. "Don't you believe for a moment that Mellery's still in it for the pursuit of some elusive dream. He's done remarkably well from his horseflesh for quite a number of years."

"Very kind of Charles to say so, but the racing business is getting tougher by the day. Last year's Newmarket sales saw a continued dive in prices. The forecast for the Kentucky sales in July isn't much rosier."

"How unfortunate," I said. "The Run for the Roses is becoming a run *on* the roses."

Mellery took it in stride, though. "Perhaps it's good in a way," he said. "Racing was once a marvelous and joyful pursuit, but as prices of bloodstock soared tenfold since the mid-seventies, it has become uncivilized. The cornering of the market by Americans didn't help the situation either. Then finally in 1986, prices began their fall."

"I don't understand something here," I said. "If prices are down, then there ought to be buying opportunities?"

"Yes and no. Besides a surplus of bloodstock, another reason for the decline is the new and tougher tax code, resulting in the racing business being all the less attractive."

"Do also keep in mind the lag from investment to payoff," Charles interjected. "Mr. Mellery had spent a great deal of money in the mid-eighties at the yearling sales, based on expectations of higher future stud fees. The Vagabond, his hopeful two-year-old, is an off-spring of a yearling bought at the 1984 Keeneland sales; one which

Mellery had paid millions. But as prices have fallen, even a winner will need luck to be able to recover the original purchase price in stud fees. And when one considers the fact that most of the horses are duds and flops, the outlook is dreadfully bleak."

"Monsieur Martin undoubtedly knows how to make a person feel wonderful," Mellery said sarcastically. "I don't know why I keep sending him invitations every year."

Evidently, Charles had been cutting down at the spectator front as well. He told Mellery that the chances of him showing up for the Epsom Derby were slim; however, he would try to attend the Royal Ascot meetings in July if he could squeeze it in. Clearly, Mellery was far more the sporting ol'sport type of the two. When Charles went away, he preferred the more reclusive surroundings: friends' parties at palazzos in Venice and palaces in Dusseldorf. He also tended to favor those high level economic conferences to a fox-hunting weekend. Like my boss, Charles was a sought-after speaker. Unlike Warren, Charles could be seen at Davos promoting capital markets one day, then turn around to defend nationalizations at the next Bilderberg meeting.

After Charles went upstairs to dress, Mellery and I had a little chat about consulting. He showed some interest in the corporate restructuring projects we had done. Thank Wall Street for that, I told him. After years of the whole being worth more than the pieces, the pieces are suddenly worth more than the whole. Although I was no rainmaker, I did put in a good word for our firm: the strong presence we had in London, and the successes we had had in turning companies around. Mellery was intrigued, especially upon hearing how speedy and efficient we were in carrying out the reorganizations. He said he would soon be exploring ways to expand his firm's reach in America, and that he might very well give us a call. Anytime, I told him.

Mr. Mellery, more so than other members of his family, which has a large presence in Asia, had always been pro-Europe. It is said that doing business on the continent could get very tricky. Besides the different languages and laws, you have corporate structures that are difficult to decipher, and disclosure laws that are far less strict than in the U.S., even for the biggest companies. It is a very popular sport, the shell game, played by owners who form various shell companies with cross-locking relationships—as a way to protect, conceal and deceive.

Through Mellery, I became better acquainted with Charles the banker / financier. Most private banks, particularly in Switzerland, set their main objective as the preservation of capital. The clients, at least the traditional ones, were more concerned with not losing their fortune than with multiplying it. But Charles had other ideas. He wanted to do more than just woo the rich; he wanted to expand and make things happen.

However, it wasn't all smooth sailing for Charles, especially in the beginning when the resistance was great. The notion of capital preservation had always been deeply entrenched in the Swiss investment philosophy. But Charles had a weapon that many investment managers didn't have. He was one of the owners, and with that, came a sizable capital base made up of himself and a loyal group of friends and devotees. Subsequently, an affiliate holding company was set up in neighboring Liechtenstein with the intention to aggressively put the capital to work. Since many of the wealthy had more than one institution for their deposits, Charles was able to bring in new business as well as maintaining the old. He could be seen reassuring Latin Americans on the virtual safety of their flight capital in the morning, then turn around to convey to the Arabs the advantages of acquiring Western assets in the afternoon. Dictators and Sultans, he'd had'em all!

"Although outwardly appeasing, Monsieur Martin's inner courage was that of a giant," said Mellery. "He had a tremendous capacity for information. Besides the reading of newspapers from Europe and the rest of the world, he regularly went through everything from major periodicals to obscure trade journals, as well as the digesting of stacks of detailed reports. Hardly a moment was wasted with him. At times, he could be so preoccupied with his analysis that he became absent-minded with normal business at hand."

Through a combination of intuition, courage and luck, Charles's investments achieved phenomenal returns. He had good timing. The 1970s created some great opportunities. Not only were many of the industries in transition, but just as important was the emergence of financial innovation. There was a plethora of new investment products that came on the market; some mere gimmicks, while others tapped a vast reservoir of international capital itching to be used. But Charles was no fool, he hedged his speculative sprees with a long bet on gold, lots and lots of gold. And gold, of course, only went from $35 dollars an ounce to $835. Such was the craziness of the Seventies.

"One must imagine that Monsieur Martin has traveled millions of miles visiting companies and clients the world over," Mellery added. "He has an aura about him that makes others want to do business with him." Another strength of Charles's was his exercise of independent judgment, Mellery told me. Some of his biggest scores were made against popular opinion. "It is this cockiness, this willingness to go against the flow that separates him from the rest. Seer one day and savant another, his reputation was such among his clientele that any advice from him became the voice that must be obeyed; not least among the ladies!"

"Ain't that the truth," I smiled in agreement.

Mellery continued: "Socially, Monsieur Martin strikes one as a crazy man when one has just met him; and if one knows him, he is infinitely crazier than any other craziness that one cares to remember. Some of that has carried over into business as well. He is a statistician who doesn't believe in statistics; a philosopher who doesn't believe in philosophy. It is almost as if he can't possibly prove himself right unless the others are also proven wrong."

It was at that moment that I found myself in total agreement. When the game is played at the highest levels, it is more than just who wins, but how the victory is achieved. For not only the ends have to be conclusive, but the means skillfully orchestrated, as well. A default by the opposition just isn't good enough; neither is a victory achieved through sheer luck or randomness.

When Charles came back down after putting on his dinner jacket, I had trouble picturing him as the ferocious investor that Mellery had described a moment ago. A distinguished gentleman, maybe; but in his black tie and cummerbund, he could look only so tough. In fact, he had to be doubly convincing to make his points stick.

We moved on to various financial topics, some general, others obscure. Mellery, being a capitalist, liked to see an eventual world where even the largest corporations can be taken over—at the right price. I agreed, but only if the playing field is level, especially when it's a foreign buyer. Charles, on the other hand, was uneasy with the idea of millions of shareholders. He would rather see companies having a dominant group in control, be it the founder, his family, or even a bunch of institutions—as long as they give the investors a clear idea of who is at the helm, or what faction is calling the shots. I had some problems with that: "Uncle Charles, if there are no checks on the founder's authority, his autocratic ways could easily lead to fraudulent acts that might ruin the company."

"True, but let's not forget that if the owners do cause a scandal, they themselves will have the most to lose. Call me traditional or old fashioned, but I'm not a strong believer in the idea of limited liability. Not unlike Rommel leading his own Panzers, if the owners are not willing to put their own personal wealth at stake, then why should the outside investors do the same with their capital?"

"All right, let me ask you both this, then. I have some mixed feelings on it: that is the idea of capital formation. On one side you have the Anglo-American tradition of looking for equity—you know, stockholders. Then you have the Continental European way of heavy lending from the banks and bondholders. Why so different?"

Mellery responded first. "As I am in the securities business, it is naturally in my interest to see Europe as one large capital market. The free flow of capital will help, so will the establishment of a single currency. Now, as to the best way for a company to attract capital, opinions vary. But from a strictly self-serving point of view, I would recommend this: if one feels that one's company will be going up in value, then one ought to get as much finance from banks as possible. However, if one feels the value of a company has peaked, then go to the equity market to find new investors and cash it in. Easier said, of course."

I liked Mellery's bottom-line driven instincts. Charles, though, was more elaborate. "The clash between capital market finance and private finance represents a convergence of two capitalistic philosophies. In the German-based model, the close links between banks and industries make the both sides mutually dependent. While this provides stability, it could only work in an environment of limited competition. What it essentially comes down to is a preference for a single strong outside partner such as a bank as opposed to thousands of unpredictable shareholders from within.

The danger in siding with the banks, of course, is the prolonged survival of not necessarily the fittest, which in turn would set off some rude awakenings when such companies eventually fail. The capital markets, on the other hand, are more incremental. Bad news is harder to hide for extended periods of time."

"Isn't the marketplace also less elitist?" I asked, "More everyman for himself—sort of a zero-sum game?"

"Yes," Charles replied. "The cozy relationship between the bankers and industrialist has made them distrustful of the masses. They see themselves as superior to the man on the street—who is often viewed as an opportunist incapable of rational thought."

Got to credit Charles for his honesty, especially considering he has undoubtedly been one of those elitists himself. That's the reason I like the market. It's more accessible, more in line with the democratic spirit. It gives us small folks a chance to beat up on the big guys. With that in mind, I had a question all lined up: "What was the most you have ever lost in one day?" I asked Charles.

No answer. Perhaps the memory of the wound was too painful to rehash.

Mellery, though, had no problems with the question: "In 1974 dollars or in today's?" he said, jokingly now. But back in those days, capitalists actually dreaded waking up in the morning. In fact, due to the preceding bull market running out of steam and the sudden OPEC oil shock, the markets worldwide took one of its greatest nose dives.

"It's easy to make money," Charles began. "But it's even easier to lose it!"

"You know what my problem is, sir? It sounds like the easiest thing, but time and again, I don't know how to properly take a profit. I mean, even when my head tells me to let the profit run, I'm usually out of a position at the slightest correction. And once I'm out, its difficult for me to get back in again, as if some rhythm had been broken for good."

"If I'm not wrong," Charles said to me, "this may be a blessing in disguise, for you have already mastered one facet of investing: knowing how to cut your losses."

"Oh yeah, that to me is instinctive. I'm sort of a cynical trader. I only wish I can be a little more greedy on the upside. It's almost as if the sole purpose of corrections is for the market to intentionally shake me out."

"If I may give you a small piece of advice," said Mellery, "Resist letting the price at which you had entered determine the point of exit. Let the general trend of the market dictate when you should get out, not whether you've already received your expected returns."

"That's great advice," I acknowledged. "Only wish my mind is strong enough to ignore the price at which I paid. If I could ever do that, then maybe I could *really* let the profit run."

"Don't be too hard on yourself," Charles said to me. "Stage fright is not the exclusive domain of beginners. I've seen many brilliant analysts incapacitated as they attempt to execute in real time."

"Thanks for the reassurance," I said, still somewhat frustrated.

"Now, when I first began in capital management," Charles said, "I made every call on my own. Needless to say, it was a 24-hour proposition."

"You don't trade anymore, Uncle Charles?"

"Rarely now. As the capital base grew, I began parceling it out to professionals, from hedge funds to money funds, in part so I could devote more time to my investment firm. But in the early days—and perhaps this could be a guideline to you, as well—I did not put any capital in play without first fitting the target into one of the three categories: whether its price movement was in an uptrend, a downward trend, or more importantly, whether it behaved like a wave. Not all of my hunches were right, far from it; but the method gave me discipline: what I didn't know, I didn't play. And guess from which trend I extracted the greatest return?"

"From long upward trends, I would think."

Charles shook his head and smiled, "Inflation aside, I probably made more money by finding breaks in the wave."

"You're a genius!" I said with admiration.

"Truly a genius," added Mellery. "One reason your uncle was so successful when he traded was that he could hold on to some positions for years, yet dump other positions in a matter of hours."

"I thank Mellery for his kind words," Charles said rather humbly. "Yet I will have you know that one of the biggest losses I have suffered was indeed a position I had held for very many years, and still hold today, to some extent. I had, in the late-seventies and early-eighties, stepped up my investments in South Africa. For a while at least, the returns had been stellar. Backing it all up, no less, was their rand, as powerful a currency as there was, to a point where a dollar was trading at only three-quarters of a rand. Then it started: the Western embargo, the racial unrest. The upheaval in Uitenhage in 1985 was one of the worst since 1960."

"Really, and you couldn't get out during the free-fall?"

"I could have lessened my exposure, but I was under the delusion that I didn't have to. Soon after the Pretoria government instituted a state of emergency, I flew down to Jo'burg to meet with friends and advisors and to assess damages. Upon returning, I became as convinced as before that the fundamentals were still intact; that the panic was premature and unwarranted. So while the Americans began their divestitures and the Brits and Swiss were busy calling in loans, I increased my holdings; eventually *doubling* my position."

"The rand never regained its past glories, " Mellery said gloomily, "The dollar had risen to nearly three rands, quadrupling what it was."

"One of the reasons for my mistake," Charles said, "was my reluctance to face reality—not dissimilar to the views of many of the whites down there. For throughout the downturn, I kept reassuring myself that the rand was still a Western currency, meaning its movements were more cyclical and wavelike in nature. But instead, it had taken on characteristics of a Third World currrency...politically speaking. And I didn't see it. I refused to see it."

"Wow, what a story." Charles suddenly became a human being after that slow deliberation. A man with faults. The irony being that he erred by trying to detach himself from the human side of him: a man who could look the other way from even his own self.

While we are on the subject of currencies and the inflationary 1970s, I want to see if I can properly explain what Charles meant by his so-called implicit deflation in the modern era. Although a little abstract, it was the best news I had heard all day. What Charles said was that, despite the constant rise in consumer prices—it having gone up three hundred percent since I was born—our standard of living is nevertheless still improving, even though many of us think it has not been. And the great thing about it is: not only are the rich living better, but the poor are living better, as well. Everybody is better off, far better! The reason: technology. Just think, we would not have been able to buy a 21-day programmable stereo VCR twenty years ago even if we had had all the money in the world; it simply didn't exist. Or, to put it another way, even if they had made such a thing, its price would have been thousands of dollars instead of merely the couple of hundred that it would cost today. I still remember that classic ad of Sony's when they introduced the Betamax console in 1976, the price—$1999—inflation not included. Expensive as hell, but I still wanted it. Even wished I could recite the Torah so I could blow my Bar Mitzvah money on it. All right, stop it. I'm starting to get carried away again. Let me just wrap it up by saying that, in spite of the consumer price index zooming through the roof, it only tells part of the story; that there is implicit deflation everywhere we look. Implicit because we have to presume that had those products been available way back when, they would have cost an arm and a leg. I mean, when I got an AT&T telephone my first year in college, as a present from Grandpa, it was incredibly expensive. Now, eight years later, you can go to some crazy place on Canal Street and get a cordless phone with ten times the features for much less in real terms. Or, imagine all the people in the old days who wanted a phone with answering machine, auto-dialing, voice mail, fax connections and speakerphone and so on and so forth. Why, they would practically have to hire a real-live secretary to perform all those tasks. Now if that's not an example of deflation, I don't know what is. And you know what's even better? The best part is, this is not a one time phenomenon but an ongoing process. Many items that we see today as out of this world will be taken for granted in the next century—by the rich and poor alike! A laptop flying saucer, anyone?

Our talks were interrupted by Alexandra, who came walking in with a stack of mail for Charles. She still had her books with her, having just came back from her school. Charles then told Mellery that he was going to need a few moments to go through the mail before they go. He also gave me another chore to do: "Be a dear and help Mr. Mellery with the cover to his motorcar. After you've folded the tarp, I'd like you to please bring it down to the cellar for storage."

So that was Mellery's car being kept out there. Even though he had a spread near the Place François I on the other side of the Seine,

Mellery still preferred to leave the car with Charles when he wasn't around. That afternoon, after a few hours in his Paris office, he used the excuse of picking up Charles to duck out of getting high on tea leaves with his wife and her friends at a Right Bank hotel.

"So nice of you to come and drag Charles out of the house," I said to Mellery, "despite him looking as though he was about to face a firing squad."

"Ahh, a bit of dancing on Friday night won't kill him; to say nothing of some frivolous card games."

"Well, it would depend on the stake," I said, while pulling the car cover further away from the front grille.

Mellery then opened the car door, got in, and started the engine. The car was a light blue Facel Vega, circa late 1950s. It was huge, way surpassing the adjacent Saab in size, though still pretty racy-looking. I told Mellery that the car looked more like it belonged on a movie set than on the streets of Paris. And, like a '57 Chevy, the engine gave out one of them 1950s drag-racing kind of roar. Supposedly, the Facel Vega was an extremely valuable car. According to Mellery, very few of them were made, and only a handful still exist. Yes, Facel Vega, another proud symbol of French elegance; however, unlike Louis Vuitton, it eventually disappeared when nobody wanted to copy it.

On the way upstairs after I stored the tarp in the basement, I overheard a minor squabble taking place between Ally and Charles in the vestibule. What Charles wanted was for Ally to write a letter to an American acquaintance from Palm Beach who had asked him to pull some strings for her daughter. Ally was upset; she wanted Charles to write the letter personally: "Why don't you write it and I type it," she said.

"No, no, you do it for me in your name. I want to avoid direct contact at all cost. I know what we'll do: I shall quickly dictate a letter to you before I go. Just say...have you got some writing paper there? Just say that: Monsieur Martin was most pleased to hear that Amanda is in Paris. But he regrets very much that he cannot do anything for her at this time. However, he will no doubt keep her in mind and get in touch with her the moment a suitable opportunity should arise. Yours faithfully, Alexandra Lachapelle, Monsieur Martin's personal assistant."

Ally put her pen to paper and was totally professional in taking down the note. She had a powerful writing script—very quick and fluid—totally opposite of my secretary Connie, who writes slow as hell and in big letters, too: with her *M*'s twice as wide as her *N*'s. Ally then read back the letter to Charles, and, except for misspelling the word "suitable," she was otherwise perfect.

In spite of her professional performance, Ally was glad when it was all over. In a quiet tone, with her anger subsided, she said to me, "This is how I have improved my English lately." That just brought the poker-faced me to a burst of hissing laughter.

After I said good-bye to Charles, I turned to Ally and said, "The boss is really putting you to work, aye?"

"Uh, nonstop! Did you see what I did in the dining room after you two had left me?"

"Hey, yeah, that's right. Did you do all that by yourself?"

"Who else?"

"Wow, that's *b-u-tee-ful.*" I don't know if you remember all those plates and silverware we were sorting just before Charles and I headed out for lunch? Well, Ally then went on and set everything up on the whole table—linen and all. "Look, there are the two champagne bottles I brought in from the kitchen, sitting pretty in their buckets," I said self-congratulatingly.

"You? I was the one who did all the work," Ally said. "The minute after you left, I realized I had forgotten to tell you to put the two tables together for me, so I had to push them together *all* by myself. They were very hea-vee!"

"Owww, Ally, I'm so terribly sorry," I truly was, too. It was a pretty big job, putting together a table for twelve. And she did it splendidly.

"You were right, Ally, working for Charles *is* hard work."

"Yes, it's a hard piece of cake," she said.

A hard piece of cake; she's too much!

6 / JUST ANOTHER *CINQ A NEUF* IN MONTPARNASSE

Ally and I decided to go to a movie to kill the early part of the evening. I didn't mind a French flick, but she'd rather go see Tom Cruise or Mel Gibson. So we compromised and decided on *New York Stories,* a Big Apple flick.

"O-kay, let's go," she said enthusiastically. "It's playing near the Tour Montparnasse."

"Is there a place any closer?"

"That's a good theater, and the closest one."

"Are you sure?"

"Am I sure?" her eyes rolled up in disbelief. "Of course I'm sure! I know every theater in Paris. Ask me any movie theater and I will tell you where it is."

"Is that so? We may have to see about that." I began flipping through the Reprises section of *Pariscope*, which lists the revivals. To my pleasant surprise, there were quite a few older American movies being revived, like *Jonathan Livingston Seagull, Garp,* and *Brazil.* Also to my amazement was the showing of Pink Floyd's *The Wall*, which required almost an Anglo-American spaciness to be truly appreciated, something I felt the French still lacked. Boy, that Wall concert at Nassau Coliseum which I comfortably numbed through...it was beyond words, unreal! Yes, I am still saying that after more than a hundred Dead shows.

"Okay, Alexandra, where is Action Galande?" I proceeded to give her a little quiz.

"It's in the Cinquieme Arrondisement, on Rue Galande."

"Right on. You know what it's playing—*The Rocky Horror Picture Show.*"

"Never saw it. Have you seen it, is it good?"

"Only on a Friday night at the Eighth Street Playhouse in the Village, and be sure to wear a raincoat if you decide to sit near the front." I spotted another revival house called Studio Christine that was showing the great Marx Brothers. It was a double feature of *Monkey Business* and *La Soupe au Canard,* which was *Duck Soup.* Don't ask me why the French translated one title and kept the other one in English. "Okay, Ally, here is another one for ya: where is Studio Christine?"

"It's on Rue Christine, a small street not far from here. It's another easy wooooone!" She said, wanting a real challenge.

"That's okay Ally, I give up! You've already convinced me that you know'em all." There is a time to challenge, and a time to surrender. My decision then was to declare her victorious.

Actually, I used to know a little about movie theaters myself. The Thalia, the Metro, and the good old St. Marks where we saw lots of double features for three bucks. None of them are around anymore. About the only place that's still at it is the Cinema Village on 12th Street, which continues to show old movies like the *Valley of Dolls, Beyond the Valley of the Dolls*, way the hell beyond the valley of guys and dolls and so on. They'd also do some serious stuff every so often like Bergman and Fellini revivals.

"Ally, did I tell you I was a film student for a year at New York University."

"I love cinema. What happened to you, you gave up?"

"Well, let's just say I couldn't see myself making a living with a film degree. I wasn't about to waste several years of my life to find out I hadn't any talent." I then told Ally of how I made a go at film-making after transferring out of Penn my sophomore year, not long after Grandpa died. It was partly at the suggestion of my mother and her husband Ira, who had moved out to Los Angeles to help resuscitate a studio.

"Was he successful?" Ally asked.

"Euh, so-so. Ira's timing was pretty good. The movie industry in the Seventies was in the toilet, so he really couldn't do much worse. But if you ask me, he should have stayed in New York as an officer and counsel to the parent company. But nooo, he wanted to *go* Hollywood!"

"Who wouldn't?"

"Lots of people. Ira was lucky. He made a fortune from the stocks and options he had been holding when the company was eventually bought out. Then he joined up with an entertainment finance firm, making his little deals here and there and getting some occasional credits and what not."

Ally wanted to know more about Ira the "producer." I didn't feel like going into it. I told her it's so easy to be a producer these days. Hell, there are almost as many producers in a film as there are senior vice-presidents in a corporation. The difference being that most producers do absolutely squat. They just talk to their backers, get their cut and pass the cost on to the moviegoers. Very big deal, being a co-associate producer of Cold-as-dice Productions.

"Do you want to know what I think, Mark? I think you are jealous of your step-father."

"But Ally, have you seen the price of a lousy movie lately? It costs more to go to a movie than to go to the cleaners. And dry cleaning is one of the biggest rip-offs of all time."

"But how can you be a film student and not love going to the cinema?"

"Easy." I told her I've always liked the older movies anyway, the ones you see on Turner Cable all the time. Blame it on Rocky II, Rocky III, and Rocky IV.

"You haven't seen any new ones?"

"Only obscure B-movies, no major studio releases at all. However, when HBO or Cinemax run their free promotion weeks, I'll catch enough new flicks to know what's going on."

"Ah, so you're cheap! I know now. You just don't want to spend your money on movie tickets." Even though Ally had her finger pointed at me, she wasn't trying to be mean; more like trying to both accuse and make fun of me at the same time.

"No, Ally. It's the principle," I said, in an attempt to defend myself. "And the great thing was, the longer I stayed away from the movie theaters, the more I wanted to *keep* staying away."

"Tu es si obstiné!"

She said I was stubborn; but I think it was more like a phase. Another phase I was going through at the time was that, despite being on the road a lot, I hadn't stepped into a fast-food chain in ages. Like Joe DiMaggio, once I'm well into a streak, I like to keep it going. even just for the hell of it. Of course if a zesty Parisian girl wanted to go see an American movie, then viva Hollywood it is.

But boy, was I hoping she wouldn't be into those American fast-food joints. "Hey Ally, we won't be eating fast-food later, will we?"

"Why not, it is very cheap on your wallet!" She didn't mean it though, smiling as she said it. She was just playing with me.

I don't know—maybe I am a cheap bastard. I would watch complimentary movies on flights when they are offered. But never ever have I paid cash for earphones just to hear the sound. I remember seeing *Wall Street* the old fashioned way—in silent movie mode. In fact, I'm still waiting to hear the rest of that speech after Gordon Gekko opened with "Greed is good." Look on the bright side, at least Hollywood was spared of my 'most likely to be unfavorable' review. One less thumb down its throat!

Ally and I talked about movies as we walked toward Montparnasse. I told her of some recent French movies I had seen on television: *Entre Nous,* a film about a friendship between two women who met at a concentration camp; *A Man and a Woman,* about a man and a woman; and *The Man Who Loved Women*, yes, you guessed it, about a man who—just happened to love women. Unbelievable! Suddenly, I realized one of the main reasons why French movies were no longer popular in America. It was apparent from the titles: too much relationshipnal mushy-mushy in an age where the audience wants action; wants titles that *spell* action.

I then rattled off a bunch of other French movies: *Borsolino, Breathless, 400 Blows* and the like. That darn girl had seen them all; and many times over. Then again, most of the French movies I had seen were shown on either A&E or Public TV; not quite the arena for unknown pictures. But then I suddenly remembered a film I had seen on a French class field trip in high school, it was my one last chance to stump her: "Alexandra, did you ever see *Rabbi Jacobs?"*

"Eh, Les Aventures de Rabbi Jacob—of course, I have! It was a very funny wooone! When I was little, I saw it so many times. I used to tell my mother *'Maman, maman, il y a Rabbi Jacob à la télé!'* Another good one was *Le Gendarme de St. Tropez,* have you ever seen that one?"

"No, but I'll take your word for it," I said to the joyous Alexandra. How beautiful she looked as she practiced one-upmanship with me;

and how cute she must have been as a child as she sat on the floor of her room, with her legs all curled up, and eyes glued to an antiquated French television set.

Ally was also at her childlike best as we were walking by all those boutiques and shoe stores on the boulevards. She had the ability to look at the window display for a tiny second, and immediately know what she liked. The only problem was: she couldn't afford the merchandise.

"Well, Ally, I guess you're relegated to a lifetime of following Imelda Marcos around, hoping she might drop a pair or two while walking out of Maud Frizon."

"Or I can wait for a big sale," she followed.

Ally didn't have to wait for any sales to buy anymore garbage. I thought she already looked good as she was. She had on a jadish green cabled cardigan with white stripes around the edges, her mandatory Parisienne scarf, and an old denim skirt. She told me she made that skirt herself, from a batch of Levi's she had outgrown.

"Very resourceful, Ally, and a fine job you did; they certainly look to be very nice," I was not exactly sure if I had meant her legs or her dressmaking skills.

"That's what happens when you're poor," Ally shrugged. "You try to make the best out of the leftovers."

Despite Ally's skirt looking as good as used, her shoes were a bit unusual in design and far from homemade. They were basically classic-looking flats except for a piece of braided leather stuck onto the back end.

"Hey, Ally, what's the idea of that funny-looking piece attached to your shoe."

"It's decoration. This design is very fashionable in Paris now. I really should not have bought it; but my friends each bought one, so I could not just stand there and watch, so I made a *folie!*"

Faire une folie is a French expression meaning a sudden burst of emotional desire to make a purchase—as if they *have* to have it at that instant—and they'll worry about the consequences later.

Ally almost made another folie when we passed a fashion jewelry store and she saw some thick silver bracelets with triangles engraved on them. She liked the one with the red triangles the best. "I love that. It's cool yet sensual. Other than the price, it's perfect."

"I don't know. I think it looks better on Wonder Woman."

"Oh, come ooooon!" Ally said with a little frown. "By the way, Mark, do you remember *Wonder Woman,* the TV show?"

"Sure I do. It starred Diana Prince, a former Miss America."

"Do you remember that she had a sister?"

"Very vaguely. Let me try to dig into my image files. Hmmm...I do recall a sister, but not in every episode. I think she was chubbier than Wonder Woman: clumsier, too—always getting herself into trouble and needing Wonder Woman to bail her out of it—a far cry from Robin the Boy Wonder!"

"Did you know her sister was played by Debra Winger, one of my favorite actresses?"

"Oh yeah? I cannot visualize her at all. Perhaps she had shorter hair back then. You really like Debra Winger, huh?"

"I loved her and Richard Gere in *An Officer and a Gentleman;* she was also great in *Terms of Endearment.* I just love her voice and she's such a natural on screen."

Well, la-di-da, here is a French girl who knows more about American movie stars than I do; the newer ones anyway. But I bet she's got a while to go to catch up with me on the oldies. I'm pretty knowledgeable in that category for someone my age, even before I became a film student at NYU. Credit partly goes to friends of my grandparents, who were some of the biggest film and theater buffs I know. But Ally was undoubtedly quite a film buff in her own right to have known some of the things she knew. It reminds me of a time in junior high school when I went to the Port Washington public library to look through some seventeen years of New York *Times* microfilms, just to count up all the third basemen who had ever played for the Mets. It was for a bet. Boy, was I a sick kid.

Jutting out single-handedly into the Left Bank skyline was the Tour Montparnasse. A towering salute to modern architecture to some, a dark tombstone to the old neighborhood to others. The Montparnasse vicinity in the early part of this century was known as the center of bohemia (whatever that means) though I guess it was where starving artists met their wealthy patrons at the apartments of those well-kept mistresses, and where anarchists met journalists through their mutual ladies of the evening and so on.

The steamy cabarets and watering holes of the past are there no more. Nowadays, Montparnasse appears more conventional with its modern hotels, department stores, and shopping malls. Even the *gare*, the old railway station, is hidden behind the office buildings that wrap around it. As for our cinema, it was located on Boulevard Montparnasse. Besides *New York Stories*, it was also showing *Monsieur Hire, Jesus of Montreal, and Lauren d'Arabie.*

"This is where I saw *Working Girl*," Ally said. "Did you forget to see that one, too?"

"Well, all I can say is that Mike Nichols hasn't been the same since *The Graduate*. But that's asking a lot since it's one of my favorite films of all time; so he's off the hook."

"I'm sure he will sleep better knowing of your approval," Ally said, making one of them Parisian faces while at it. Then she turned her voice up a notch and said, "Someday Mark, I, too, will be a working girl."

"But aren't you one already?"

"No, I mean a real woooone!"

A real one, that cracked me up. As much as I thought Ally would make a good businesswoman someday, I just couldn't visualize such an animated girl in a dark pinstripe suit with a small bow tie. "Ally, as much as I think you have a head for business, I can't quite imagine you being transformed into a Young Urban Parisienne Professional."

"Why not. I'll get my degree, and then I'll get a job in marketing or advertising and be a big success."

"Just like the characters in *Working Girl*, with secretaries and everything?"

"Yep. With my own office on a high floor in the Tour Montparnasse, overlooking *tout le Paris*."

"*Formidable!* Then you can hire me as your management consultant," I teased her. "By the way, Ally, speaking of views, did I tell you our office was almost a setting for a movie shoot?"

"Oh ree-lee?"

"Yeah, it was a recent hit movie about a female management consultant. For authenticity, they were going to film the elevator lobby and some of the office scenes at our firm. We have Central Park views as well as a spacious double-height reception area with a really circular staircase leading to the upper floor."

"So what happened?"

"Well, as it turned out, we later learned that we were not the first choice; that they had previously sought to do the shoot at our competitor's office, but were turned down. And we don't take leftovers from anybody, at least we had to act like we don't." It was a shame, too, for I missed out on seeing one of my favorite actresses in action.

"If I'm ever asked for permission to do a film, I would say yes, especially if they pay us."

"Yeah, but the thing is, Ally, if you happened an ad agency in Tour Montparnasse, then it's sort of glamorous. But high-level consulting is quiet, not flashy—so quiet it's downright dull." I told Ally of another recent movie that initially wanted the characters to be consultants. They had even sent an advance scouting crew to one of our competitors to see what consultants actually did. But, boy, were they surprised. They quickly concluded that our work was too boring to warrant the portrayal of the main characters as such. So they turned them into I-bankers and takeover artists instead and made the movie into a huge success.

While sitting in our seats and waiting for *New York Stories* to begin, we talked about one of my favorite subjects, the Big Apple. Ally's been there twice, but neither time for very long.

"The first time I was there was during the weekend of the New York Marathon. My mother and I were in Chicago visiting a friend. So on the way back to Paris, we stopped in New York for a few days"

"When was that?"

"Long time ago. It was the year an Italian guy won the marathon."

"Oh, yeah, Pizza-lotto or something. I was still an undergraduate then. It was a very hot day, right? I remember that day. We all thought that Italian guy was not going to hold up. Hey, that was good timing, Ally, your trip. Marathon Sunday is like the one day out of the year where New Yorkers turn into the nicest people. Especially after word got out of a major Italian victory!"

"You know where we went? All the French people in New York went to cheer for the French runners right off the Fifty-ninth Street Bridge—"

"*All* the French people?"

"Yep. We were all screaming, *'Allez France! Allez!'*"

"That must've been fun."

"Yep. And then we went to Serendipity for lunch, and Bloomingdale's for shopping."

"Alexandra Lachapelle, that was about as perfect a way to see New York as any. If every kid could spend a Sunday like that in New York and leave, she'd already be walking away with plenty. The only other things that brings to mind are perhaps the Staten Island Ferry and then Chinatown."

"I love Chinese food. All I did was order out for Chinese food the last time I was in New York."

"Why? I mean, I like Chinese, too; but only a couple of times a week."

"Because we were broke," she said. "We had spent most of our money in Quebec, and I wanted to use whatever I had left to buy a compact disc Walkman. So we stayed at an apartment of a friend on Riverside Drive; she was going to school at Columbia. We all lived on Chinese takeouts and pee-zaa."

"Ma pauvre Alexandra," poor thing, I said, "You shoulda called me up."

"You should'ah given me your numb'ah." Boy, could that girl talk nonsense as easily as me. "But don't get me wrong, Mark, I love pee-zaa; and the fried rice of New York is the *best*!"

I love pizza, too. One of my saddest days was when Mario's Pizza on Eightieth and Madison moved away. It was an institution. I just hate it when landlords disrupt my neighborhood like that. But as with my grandfather's old store, the pizzeria was sitting on a piece of real estate that the fashion boutiques were willing to pay many times the rent for. Thank god our local greasy spoon is still there. Me and Edwin sure have done our best to try to keep it there. We patronize that Greeksy Spoonful coffee shop as much as anyone during its evening hours; or so they said. Once we even ran a streak of several weeks of at least an order a day. That's how much we *love* cooking and cockroaches.

Speaking of cockroaches, actually, I really do have to go on with Paris; all right, let me just tell it real quick. I mean, what's a true New Yorker without a *cuca-racha* story? I don't know if I've mentioned this, but, I enjoy smoking pot; not heavily, though. My friend Dave, a musician, he's a real pot head—up to five joints a day till his money runs out. He has frequent mood swings and paranoia attacks and stuff. But I'm not bad. I do it in small doses. Just a bong hit or two a day; lately—not even. And I don't touch any of the heavy shit like coke or crack. I'm not addicted. I can stop grass even easier than alcohol, and I can *easily* not booze for days.

So anyway, Edwin had quit smoking pot for a while, and he detected an immediate drop in cockroach sightings when I went out of town—even after just a couple of days on business. At first, I thought he was just bullshiting me to get me to stop. But when I came back after having been away for a while last Christmas, I decided to sit it out and *examiner la situation*. Low and behold, that cocksucker might have been right: cockroach sightings did drop significantly. And although no control was used, the correlation between roach-free and smoke-free in our case was tough to ignore. Edwin thinks it's the aromatic smoke that permeates the nooks and crannies beyond the walls—attracting men and insects alike. If Edwin were right, which I doubt, then I would have to face a forecasting model dilemma: I'm going to need to determine the trade-off between the pleasantries of a roach-free apartment and the consequences of impotence and low sperm count. So far, I'm still opting for the latter.

New York Stories was delightful. Almost as much fun were the commercials beforehand. You want to know how civilized the French are? Well, they give you two starting times for a movie. One is called the *avant-premiere*, which is like fifteen minutes before the movie begins; that's for commercials and coming attractions. Should you not care for it, you don't have to sit through it. But the commercials were very slick and entertaining—definitely worth showing up for.

If there was one theme that united all the commercials, it would probably be sex, sex, and sex. Nothing outright offensive, just very suggestive: men looking at women, women looking at themselves; a lady in a bubbly bath soaping up her breasts, a room service man looking at her with his own hands around a hard boiled egg and so on. No, it's not going to amuse many feminists, but it was all good clean fun. Well, maybe not as clean as the soap operas, but you gotta love that funky background !

New York Stories is composed of three short films: by Scorsese, Coppola and Woody Allen, in that order. I liked the ending of the Scorsese film, where Nick Nolte picks up a new young admirer—his-soon-to-be assistant, hero-worshipper and bedmate. Kind of like Phoebe at the end of *All About Eve*. Ally, meanwhile, liked the film's choice of music, including a classic Procol Harem number. Scorsese, a product of NYU film school, has always been a hell of a rock and roller. *Taxi Driver, Mean Streets, The Last Waltz*—all musically filled. Ally also liked how Nolte, the artist, was playing incredibly loud music in the middle of the night to inspire himself to paint.

"Ally, did he remind you of some one you know?"

"Who?"

"You."

"No, not me. I know nothing about art!"

But Ally knew enough about being late to school to identify with Zoe, the little girl in the second film. Being a New Yorker, though, I found the locational choices of Coppola's film annoying. He was probably trying to be expedient, but still, kids who live on Fifth Avenue take their school buses up Madison, not way the hell across on Central Park West. And Zoe's school, Fieldston in real life, is sort of a...I mean, why not Horace Mann, the alma mater of Major Anthony Nelson, for the richest Arab kid in the world. "Clearly the work of a California film student," I told Ally. In fact, the whole story could've been told better in an L.A. setting. Sophisticated New York mothers don't go off to—of all places—India; they go off to lunch—a far more spiritual undertaking. Save India for California Stories. And don't try to pass the Metropolitan Museum off as an Arabian palace, either; it's a sacred place—a place to dance like an Egyptian mummy. Now don't get me wrong, I thought Coppola's story was the most endearing of the three. The character of Zoe, the adorable little girl, was played to perfection. "I'll cast my shadows on the Acropolis!" she said, swinging her arms out. And a feel-good happy ending didn't hurt, either. But I'll bet you the critics probably liked that one the least. Professional critics are a strange breed; you just can't please them. You know what they are? They are like frigid nymphomaniacs—impossible to satisfy! They will call Coppola's film too sentimental, guaranteed. And if Zoe were portrayed instead as a spoilt little nasty brat, the critics will call such a film "harsh." They want everything unbiased, them critics, like a dry newspaper article. And when that happens, they will totally trash it as dull. Okay, so I agree that an adult shouldn't get too touchy and feely about things, but young people do get very sentimental, myself included. A part of me had totally identified with Zoe, as I, too, had lived by my lonesome in Ira's hotel apartment for a summer—the summer before I was sent away to a school in the Connecticut woods—and understood all too well her longings and loneliness.

I told Ally that if you like to associate movies with fantasyland, do not study them too hard. Film schools tend to make people over analyze—sort of like at a basketball game, you're constantly questioning the shot selections. What's more, sooner or later, you start seeing a movie the way *you* want to see it, not the way the director would like to trick you into believing. Personally, I have a tendency to time how long each shot would take, and guess what the next shot might look like and so on. I also have a tendency to go beyond the picture on the screen and visualize the whole movie set. I end up seeing lights, dollies, cameras, and all the peripherals; even of stars quickly saying their lines and then a beeline to the dressing room. "Bring on the script girl!" as they say.

One other nasty habit I have is that I love to catch the director as he tries to make some short cuts. For instance, in Woody's film *Oedipus Wrecks*, there was a totally smooth and acceptable transition scene of Woody's mother as an eternal nag. Woody did it by taking his mother to an outdoor section of a restaurant in Central Park, and had her whine and complain about not wanting to dine al fresco—saying that it was too cold outdoors and so forth. I felt like barging onto the set and telling Woody to tell her to be quiet: look mom, we are sitting outdoors because it's far easier to shoot outdoors, despite the cold. Back inside, the ceiling is too low and lighting too difficult. This is a very short scene, mom, in a short film. It ain't worth the time and money to set everything up indoors just for you.

But that was a minor item. *Oedipus Wrecks* was vintage Annie Hall-ish Woody. Lots of funny lines, a little weak in the middle, but always a strong finish. Treva, the psychic, stole the show; "I'll boil you some chicken," she says at the end. Look, Woody does get a little predictable after a while, but that hadn't stopped my friends from watching bits and pieces of *Love and Death* for only about a zillion times. He'll always be one of my favorites, too. The fact that he lives in my neighborhood doesn't hurt, either. We even have the same...well, I should respect his privacy, I'll just say that despite Woody's overall reclusiveness, no one on earth, not even me, adores and idolizes New York City in such proportions; and that's good enough for me!

After the movie, a most unusual sensation occurred as I was leaving the theater. It was a feeling of being instantaneously transported from a New York movie-house into the streets of Paris. Sort of like that Star Trek episode where Captain Kirk had to pass through a set of doors to escape an impending doomsday. It's like—poof!—suddenly you are in another time and place. I think this sensation of virtual travel had a lot to do with my having just seen a contemporary New York movie; it reminded me of home, of walking out of the Beekman after a Woody movie and straight into the thick of Second Avenue. But in this case, I was thrust into the excitement of Montparnasse instead: of sidewalk cafés and French advertising billboards and funny little French cars battling for positions. No, what I was seeing before my eyes was no New York, it was grand old Paris in all its splendor.

It was an incredible feeling. The New York portrayed in the movie was so realistic that I wasn't sure if the Paris that stood before me was dream or reality. It was like, wow—here we are in Paris again. We were just on the streets of New York only minutes ago. Funny how we always thought that movies themselves were the escape, not what happened to us after we've left the theater. But such was precisely what I had experienced. It was like waking up to the pleasures of reality, a rare case of reality transcending the make-believe.

In a way, the experience was similar to walking out of a Dead show at the Garden. I have been so used to the apres-concert stroll in the parking lots of Nassau and the Meadowlands—Deadheads selling T-shirts; Deadheads cooking and setting up tents; Deadheads replaying the show they had just taped—that I was not ready for the sudden appearance of dark-as-dead concrete surrounding Madison

Square Garden; not ready for the reality of the squalid Penn Station late at night; not ready for the reality of getting in a cab and being in my apartment just minutes later. Deadshows are not supposed to be over *even* when the music finally stops!

Contrary to feeling let down, that jolting change of scenery from New York to Paris was a pleasant surprise. Now I'm not saying that if I watched another American movie abroad, I would get a replay of instant time travel. Everything diminishes with repetition and, in this case, anticipation. But at that particular moment, I was totally high on Paris. It was, like—as if a genie had just blinked and given me Paris. I was incredibly rejuvenated; and couldn't wait to be out and about the city all over again!

SEVEN

Ally was in a good mood as we headed down Boulevard Montparnasse toward the Jardin du Luxembourg. After I made a remark that it was still surprisingly light out, she responded by saying, "The longer it takes to get dark, the later we stay out at night." Did she have that Parisian partying logic ingrained into her brain or what?

When we passed by the Café Dome, I mentioned to Ally that my grandpa had once taken me there. She chuckled mockingly and said, "Bhuh, everyone's grandpere takes his kids to these places... for old times."

"Yours, too?"

"We used to go to La Coupole. We just walked by that one. Same thing."

"Me and my friends were across the street at the Rotonde the last time we were in Paris—led on by Hemingway's observation that 'Taxi drivers take you to the Rotonde no matter which café in Montparnasse you ask for.' Let's see, that night, it was first the Rotonde and then the Pub Saint-Germain."

"Bhuh," Ally again made a funny noise with her mouth. "Pub Saint-Germain, it's so full of tourists."

Boy, did she have an attitude for a young girl. Yet in a way she was right. The Pub was huge and dark, darker than the darkest dark beer. After some of the frat boys had had a few, they started coming on to the girls with the only French they knew: *Voulez-vous coucher avec moi?* The funny thing was, many of the girls there didn't speak any French, either. But no harm done—certainly less harmful than if the boys had uttered the English equivalent.

We were on Rue Vavin heading toward the Luxembourg Gardens when we stumbled upon the Lucernaire, an old movie house that, well, if I hadn't just seen a movie, I would have wanted to see the film that was playing there. The place was showing *Camille Claudel*, with Isabelle Adjani as the sculptor. The only film of hers I had seen was *Subway*, in my senior year in college. Personally, I prefer the steamy Valérie Kaprisky of *Breathless* remake fame. But Ally told me something that gave me the urge to see all the films Adjani had ever starred in. No, it's not the fact that she's a French Deadhead, rather that some years back, Ally was almost chosen to play a part in a film as Adjani's character in the teenage years. "I was supposed to take her place in a childhood flashback," Ally said. "One day, I was in a roller skating rink, and some guy came up to me and asked me if I wanted to play a part in a movie. At first, I thought he was a fraud; I've had people come up to me before. But he gave me a card and everything. So my friends convinced me to go and see."

"Did you get the part?"

"Almost. They took many pictures, and I was one of the finalists. But in the end they decided to pick someone else, someone with darker hair."

"That's right. You are dirty blonde, and Adjani is a brunette."

"But she has blue eyes. They were going to dye my hair. It's easier for them to do that than to find a *brune* with blue eyes."

"Yeah, that's too bad. But you know what, Ally? I bet if you had the persuasive skills you have today, you might have talked them into giving you the part."

"Yep. Can you believe it, I almost became a star. Maybe I will get another chance."

"Oh, I think you will." It was more than mere encouragement when I said that. Ally did possess a certain star quality. Reminds me of an older version of Jodie Foster in *The Little Girl that Lived Down the Lane,* lively and headstrong, with a voice that's well projected yet not so girlishly high. And what's more: like Adjani, Ally also has that classic nose. Delicate and shapely, with the cutest little nostrils I've ever seen—so perfectly round that they were addicting to look at. If I seem a bit superficial, it's only because my own nose is more on the large side. While I don't have that big French nose, my head is kind of small, so proportionally speaking.... I can't believe this, after seeing Woody in *Oedipus Wrecks*, I'm now sounding like Pinocchio Wrecks.

Although Ally hadn't been much of a tour guide in the classical sense—her having been the head usherette at Eiffel Tower and all—she still managed to point out to me some buildings of educational interest which not only enabled me to understand France better, but also led me to learn something about her family that was absolutely hilarious.

One of the buildings we passed was the University of Law, France's top law school—commonly known as Assas, named after the street it's on. Unlike America, where Law is a graduate degree, the program in France starts right after you graduate from high school, and lasts at least six years. Ally told me that her mother graduated from there, and after she had the kids, became a practicing lawyer.

"Ally, is that how you became so good at arguing, by fighting with your mother all day?"

"No, I didn't have many fights with my mother. It was mostly with my father."

"Is he a lawyer, too?"

"No, he's in insurance. He was a sous-directeur of an insurance company before it fused into a larger company."

"Alexandra, your father was in insurance and you didn't even have insurance on your car?" Again I found myself shaking my head.

"My father and I have been in a cold war," she said. "After he retired, he was always home, and became more irritable than ever. He was getting so much on my case that finally I just couldn't take it anymore: *J'en ai plus que marre!* I was too fed up!"

There was real emphasis in the way she said 'fed up', her head pointing down and her face very angry.

"What happened, did your father retire to a life of leisure after his company was sold?"

"Oh, no, he retired because he's an old man. He is in his sixties."

I was like, "What, you have a father that age?"

"Yep. My father's been married three times. The third time to my mother."

"Ally, that's amazing. I mean, that's unbelievable! Did your mother meet your father while representing him in his divorce?" I was on the verge of losing it again. So her father was a Frenchman enough to cheat on his wife, I thought, but dull enough an insurance man to marry the mistress instead. The old *cinq à neuf*, as they say, had turned into a twenty-four-hour affair.

"You want to know something crazy?" Ally added, "My half-sister, who is also a lawyer, and works with my mother, it was my half-sister who was friends with my mother before my father was."

I shook my head and laughed. As tragic as I'm sure some of the detailed events might have been back then, I also had the feeling of everybody else eventually getting along, becoming one big happy family. Everybody except Ally that is, who had gotten quite "fetup" going *tête-à-tête* with her father and left the homestead.

Just outside the Jardin du Luxembourg Ally tried telephoning her friend Olivia to see if she wanted to join us for dinner. But her line was busy, so we decided to just walk there instead, since it wasn't far away. Olivia's place was on Boulevard Saint-Germain, but on the opposite end from where Charles lived. While not as long as the Boulevard Raspail nearby, which, I believe, is the longest street in Paris; Boulevard Saint-Germain nevertheless goes a long way, cutting through the heart of literary and educational Paris.

Although most people know of the Sorbonne, the historic university where many of the greatest Frenchmen had their schooling, right behind it are two *lycées*, high schools, which have graduated their share of legends as well. "See the old building with a tower, behind the Panthéon? That is the Lycée Henry IV, where Olivia graduated. And on our left is Lycée Louis-Le-Grand, where his eminence Charles-Le-Grand went to school; he's your host."

He's your host, that cracked me up. "Which school's better?"

"Which lycée is better? I don't know; you'll have to ask Olivia that. They both have great reputations."

"Where did you end up, by the way, after getting kicked out of your Catholic school?"

"Eh, Lycée La Fontaine, it's far from here, but almost as good. The two over here may have better teachers, that's all." Yeah, right! Their loss for not having Ally as a pupil. I think that deep inside, Ally truly believed that anywhere she ended up was the best place to be.

I then went on and told Ally a little about the Lenox Hill School in New York—much smaller in comparison and architecturally far less impressive. There were only two sections for each class, with about fifteen students per section, so people got to know everybody. But because we had students from K through twelve, there were naturally many students whom we didn't really want to know. In many ways, going to school in the city was, well, an education. It was almost like going to work except you didn't get paid for doing it. Instead, you're the one who had to dole out the thousands in tuition—if and only if they let you in. It really could get very pretentious at times, worse than a boarding school up in the boonies. The fault, in many ways, was that of the parents, who shower their kids with this and that not because they love them, but as a way to impress their own friends. If I had stayed at Lenox Hill instead of moving back to Port Washington, I might have been a sociologist by now. It was certainly good enough a training ground: spoiled brats of tycoons mixing with scholarship students from Harlem and dysfunctional wackos like me.

I remember this one girl in our class, Michelle was her name. She was chauffeured to school each morning—in her father's stretch limo no less. But the funny thing was, she was kind of ashamed of it, not embarrassed enough to walk to school, mind you; but enough so that she'd always get out of the limo at the corner intersection and walk the rest of the way. But her little brother was another story: he'd make the driver continue driving to the middle of the block and park that sucker right smack in front of the schoolhouse. Then he'd roll down the windows and hail his little friends to come inside to watch TV. If there was anything funnier than a bunch of kids charging at a limo, it was the sight of those little shrimps after they had gotten inside. Christ, the back seats of that car must have packed in his whole class. Just think, when I was that kid's tender age, all you needed was the biggest Lionel train set to be the most popular kid in class.

Ally's friend Olivia lived with her parents in an ornate looking apartment building. But she wasn't home. The concierge said she had just left a short while ago. The concierges in the residential buildings of Paris are not the same as their New York counterparts in those modern Third Avenue condos. They are closer in relation to a superintendent/watchman than a uniformed white-gloved man with an accent. They are also predominantly women. And, as far as I know, the concierges know everything about everyone that lives in the building—at least they do in the French movies.

In a sense, I was sort of surprised that Ally had just dropped in like that. I've always been told, even in high school French, that the French rendez-vous in cafés, clubs and stuff; that the family dwelling is considered private and, therefore, people shouldn't just casually stop by, especially the friends of children, not to mention dragging along an American. Perhaps times have changed.

We Americans, myself included, have always been kind of casual. Only when Edwin throws one of his afterwork cocktail parties does he then officially invite some friends over. Otherwise, people just stop by our place all the time without warning, especially Edwin's friends from the neighborhood. But it definitely wasn't due to his being so hot a host or anything. Believe me, he often ignores his guests, leaving them alone to watch TV in the living room. When I'm in a good mood, which is to say when my bets are paying off, which is to say all the time (uhum, uhum!), I'd go out there and try to be polite and shoot some bull for a while. But more often than not, they are just left out there to find their own amusement. It's better that way. All they needed was to get away from their parents' places for a while—you know, to relax, smoke a joint, mellow out and what not. Completely understandable.

My apartment has the advantage of being on the lobby floor, but high enough to be above the eye level of pedestrians. It's a convenient place for people to come and go without disturbing the neighbors. When Grandpa lived there, he even used the reception as a workroom in his final years, to serve his long time clients. He would have retired otherwise as his eyes couldn't quite hold up anymore. Watchmakers require lots of precision, and also very steady hands. Another reason he closed shop was due to the astronomical rent increases sought by the landlord of his Madison Avenue store.

From hindsight, there was nothing wrong with landlords trying to get a higher rent. Artificially low prices are against everything I believe in. But back then it was a different story. I fought like hell after Grandpa died in order to take over the apartment. Not only was he paying a very low rent, but the place meant everything to me—the only space still held over from my childhood, and a fairly big one at that: a double room for living and dining out front; a kitchen, bedroom, and bath along the hall, and a larger bedroom with bath in the back. Although my present rent is still low by comparison, it isn't dirt cheap anymore—almost triple what Grandpa was paying. Part of the hike was due to my having negotiated with the landlord to renovate the place first. I didn't want him to get too sore at me; and the time was right for new bathrooms and kitchen as well.

When Edwin moved in a few years ago, I told him he'd only be responsible for his half of the rent. I could have charged him more, but then I had to be nice to him, so hell with that. Hell with getting a VCR, too; as I convinced him instead to dole out some dough for a vertically designed washer and dryer set. While I wait anxiously for the era of disposable clothing to arrive, I have settled on the second best thing: doing laundry in my own apartment, especially with no clothe on. One of my little quirks of irrationality is that I need to take off all the clothing from my body and dump it into the washer. I absolutely hate to see dirty laundry lying around after I do my wash. Everything down to the shreddiest underwear must not get left behind. Man, the self-loathing and disgust I'm liable to display upon even finding the tiniest smelly sock I'd forgotten to wash.

But nine times out of ten, I'm reasonably rational. I also think I'm a reasonably fair person. Fair as in equitable. Fairness basically comes down to consideration for others, in the sense that you don't try to be a ball-breaker. For instance at work, I'm always on call, and am always prepared to work into the night—not to get a pat on the back, but more out of a sense of duty. However, when dealing with a bunch of co-op students whom I help to manage, all I require of them is the minimum. Anything above that, I see as a bonus, and it's always appreciated. I still belong to the old school that thinks most people would rather have fun than go to work.

My roommate Edwin, though, is a little different. He had more of a full-service type of upbringing. Although we have opposite personalities, we get along well because we are both pretty laid back. Well, he actually thinks I'm a little neurotic and quick off the handle, especially for a Deadhead, so let's just say that...let me just say that we seldom get into each other's way; that we rarely get upset over the same things and at the same time. Still, sometimes, his simplistic mind really pisses me off. Take our grocery bill for example: we Vermonts have had an account with our local grocer for years. I find it a great convenience to buy on account and pay monthly. Although our normal food bill isn't much, after adding in the party platters and all the mushrooms and beers, we are a good piece of business. Yet, to use my secretary Connie's favorite expression, *it irks me* to no end when Edwin makes his little candy store-like purchases and puts it on the monthly tab. He likes to buy his Kit Kats and his Mounds of Reese's and Almond Joys one bar at a time; then has the gall to tell the cashier to charge it.

"Dammit, *Edna*, show some consideration to the cashiers who have to do all your paperwork!" I've told him countless times and it still doesn't help. I hate to sound like a broken record, but with certain things, you just get pissed off every time it happens. "If you don't have the cash, *Rock Star*, then buy an extra six-pack of Bass Ale or something, make it a bigger purchase for crying out loud!" I would tell him over and over but I swear to god it doesn't help. Sometimes, he would retaliate by calling me names and make fun of my skinny legs. That doesn't bother me much, not at all, not one bit. But the thing that always shuts me up is when he uses his head and says something intelligent like: "Li-shen Zh-ippy, if you don't sh-tart shutting your trap, I'll just go to the store and open my own frigging account!" That always worked, boy, despite my knowing full well that he would never follow it through. He hates paperwork even more than those cashiers do. See, Edwin has this condition which I coined as wallet-phobia, it's crazy but true—he can't stand carrying things on his body or in his pocket. I have a phobia, too, except mine is called the wallet-*less* phobia, that's when I literally get a heart attack after I slap my ass and find my wallet isn't there. Edwin also hates to carry things when he is walking, save his candies that is. How-can-you-be-a-New-Yorker-without-making-a-habit-of-carrying-bags-till-the-tip-of-your-fingers-gets-so-pale-and-numb-as-to-be-mistaken-for-icicles?

"Alors. Café, bistrot, ou resto? Choisis!"

"Let's go bistro food. I had *brassero* last night"

"Bon. J'ai faim."

The more you get to know the Left Bank, the more fun it is; just teeming with activities and things to do. I don't think there is a place in America quite like it. New York has some of its flavor, especially if you combined the Village and Chelsea, then tack on Soho, and age the whole area architecturally for a couple of hundred years. But Paris, by virtue of it being the capital city, delivers quite a bit more on the grand-project end—to make up for what it might lack in East Village's tongue-piercing eccentricity.

Ally and I were walking on St.-Germain toward St.-Michel when we went past Rue de la Harpe. I wanted to walk up that street for the hell of it. We had had some good times there a few years ago hanging out with street bands and entertainers. While Ally didn't mind us walking through, she told me we were not going to eat there. She was going to take me to a place where she and Olivia had been to before.

Rue de la Harpe is a narrow street dotted with ethnic restaurants, especially near the St.-Michel end. Most of them also have tables that expand on to the walkway. Even though the street leans a bit to the touristy side, it is the young Americans who are the tourists, which sort of makes it happening as well. Yes, Rue de la Harpe: exotic as Arabia, and civilized as Reeboks and the Air in Jordan.

"Do you know, Mark, what we call this street?"

"What?"

"We call it Rue de Couscous!"

Rue de Couscous—she took the words right out of my subconscious. How true indeed, all those Middle Eastern and North African joints, with couscous and shish kebab galore. Yes, me, and thousands of others have eaten there and assumed that couscous, which sounds almost as weird as it looks, is authentic French food.

"Ally, I'll bet you that at the end of Couscous Street, you'll see a band playing American tunes."

"Okay, we bet!"

For some reason, I thought I was going to win. I mean, it was Friday night on Yankee boulevard; I couldn't miss.

When we walked past a movie theater, my memory was triggered once again. "Ally, I almost forgot; four years ago, we went into this movie house just to the right of the next cross street."

"*Eh, bien.* It must be the Salle Huchette."

"It was a Salle all right, no bigger than a room, with the tiniest piece of cloth passing for a screen."

"What did you see?"

"We saw a movie about two chess players, of how they were making a ridiculously big deal out of a chess match."

"I remember hearing about that one. But I didn't care for it."

She didn't miss much, I told her. Only a French filmmaker could convince himself into thinking that people would line up to see a flick about a chess game.

But Ally disagreed. She said that if you can get Tom Cruise and Richard Gere to play the leads, she'd go see it in a second. That was how we got into this big argument about films. Ally liked the Hollywood emphasis on actors being given lots of space to show off while I favored the French and European style of the director controlling and determining how a picture ought to look. To me, actors in general must convey the desired effect, not change the movie.

"I don't want them to change the movie, Mark. I just think they should be given more room to display their talents."

"Well, maybe for stars. But everyone else must perform specific tasks, not to steal scenes and show each other up. And above all there must be order, as well as a clear command structure. Anyone who talks back to the director is to be shot! Any director who runs overbudget should commit hari-kari!"

"Mark-uh, you are talking like an unmanageable consultant!"

Boy, can she attack without warning. I tried to salvage myself: "Well, I'm not saying that every film must have a planned effect. If a director starts out wanting a more participatory effort, then it's okay for actors to go off on their own a bit. Otherwise, they ought to be on a tight leash; especially when the camera is rolling!"

"But Mark, the director must cater to the talent he has, or the film is going to look too predictable."

"I agree with that. I only want to add that a director should not be forced to work with people he can't get along with, especially when it's a box office star brought in by some opportunistic producer. That's why I like Woody's movies. He incorporates his directions with actors he understands and works well with. So you get the best of both worlds. You know it's a Woody movie, yet you really like the acting of the characters at the same time."

"But Mark, you make acting sound so easy. It is a very special talent. Look at Meryl Streep in *Sophie's Choice* or *Out of Africa*? She was incredible! It takes years to learn to act."

"It might have been incredible, but in most cases, I'm not there to see so-and-so act. I'm there to see a movie. I don't want to come out of the movie theater and say: wow, can he or she act or what? Wow, the acting was so brilliant that I totally forgot what the story was all about!"

"O com'on, you just don't like stars!"

"Stars spelled backwards is *rats*."

"No, it isn't."

"All's I know is, we in New York make money for America, while they in Hollywood make money for stars. And everyone else that hangs on their coattails. I mean, why can't every movie have new and fresh talent. I want to see new faces. I want to say it's a good movie. If I want to see over-acting, I'll go to a Broadway play. Movies are supposed to be real."

"Movies are supposed to be real?" Ally laughed sarcastically.

"Movies are supposed to make you think—"

"I know, I know." she said. "*Dans la même temps*, I welcome any actor to be funny. The French filmmakers, they take themselves soooo seriously: *What? You want me to make a movie that is entertaining, that makes people laugh? But I'm an artist!*'"

"Ha ha ha, thank god you're no artist."

"But I *am*...a humorous *wooone*! I think no matter how serious the role: blind or deaf, or even paraplegic; if you can make a few jokes, it's more entertaining."

"But Ally, if the scene is tragic, like someone who's near death, then it ought to take on lots of seriousness."

Ally shrugged. Then her eyes lit up as she said, "Oh, I have an American joke for you via a California surfer. Let's see...what did one guy on death row shout to the other as they both headed for the electric chair?"

"What?"

"Hey, more *power* to you!"

Gee'sus H Krist, did that take me by surprise. There was about a one second delay before I started laughing out loud. I didn't know if I was laughing at the joke, or that thick French accented delivery of hers, or both. Oh maaaaan!

EIGHT

La Petite Ollioules was a bistro on a quiet street near Rue Saint-Andre des Arts. The decor of its dining room was a mixture of old and new. The tin-topped bar and the engraved mirrors were perhaps held over from the original mamas and papas of the joint. But to convey the sentiments of the new owners, laced curtains were replaced and slate tiles added. Other modern touches included tables that gave off a fiberglass shine and black chairs with curved seat backs. The crowd appeared to be mostly Parisians—a far cry from the *couscous* street on the other side of Boul'Mich. Oh, by the way, Ally won the bet. There weren't any street bands playing at the other end. Starving artists have to eat, too; though probably not as well as the last supper of prisoners on death row.

While waiting for a table, we got a bottle of wine recommended by the house. It was a Saumur-Champigny, from the Loire region. My grandmother liked Loire wines, but white ones. "Ally, I didn't think they made reds in Loire, sort of a lightweight district."

"I don't know, maybe it's not exported to the U.S.; but it's very popular in Paris. It costs no more than a Beaujolais and tastes like wine."

"Tastes like wine. Good one, Ally." Red, red wine…it was comforting to know that Ally knew about as much, or was as ignorant about wine as me.

We only waited for a short time before we got a table, which made Ally pretty happy. She and I both hate waiting. A young man came by and greeted us and gave us a run down of the specials. But we had already read the menu-filled mirror while at the bar and knew pretty much what we wanted. For starters, Ally was pleased that they offered the *grenouilles*, or frog legs, which I didn't mind trying; and we both agreed on the *aigo sau*, their special fish stew. So that was quick enough. I'm sure their stuffed chickens and over-stuffed veals were all well and good, but the house fish stew must take precedence. Besides, it was Friday, the day to eat seafood.

"So, Ally, do you come here often?"

"Not too much. But Olivia likes this place. It's a little expensive for students like me. Plus there are many other good places to eat in Paris. Unlike parts of the U.S., unlike L.A."

"Sure 'bout that? You've never heard Johnny Carson raving on and on about Burbank's Restaurant Row."

"Bhuh, every restaurant row in L.A. is just cheese-bigure after cheese-bigure after cheese-bigure."

I laughed. "Other than Live cheeseburgers on Saturday Night, what do you think of California, the Left Coast?"

"I lovit! I had so much fun there last summer."

"I must say you do travel a lot."

"Eh, one a year. I have a half-brother who is with an airline, so it's great. My friend Sophie and I, and Olivia a month later, we all went last year; and spent mcst of our time in Los Angeles."

"Oou la la in LALA land! That's so um...well, let's just say that I personally prefer Sinatra singing "New York, New York" after a Knick game than Randy Newman doing "I love L.A." after a Laker game."

"No, you're wrong. You have family there so you should know—it's the center of music and show biz, center of beach life, center of modern culture."

"I know, Ally. I've seen enough episodes of The Beverly *Flat-bellies* to truly, *truly* appreciate modern culture."

"Good, then you can appreciate the fun and the sun."

"Yeah, right. Tell me, Ally, did you become a member of *Three's Company* too? Riding bumper cars around Santa Monica?"

"No toy cars for me this time; but skateboarding, that's fun. They have the best skateboarders there. They do flips and turns in the rink all day, and then they invade the Venice boardwalk by jumping over benches and trash cans. It was incredible. They can kick around a skateboard in more ways than Europeans a soccer ball."

"Is that correct English? Well, I wouldn't know, anyways. So it sounds like you seriously got into some skateboarding."

"Yep. But you know what I love even more? Surfing!"

"Well, surfurbia, USA, that's the place."

"Do you know Huntington Beach?"

"Uh-huh, right up the road from Newport Beach, where my mother now lives for most of the year."

"Huntington Beach is where they invented surfing."

"Well, I wouldn't say they inven—"

"Okay, okay," she interrupted me. "But they hold some big surfing contests there. We were going to *all* the different beaches and catching their waves."

"Well, waves indeed are bigger out there than in the South of France."

"Oh, by far. We watched our surfing instructor surf through tubes of waves. It was bitchin', man!"

"Ally, where d'ya learn to talk like that," I said of her Franco-beach-bum speak. "Did they like French girls out there?"

"Naturally. California is very popular to the French. And they loved us there. That was how we were there for so long: Sophie's sister was doing a program at UCLA, and she invited us to join her for the summer."

"The University of Children Longing to be Actors?"

"Yep. They have *such* a beautiful campus."

"How did you like living in the center of the splash and flash of cul*ture à la Californie*?"

"It was great. Lots of entertainment and fun in Westwood Village."

"You mean spiritual book stores."

"Oh, com'on. I mean stores, bars, clubs, not to mention all those drive-ins. They are so California, the drive-ins: you pull up, sit in a car, and order your French fries with chili and—"

"And all the while your engine is running and your stereo is blasting."

"Always. Unless if it is the drive-in movies. But most of the movies we saw were in Westwood. There is also this other place, where they have twenty theaters showing at once. Can you imagine the choices I had to make? I wanted to see every single one."

"Yeah, but none of them any good."

"Sure, they were good. Tom Hanks, Tom Cruise, and the Brat Pack, and of course, Debra Winger, on the first day."

"Of course. How about some other stuff, like souvenir shopping by looking through trash cans of celebrities, or luxury car shopping on Rodeo Drive?"

"Yep, we did that. We saw lots'a lots'a cars, but nota lota sta's."

"Well, thats'a problem with tourists, Ally. They mistake one another for movie stars in Malibu, and they expect to meet more celebrities in Beverly Flats than they do watching I Love Lucy."

"Hey, I was *not* your typical tourist."

"But you still have to wait at the right tables in the right *resto* to kiss the plates of the stars."

"Well, maybe next time. I'm going to go again. Los Angeles was great. Everyone was so happy there. And les beachtowns, they were unbelievable. Schools having classes on the beach, people hanging out and listening to music on the beach, it was really cool; but the volleyball action was really, really hot!"

"Oh, fer sherrr!" I cracked. "Hey Ally, did you learn to speak any Valley speak?"

"Ah, Valley girls in shopping malls?" she made a face. "No, we didn't, *lake*, spend time down in the Valley. Traffic is, *lake*, always the other way—the Valley invading the beaches."

"Ally, Ally, Ally." I was shaking my head and laughing again. "So *you* were the one that starred in 'The Invasion of the Valley Snatchers!'"

"What do you want from me, Mark. *Lake*, it was not totally rad enough for me, dude. The beachtowns are much more tubular to the max!"

"Whatever you say, dudette. Ally, are all Parisian girls just like you? Or is that a stupid question." Boy, what's this world coming to? Even French girls are speaking broken L.A.-speak and wanting to be California beach bums.

Despite Ally's enthusiasm, my impressions of Los Angeles were not nearly as favorable. I find that city annoying and a let-down. It tries to be so impressive and overwhelming to visitors, but it really overwhelms with emptiness. Downtown L.A. is like a ghost town most of the day, even high noon on Flower Street has hardly any pedestrians. But ghost town or not, you still have to cough up the money for parking everywhere you go, even to go to a stupid mall. You know what Los Angeles is? It's like a suburbia inside a city;

as if they took Nassau County, added a few more freeways and tall buildings, and tried to pass it off as a city. Yet unlike suburbia, the package also included all the crimes and blight that the big cities are famous for.

I believe it was in *Annie Hall*, where Woody shows quick shots of a plane flying back and forth from L.A. Well, that's still the way I feel about it. Despite, or perhaps due to the fact that my mother used to live there, I earnestly try to avoid that city whenever possible. Even when I do head out West, I do my best to arrive at John Wayne in Orange County. But sometimes, there's just no way to avoid LAX. You know the old LIFO FIFO rule of accounting? Well, LIFO is definitely the preferred way I deal with L.A.—last in and first out! But, boy, did I almost screw it up the last time I was there. It was when I made a detour after a weekend in San Francisco, to assist my boss and our Washington man, who was an expert on government contracts, in a go or no-go feasibility study for a defense contractor.

I was ticked off the moment I got off the plane. There wasn't even a taxi available at the airport to take me into town. So I had to rent a goddamn car at this gigantic rental complex. And since I did not reserve ahead with an express account number, I couldn't get the car under a canopy with trunk open and engine on; instead, I had to wait on a goddamn line for a car that was way the hell over on the far end of the parking lot, *baking* in the sun. Then I had to battle the freeway traffic forever just to get to the corporate office on South Grand. I've never seen a city with so many cars and even more bad drivers. You turn the radio on and you hear accidents on every single freeway. So due to the damn traffic and the confusing way they laid out their office buildings, I missed the rest of the engagement team, who had already gone to the company's research complex. So again I put my wheels to the freeway and hit the road. Then, after a long and grueling day of work that went into the night, I didn't even feel like driving back to our downtown hotel any more, not to mention driving out again to LAX the next day. However, my screwed up day finally turned lucky when I realized I still had a chance to make the last red eye out. Suddenly I had become a man possessed—rushing to my plane as if it were the last flight from Saigon. You know that song "You Gotta Get Out Of This Place"? Well, it never sounded more anthematic than that night, boy.

Remember what Woody said about L.A. in *Annie Hall*: "Don't tell me I have to walk from the car to the house, my feet haven't touched pavement since I reached Los Angeles." Well, my brain definitely had. It had been touching the pavement and frying on the freeway concrete since god invented the cocaine rush hour. Why else are those fruits out there all into that meditational shit? No wonder my mother moved farther out, albeit to a different form of suffocation; to one of them overpriced, guard-gated communities overlooking Newport Bay. She and Ira used to live on the Westside, not as glitzy as the neighboring Hills and Airs, thank god. The folks on the other side of the 405 renovate their existing homes while the egomaniacs across the freeway like to raze the original and erect palatial haciendas from scratch. Whop-dee-do! If I were ever given a choice between overlooking Sunset Boulevard or overlooking Sunrise Pond in a sleepy New England town, I'd take the Pond in a second—especially when you factor in the air quality. For example, take this house where my mother used to live, that chunk of California contemporary on the side of a hill: the first day I was there, and that was many years ago on the pollution ladder, all I saw was this brown haze blanketing over the Downtown skyscrapers and Century City. Very big thrill, let me tell you. More million smog views than million dollar views, and certainly more breath-choking than breathtaking!

Ally and I were sharing wine and L.A. stories when the frog legs arrived. Back to bon appetite, I guess. It was the first time I'd seen such a dish. Tiny little creatures they were, looking a bit like fried chicken wings. "You know, Ally, I was kinda expecting a slipperier texture, like the frogs we used to dissect in biology."

"But these are *French* frog legs."

"Okaaaay," I nodded in slow motion. Whatever they were, they smelled pretty good. But you've got to work at it as each leg had very little meat—all wrapped around those teeny-weeny leg bones. As for the taste, it was sort of a mixture of chicken and fish, with tender white meat and a nicely spiced flavor. The frogs were an ideal appetizer; giving your tastebuds quite a workout and leaving your stomach with room for more. Or, in American advertising lingo: taste great…less filling.

Well, plenty of room in the tummy was indeed necessary to participate in the consumption of the *aigo sau*. Boy, you talk about a fish dish that was filled with excitement; and anticipation! The way they did it was, instead of having the fish together with the broth, they separated them after birth by placing all the fish and vegetables in a raised platter while they served the soup first. What a great move it was; for along with the soup came a side plate of French ketchup called the *rouille*—a red and hot and chili pepper and olive oil and garlic flavored concoction that you mix in with the soup. And boy, did I mix it up. It was so good that, not only did I put it in the soup, but on the fish as well. *More red tartar sauce, Mom. Pleeease!* Red sauce together with white fish? I know, I know, but tasting is believing. What a combination! The *aigo sau* is exactly the type of dish that makes me proud of the red-hot seafood lover in me, and sad for all those non-fish eaters: the things they are missing out on. And there are still lots of people out there who don't eat fish. A tragedy! "Flavorless fish and chips is about as fishy as some of my friends can tackle," I said to Ally. "You can't really blame them though, especially after hearing stories about polluted bass and bluefish from the Long Island Sound."

"Long Island Sound, you mentioned it this morning."

"Yes, with New England on one side and Long Island, where I grew up, to the south."

"How did you like living on Long Island? Did you like it as much as I liked California?"

"Well, growing up on Long Island is kinda like growing up in Southland. You know, guitar jams in the basement, keg parties on the patio, and getting high up in the attic. The exception being that we don't drive all terrain vehicles up the Pacific Palisade cliffs in the middle of the night just for kicks; and we had better things to do than spraying the speed limit signs on Topanga Canyon from 35 to 85."

"Did you go in to Manhattan often?"

"Oh yeah, me, personally—all the time. The trains are very convenient. But lots of people just hung out in bars closer to home," I said, remembering those fake I.D. nights at U.S. Blues, Raffles, and Sprats. Those were the days!

"Mark, how is your Hampton Beach in New York, is it anything like California?"

"The Hamptons? Can't help you there. Never went. Wait, I did once—visiting somebody who was taking summer courses at

Southampton College." At least she got affordable housing, I told Ally, a rare thing in the Hamptons. For unlike California, it ain't so easy to play homeless beach bum there.

"You let me worry about that," Ally said in a sly tone. "You just worry about getting us there."

"For you—anything!" I said with a smile. "Come next summer. Next Memorial Day. Me and my roommate will take you sailing out there. Maybe you'll like Malibu on the Atlantic just as much. On second thought, it ain't so easy to sail out to the Hamptons. It's pretty far, a good part of a day."

"That's okay, I'll have time," Ally said with confidence.

"Yeah, but sometimes, there is absolutely no wind. You want to hear a funny story? It happened last year off the shores of the Hamptons...."

I went ahead and told Ally about the Around Long Island Race last year, during a weekend in late July. The race's starting point was in New York Harbor, with all the boats gathered against the Manhattan skyline. The wind in mid-summer is not overwhelmingly strong, which suits me just fine. Slower wind actually bends the best around the sail and fills it up nicely. In heavy air, wind just flies right by the sails so there isn't that much finessing. But nobody wanted no wind, which was what happened on the second day of the race, when the wind just came to a sudden halt somewhere off the Hamptons. Aggravating the situation was the presence of many other boats clustered around us, with no one able to break away. True, we have an engine on board, the iron jib as it is called, but you can't use it in racing; a definite no-no. Personally, I think the engine is a great addition to a sailboat, particularly for docking and serving as a backup. But them old-timer sailing purists? Forget about it! They are so adament against using it that I've seen beautiful, beautiful boats with engines that are rustier than a car in a junkyard.

So anyway, we were sitting on our butts in the calm sea and waiting for the wind to pick back up. As Edwin's navigator, I didn't have a hell of a lot to do when the boat ain't goin' no where. But the thing to do as a navigator is to absorb lots of reading material, whatever there is that might help you plot a course. One of the books I had around was a tide guide. It tells the movement of the currents and stuff—things nobody wants to read, and therefore relegated to the geek on the boat—me. Not so much to boost my ego, but Edwin occasionally underestimates just how much sailing I knew, especially in racing. I'm never forceful or commanding on a boat—leadership qualities are virtually non-existent in me. But at times, I contribute by using my head.

Well, after I reviewed the charts, I had a hunch that the boat was not only *not* moving forward, but was actually being pushed backwards by the currents. When I informed Edwin of my suspicions, he pulled off one of the best moves of all time: he told me to quietly untangle the anchor and discreetly drop it in the water. I swear to god, what subsequently happened was absolute sheer delight. Low and behold, our boat, the *Slipknot!*, began distancing itself from the pack. It was especially sweet passing our pals on the *Easy Wind*, with whom we had a friendly wager. Boy, I can still hear the crew on that boat cursing it up in total bewilderment. They thought we had the engine on or something. But dropping your anchor, unlike insider trading, is one-hundred-percent legal; though like insider trading, everyone sooner or later wakes up to it and eventually catches on. Still, it was great while it lasted. Oh, the look on the faces of our opponents!

So anyway, Ally and I had a somewhat messy but nevertheless marvelous time eating the *aigo sau*. I thought the light red wine we ordered went rather well with the food. But you can drink whatever the hell you like. Some people might treat the dish as a fish stew and accompany it with a white, dry Chardonnay. As I had learned at lunch that day, whatever turns you on.

A dinner, even at the neighborhood shoe-box bistro, is not over until the dessert lady is seen. So Ally ordered a *tarte tatin*, while I went for the *Charlotte aux Poires*, a creamy cake topped with pears. The *Charlotte* was fork-licking good, especially those home soaked pears. Ally's apple tart wasn't bad, either. It tasted closer to pastry than to an American apple pie. Far less pie-ish dough and far more tasty apples—especially the top layer which was caramelized to a golden brown.

"Mmm, yummy yummy!" I said of the deserts.

"Yum-me Yum-me? Is that how you say it? It sounds funny. In France, we say *meum meum*."

"Close enough," I liked Ally's attitude. She had a real healthy appetite and a good time eating. The girls in New York, well, they always seem to skip dessert when you take them out. However, they often talk you into ordering a big one for yourself. Then they'd take a fork and start chiseling away at *your* cheesecake. That makes you feel bad, so you tell her you'll order one just for her. But *noooo!* "Oh, Mark, please don't; you are trying to get me fat so you can dump me." Women!

Although the check came out to a lot more than fried rice and pizza, it wasn't bad if you included wine and service, perhaps even a bargain due to the authentic local backdrop. And, despite it being labeled as bistro fare, I think if they used choicer seafood and paid a little more attention to presentation, the food was good enough to be served at posh French restaurants anywhere.

As we were winding up a meal at a Left Bank bistro, me and Ally talked about, of all places, her traveling and dining experiences in the Wild Wide West of America. She and her friends took a couple of weeks off as beach bums and toured the Great American Southwest. She found the *grande espace*, the vast openess out there, a *colossal* experience. The only sad part was, I knew very little about that part of America, and was unable to match her anecdote for anecdote. Vaguely recalling the Brady Bunch encountering some Indians after getting lost in the Grand Canyon just wasn't good enough.

"Mark, have you ever gone to a dude ranch? One right in the middle of no-where?"

"Can't say I have, though I imagine it'd be something like a forerunner to the Club Med, *sans* yuppies and bikinis." I remembered an episode of *Happy Days* where the Fonz and the Cunninghams headed out West to save a dude ranch from foreclosure, but that was it.

"We spent two days at a dude ranch in Arizona," Ally continued, "It was almost like a family bistro in France, only on a bigger scale. Everything there was big, big, big."

"Well, that's the great Southwest for ya. It's so big that people don't even bother to say how many miles from here to there. Instead, it's how many tanks of gas. If somebody is asking around for where the next desert party is, and you tell him it's less than a tank of gas away, then he'd be happy as a cactus and say: *Ya-hoo! What'a y'all say we be mozzin' on outta here, pard'er!"*

Ally liked that one. "You did that great, Mark: *howdi pard'er!*" She mimicked me mimicking a cowboy. "But have you ever been to a *real* Western party? A *real* Sunday barbecue?"

"Maybe not Western style, but clam bakes, sure."

"No, no. I'm talking about a big Sunday barbecue pique-nique at a dude ranch. There is no television and telephone at the ranch, so all you do is horseshoe around and eat—"

"Horse around," I interrupted her.

"Yep, horse around, go to a rodeo, then watch the cooks prepare for the barbecue. I tell you, they were already preparing to cook this huge roast pig when we arrived, and they cooked that thing for a whole day before it was ready to eat. Can you believe it? That was how big it was."

"And the pig wasn't burned?"

"I don't think so. There was so much food it was unbelievable. The salad bowl they had was bigger than this table."

"Wow-wee! Ally, did you all eat till you dropped?"

"We all roast-pigged out. There was no other way."

"Pigged out, good one Ally. Did you also get that mandatory end-of-picnic watermelon?" I was cracking up as I said it. I shouldn't make fun of everything like this.

"I don't remember watermelon, but you know what I love: the corn on the cob."

"That's very American of you, Ally."

"Yep, corn on the cob, Willie Nelson, and cowboy boots."

"Not necessarily in that order, I hope."

"Of course not, I like my cowboy boots the best. I got them at a Tony Lama factory outlet in El Paso."

"Down in the West Texas town of El Paso, I fell in love with a Mexican Girl." I didn't know what drove me to break out in song, I guess I just felt like it. But I quickly explained away. "I'm free associating, Ally; just like Zoe in the movie when she mentioned a Maserati, and the rest of the girls started singing *'my Maserati does 185.'*"

"Our old mobile couldn't do 185, but we managed to get speeding tickets at every state we drove through. Arizona, New Mexico, Utah, Nevada, Texas. No not Texas, we only went into El Paso and came back out."

"Did you like the Southwest more or California?"

"Oh, California, by far. It's no contest. But I also wanted to see your Southwest: the Natural Bridge, the Petrified Forest...all the things I saw in the cowboy movies. It's a completely different experience seeing it in person."

"What's different, Ally? You have a semi-ghost town somewhere, its only intersection being a malfunction junction with a 7-Eleven type convenience store on one corner, a Mel's Diner like joint across the street, and an old gas station that's never open."

"Oh Mark, you are always stereotyping. Of course, it was not like France, where even the next town has its own personality. But it was still inter-sting. One day, we went to this club with sawdust so high on the floor it was like walking in snowflakes; and they used big wooden boards as table tops, tied big trash cans to it as support, and stacked up milk carton crates to use as seats. Isn't that great?"

"Umm...I can see giving them a point or two for originality." I almost had to, considering how enthusiastically convincing Ally was, and how she absolutely saw no possibility of anyone possibly disagreeing with her.

Still, not everything she saw was herbs and roses, particularly around an Indian Reservation near the Continental Divide. While shopping for Indian jewelry was fun and good, Ally was nevertheless shocked by how backwards a part of America still remained. As if the widespread poverty weren't enough, how about tacking on the rampant alcoholism: "People were trading in food coupons at discounts to buy more liquor—just so they could drunk-drive themselves off the road."

Not to sound apologetic but the truth is, as much as I'm aware of urban decay, I'm virtually oblivious to rural poverty. While the down and out in the cities could at least see some light through select schools, athletics, part-time jobs—and yes—even pushing drugs or prostitution; those on the reservations, however, face a much tougher challenge—for they have been robbed of a most fundamental right granted to us all—that basic American ideal known as hope.

9 / LE ZIGZAG, S'IL VOUS PLAIT; AND DRIVER, I'LL PAY YOU TWICE AS MUCH TO DRIVE HALF AS FAST!

One of the better reasons for living in New York City, or at least a consolation prize for the high cost of eating out, is the digestive stroll after a meal. It does the body much good—both mentally and physically. I remember the first years at NYU: a bunch of us would walk down to Chinatown, share a tableful of dishes, then on the way back, we'd go through Little Italy, stopping at Ferrara's for cappuccino and cannoli before heading back to the Village. It was altogether quite a metabolic workout, so much so that by the time we got back, we were hungry again.

Now, contrast that with, say, Jack Straw from Wichita, and see what he does after eating out. First, the drive back: with the advent of automatic transmissions and automatic garage-door openers, Jack would be on his couch turning on a ballgame with a beer in hand before the enzymes have even had a chance to breakup the T-bone. No wonder my ol'buddy's been moving much too slow.

Solid walking mileage can also be had on the Upper East Side. Although the blocks around my apartment are pretty busy during the day, it's almost as still as Wall Street at night. So when I go out, I usually walk over to at least Third Avenue to find restaurants and stuff. Incidentally, between First Avenue and Third Avenue, from the sixties to the nineties, lies one of the highest concentration of bars and restaurants in New York. You can go out to a different place each night for months and still not get through them all. Then again, who wants to? As much as I like Italian food, to sit at one of those trendy twenty-dollars a pasta places in Armanis just isn't what I crave to do in *my* neighborhood. I don't even own an Armani, for Christ's sake. Same with my roommate Edwin. When we go out, we often end up at Stella's Brew, our regular bar and grill with the balconied windows. Not only is it a good place to watch all the games, but it's easy on the wallet, too. Kind of like a Cheers Bar ambiance at coffee shop prices. And, when you bump into Edwin's friends—those cash-rich nitwits who know nothing about sports—then the night is practically on them!

While I'm at it, let me just see if I can cleanse my soul a bit on my feelings about New York City. Ever since the departure of Tom Seaver and Reggie Jackson, the town hasn't been the same. I mean, they virtually took the Base out of the Apple. And the exodus has been non-stop—the Giants and Jets, and who knows—maybe someday, the Mets and Yankees. And that's only in sports. There are Fortune companies relocating elsewhere in search of lower rents, and fortune seekers taking their place with quick killings in drugs and car stereos. Hell, every time I turn on the local news, I get inundated with tales of tragedy after tragedy. It really sucks. There have even been times when I have wondered: could Ed Koch and Woody Allen have both been wrong? Could I be wrong? I mean, without New York, we are like fish out of water, sushi without seaweed. God forbid if the middle class really starts to pack up and leave. For if that should ever happen, then there goes the tax base. But you know, every time I get depressed about New York, all I have to do is to just ask myself: "So what are you gonna do, Vermont, move to Los Angeles?" And boom! Like lightning, it picks me right up. No way L.A.! If you think I'm going to trade in Grand Central Station for valet parking, you've got another think coming. And you know what, it works every time. Half a dozen warm bagels will always beat a dozen of their smog-filled donuts: Every! Single!! Time!!!

As I turned onto Rue de Capet, there was a sense of retreating into familiarity. Although not quite as routine as turning onto Seventy-eighth Street from Madison, I felt homey. The dim lights, the solid walls that surround the property, the crooked double door entry gate. Hard to imagine it was only last night, just yesterday, that my feet first made contact with those uneven cobblestones in the courtyard.

All was quiet inside the house. Quiet but not undisturbed as there was a smell of cigars mixed with sharp perfumed fragrances. We must have just missed Charles and company after they had come back from their outing. Ally was glad they hadn't made too big a mess: just a few glasses scattered about; and in the vestibule, resting against the staircase, were two designer hat boxes—opened, with the hats removed. Showering gifts again, that Charles, for kisses and kicks.

To complete the hat trick, there was a box of Dalloyau chocolates on top of the bureau for me, unopened. Next to it, under a half-finished cigar, was a note from Charles, saying that although he won't be returning until quite late; tomorrow night, a feast awaits. Guess I'll just have to pace myself on the chocolate truffle front, to make sure those calories would tie me over till tomorrow night.

Now this was more like the Charles I knew. The rushed letter he had dictated earlier to Ally was somewhat uncharacteristic of him, or at least uncharacteristic of the old Charles, the suave banker to the international hostess set. Careful as I was not to speculate, I had always assumed that one reason Charles had never remarried was that he couldn't quite fit it into his schedule. For one thing, his client base had consisted of some of the wealthiest women in the world. He knew everybody, and cared for them all, or so it appeared. And they, in turn, adored him; confided in him; and surely there had been instances where they were very much attracted to him, despite knowing he was probably a man they can't always have. But it is not necessary to have *all* of Charles to get the full effect. To some, a couple of days with him could equal weeks and months in the company of another, as he had shown on that day in my living room with Theresa. When Charles was not honing his skills as a psychologist, he could be found serving as a social advisor: writing a recommendation to a Swiss boarding school for a Hong Kong dowager here, providing the right property agent for a Brazilian heiress there. And, should his clients have a need for art dealers or antiques and furniture makers, Charles could, literally, open his own doors and show them around. Finally, for those who needed even more one-on-one attention, then off he goes for a few days of island hoping in the South Pacific. Line them up between Bora Bora and Pago Pago, spread them out from Fiji to Tahiti—no island too small, no seaplane too big. And, to mix some business with R&R, the more his clients chose liquidity, the more he went on a buying spree—when the price was right, no doubt.

"Mark, do you mind if I change my clothes and make some calls?"

"Not at all. You know what, Ally, knowing how long you can be on the telephone, I think I'll take a shower to wake myself up a bit."

"Bon, parfait!"

I wasn't really tired, but felt I ought to feel clean before going out, just to be on the cautious side. Sure I knew that the Parisians didn't have much of a deodorant habit; but that didn't mean I had to stoop down to their armpits.

The bathroom connected to my bedroom was fairly conventional; all except for the tub. First, it was decorated with water faucets that looked like the heads of two golden ducks, with a set of flat beaks pointed straight down to serve as the hot and cold faucet heads. In addition, the edge of the tub was made from marble that was nearly a foot wide. Why, you can even sit on the edge of the tub if you wanted to; or, if you prefer, do what that woman in the commercial before *New York Stories* did, have a tray of breakfast sent up—bathroom serviced up!—as you plan out the seduction in your tub.

As for an expensive fixture that I could have done without (no, not the ubiquitous but useless bidet; that just comes with the territory), but an item which I didn't see a need for was that antique-styled mirror on the back wall, part of it right along the tub. In truth, I don't recall having seen myself taking a shower before. I mean, I've seen a few familiar angles as my eyes look down on my body, but certainly not all the shots at the disposal of the eye on the mirror. In addition, the showerhead was placed in the center of the tub, which was also a little strange. But that was kind of cool, too. Why use only one end of a tub if you can use it all? I can also see a center showerhead as just the thing should there be a *douche à deux*, a shower for two, if you know what I mean.

To my relief, the steam took care of the mirror and I was in and out of the shower in no time. I think we Americans are probably the fastest showerers on earth, though we make it up in frequency. I could just picture the Europeans soaping it up in a tub-full for their baths-of-the-week, and admiring themselves in the mirror for hours on end.

After showering, I changed into a fresh pair of boxers but still wore my old pants and shirt. To wear my old socks after a shower, though, was completely out of the question; and so was putting on a fresh new pair. So that made it barefoot and loafers by default.

Add my unshaven face and a little hair grease, I might have even passed for Don Johnson—yeah, in my next life! That's all right, though. When traveling solo on the road, there is little need to get too fancy and dress into a cutting edge personality. Just the straight forward easy to wash'n pack stuff will do—clothes that can be worn day in and day out.

The first thing I did after I went outside was to open the doors to the front gate. They were quite heavy; and squeaky, too. Not to mention that, unlike garage doors, there was no motor or even pulley to give some assistance. "Mark, can you do me another favor? After I get the car out of the *cour*, just close the doors behind you."

Yeah, just leave it to ol' Mark here to do the dirty work.

Unlike other guys, who might feel a bit uncomfortable at having a girl drive them around, I was more than happy to yield, especially after witnessing Ally's talents in the Paris traffic last night. Not that I'm a bad driver or anything; but even so, Paris has enough landmarks to help out the directionally challenged. Just remember Dean Smith's North Carolina Tar Heels and their "Four Corners" offense. Paris has four corners, too. Sacré Coeur on top, Eiffel Tower and the Bastille on the two flanks, and Montparnasse on the bottom. Venture out of those quadrants and you're on your own!

We crossed the Seine and drove through the Place de la Concord and the Madeleine. "There is Restaurant Vignon, where we had lunch." I said to Ally. Damn! We sure got there quickly by car.

"How was your lunch, Mark? Was the food what you expected from French cuisine?"

"Beyond expectation. The food was phenomenal! You should ask Charles to take you there sometimes."

"Oh, no. It's not my cup of tea. Did the old man take you upstairs or down?"

"The main dining room, why?"

"Nothing. Usually, I get calls for him to meet people upstairs."

"Tsch, uppers or downers, either way blood flows!"

We drove by the Opera; as impressive looking as any opera house anywhere, especially at night when it's all lit. But word had it that Paris was soon to join the likes of Lincoln Center of New York and the Opera House of Sydney. The French government was about to complete the construction of a huge, ultra modern opera house near the Bastille.

"Ally, what are they going to do with the old Opera house once the fat lady is carried into the new one?"

"I don't know," she shrugged.

Ask a stupid question, get a stupid answer. I got the feeling that I was more curious about Paris than she was; though she sure knew her movies: "Do you remember, Mark, in *Legal Eagles*, when Debra Winger was trying to tell Robert Redford how to drive and chase a bad guy? Then Redford got really *fettup* and left the car and told her she could do her own driving?"

"Yeah, I remember that. Then she admits to Redford that she doesn't know how to drive. That was pretty funny, almost as funny as that scene where Daryl Hannah was chanting up a fire dance."

Unlike Debra Winger, Ally could certainly have given Redford a drive for his money. She was fast—almost race car like—with her ass all the way back, her palms on the steering wheel, one foot abusing the accelerator, the other foot gripping the carpet for support. I told Ally that she definitely made her turns too sharply. I don't mind when someone changes lanes quickly, it looks dangerous, but is actually safer than indecision; but turns on a city street ought to be done more conservatively, without so many neck bending lateral *G*'s.

"My turns are fine," Ally defended herself. "It's just the crying sound from the brakes that make people *think* I'm turning too fast."

Well, about the size of a regulation seat-of-the-pants Ally-logic. If I may lift a line from Jerry and the Boys: *Nine mile skid, on a ten mile ride; hot as a pistol but cool inside.*

"You know, Ally, if you had gone to a high school in America, you would not have passed the drivo-trainer course. In fact, you wouldn't even come *close* to passing it."

"It's not the driver...It's the Saab!"

Boy, could she go on a counter attack, channeling my criticism into the exhaust pipes—even turbocharging it back through the valves of praise. "Ally, perhaps you do have what it takes to go into advertising. That was almost as good a line as Tom Cruise saying "Porche, there is no substitute!"

"Oh, I luv Tom Cruise."

"And I'm sure he would love you."

"I want to do a movie with him one day."

"As long as you don't forget me as your cinematographer."

"Only if you don't forget *me* as your stuntwoman."

"How can I if you keep driving like this. Ally, it's a good thing you're French, for if you were American, you would've been single-handedly responsible for raising women's car insurance rates."

"Oh, com'on, I'm not that bad," Ally quickly adjusted my claim. "Did I tell you, Mark, about the time we drove through the States, with Sophie and Olivia, and we got tickets for speeding."

"*We*, or you personally?"

"Me, okaaay? But that *flic* was so stupid, he did not even write down the correct address."

"So naturally, you did not pay?"

"Naturally, not."

The thought of Ally getting a ticket cracked me up. I could just picture myself being a cop pulling her over. As I walk up to her car, she would give me that most innocent "whoops!" kind of stare, with her eyes sad and wide. A girl like that going as fast as a Major League fastball? Nah!

"It was fortunate that you were driving out West," I said. "Had you been driving through the South, they might even put you in the slammer. My freshman year at Penn, we drove down to New Orleans for Mardi Gras, and we nearly got locked up with the devil that went down to Georgia."

"What's Louisiana like?"

"Don't know much about the Cajun Country. It's pretty weird down there. They're all into collecting rocking chairs and porch swings'n shit."

"Ehh, you're ow'ful! Is that any way to talk about your own country?"

"I've said plenty worse, Ally; plenty more worse! But I do like New Orleans, though. It's a crazy place, full of alcoholics. You know there's a bar down there without even an entrance door?"

"Oh, *ree-lee*?"

"Yup. It didn't need one. That bar hadn't closed its doors for years. Big partiers down there, them natives. They put in more hours drinking than the Japanese spend working. It's incredible, everybody seems to get into the spirit of things once they're there. Just ask all those kids from my high school who went on to Tulane, one of the better schools in the South, by the way."

"Do they have an MBA program?"

"Think so. But boy, what a party school and city, especially on nights when the Radiators play at Tipatina's."

"Did you see the *Big Easy* with Dennis Quaid?" Ally asked.

"Parts of it, and that's the kind of music they play—Fishhead music, and lots and lots of street jazz. The musicians don't sleep in Noir'lense. They play on the streets for money during the day, and play at the clubs for food at night. It's a crazy place. I think you'll like it. It's probably the most friendly city in America, to the French anyway."

"Great, I can't wait to go!"

If you think Ally is merely a crazy driver on the road, you are only half right; she's a hell of a crazy parker, too. We were on this street near a cemetery, and the only space we could find was about two-thirds of a car length between a Renault parked in front and a driveway in the rear. But not to worry. Ally first drove up past the Renault, estimated the extra space in front of it and said, "I think we can give the Renault a push." Next she parallel-parked the Saab, to as far forward as she could till it kissed the bumper of the Renault; then low and behold, she shifted the Saab into a lower gear, stepped on the gas, and, like a tugboat, our Saab was slowly pushing the Renault forward—right before my very eyes! It was one of the most unforgettable things I had ever witnessed, sitting there next to her and watching the Renault inching up inch by inch. Whatever happened to parking brakes? Christ almighty, was I in shock. I had never seen anyone do that in my life; didn't even think such a stunt was even conceivable. Believe me, with New York's parking situation the way it was, I thought I'd seen every creative parking trick in the book. Jesus Christ, that was hairy. I felt almost like a criminal, praying that nobody would walk by with sticks and stones. But dammit, it sure worked all right. That Saab was now within its bounds and no longer blocking someone's front gate. And how was Ally through all this? She was as cool as her linen jacket—just another day at the motor vehicles office. "My friends do that, too. You will meet them soon. So, as we say in French: *La nuit est à nous!*"

Yes, we've met the night, and it is ours!

10 / Ten

Le Zigzag was a night club on a side street off Boulevard de Clichy—Boulevard de Moulin Rouge as it's been known to the tour bus trade. Despite the area being as neoned-out as Times Square, it didn't appear to be half as seedy, only twice as weird. When Ally and I walked by a huge theater-sized discotheque, I noticed a long line of people in outrageous costumes, as if they were part of a wild fashion show, except that many of the dressed-uppers were...well, let's just say that the line between Jack and Jill was hazy at best.

"Hey, Ally, you're not taking me to this multiplexed showplace?"

"Not tonight. I'm supposed to meet some friends at a boîte farther down. It's not as big as this one, but we like it better for its music." The French call their night clubs *boîtes du nuit*, night boxes. Not a bad description, even though I've always thought of my bedroom as my night box. Then again, perhaps I was the only one on that street who actually *sleeps* at night.

There was a fair line outside Zigzag, so Ally told me to queue up first as she headed toward the entrance to check out the scene. A bit later, she waved me over and saved me from a stiff admission charge.

"Thank you very much."

"No problem. You know, the doorman almost did not let me in. He said I was too late for my meeting."

"But you charmed him into it anyway, huh?"

"Always!"

Maybe it was due to my lack of exposure to the nightlife of New York, but my first impression as we got inside was dark, dark, dark! I guess everything seems much darker when compared to the fluorescent lights in my office. It took a club in Paris to sink in the thought that I hadn't been much of a happening man-about-town. Why, I could probably count on one hand the clubs I've gone to the whole of last year.

Le Zigzag, contrary to its name, was squarely laid out. A red-walled foyer area as you enter, then you walk through a corridor with a long metallic bar on the right, and tiny tables on the left. Past the bar was a rectangular dance floor hung with disco lights, under which a handful of people were dancing to an old Stray Cats tune. From the dance floor, you could see a loft area built into the space above the bar, which explained the bar's rather low ceiling. Then, at the far end of the dance floor, there was a little stage, then another bar, and a couple of small rooms. Ally and I went into one of the rooms, but not before she gave her body a passing wiggle at the "she's sexy and seventeen" music.

"Bonsoir, Alex."

"Bonsoir, ça va?"

There were greetings all around. I didn't know anyone, so I just followed Ally along. She greeted every single person in that room with a kiss on both cheeks, even the ones she didn't know. Oh, there was Sabine, Babette, Florence, Valérie, Olivier, Vincent, Stéphane Cyril, and Sébastien. The French, it became clear, take too much time greeting everybody. Christ, if you're at a big gathering, by the time you've cheek-to-cheeked everyone present, the party's over already.

After I said my hellos, I planted myself on one of the red sofas, took a few periodic whiffs at all the perfumes in the air, or rather the mixed-flower salade du jour, and watched Ally and her friends chat away. I say watched because, amidst the music and lightning quick French accents around me, that was about all I could do. But what fun it was just watching them kibitzing up a storm. In fact, I don't know if I mentioned it earlier, but the French talk with everything they can get their hands on. Literally. Take this guy at the other end of the couch, the way he kept nodding his head while making karate chops with his hands in front of his body, and this was all talking to a girl. Imagine if we ever got him to talk about the life and times of Gustave Flaubert. Ally was up there, herself. She was flipping through some papers with one hand and gesturing with her other hand. Her leggy legs, too: one minute they were stretched out on top of the coffee table, another minute she had them one cropped over the other just like me, and soon afterwards she had them in a more grownup cross-over-the-knee position. I didn't mind it at all, her restlessness, even her tendency to slam her feet on the floor from time to time, especially when she got emotional.

That was the thing, though. Ally was discussing with some of her fellow students on having an end-of-the-year party at Zigzag—a *Sacre du Printemps*—for her class at Dauphine. Sort of like them Spring Flings and Booze Cruises we have in American business schools. And like us, the Parisians had their disagreements. Some of the organizers feared that Zigzag might be too small; Ally disagreed. There were also others who felt that its music was too mainstream; Ally again disagreed, saying if they wanted to, they could bring their own. Finally, there were those who wanted to have the party at a pavilion near their university, which Ally didn't mind except it would be too expensive. "We will never break even there charging only one hundred francs per person, *jamais!*" She said that as she tightened her lips and gave off this real irate look. As I said earlier, it's very easy to stir her up. Her *copains* seemed just as contentious, dismissing her with equal ease. Yet moments later, after Ally got some of the things she wanted, she became agreeable again. "*Bon, c'est* cool," she said, slicing her hand across her chest. "*C'est* super cool! *D'accord, parfait!*" You should've seen her in conversation. She spoke very expressively, with lots of emphasis: loud one moment, soft another; slowing down a bit, then rapid fire. She could really talk breathlessly fast, that Ally. So fast that I'd run out of breath just listening to her. But once she was content, she would mellow out: take a big drag from a cigarette and be in that patented, wide-eyed daze again—with almost no cares in the world.

The same could not be said for her friend Sophie, who came into the room with a drink. "Eh, Sophie!" Ally got up and kissed her and said something as she patted her affectionately on the shoulder. But Sophie was carrying a full drink, and it damn near got tipped over.

"Je vous présent Mark Vermont, un ami de Charles Martin de New York," Ally said.

"Hello, I'm Sophie. Nice to meet you."

We exchanged greetings.

"Un New Yorkais! Alors, vous n'êtes pas Americaine, non?" A New Yorker, then you are not really American then, Sophie said.

I reacted with a quick laugh. *"Mais...est-ce que les Parisiens sont vraiment Français?"* But are Parisians really French, I said.

"Absolument! Nous Parisiennes sommes l'example même de tout la France!" Sophie replied.

Well, at least she didn't say tout le monde. *"C'est bien ou mal?"*

"Très bien, naturellement."

Sophie was different from Ally. She had a quieter voice, a milder manner, and appeared more refined and sophisticated. Her hair was also shorter and more styled than Ally's. I think Sophie's the way most people imagined a French girl, demure and elegant. She also smiled a lot more. Ally could really be quite feisty and disagreeable at times, a little rough around the edges.

We sat around and talked about this and that. Like Ally, Sophie was also bilingual. But her English was more reserved and correct. She thought first before she answered, while Ally improvised as she went along, even at the cost of mixing Valley-speak with Franglais. Not surprisingly, Sophie was interested in a career in public relations; she was going to do an internship in the coming summer.

"Public relations or public deceptions?" I said with a smirk.

"A little of both, but at times neither."

"That's right. PR firms get paid millions of dollars to answer questions with two words: *No comment*!" It is often with a smile on my face that my remarks are at their cutting best.

"That is an American specialty, the short no-comment response," Sophie fired back. "Here in France, the art is in the creating of a complicated response."

"Yeah, but complicated responses to a simple matter like adultery would only generate bad publicity. Look at Gary Hart."

"No, what you in America think of as negative publicity may not turn out to be such with the French public. Sometimes, it is better to have a little controversy than no news at all. Just look at Piccasso, or Hollywood—"

"Or terrorists," Ally had just cut into the conversation. Then she took a sip at Sophie's drink, "Yuhhhuh."

"Donc, ne la bois pas, alors!" Don't drink it, then! Sophie snapped at Ally. "Alexandra thinks it is ice water from an American restaurant." Sophie added mockingly.

I decided to let that minor slight slide for now. "What are you drinking there, Sophie?" I was curious.

"Whiskey and cola,"

"No, it's Jack Daniel's and Coke." Leave it to Ally to give brand names to generic products.

"Sans blague," no fooling, I said. "You're a JD man?"

"Woman," Sophie corrected me. "It is my drink sometimes. Do you like JD? Care for a taste?"

I admire girls who can drink; especially a soignée French girl who could drink like a Blue Ridge redneck. "Freshman year in college was my mixed-drink days," I said. "Whiskey bottles just lined up one after another on the dormitory's window sill. Ever had this whiskey called Casey Jones Locomotive?"

"No."

"Been my sentimental favorite for years. Nowadays, I just gin up a little vodka martini when I'm bored with life."

"Absolut *et* Tanqueray!"

"Thank you, Ally. Thank you for that clarification!"

But Ally wasn't quite through just yet. "Listen to this: A dry and tangy martini...no, no, no—once more: A shaken Tanqueray martini, from Charles *le Absolut* Martin, to Mark *le Tang-drinking* Martian!"

"Is that a French haiku?" I shook my head in disbelief. "Listen, Ally, you must promise me not to be so witty; otherwise, you might end up a starving poet Pernod-ing it up in Montparnasse than a sales manager perusing it up at Galleries Lafayette."

"Uhuh, I hate Pia-know."

"Then what do you drink, tanned California beachwater?" It was then that I remembered something. "Oh, by the way, Ally, forgive me for being so rude; with all this talk going around, I didn't even ask you if I could get you anything from the bar."

"That's quite all-riiight," she said, dragging her accent a long way. "But you know what you could get me, a Marie Brizzard with O.J."

"What's a Marie Brizzard?"

"It's an anisette. I tell you what, just a screwdriver will be easier."

"Nope, *pas de problem*, I'm sure I can manage. Anyone else need anything? Well, then like MacArthur, I shall return."

While waiting at the bar getting drinks, I bumped into Stéphane, who was fidgeting with the soundboard on the platformed stage near the bar and talking to one of the disc jockeys. Stéphane and I had already been introduced a bit earlier back at the little room, and he seemed like a friendly, laid back sort; so after I got Ally the drinks, I went back to the area around the bar near the stage and hung out there with him for a while.

I quickly found out that Stéphane and I had one thing in common: we were both from North America. I sort of felt his French accent was more relaxed: more Canadien; or rather, Quebecois! Stéphane was also one of the biggest guys at the place—he towered over most of the French people there. I have never understood that about the French: despite them eating all those rich foods, they don't look big, most of them. No bigger than me.

Stéphane was also attending Université Dauphine. But after graduation in July, he would be going back to Montreal to work for a French firm. It is important, when dealing with a French Canadian, to respect his politics, even if they differ from your own. They are also very protective of their language. When our firm did a study on Canadian export opportunities in the US market, the report was not only twice as thick to accommodate both English and French, but we also had to be very diplomatic and do a double cover so that the English and French versions were on opposite ends.

To my relief, though, Stéphane was for free trade. He believed in a united Canada. "Ontario is the richest province, it would be foolish for us not to do business with a rich neighbor."

Stéphane had a point. Our only office in Canada is in Toronto. A big yet livable city. Beautiful and clean, too, with lots of young people and a lively night life; kind of like Chicago. And, like the Windy City, if only Toronto weren't so damn cold in the winter, I'd rank it high up there as one of my favorites. To be fair, though, even in the winter, you won't feel the cold if you are careful. Take the tower our office is in, located near Bay Street and the waterfront, our building is connected to a bunch of other buildings and shopping centers via underground walkways. In fact, most of downtown is like a city underneath a city. Why, if you really feel like it, you can spend a whole winter not taking a single step outside. Although I haven't been to Montreal since I was really little, I would assume it has a similar set up.

"So Stéphane, missing the hockey action back home or what?"

"Definitely. Besides the Canadiennes, I'm also a little bit of a Nordiques fan. An eternally hopeful Nordique fan."

"Are you able to play hockey in Paris?"

"Not in Paris. I'll have to wait until I'm back home. Every New Year's Eve, we play hockey in Mont Royal, and then we get drunk."

"I take it you take Montreal over Toronto any day, huh?"

"Hands down. I also love Quebec City. I have relatives there—real French-speaking ones—some are not even bilingual."

"But you don't mind the English, though?"

"Hey, English is the language of business. That's the way it is."

More resignation than approval, I gathered from his tone. I was also surprised at how little he had been to English Canada—the other side. In fact, he was telling me that when he does go away, it's usually the United States, especially Maine. Well, at least he likes America. We went on and talked for a while about Maine, where his family kept a second home. With sentences like "Come to Maine in September, when the tourists are gone and prices are down," he could've almost passed for a native. Yet only yours truly, Lumberjack Vermont, not the Canadian with the log cabin, knows that Maine has the highest percentage of forest per acre than any other state, the Pacific Northwest inclusive. I spent some time in Maine some years back, when me and Edwin sailed down from Nova Scotia, a land which Stéphane had also denied ever visiting. He thinks English Canadians can't think for themselves. "In Montreal, half of the top-ten television shows are in French. In Toronto, it is all a copy of America. No originality to be found."

Unlike most Canadians in Paris, Stéphane wasn't here as an exchange student. He applied to the Université Dauphine soon after high school in Montreal. An aunt of his had been posted to Paris as a member of the diplomatic corps; so Stéphane gladly took the opportunity to come along for the ride, having wanted to learn something about life in France in the first place.

By the way, that was also how my grandmother first came to Paris in the 1930s. She could have studied her fine arts in New York, but since her father was working for an American bank in Paris, she also came along for the ride, then held over and stuck around because Paris was so much fun and so very cheap. It was even cheaper, in fact, during the 1920s, when all those young Americans crossed the Atlantic to drink Pernods, as well as to write and paint. The dollar was so incredibly strong back then that it stretched a long, long way—all the way to the overseas banking department at 40 Wall Street.

Fact or fiction, that "lost generation" of Americans who found Paris really hit a jackpot. Not unlike the sixties, the twenties were as well a once in a lifetime offering: the endless parties, the endless exchanges of wit, and if I might also add—the endless orgies—both AC and DC. That's one good thing about being an *ar-tea-st*, you can do whatever the hell you want and claim it's for the sake of art and get away with it. And back then, there were plenty of newly rich Americans setting up camp in Paris, trying to crash Paris society by throwing the weight of their money around—especially after they'd been snubbed back home. So if the expatriate mingled in the right circles, had the right benefactor, he could have lived the high life on practically nothing. Hemingway probably was not a financial genius if he had to resort to stealing pigeons from the park for food during some of those days. Every other dashing American was going to three-star restaurants and vacationing on the Riviera and totally partying it up.

If a time machine ever got invented, I'd still pick San Francisco of the late sixties and early seventies. But the Paris of the Roaring Twenties isn't far behind. Although those two eras are on opposite ends of the social spectrum, they both share sort of a liberating, to-hell-with-the-rest-of-the-world mind set. And that's appealing to me, at least to my imagination: to live in Paris, frequent the cafés on the grand boulevards in their prime; drink Chateau Laffites for a dollar a bottle; meet an outrageous girl or two and swing deep into the night with the big-band sound; perhaps even to squeeze in an up-close and personal talk with Gertrude Stein, asking her to please elucidate on what the hell she had been trying to say with all those alphabetical combinations of hers. Let's see, what else...and, of course, to not let Picasso, Rodin, and Toulouse-Lautrec walk away without bribing them into painting, sculpting, and caricaturing me into immortality. Yes, I'll even take steroids and work on the Nautilus for a whole year to transform my skinny body into that bulky, muscular, manly powerhouse that Rodin had sought. All this and more—to live in Paris—even at the expense of putting on one of those silly-looking suits they wore back then, with a tall hat, a cane and all the trimmings.

11 / "ANYTHING TO DECLARE, MR. WILDE?"

The night was going along smoothly as we slowly wasted away in Champagneville. The club was getting crowded. People conversing in small groups all over the place. Judging from the way most of them looked, I'd say this was a more subdued place than that disco up the block. Oh, there were a handful of outrageous outfits and hair styles here and there, but most folks looked normal—normal enough to allow the wool on my sports jacket to blend right in with the silk on their scarves. When you are an outsider, much less a foreigner, you don't mind being able to blend in with the natives. In places like India and China, it would even be a challenge. But in New York, if I have to walk into one of those joints where people are more interested in star-gazing than drinking, I'd be schmoozing for a bruising.

The music at Zigzag was tolerable, though being a semi-retired Deadhead, I was pretty much ignorant of what was happening on the top of the charts. I mean, not only can I not tell the difference between UB40 and Ziggy Marley; but, for the longest time, I had myself believing that Whitney Houston and Sheena Easton were the same person. Leave it to Ally to run down the hit-list though, just like she did with the movies. Who the hell are the Fine Young Cannibals, she'll tell you, and she'll just about drive you crazy doing it. "I like Zigzag the best," she said. "They play very good songs in English with just enough French pop mixed in."

Yeah, if you call those unrhythmic sounding Gypsy Kings French. They sounded more like a bunch of island natives doing some rain-dance number. Couldn't believe they were so popular. I, for one, was unable to get excited enough to dance to that shit. I don't dance, period. I mean, I like to see girls hop'n bop and stuff, but I told Ally that real men ought to restrain themselves from dancing.

"You're a male chauvinist!" she accused.

"No, I just believe men should stick with basketball."

"*Le basket* at one o'clock in the morning? Com'on!" She liked to get on my case; or was I asking for it?

It was not surprising that I was out of touch with New York's nightlife. Except for Edwin's band and a few other local bands that I follow, noise at night usually comes from the clacking sounds of all those big blue chips dangling on the card table, especially after my winning a big poker hand. Maybe I'm getting old, for New York to me still meant the Mudd Club, Area, and Pyramid. And that was a long time ago. Even Sophie and Ally had been to more fashionable New York spots than me.

"Have you ever been to Vibes? It's a night club," Sophie asked.

"How am I gonna get into Vamp's, marry a supermodel?"

"We went there the last time we were in New York. We just spoke some French outside and smiled and they let us in."

"Lucky you! But it also helps if you're a bunch of young and sexy girls. If I was to go there afterwork in a suit and tie and start opening my mouth with broken French, it'll get me nowhere."

"Then wear a leather jacket," Sophie said.

"I don't have one."

"Are your friends...um...as inactive as you?" Sophie said. "We call them *chiants*, dull people."

"I don't have that many friends; no where as many as you and Alexandra."

"Pourquoi?"

"Well, trendy people don't like to associate with me. I'm very boring. You know, a drip."

"Non! C'est pas vrai!"

"Afraid so. The thing is, Sophie, as people get older, they start to lose track of old friends. Also, I think it's because you and Alexandra grew up in Paris, spent your whole lives here, whereas we Americans move around more often, and farther away, so we don't stay in touch as much."

"Awww, you live a lonesome life, Mark." Ally said.

"Lonely as Robinson Caruso," I said, seeking her sympathy. "No, actually, many of my friends still live on Long Island. Some of my roommate's friends are tolerable to hang out with. I mean, we regularly play poker and stuff. We just don't go out and have as much fun as you Parisiennes."

"I will excuse you for now," Ally said. "But only because you have a job during the day."

"Thank you, ma'am, for your understanding. I mean, we do go out after work sometimes, but the camaraderie is nowhere near that of you guys."

"Do you go to nightclubs at all?"

"Nah, that's for playboys and out-of-towners."

"I can't believe you don't go anymore. Where is your sense of adventure? What are you going to do if I come to New York? You are going to show me a good time by playing poker at night."

"Actually, Ally, I could take you to the Surf Club on Tuesday nights. But I had classes on Tuesdays last semester."

"Is it a good place?"

"It's close to where I live, though probably not as radical as them downtown joints; kinda mellow like Zigzag. In fact, in the middle of the New Years Eve party one year, the sound system broke down. Yet everyone remained pretty cool about it. It's the only place I know where people were not up in arms and demanding their money back, especially it being New Year's Eve."

"But still, why only Tuesday nights? Is it anything special?"

"No, not really. It's just a habit. My roommate Edwin hangs out there with a bunch of his loser friends."

"They don't go out on weekends?"

"I'm sure they do. But I only go on Tuesday night because'um... because it's free admission on Tuesday nights."

"Ah! You're cheap! You really *are* cheap! I know the real you now, Mark, you are what we call in French, a *radin*!"

Now everyone knows. How the hell did she drag it out of me anyway? I think she accused me of not even able to afford a radish, which was not entirely true. I'm a cheapskate when it comes to spending money for my own amusement. But I'm pretty generous to others, or at least I think I am. I did buy Ally and Sophie and all some nice, big drinks just a while ago, and the pleasure was all mine. Whoopee Vermont! A few lousy drinks!

Due to peer pressure, I managed to join Ally and her friends on the dance floor for a few numbers. We danced to this French singer called Boney M., whose music was high on their charts, though it was more like brainless seventies pop-shlock to me. Things brightened up a bit when they played *Kokomo*, a Beach Boys song from the movie *Cocktails*—star-ting, and ending, with Tom Cruise. No surprise that Ally liked the Beach Boys, especially after her stint as a California Girl last year. "I love the Beach Boys," she said, "Life is a beach."

"And then the *beach* gets on wheels."

"Quoi?"

"Never mind."

Amazing as it sounds, I found myself actually boogying a bit on the dance floor. It wasn't exactly Fred Astaire in *Let's Face the Music and Dance,* but for me, it was a pretty big step. I guess it was partly because I was mingling with foreigners in a foreign city; so any American tune got a positive reaction. In a funny sort of way, and I say this hypothetically: I wonder if, after an extended period overseas without hearing any American music whatsoever, I would possibly become tolerant, or indeed even receptive, to the sounds of Barry Manilow. I dearly hope I will never be in a position to put that scary thought to the test.

Well, as long as Hollywood restrains Madonna from acting so she could concentrate on her main line of business—that of singing and being herself—we'll have nothing to worry about. She sure had come a long way since she made that amateur film about a bunch of loafers in the East Village. In fact, she's probably more famous abroad than in the U.S., kind of like Marlboro cigarettes.

"Do you like Madonna?" Ally asked me.

"Don't know much of her music. Just catching a video or two of hers here and there. But you know, I did go to this joint called Danceteria back around the time when she used to perform there, during her pre-Madonna days; though I doubt I had ever seen her on stage."

"I have many of her records."

I did not want to tell her I didn't have any. "Yes, I do like the video with her on stage being carried around by a bunch of guys."

"Oh, that's *Material Girl!"*

"That's the one...*Li-ving with a material girl...*, Ally, *es-tu une* material girl?"

"Down-to-earth material only!" she smiled and said. "Well, maybe there are a few things I'd like to buy when I really start to make some money."

Not if, but when she makes her money. A bit of over-confidence there you might say. Yet I couldn't help thinking it was so. Sometimes, you can really spot a winner at the starting gate.

Ally was not the only bright girl present that night. A bit later, in the café downstairs, she introduced me to Olivia, the girl who had missed having dinner with us earlier.

"So this is the other girl who went to California?"

"I am *tired* of being the other girl!" Olivia said in fake anger. "Just because I didn't go to the same school as Alex and Sophie, I am labeled the other woman!"

Ally laughed. "No, my dear. You are the other woman because you are too grown-up for us." Ally then turned to me and said, "Olivia is one of the top girls in her class; she is *so* intellectual."

"Then why does she want to have anything to do with me?"

"Oh, com-ooon, you are a guest of Monsieur Martin. If you can talk to him, you can talk to anybody."

I looked down and shook my head.

"Also, you will be glad to know, Mark, that Olivia has the best English of all my friends."

"That's another thing, Ally, I'm truly surprised at how versed in English many of you are. I thought the French only spoke French."

"That's true for the older and less educated. The new generation is different. Also, many of my friends are business students so they have to know English. *And*, let's not forget, Mark, that most of the people you end up talking to will speak English." Then Ally gave me one of her smirks and said, "Otherwise, they would not want to have any conversations with you, which is about ninety percent of the people in this place."

"Thanks a lot!" Boy, can she be bad. "Well, Ally, now that you've reduced me to Mr. Personality, I'll just have to simmer a few more days in Paris till my French gets to be as good as yours."

"A few days? Huh! Try a few lifetimes. You might beat me in English, Mark. But you will never beat me in French; not in a million years!" It was those Ally-gant eyes again. "But Olivia is nice," she continued, "You don't have to worry about your vocabulaire the way you do with me."

"Nice to meet you, Mark."

"Nice to meet you, too, Olivia. But if one more person tells me it's nice to meet me, I'm not going to make it nice to meet me anymore."

"Ou, my American friend has a temper," Ally said to her friend.

"Takes one to know one, Ally. So Olivia, tell me, how come you are not somnifacient at this time of the night." I tried to give her a vocabulary test.

"But I am. I have been studying all day until Alex called to tell me to come along to say hello. I am actually sleepwalking as we speak."

Olivia told me she was preparing diligently for the entrance tests to the École National d'Administration. She had graduated from Institut d'Etudie Politiques, popularly known as Science Po, the year before. Both schools are located in St.-Germain, by the way, not far from Charles's house. Science Po, catering mostly to undergraduates, is sort of like a Harvard, Yale and Princeton rolled into one, with entrance going to only the students with the highest test scores. And only the best students from Science Po have a realistic shot at the couple of hundred places in ENA. However, unlike the Ivys, a wealthy father donating dormitories and gymnasiums don't mean squat. Entrance is strictly based on merit.

"So, Olivia, what do you think of your chances of getting into the ENA?" I love to personally analyze the odds on things like this, even when there's no money involved.

"I'm somewhat hopeful," Olivia said.

"She will get in; I know she will," Ally added.

"Don't jinx her, girl, for god's sake!" I shouted to Ally. "Incidentally, did you tell Olivia that Charles Martin has taught there."

"I deedn't ave to tell herrr," there was that defiant French accent again. "She already knew!"

"Yes," said Olivia. "Actually, Monsieur Martin was one of the people who interviewed me."

"*Ah bon.* Did you tell him you know Alexandra?"

"Are you joking?" Olivia laughed. "That would have ruined every chance I had of getting in,"

"Thanks a lot!" Ally said loudly as she gave Olivia a quick slap.

"So, Olivia, what kind of questions did Monsieur Martin ask you, impossible translations of Latin and Greek?"

"No, but he did ask me about reacting to hypothetical situations. At one point, he asked me if I were to accompany a VIP from an exotic land to an important dinner party, and the foreign dignitary mistakes the butler, who resembles the host, as the actual host of the dinner—namely, after the butler opens the door, the foreign guest gives him a big bow, then hand delivers a personal gift direct from his emperor and so on. If such were the case, what, if anything, could I do to prevent my guest from finding out that the man is merely a butler, and save my guest from total embarrassment?"

"That is such a typical Charles Martin question," Ally shook her head. "I would say '*cut*!', then tell that VIP to go back out the door and do a second take."

"Good one, Ally! That, and an attitude will get you a rejection slip. And you, Olivia, what did you say?" I was intrigued.

"Well, I said I would consult the host, explain to him the gravity of the situation, the strategic importance of his country to France, then kindly ask the host to arrange for one more person at the dining table—an unexpected house guest—the butler himself, who shall play the role of the father of the host for the evening. Of course, I would also make arrangements to have the rest of the staff fill the void, and find a way for them to still have access to the butler should they run into problems."

"That's brilliant!" I said, admiring her plans to delegate a delicate situation. "Kinda like Sparky Anderson still sending in the signals after getting kicked out of the dugout." But before I even finished laughing, I realized the two girls were looking at me with the biggest blank stares—having no idea what the hell I was cracking up about. Soon, I regained my composure. "So, Olivia, did Monsieur Martin like your answer?"

"I couldn't tell. But he did remind me to not forget to make a report afterwards regarding the incident."

"Bureaucrats, all they do is make reports," Ally interjects.

"That's pretty much what the consultants do, as well," I said. "Except they charge so much money that people actually find time to read 'em."

"*Bon. Alors*, listen you two, why don't you both stay down here and talk about your reports while I go get some cigs. And Mark, like MacArthur, I shall return."

Boy, can she pick it up in a hurry.

The downstairs café we were in was more like a cozy snack bar. The mirrors made the place look larger than it was. Although the music wasn't so loud down there, the conversation was. Put a bunch of French people in one place, don't matter where, and you're gonna hear'em, whether you like it or not.

Take Olivia, slim and trim, with long dark hair and a small soft face, she appeared at first to be rather delicate, perhaps even a bit shy. But how very engaging she was, displaying tremendous confidence and passion as she spoke, like when she was explaining the intellectual fervor of French women. "Simone de Beauvoir was one of the great feminists of her time, a pioneer in the woman's movement; yet, she was also at Jean-Paul Sartre's beck and call."

"We call that hypocrisy, Olivia."

"No, I disagree. I think she was rather a genius."

"Yeah, a genius in disguising the real her."

"Not exactly, Mark. I define a genius as someone who not only understands proper behavior, but also knows how to disregard it."

"Why didn't she follow what she preached?"

"Perhaps she was above what she preached."

"But *that* is hypocrisy."

"No. Hypocrisy is telling others you live one way while instead you live a different way. A genius, however, is someone who could convince others of the right way even if she chose not to exercise it herself."

"Come again? Did you just make a distinction? I mean, we do have to practice what we preach?"

"It's not always black and white, Mark. All right, let's tackle a controversial subject: abortion, for instance. Let's say there is a feminist leader, who, as a staunch advocate of abortion rights, has been fighting the pro-lifers and their legislators every step of the way—citing everything from rape and incest to 'ourbodies, ourselves'. Her arguments are unrivaled, her judgments sound as can be. Mark, you have to excuse my English, I'm just thinking as I'm going along."

"Oh, you are doing just fine. Far better than I might ever do. Okay, so she is seen as the hero of the pro-abortion lobby."

"Yes. Then one day, she gets pregnant, accidentally, from a date rape of all things."

"Wow, from a rape. That's perfect, then."

"But she decides to keep the baby."

"Whaaat?...Why?"

"Why? Because the man who raped her was the most famous and handsome prince in all of Europe. So how do we treat such a case, is it hypocrisy?"

"Mmm...nope, I guess not," I said. Similar to the idea of a trade-off in economics, I understood that decision perfectly. "Self-interest in this case, Olivia."

"Absolutely. She's a woman first and an advocate second. Her own case is above the norm. Perhaps she also feels superior to her subjects and could, therefore, make her own decisions and not be overly concerned with her own consistency. Simply put: her desire to have this particular child was even greater than her conviction for social justice."

"That's fascinating," I said. But my excitement was also marred by confusion as various scenarios entered my head, randomly and confusingly. My thoughts were not so much of that woman contradicting herself, but of whether she wanted the child to be a boy or a girl, the pros and cons of each, and how might the child think and feel one day in view of it all. "Olivia, that woman would make a great character in a movie. Did you just invent her?"

"Perhaps…but perhaps not."

"If she is alive, I would love to meet her. A conscientious yet clever woman; it's so classically European. Still, how much should we trust such types? Your so-called geniuses?"

"Their genius, I think, is in their ability to distinguish and their ability to exercise the most human of traits—flexibility. That is, once a person understands the general guidelines, he or she may include footnotes, exceptions, and so forth. Another way to view it is that while the geniuses are teaching arithmetic to the masses, they are themselves practicing calculus in real life, a much higher form of mathematics. It is not that they don't agree with arithmetic, but rather that they have already understood it all too well; and it is their wish that, eventually, one day down the road, more and more people would also come to know calculus—rendering arithmetic unnecessary."

"So perhaps arithmetic, shall, one day, just be taught to the kids."

"Precisely."

"Then everybody will be geniuses," I cracked. "And therefore, nobody is. A bit of self-destruction there, don't you think, that the final goal is ironically to render the geniuses themselves obsolete?"

"In a sense, Mark, that is what being a real genius is all about—to live as pure a life as an individual possibly can. But in order to do that, one must go through a certain process; the society must go through a certain process—one which would enable us to custom-tailor our laws into each person's life. Then and only then shall we see the day of true existentialism."

"Wow! That sounded good, Olivia, a custom-designed society. I don't quite understand it all, but it's graspable."

To my surprise, Olivia was not merely an existential junkie, but one who seemed interested in big business and management as well. It shouldn't come as a surprise since many of France's industrial and financial giants are state-controlled. It also wasn't surprising that Olivia and I didn't see eye to eye on the precise role of multi-billion dollar companies in society today.

Olivia believed in the idea of stakeholders—that the obligation of a business must go beyond that of making a profit; that it must also be responsible for the welfare of the employees, the communities, the environment, and a whole slew of other public service constituencies. This is not merely because Olivia is an idealist from France; much of the academia in America express a similar view—that making money is only one of the objectives of a big corporation.

I expressed to her that that is not the way capitalism ought to work. A company must solely be responsible to its owners and creditors—that's all. No further obligations are necessary. If there isn't enough money to go around, the various stakeholders can go to hell: charity starts at home!

Olivia disagreed. She said I was making a company more important than a life, an entity more vital than a being.

"I don't think so," I responded. "The key here must be profitability as an ongoing concern. I don't want the so-called stakeholders to carve up the meat and leave the company with just the bare bones."

"But, Mark, what is a company but a distributor of wealth?"

"Well, fine. Get the stock price up. Then, should any of the investors wish to act charitable, they may indeed do so by selling a part of their holdings and donate the proceeds to whatever the charitable whim they have in mind. Give it all away for all I care, or stuff it all under their mattresses. Only thing I ask is: don't practice altruism and democracy with other people's money."

"Sounding like a true, heartless capitalist," she said, with a hint of disappointment.

All right, perhaps I shouldn't have sounded so uncaring. Let me just backpedal a bit by saying that while it is up to the managers and, ultimately, the investors, to decide where the money goes; it is in their long-term interest, *and* benefit, to be sensitive to the needs of the various stakeholders. But it should be done through a vote by the investors, not through blackmail or government legislation. In other words, the public has no right to force the investors to look long-term if they feel impatient and elect to take short-term profits. The marketplace has to dictate that sentiment by reflecting it in the stock price, and they have. Lawsuits and ugly labor strikes have indeed crippled many a company preoccupied with nearsighted vision. On the other hand, short term thinking isn't always all bad, especially when resources are limited. This is another forecasting dilemma, by the way: how to accomplish the balancing act between long-term and short.

As a rule corporate America is generally risk averse. Given a choice, they would rather see their share prices go down bit by bit than for them to take a sudden plunge. But a private company could ignore Wall Street and act more long-term, though that is riskier because when you make the wrong decision long-term, you screw up in a big way. The problem with much of the media, save the *Journal*, is their tendency to tell success stories of long-term vision, but very few investigative reports on long-term strategies that have failed—sometimes by the billions. Blame it on corporate advertising dollars.

The thing is, if the investors are patient and profits are rolling in, like the Japanese, then you can afford to be long term. But America isn't Japan. We don't take out multi-generation mortgages because we know that in the long run, we'll all be long gone.

Olivia said that from the way I sounded, I apparently favored the American approach of valuing each subsidiary as a separate accounting entity inside the corporate umbrella, so that, at least in theory, any division can be bought or sold 24 hours a day, 365 days a year.

I told her it was not completely true. "As an outsider looking in, I'd be more secure in dealing with a professionally managed company with an open set of books than a more European or Japanese-like outfit controlled by a god like father figure founder with one hidden asset layered over another."

"Are you saying, Mark, that you would rather not be subjected to shareholders scrutinizing your every move."

"D'accord!" You got it!

"I would also take it, then, that if you were an owner, you would not hire outside consultants."

"It depends," I said. "If I had a privately held company, no. But if I were the CEO of a public corporation, the answer would be yes. It's part of the job of being a CEO, to read reports turned in by outside consultants."

"But not necessary to act on it."

"Oh, certainly not, especially if it's not financial analysis. That's why more and more of the CEOs are financial people, and why investment bankers make more money than lawyers and consultants. The fact is: the buying and selling of assets effects the bottom line far more dramatically than operational adjustments. I mean, you can improve operations from a Swiss cheese to a Swiss watch for all I care; but still, if you don't know how to acquire key assets for growth, you're nothing."

"What about managing?"

"Oh, I don't want to belittle operations in any way. After all, standard operating procedures have made consultants part of the system. See, many of the corporate top brass got there through experience. And, as unnecessary as they might think outside consultants are personally, they must show their knowledge of their existence, almost like dealing with your bankers and auditors, it's part of the job. Ignorance and arrogance are okay if you plan to spend the rest of your life with one company selling one product. But the top people are moving around with far more frequency today and into totally different industries. They need to know where to get advice."

"And knowing when to refuse the advice given and go with one's own instincts; isn't that the heart of leadership?"

"You are asking the wrong man. But I think it's safe to say that the future belongs to professional managers, not visionary founders of businesses with abrasive, Social-Darwinist personalities. The CEO or the French PDG of tomorrow truly needs to be skilled in all areas. Like the CEO of the conglomerate who recently hired us. He came into the company as the second in command from the outside, with the implicit knowledge that the top job was to be his in a few years. I mean, his resume was right up there with George Bush's. Along the way, he's walked through stock offerings, acquisitions, strikes and walkouts, class action suits, etc., etc. And third world nationalizations, too—during his stint as the top international man, since global vision is being so touted these days."

"Do you not believe in globalization?"

"I do. But many executives are just paying it lip service. The sad truth is, not everyone wants to take a chance leaving the headquarters for some foreign destination: it's a risk. Because once you are gone, then someone else moves into your corner office; and all of a sudden, you cease to matter anymore."

"If you come back strong, you are sure to be on the short list."

"That's right, Olivia. You get back your turf and more. Not to mention you've learned how to eat a hundred different kinds of cheeses and sausages."

"I think I smell an internationally-minded young man sitting here with me," Olivia said with a smile.

"If only you know how much I love New York, Olivia, you will know not to say that. I can't see myself moving. Everything's so set where I am, got my routine down pat. Besides, I've got bartenders who are depending on me."

"I've got a mother, two ex-wives and three bartenders who are dependant upon me?"

"Ohhh, Olivia, you are a gem," I said admiringly. "All I need now is another wife. Wanna be my second wife, Miss Hitchcock... Mrs. Thornhill?"

"Only if you divorce your first one, Miss New York City."

"And leave Lady Liberty? Impossible! Come to think of it, I must have gone away countless times since I began working, for business and personal matters; but it's mostly just a few days at a time, seldom more than a week. I hardly know what it feels like to be without my weekly fix of pastrami and rye, with pickled tomatoes and New York rudeness on the side—free of charge!"

"Mark, I sense that food and sarcasm are very important to your psychological well-being."

"Mere attempts at'em, m'dear. They are so crude at times that they're not even amusing enough for my own taste; and I'm easily amused."

"That's all right, practice makes perfect."

"And perfection makes you very lonely."

"See, there you go again!"

"I know, that was pretty bad. But what'a ya gonna do, Olivia, you're gonna tell me that I haven't passed my oral and anal phases yet?"

"No, but if you insist."

"Oh, Jeez's. Which one comes first by the way?"

"For you, Mark, they both arrived much too late!"

"Ha...Funny girl!" I gave her a grimacing look. "So Olivia, you seem to know me very well already."

"It's my job to know where people are coming from."

"You mean to assess an American to see if he's worth his salty pretzels."

"No, silly, to see if I could like him."

"Well, in that case I better put on a good performance."

"Don't worry about the performance, just be yourself."

"That's what my *ex* used to say, though I never quite believed her."

"And you ended up performing badly anyway."

"Yes, how'd you know?"

"Because you weren't relaxed and being yourself. Now tell me Mark, reach deep down inside and tell me something about your goals and aspirations. Do you like your work? Do you believe in it? From what you have told me, I get the feeling that you have not quite made up your mind yet as to where you truly stand. You say CEOs need to possess leadership qualities, a good package of skills, and so on, but then you also say that the only thing that matters is the bottom line."

"Well, if I had to pick a single quality in the CEO of tomorrow, it would probably be an ability to act fast, almost instantaneously. This may sound somewhat biased due to my trader's instincts, but reaction time *is* crucial. So how do you train that? You can't, really, not in quick lessons anyway. The reason being that to make quick decisions, you have to have a firm set of principles: ethical, financial, social, etc.. Once you have the principles, the decision-making process is simplified. But if you can't distinguish right from wrong, then you will have taken too long to make up your mind, and sooner or later, you will have sought the wrong advice. Also, keep in mind that if you screw up on the assembly line, it's a couple of dollars here and there. However, if you make a wrong decision at the top, it could well cost in the millions."

"What about knowing how to prioritize? Especially when your principles are interlocked?"

"Oh sure, prioritizing is crucial. If an executive doesn't know what's most critical, he's lost. Everything today has constraints built in: seldom is there enough time or sufficient data to look at a situation in full. But what makes prioritizing tricky, Olivia, is that nobody wants to be told of that word, and everyone you talk to thinks he or she is prioritizing better than the next guy. Therefore, prioritizing is too general a term. Personally, I favor a solid grasp of game theory, and some precise microeconomics concepts like efficiency, opportunity cost and a feel for the supply and demand. I mean, if you can't assess the tradeoffs in a given situation, then you are doomed; if you can't foresee diminishing returns from a project, then you are incompetent; and lastly, if your strategies are contradicting and inconsistent, then your decisions will eventually cancel out."

"So decision making to you is more science than art?"

"Yeah, but each situation is unique, and at the highest level it's probably art. Also, I tend to be very skeptical by nature, especially when everyone is out touting one management style or one race or one country or one whatever that's superior to the others."

"Does that mean you aren't threatened by Japan overall?"

"Certain Japanese companies, yes; but not the country in general. I was just discussing this with Monsieur Martin at lunch."

"And...?"

"Well, he assured me by saying that if the Japanese should pull all their money out of America, where are they going to put it? They don't even sleep on mattresses!"

"I almost got that one, Mark."

"Then you're the only one." I laughed. "Oh, *th*-dop worrying about Japanese already. Look, let's get serious for a sec: on the productivity scale from 1 to 100, we may be at 33%, but the Japanese are, at best, around 50%, so there is still tremendous room for improvement on both sides. It's still anybody's sumo match."

"Do you think America should copy Japan more?"

"Not by verbatim. We should be selective. Not everything that works there will work here. The other day at our client's office, I was just thinking about what the single biggest leap could be. And you know what, it involves almost no capital investment; yet my gut feeling is, it will boost productivity like a skyrocket. What it is is simply putting the right people in the right places. So many people are in the wrong jobs and positions it's sickening. To separate the hard workers from the bullshit artists, all you have to do is to just talk to them. Get rid of the ass-kissing political animals in the work place and listen to the true, dedicated workers and you'll improve productivity by leaps and bounds."

"I see you are quite emotionally charged up over this."

"Well, it struck a chord. Did it really show?"

"Yes, you were spitting…into your drink."

"Sorry about that. A faux pas a day, I guess. You know what else I hate? People who are blind and headless followers. At least you should voice your concerns and objections off the record. Take me, I pitch and bitch all the time, but only to people higher up. I don't *think* it's being disagreeable. I mean, otherwise you are just another dispensable robot."

"I would think that you much prefer robots?" Olivia said.

"Yes, I like their dispensability...almost as much as I like their dependability."

"Good one, Mark!"

"Thank you; and *thanks* to you," I said. "But in a way it's true, robots are not the problem; it's the people who are the wild cards, the ones that give you the most sleepless nights."

"I'm sorry to inform you, Mark, that we have more people than anything else; and many of them want to work."

"Many of them might want to work, but most of them don't want to work hard unless they are forced to do so."

"How peculiar you sound!"

"Well, it's surprisingly true. Following up on what I just said about placing people in the right places, almost every workplace I've been to, I see two types of people, ones who are overrated, and ones who are the unsung heroes. And it doesn't take a brain surgeon to figure out who's who, either. The best workers, inevitably, are the ones who take their work seriously; the ones who aren't constantly complaining and making excuses. The fault, dear Brutus, is *not* in the land of the rising star but in our stars and stripes, Shakespeare."

"So, my dear rising star—"

"Umm, I'd rather have the rising yens instead if you don't mind."

"Okay my dear rising yen from the land of the rising, sunny, and shining star; how's that?"

"Every sun is a shiny star; but not every star is a sunny star."

"You know, Mark, I was about to ask you if you ever have aspirations to climb the corporate ladder; but seeing how absurdly you can carry on, I'm seriously considering withdrawing my question."

"I'm sorry, I'm really sorry. That's one of my major weaknesses. 'Don't get wise with me, Vermont,' as my roommate likes to say. But sometimes I can't resist. It has to do with my resistance level."

"Or the lack of it."

"Thank you. Now back to your question, do I want a career in management? It's a fair question, especially now that I'm out of school. I guess I like consulting, but wish it were geared a bit more toward acquisitions than organizations."

"So, in your heart, you want to buy and sell."

"Not as much as the guys on Wall Street. They are so transaction-oriented that they can't seem to make the adjustment to consulting. We've taken in some brilliant Wall Street people and seen them fail as consultants. 'Look, Mr. Wall Street, this is a flawed estimate... No, not a *floor* estimate, but a flawed one.' This is a typical conversation when you talk to them. They have a one-track mind."

"And you, Mark, don't, have a one-dimensional mind?"

"Not yet anyway. But you know, Olivia, the sad truth is, that as much as I might be able to bullshit all day about management, and even tackle my share of problem solving, I can never see myself as a hands-on manager. I'm very impatient, and despite my knowing how employees ought to be treated and would like to be treated, my own buried-under-the-surface views on people scare me."

"How come? Are you constantly thinking of ways to exploit the proletariat."

"Worse. The *elimination* of it! But the problem extends beyond what I think. Realistically, even I, would never hire myself as a manager. One, I'm not a leader and terrible at politics; two, I'm not tough enough. I have never fired anyone in my life nor do I have a desire to. Yet, if I were a headhunter, I would be reluctant to hire a man who had never laid off a sizable number of workers, or closed some unprofitable divisions and instituted across the board salary cuts. It's just that I, personally, don't thrive on instilling fear into people."

"Could it be that you have a compassionate side?"

"Don't count on it. Another part of me just hates labor and hates to manage the workers. As I said earlier, I wish I could operate a factory full of robots, move them around as the production goals see fit, and be able to send them packing anytime without worrying about their feelings and their families. I'm big on precision and control: JIT, SPP, you name it, I'll try it. But human resources is something you can't calibrate to the same extent as robots, although in some ways, I wish we could."

"Again, speaking like a cold, heartless capitalist."

"Uuh...not really. I run from initial capital investments. I'm far more a variable cost man—went to school for that, cost accounting and finance and all that. I shake when I hear millions being thrown at projects whose payoffs are years and years away. What if something were to go wrong? Who the hell is going to buy my half-built plant? So in that sense, I am as far from being a capitalist as Karl Marx. I'd rather exploit a poorly performing stock than the working proletariat."

"But monetary capitalism is still capitalism."

"Well, yes and no. In a perfect world, one investor actually pits himself against the next pit bull. Almost a zero-sum game in relative terms. I win at the expense of someone else and vice versa. So my objective becomes trying to pick and time the markets better than the competition. My problem with industrial ownership, however, is in its unpredictable randomness: crisis can happen to the best of companies, and at anytime. Look at Tylenol, or Bohpol, or that bomb aboard the Pan Am, and last but not least—the Exxon Valdez fiasco. One single disaster could disrupt the most carefully laid plans. As an investor, I can protect against these extraordinary crises better than a principal participant."

"But crises happen in financial markets, too. Look at the stock market crash."

"Well, yes and no again. It's true that the one day drop in the overall market in '87 was unprecedented; but individual stocks, of even the largest corporations, will see swings like that on a regular basis. You know which two Chinese characters make up the word crisis?"

"Maoists and Taoists?"

"No, *dummy*!" I finally won a chance to tease her: "Characters, not people—symbols! Nice try, though. But anyway, it's the word *danger* combined with the word *opportunity*. People who had the balls to buy in the days after the '87 Crash picked up incredible bargains. So you have to look at it both ways."

"How did you do, Mr. Great Wall Street of China?"

"Ah, heck, I'm still young, still at the learning stage, still able to take my losses and bounce back—as long as I can learn something meaningful from it, that is. Lots of times, I would simply put some money in play to test a theory or two; and believe me, there is no better way to learn than with your own money. I mean, when you take a loss on your own account, you most definitely feel it; but on the flip side, nothing in life can beat the excitement of timing the market to perfection."

"Why not put your money into other excitements? Ever tried climbing Mt. Everest?"

"I'm not crazy about heights. Besides, the thousands of dollars that's needed to finance that two week trip—to buy such an adrenaline rush—could just as well be spent trading futures and options. What's more, the latter is almost as thrilling. And chances are, the money is going to last me a hell of a lot longer than two short weeks; and Olivia, if I get lucky..."

"Yea-ss...?"

"And if I get lucky, I might even get lucky!"

12 / I HAVE NOTHING TO DECLARE EXCEPT MY PENIS

So Olivia and I were hanging out in the club's café and doing a bit of munching out. Although the café at first sight seemed more trendy than comfy—the sleek brass and glass, the geometrically odd furniture and so on—it was in reality a good place to linger. It reminded me of those art deco-ish downtown Manhattan diners—sans the tasteless open-faced turkey sandwiches that is. Instead, it was pig's feet and *tête de veau*.... But we didn't go for any exotics: just a Prosciutto with Melon for Olivia, a vegetable platter called *crudités* for both of us; and, to give my stomach lining a workout, some apple flavored French sake called *calvados*.

With just as much style and polish as the café's decor was my salad mate Olivia. There was this marvelous sense of refinement about her, and so thoroughly engaging she was that I loved hearing whatever she had to say. And you could never be sure of what she was about to say. One minute, she could be as hard as our chrome tabletop; then another, soft as the lighting on the wall; like when she was telling me about the future of woman-kind.

"We women will have a chance to take over the world one day," Olivia said. "Or rather, that the next century will be the century of women. I'm not saying all women, but you will see us outperforming men in many, many areas."

"But will men ease off and lay down the red carpet just for you?"

"Red carpet?" Olivia said cynically, with a smile as thin as her prosciutto. "We will be lucky if you didn't scatter the road with slippery little marbles."

"Come now, Olivia, men aren't that bad, are they? Though I do see what you are saying about women: that there are certain professions out there that women will easily excel in. The question is, when we say women, what do we actually mean, the physical entity itself or the generally accepted female personality?"

"The general female attributes and qualities for one; but in certain cases, the physical entity itself also matters a great deal."

"Well, that's good. Because personally, I'm gender-blind. I only believe in finding the talent I'm looking for, not tokenism. I also don't believe in all those feminists who preach that women should be networking with other women, and women are the only ones who truly understand other women's needs and so on. That's just a bunch of garbage."

"Not all of us are like that. The truth is, many women are far more fierce in defending their turf against other women than they would be against most men. But as we look to the future, as the world becomes more civilized and less violent, as the threat of force becomes less and less a factor, and—"

"And without the threat of force, men can no longer get what they want by intimidation alone."

"That's right, Mark. The future will not be the rule of man, but the rule of law. The new generations of women will be brought up by working mothers, who will in turn set examples for their daughters. And once a woman shows that she is able to manage both work and the kids, she will have become the most indispensable part of the family. To be sure, not every woman will be able to manage both; but for those who do, they will have in their possession skills and instincts that are just as sharp, perhaps even more so, than their male counterparts."

"Sort of like Holocaust survivors, or POWs: after overcoming great odds, life's remaining obstacles seem pale by comparison."

"That and more—as even greater mental stamina is needed for a woman to compete and succeed year-in and year-out. But we can do it. The truth is, we women are capable of bearing tremendous hardship. It is society that is constantly pulling us back. Yet as society progresses, as more and more women become role models, even more women will change the way they see themselves. Think about it, Mark: there will come a day in the future when we women can not only have all the babies we want, but to also have the means to provide for them. We will have possessed both the power of production *and* the power of reproduction."

Wwwwoow, did Olivia unnerve me there. I became totally envious of the opposite sex for a moment. Hell, if arm-wrestling and hand-to-hand combat become less and less of a factor, and if women are just as capable as men otherwise, then they possess an edge at birth, especially the Helen-of-Troy types that no man can resist, or the genius types that Olivia had spoken of earlier—the Madame Curies and the Simone de Beauvoirs. A woman like that would have so many cards at her disposal, the trumpest of them all being that she could have our baby all to herself. Heck, if she is conniving enough to hide her pregnancy from him, he wouldn't even know if that the baby is his. And that's the most treacherous form of robbery of them all, taking it from him without him even knowing.

Yet all you hear in America's women's lib circles is how burdened women are by the fact that *they* end up getting pregnant and men don't; and how little the society appreciates the sacrifices to *their* careers they must make to bring up the children. While their gripe is 100 percent valid, their loss is far from 100 percent. I mean, don't they see, their sacrifices would not go unnoticed by their children. In fact, it would be the next generation's gain. Those moms would be heroes for life—for eternity! That's why it was so refreshing to hear this Parisian girl talk of pregnancy as not so much a hindrance but as a power. A power that men will never, *ever* possess. A power women could use to their great advantage, including not using it at all! I sensed a certain similarity between Olivia and Charles in the way they do their analysis: a bit farfetched, but not totally inconceivable. Why, I could easily picture a scenario where, for a man who desires a family, and if the female has just as much earning power, he will be dealing with someone holding far more cards, someone with far more leverage—someone with the power of giving birth!

"But Olivia, I have one more question; that is, will women ever settle for someone beneath...what I mean is, why are even many of the successful women always looking to snag some older, richer man?"

"You have a valid point; and deciding that is crucial—not only for her, but for her children as well. In my view, regardless of how successful a woman appears, if she insists on a partner with greater power, money, or fame, then she would still be more or less subjugating herself to his dominance."

"Are you suggesting, Olivia, that women might want to look for sexy young men as trophies to hang on their *own* walls, just like the way men have been doing to women for all these years?"

"If a woman wants total control, yes. But she must also be willing to constantly serve as a pillar of strength. Personally, I'd like to show some vulnerability and weakness from time to time."

"Gosh, if you didn't admit it yourself, Olivia, I certainly would not have guessed it. You seem so...so self-assured."

"I try to be self-reliant. My mother is a journalist so she has always been very independent, and that has made me such as well. Honestly, when I'm older one day, I will not be afraid to love someone who is younger and starting out. I'm not afraid to be both the provider and the nurturer."

"Oh, you're so brave! And right you are, too, as I think you've smacked dead on into the keyhole. It's not only how talented or rich the woman becomes, but whom she chooses as her partner, or partners —if one at all!—that will determine the trend in future generations."

It's not all a woman's choosing; man's attitude must also change."

"Well, I, for one, am perfectly willing to be a house husband."

"Then me and you, Mark, we could be perfect together."

"Yes, Olivia, you bring home the paycheck and I'll invest it... I'll multiply it!"

Now, before you start thinking that women are out to conquer the world, let me just say that such a view was from our table only. For even at the next table over, you get a completely different picture. Literally. The table in question was the round-corner booth a few tables back from me. There was a group of Frenchmen sitting there, singing and drinking and getting pretty loud. They were talking mostly about other men and women—what else—and dishing out some heavy and hefty insults.

I didn't pay much attention to them at first, but when the couple occupying the table between us got up and left, the group at the corner became more audible. It was then that I realized what they were up to: there was this TV monitor over their heads, and what they were doing was watching the closed-circuit TV screen of the action at the entrance foyer to the club—seeing who's coming in, and who's going out.

The group got even rowdier when Jacques, the guest disc-jockey came down. He was that macho-looking guy whom Stéphane was hanging out with earlier upstairs; the one with the dark leather vest, dark shirt, and dark tie. He pulled up a chair to that round table, took out a cigarette with his lips, and was quickly pal-palling with that whole noisy bunch. They were talking in slangy French, so rather than translating badly, I'm just going to convey the flavor by taking some key words and giving it my own spin—authentic or not.

"...Oh, baby, I love you so much I will even follow you down to the sewer," one guy said into the monitor.

"Oh darling," added another, "You are like a mermaid floated ashore by the tides of love!"

"There is So-and-so, *quel gâchis*! The only piece of ass he ever had was when he put his hand in his back pocket!"

"Hey, idiot, tell us about your first sexual experience—and are you looking forward to it?"

"Regarde! Regarde! I told you she had a propeller on her head: everything just swirls around but never in."

"Precisely why she needs you to hammer it in for her!"

"Check out *ce mec* in that peasant outfit—the guy with the pot belly of a gorilla!"

"Tiens, it's Jean-Pierre walking in. Is he still with that old bag who drives with a broom?"

"Is he? I hear they are about to be married!"

"Non, quelle catastrophe!"

"You want catastrophe? Look at Mademoiselle Bulimia, flat as a crepe and tastes like hell!"

"But there is her friend Mae West, *avec les tits gigantesque"*

"Ah yes, she excites me as energy excites an atom."

Holy shit, what a line. The guy must have been fresh out of the Polytechnique or something. That was too ultraviolet even for me. And so it went, on and on: one kiss on the cheek, two stabs in the back—the Gallic version of spit-balls to the face and towel-snappings to the ass.

To close out my quality time spent in the downstairs café, I will just go ahead and offer my own rendition of an old familiar song we used to sing as kids—on our interminable school bus trips to nowhere: ninety-nine French egos in this place, ninety-nine egos here; and what would happen if one was to shut up, still ninety-nine egos there.

A while after I had gone upstairs, Stéphane joined me for a drink. We were hanging out at the bar where we had been earlier, the one near the sound system, which also happened to be the one corner of the joint where I was most comfortable: somewhat out of the way of the sight lines; an ideal place to hide with a drink.

Stéphane had come to get a drink to regroup himself, after having made an unsuccessful pass at some girl. He blamed it on his lack of patience, and Paris being not exactly Florida, where he had been the year before.

"I should hope not," I said. "Otherwise, this place would be like a Daytona Beach meat market. Still, what do you think of American girls?"

"Fun-loving but not too bright: 'Oh, no! My poor grades are going to strip me from being the head cheerleader.'"

"Perhaps you are generalizing, Stéphane," I shook my head, "based only on a few bimbos in the sun."

"Not true. I have been up and down America and it's more or less the same. But Florida is the worst, or should I say the *best*! So many young girls to prey on down on your Southern tip."

"That's certainly news to me," I said. "Perhaps a little foreign accent boosted your odds there. Let's see...," I was thinking of something to say in broken French. "How's this: *'Pardonez-moi, ma'memoiselle, directez-moi vos zones erogènes, s'il vous plait?"*

"Montrez-moi," Stéphane said, "Not bad. It won't get you anywhere, but...I tell you what, I'll buy you a drink if you go up to... where is that vixen I spoke to earlier...ah, over there next to the stairs—see her, the one with that almost see-thru top—"

"No way, pal. I don't do suicides. She's got a hell of a body, though."

Stéphane sighed, "Some girls, their bodies curve to such perfection that I can just picture myself on top of them."

"Yeah, and some other girls you can only picture yourself in a restaurant with them, wining and dining them for the rest of your life!"

"I'm not interested in wining and dining," Stéphane said, "only a test drive."

"And there lies the problem, my dear Watson. While there is such a thing as a free lunch for girls, there ain't no such a thing as a free test drive for us! Not in Paris, and not even at the Daytona Beach 500."

If you think Stéphane and I were deliberating with profoundness at all that was around us, wait till I tell you about my close encounters with Jacques. The monsieur with the dark silk shirt and narrow leather tie; the man whose mouth pulls out two cigarettes and lights them both up at once; the *dude* with the wild looking hair. Stéphane and I were still rapping in English when Jacques came around. He had his headphones on, along with a pair of sunglasses. But he took off his shades as he gestured to some girl on the dance floor, with fingers parting his lips.

"Tu la connais?" Stéphane asked.

"Knowing is not the word, guy," said Jacques; now all of a sudden he wanted to be one of the fellas. "Her soul and my body had, once upon a time, been rolled up in ecstasy."

"Must've been a pretty *hard* roll," I said, "Or did it get *soft* a bit too soon?"

"Hah, never!" Jacques responded loudly. "She once called me the measuring stick in the oil of life."

"Holy viscosity, Batman!" Get a load of the dip shit. I was more amused than impressed, so I played along. "So, Jacques, was the measuring stick dry or was it filled to the top; or better yet, was it hard as ice or was it soft ice cream." I got him about belt high...the lower half of the belt.

"You crazy American, you are not supposed to talk like that!"

"Well, maybe I had some good teachers, especially around the roundtable in the downstairs café, watching tell-a-bitching."

Boy, when Jacques heard that, his expression changed. In fact, he was glowing gloatingly all of a sudden. Ah, so this kid knows of our little TV set was the expression from his eyes. Pretty soon, his mood went from being cool and arrogant to that of a peculiar generosity. What he did was he got both me and Stéphane drinks and took advantage of such an opportunity to do some additional self-boasting. The thing about the French is, they love to boast—even to people they don't need to play up to. It turned out that Jacques was actually one of the partners that owned the joint. But it was probably a very small percentage since this was not even his favorite hangout, or the only club he had an investment in for that matter. He just moonlights there a couple of times a week to check up on things and, according to him, "to give it enough life to keep it hopping and happening."

"From what I see of the crowd, Jacques, I'd say it's a successful operation."

"As long as I let my success go over my head and failures under my thumb."

What a guy! "So it's a good job being an owner?"

"Good job my heels. I *only* have to borrow money so I can spend more money to entertain people I do not even like."

That arrogant fuck! Head over heels sucking under his own thumb. Yet I must say he possessed a certain kind of sexiness. There was a manly aura about him that girls are very much attracted to; I could tell. And that was in spite of his longish hair, or perhaps because of it. You know who he sort of reminded me of, one of those trying to be super cool, it's hip to be hip VJs on MTV. He also had a tendency to fling his hair all around, then using his fingers to put some of the strands back in place. I saw him in action earlier as a DJ on the platform stage, directing traffic with a lit cigarette in his hand. He seemed to be one of those guys who thinks he's got the power to get people in the mood or something, like when he put on this really loud party song by Midnight Oil. "It is time to wake everyone up a little," he told us.

And you know what? He did it, that son-of-a-gun. It was one hell of a rowdy number. How can you tell bum-bum, bum, bum-bum, *how can we sleep while our beds are burning....* He was even singing along and moving like a rock star.

So the guy knew a little about music...for a Frenchman. But he didn't have to brag about it, for Christ's sake. He said he was to co-produce one of them song-and-dance music videos in Paris with someone who was a songwriter for a famous California group. They were hanging out in L.A. last summer and checking out the club scene. Then he bragged about all the club owners in L.A. he knew. Fucking guy, he had the gall to assume that just because I've driven up and down Sunset Boulevard, I would automatically be familiar with all the joints along the Sunset Strip. Try again, Sam! I have hardly ever set foot in an L.A. club, And I couldn't care less what new fly-by-day bungalow is the trendiest one in town. Or, to borrow a word from Jacques—the momentest!

Speaking of Hollywood bungalows, Jacques and I did have one thing in common: we both loved the Doors. When he was in L.A., he paid pilgrimage to all those places that Jim Morrison had frequented. I can dig that—fair is fair. When I visited Paris a few years ago, I paid my respects to Mr. Mojo Risin as well. One other thing about Jacques: like Morrison, he was also pretty philosophical about love and sex, albeit in a male chauvinist kind of way.

"Men may get free love from women," he said. "But women get free sex from men. I don't know what the problem is."

"So I guess if only men didn't have to pay so much for sex, and women so much for love."

"You see, we understand that by just being French. We show our women love, and they, in exchange, reward us for our efforts."

"But how big a reward are we talking about, Jacques? A token of their appreciation, as in rewards for lost-and-found? Or the burning and passionate 'I can't get enough of it' kind of reward?"

"Depends on how good a lover you are, my friend. If you are good, you can turn a token gesture into an insatiable need."

"And you can do that?"

"Why not." Jacques then paused for a second, lifted his head, looked up into the crowd and said: "I like to see myself as the lost and found box of love. Girls who have lost their love come to me; girls who have found their sexuality come to me as well—we all come together and live happily ever after!"

What unselfishness on display by the high priest of priestesses. Taking the rewards from one girl and giving it away as charity to the other—all in the name of love! "So tell me, Jacques, old pal, who is going to get rewarded tonight? We'd all like to know. And Stéphane will even take care of your leftovers, to get them off your back, right Stéphane?"

"Certainly. I'll smother them all—with a whole lotta love," Then he sang a couple of bars from the Zeppelin tune.

"Just make sure you don't suffocate them," I said to Stéphane. "Although, looking at how tightly they are all dressed, they can practically do themselves in."

"Ah! But the tighter they dress, the looser they are undressed," said Stéphane. "Look at that babe over there, in that body hugging one piece and cowboy boots up to her knees—scandalous! Perhaps Monsieur Jacques knows her well?"

"No," Jacques shook his head.

"She's smoking," Stéphane said to Jacques, "like a chimney of Gitanes."

Jacques also seemed to be full of lust, "I both love her and hate her. I feel like buying her a long strand of pearls and wrap it around her neck over and over until she practically chokes to death."

"Isn't that the climax to a French movie?" I wondered. "If not, maybe it ought to be. We could call it 'To Catch 22 Thieves' or something."

It went on like this for a while. Not as much male bonding as bounded by the bar—swapping stories between drinks, and drinks along with drinking stories. Stéphane was the first up. "Heard about this guy who brought a ladder to the party, because he thought the drinks were on the house." Hardly har har! Then I said I had always wanted to invent a drink called *Don't Mind If I Do*. So when I get up to the bar and the bartender asks, "Hey, you want a drink?" I'll just say, "Yeah. Don't Mind If I Do." I thought it was pretty funny, but Jacques the jock didn't think so. Instead, he tried to razzle-dazzle with some tricky way of drinking the Sambuca. First he poured some Sambuca into a tin ashtray and lit it on fire. Next he extinguished the flames by putting a snifter glass over it. After that, he placed his right hand over the glass and started shaking it up and down, like someone palming a basketball. It looked pretty fancy, his trick, with the glass suctioned into his palm, and some ooh's and ahh's from his crowd of admirers out in the stands. I, for one, couldn't figure out what all the hoop là là was all about. It was basically baby Chemistry 101, as in how to create a vacuum with smoke. Yet one of the girls was really sucking up to him, so Master Jacques used her as a volunteer to inhale all the Sambuca fumes from the snifter glass before pouring her a separate shot to drink down as well. That girl was either a bad actress or a lightweight because she suddenly looked like she was in some sorry state. What made me really puke was when she got suckered into doing it again by Jacques: "Come on, just one more sip for daddy. No, if you love me, you'll drink it all."

Stéphane, commenting on that spacey girl who was playing the Sambuca game, "Some girls, you can't take them anywhere; they just embarrass you the minute they open their mouths...."

"In public, of course, but certainly not in the bedroom."

"Such is life. All those sophisticated girls that can make you look like the most cultivated guy at a party; but in bed, if you ever get them there, they frequently disappoint. They don't open their mouth, they don't open their legs, they don't open a damn thing!"

"So that's why the French like to get away for a couple of *cinq à neufs* a week; to shack out with a sex kitten or two before going home to their 'approved' marriages."

"That's Paris!" Stéphane said. "Some here make love to women through words, others paint and photograph them. But me? I love them the old fashioned way, by simply obeying the laws of nature."

"Well, your way is certainly a lot quicker."

"Faster turnover too," Stéphane raised his voice. "And I'm going to let your low blow go for now."

"Very kind of you, sir." Boy, that Stéphane, kind of like them big jocks on campus. You'll never hear those guys utter things like "Honey, I love you so much I'll even type your term paper the night before my Organic Chem final." Yes, even in Paris, where romance is supposedly at its height, you still have guys with only one thing on their mind and are damn proud of it.

Jacques, however, was harder to pin down. With I-Love-the-City-of-Love seduction lines like "If Aphrodite wanted to come down for an orgasm, she would probably land on the Eiffel Tower," his mind was even more warped than Stéphane's.

"But Aphrodite is a goddess," I said. "She is above all that human fray."

"Nonsense. She has to fuck and eat, too."

"No, not quite Jacques. She has to liquor'em and swallow'em, too."

Either I was starting to get drunk, or the aphrodisical passion in the atmosphere was getting to us all, with some guys having all the love, and the rest of us doing nothing but champagne.

While the self-proclaimed goddess's mistress-piece was busy scanning the dance floor in his Jim Morrison sunglasses, Stéphane and I, shade-less bystanders, had silently agreed to bring some guy with all the love and all the breaks down a peg.

"So I hear the detached look is in again," I said.

"Yes, all Jacques needs to do now is to put back on those headphones he wore earlier and—"

"Yeah, and then he'd be really detached—audioly *and* visually!"

"Unbelievable. Didn't his mother ever tell him not to grow up to be deaf, dumb and blind?"

"Good one, Steffi! So good you've just bought yourself a drink."

"Am I supposed to say thank you?"

"Don't thank me, thank your wallet; or maybe thank the Sambuca flambée artist right here, who, after having unsuccessfully sought the role of the water parting Moses de Paris, is settling for the role of alcohol parting Jacques de Zigzag." Alcohol burning, actually—a much lesser feat; even less impressive was his way of using only a few fingers to both smoke his cigarette and bring his drink to his mouth. Anybody can do that shit! "Hey, Jacques," I said as I turned to the man with the roving shades, "See any new conquests? Any new leashes unleashed?"

Jacques looked in the direction of the dance floor where Ally and her friends were twisting and shouting: "I love the body language on those girls."

"Hey, girls, watch your body language. And don't dance with your body language full." I was getting loud. "What's the matter, Jacques, your bullets of love haven't yet penetrated their bulletproof chastity belts?"

"Don't worry, as soon as I puncture one of their Achilles' heels."

"Listen, you big kahuna, isn't there another way. Ever heard of the heart, my dear? The heart, Jacques, go for the heart! The way to ultimate happiness."

Jacques was silent for a second, and then said, "If you want to be happy for a few minutes, have intercourse; if you want to be happy for an hour, drink a bottle of champagne; if you want to be happy for a year, get married."

"And if you want to be happy after you're married, have lots of *cinq à neufs.*" I was really starting to like that phrase.

"What about masturbation?" Stéphane gestured by lowering his hand.

"That's right. I'm usually quite happy when I whack off," I said. "Better add that one as an amendment to your commandments, Monsieur Moses de Paris."

"Bon. Si vous voulez être heureux pour quelques secondes, branlez-vous!"

How 'bout that! While this wasn't exactly a boy's locker room scene with its nasty talks and dirty pranks, we were still just as crude. Like a rowdy bunch getting carried away at a bachelor party, or getting loud at a topless bar. Only Jacques was taking center stage as the bachelor of the moment.

"What a life you got here, Jacques, to constantly have young girls prancing around you."

"What can I say, I have a problem with girls my own age."

"*You* have a problem?"

"Put it like this: young women are not the only ones I'm attracted to, as I am also incredible with women much older than me. Older woman in general have seen their better days. But the ones that go for the younger men, they are truly in a class of their own."

"Oh yeah?"

"Absolutely! They are very sure of themselves, those polished older types, but never to the point of intimidating. They have something that is hard to describe...that desire of wanting to be both in control and in submission—*Tiens*! It is almost like making love to two women."

"Wow, sleeping with two women! That's profound, Jacques. One older and one younger."

"Age does not matter when desire's set on fire."

"Wow, Jacques, my idol! Have you ever done it with two women? How do you know which one to satisfy first? You ever got them both to come at the same time? Or do you prefer to watch instead?"

"I do not answer stupid questions from crazy Americans. That is almost as stupid as asking that if *69* is the position of ultimate passion, then what is *96*? A position of ultimate indifference?"

"Holy moly, let me see now: *96*, what kind of a twisty and turning position is *96*? I'd say it's probably when the partners are on opposite ends of the bed and looking away from one another. Yeah, that seems pretty indifferent all right—bent way out of shape! A far cry from the passions of *soi-neuf*."

"But perhaps it is an ideal position for people with back fetishes, *non*?"

"Holy shit, that's totally off the wall." That Jacques was a fucking nut—back fetish! Now everyone was getting a little buzzed; but not enough to quell our forays and mellow into oblivion. This was especially true of Jacques, whose showing up of the lone American was not to be complete without exercising a Frenchman's profound and even intellectual sensibility for the opposite sex. That could explain his popularity. Girls like confident and aggressive guys who are also pretty smart—narcissistic as they may be.

"You Americans," Jacques went on to say, "Every time I turn on the television in America, I see women complaining about their relationships, about how they are mistreated. I just don't get it. How can you be so incompetent in your sexual relationships? What man is going to be interested in a woman who is constantly complaining?"

"Well, if she's got the sexual fever of a hundred and three, I've no problems putting up with the bitching and the moaning."

"That is another thing: you Americans seem to be so unskilled at sex, and you are not even embarrassed."

"I take it, Jacques, that you don't think you'll ever have a Dr. Ruth*eau* as a national sex therapist of France."

"Never! Sex is the most overrated skill human beings have ever known. Never has such a simple thing been made so complicated. You Americans are impressed and horrified by a girl with lots of sexuality, a girl skilled at using her body to make love, but don't you see—"

"What'a ya trying to say, Jacques; it's easy to be a whore? Easy to go from Snow White at noon to Doin' Dallas after midnight?"

"Huh! No, no...not from noon to midnight. It will take less time than that. Look, you bring me a girl—any girl, and if I want to, I can teach her everything in an hour."

"Everything?"

"Let me present it to you in this way: she could come to me an hour earlier knowing nothing, but after I am through with her, after I have taught her all of my theories and theorems—my classical, timeless theorems—she will be better than nine out of ten girls out there, at least!"

"What are you going to do to her, *Jack*, give her geometry lessons? And if I might add, are those theorems foolproof, or can they even be proofed by a fool?"

That was when Stéphane cut in: "What is it I hear? The honorable Jacques is going to give her Jaclyn some geometry lessons, the same ones she failed at Ridgemont High?"

"Maybe not," I said. Sure was glad that Stéphane was siding with me, boy, 'cause I was getting riled up: "Maybe Jaclyn won't flunk her geometry after all. For I hear that this time around with Jacques, it won't be called Euclidean but rather U-Clit-In...Pardon my Greek!"

Stéphane was on a roll, too: "Jacques, *Je vous conseille:* what do you recommend as the best form of attack? Let's say we have a nice voluptuous lycéenne. No, let's make our American guest feel at home; let's call her a young American—a big-haired 'Junior Miss' contestant! What love theorems should I introduce to her? Side angle side? Umm...angle side angle? Side, side, side? Did I leave anything out?"

"Don't answer him yet, *Shia*ques the Shark. Let me go gather up my notebook. See, Stéphane, unlike geometry theorems, which are soon forgotten; once you learn the sexual theorems from Jacques, they stay with you for the rest of your life. Let's see, there's angle side side, angle of attack, degree of penetration, and let's not forget the ol'69s and 96s—that was brilliant, Jacques, just brilliant. Yes! 'tis the things that notes are made of. Better yet, let's one day spread the good word to the millions of inexperienced yet love-starved women the world over. We shall call it *La Méthode Jacques*, and have outposts in all the erotic cities around the globe. It'll be like cooking school, only with open admissions. We'll do job referrals, too. So that the only pre-requisite a thirteen-year old capitalist from Bangkok would need, before she hit the streets, is a certificate of authenticity from Jacques, with which she could then be assuredly on her way. Who knows, our franchise might one day even rival *Jacques* LaLanne, as we shall all be rich beyond our wildest dreams. And Jacques, our glorious leader, anytime you want, all you have to do is just come around and...you know, sample the merchandise—pick any girl you like, and test her for total quality control, just like what the Japanese do to their x-rated cameras. And god willing, Jacques, you might even get a Sainthood one day for your indispensable services. *St. Jacques d'Amore*—how does that sound? The one who brought sanity and order to that sleazy money machine called sex!"

Boy, was that a soliloquy or what? Sometimes I would go on these outbursts and get very carried away; and once I start, it's hard to stop. It's very irritating to people who have to listen to it, and rubs many of them the wrong way. I have a tendency to go a little overboard when I'm drinking, as I beat it on down to exhaustion. I need to exercise some self-restraint, especially in a foreign country. But it was still a great moment, getting back at Jacques at his own game.

Yeah, the battle of the sexes, girls like Olivia give women a chance; but guys like Jacques will insure it to be the longest battle in history. That's the problem with some of the girls: they allow these male pigs to manipulate the hell out of them; either out of desperation or foolishness. I know I'm a guy but, if I had to offer a single piece of advice to the girls out there, based on all the stories I've heard, it would probably be to not be so naive an eager beaver that you end up letting a guy have his way with you—don't let peer pressure push you into a helpless situation. And last but not least, unless if you are ultra horny, don't ever confess to a bad-boy that you want him to teach you everything about sex. Don't let him get to that position of power; because if you do, you may end up not learning a damn thing about what a healthy relationship is all about. It'll be more like beer bottles...or worse!

On the other hand, some girls are possessed with such venom that it's outright frightening. Man, can they break balls, those man-eaters. I mean, we're talking about major league ball-breakers here. Literally. And every chance they get! For instance, instead of being grateful to you after you have sweated away trying to satisfy their needs, they'd give you that blasé, unimpressed look and say: "I've seen bigger." One single remark, but the only one needed to take you from feeling like a big ten-inch to the smallest person on earth. I don't think there's another word a woman can utter that could top that in shock value. "I've seen bigger." It just does something to your psyche—like James Dean after he heard the word "chicken." If done at the opportune time, it could seriously damage a man's confidence, not to mention his mental well-being. And not only that, you can't even counterattack her venom with your own antidote, out of fear that she'd say it again. And again.

While we are on the subject of size, let me just get this off of my chest for now since I'm on a roll. Otherwise, I'd be too bashful to admit it later. God, I have so many insecurities, and pretty soon, I'll be too insecure to tell them all.

Remember those circle-jerk contests when you were little? Well, for the boys, that is. So anyway, I don't have a particularly large, god this is embarrassing. Well, I've never been endowed with a big penis—there! So when we had a contest to see who could shoot'em the farthest, I had to use some brain power to overcome my physical inferiority. So what I did was, because I already knew the "secret" of projectile motion, which says that a shot will shoot the longest distance if it travels at a 45 degree angle, I was able to, while other kids with bigger pricks were shooting infield pop-ups or grounding out, I always got the maximum distance. That was how I stayed competitive. All right, no more, that's it, no tasteless talk from now on. Let me just move on to wrap up the night by telling you how Ally taught me this crazy little dance called *le rock*.

When Jacques decided it was time for some rock and roll once again, I couldn't have been more relieved. I'd rather see him as Wolfman Jacques than Jacques the Ripper any day. All his inter-sexualism, curious as it was, had made me somewhat uneasy. Of course that was before I realized just how uneasy it can be when you had Ally teaching you how to dance.

She was dragging me on to the dance floor, "Don't you be a lazy snob," she said.

"But, Ally, look around, everyone else is just like me, standing around and looking at everyone else."

"Yes, but you are an American, you are supposed to go to clubs and dance like crazy."

"I am? We are?"

"Eh com'on, stop being *une andouille*. See those other people on the dance floor? We can do the same. Do you like this music?"

"Yeah, it's kinda rocking."

"Good, then you come and dance with me. You will like it, I'm sure." She was demanding but in a friendly way, which made saying *no* all the harder; which made me decide to be a good sport and take some dance lessons.

Ally was determined to finish teaching me this stupid French dance called *le rock*. I had a bout with it earlier, but still needed a lot more work. It was supposed to be a very popular dance in France, and, I have to admit, it was sort of mesmerizing to look at—with all the crisscrossing and all those tangling and untangling of the arms and body and everything.

"Now raise your arm, Mark, for me to turn under...Good, now raise it again for me to turn back to my old position."

Although parts of le rock were hard to do well, the dance was, in some ways, easier than it looked; especially if your partner is a good dancer. All I had to do was to just listen to Ally's instructions and raise my arm and let her twist and turn around me a little. And, if you are a *real* take charge type of guy like me, you can just sort of stand in one spot and do something like a stationary tap dance; stomping one foot on to the ground and trying to act as cool as the situation permits, while giving your body a shakedown here and there as you throw your partner around and around. You know what *le rock* reminded me of? One of them "Come along and shake, rattle and roll" dances à la *American Graffiti*, with some country music doe-see-doe's thrown in and some dance steps from the swingy Charleston era that my grandparents used to dance to—just a hodgepodge of Americana with a peculiarly French accent. Still, be it American or French, all dancing was Egyptian to me; every step was a march deeper into the confidence shredder. Thank goodness the music was at least a good enough of a pick-me-upper: from the *wa-wa-wa-wa-wandering* oldies to the *sha-la-la-la...la-te-da* oldies turned renewies.

It was strange having Ally lead the way—both humiliating and intriguing. I must have looked pretty awkward at first, not gripping her hand well at all.

"Don't always use the same hand!" she hollered. "Now switch to your right hand and bring me back in...."

"Next you chase after me as you swing me out, but I will also be chasing after you, so we actually change places. You got that?"

"Oui, j'ai compris."

"Okay, ready? Now swing me out!"

I swung...I chased; and my little runaway ran away. Lucky for me, after some trial and error, I was becoming less rigid and had begun to move around in a circle chasing after my partner. But Ally coordinated her body and arms so well that my errors had gone mostly unnoticed. Like the time when I had accidentally let go of her hand: now, instead of coming back and breaking up the rhythm, she just spun herself out as if it were part of her evasive maneuver. And could she ever spin herself up—as much as two full circles, 720 dizzying degrees!

That girl's got a feel for the beat that's hard to describe. And can she ever *movin' on over* when she's in a mood. Like the way she would go backwards while simultaneously swinging her body from side to side; just great footwork. Why, she could dance backwards better than I, forward. Wait, that didn't make any sense; but it's the best I can do—sort of like what that song says: Everybody but me knows that weird new dance now, *So c'mon, c'mon,* and force the locomotion on me!

She locomotived into town on that one, all right. Her movements—fluidy and springy like fluid flowing in a spring. You can always tell a good dancer from how softly her feet impact the ground; and her legs, too: nice full extensions, quick as a cat and alway in control. I tell you, looking at Ally dance, when a girl reacts to the right music—with every movement totally in sync—every part of her body just glows with sexiness.

When Ally had to take a break from le boogie-woogying to have another cigarette, Olivia and I, non-smokers both, got reunited for a couple of slower numbers."

"Care to dance, Mr. Smooth Operator?"

"Did you see me out there? Was I *smooth* or what?"

"You were...as you Americans love to say: Mark—is Mark!"

"Ha! And I thought I've been talking to a word-meistress. Shame on you for being so simplistic!"

"Simplistic? Hardly! Simply Red lipsticks...sometimes."

"Aye yeh yeh, Olivia m'dear, earlier we were talking about flawed and floor estimates; now it has evolved into smooth yet simple to operate lipsticks. What's this world coming to?"

"You've stumped me; or should I take a scoop out of Mark-speak and say: 'To stomp or not to stump, that is the question.'"

"Oooooh Olivia, you don't care how low you stoop! But I love you anyway."

"You can love me forever, Mark, but I also love this song, and *it* is not going to go on for ever and ever."

"In that case you better lay your hand on mine at once, Miss Simply Sweet Charity."

With one hand in my palm and the other hand on my shoulder, Olivia swayed gently to the tempo of the hypnotic beat. Her tender ballerina-like arms floating effortlessly in the air. We were all smiles, she and I, cheek to cheek, eye to eye, bodies swaying slowly in kind.

What's more, just as Olivia was so verbally direct earlier, she nevertheless possessed the subtleties of a seasoned stage star at work. It came into full swing during a Lionel Richie number when, every so often, she would turn her head and look away from me, as if to be just a little shy, just a little vulnerable. Them French drama queens, ever ready to add some spice to a cool fish. Not to be outdone by her theatrics, I upped the ante. At the moment I thought she'd look away again, I tightened my grip on her: closing my hold on her hip with one hand, and, with my other hand on her back, I forcefully pressed her body closer to mine.

"Hello—Is it me you're looking for?..."

13 / "MARK, HOW DO YOU PUT UP WITH ME? "I DON'T KNOW; BY PUTTING YOU DOWN, I GUESS."

By the time Ally & Company slip-slided out of Zigzag, it was nearly morning. Still, the French took their sweet-ass time in saying good-byes. Too many people to kiss and hug—some as much as four or five times in the course of a night. In fact, a number of them weren't even going home yet, as they began heading for a restaurant around the corner from the club, to feed and hang some more. And they weren't alone. Night revelers from all terrains of life were crawling into this place called Airelles—nonstop! The place looked like a total dive to me—to call it a truck stop would be too glorifying; more appropriate, perhaps, would be the label of a shabby soup kitchen passing as an after-hours bar and nosh joint. But in Paris, even a soup kitchen can be made trendy, given the right theme. Airelle's secret: it only opens for a few hours each day, from three o'clock in the morning through breakfast. Yes, a place catering exclusively to the late night/early morning crowd—perfectly up Ally's alley. But, *noctumbule* as she was, she nevertheless had to think for two and decided that we both had had long enough a night. "We will skip it," she said to me outside the entrance, "I have talked much too much for one night already."

Finally, it was down to us two, walking our way toward the car. "So, Mark, did you enjoy your night in Paris?"

"I loved it. Haven't had this much fun in ages."

"All work and no fun in New York?"

"No, just getting old."

"Oh com'on! You may dance like an old man, but you are not old."

"You danced great, though, Ally. Had I not dragged you down, we could have outdanced everybody there!"

I was relieved to find the car still in one piece. New York had really made me paranoid, especially when the cars are expensive convertibles—among the prime targets. Late nights in New York could also get a bit rowdy. Shortly after the last call, a mini-rush hour begins as people start the process of filtering out onto the sidewalks. Long Island kids who have had too much to drink, yuppies trying to finalize the terms of their one-night stands, and those impossible to flag down cabbies during the evening rush are now transformed into the vultures of the night—tagging onto your rear all the way down the block—just in case you have a couple of dollars still up your ass. And let's also not forget those Latino night owls, pumping volume into their car stereos and screeching their tires right through the red lights.

The Parisians, however, seemed to be more in control of themselves, at least on the surface. Maybe it was the lack of crack, and packs'n packs of cigarettes. The streets had definitely quieted down all right, but there was still evidence of life...or was it death. What's the difference between a wino and a bourgeois? The bourgeois passes out on the steps of a church still in his dinner jacket. No difference otherwise. I wished I could've taken a picture of those two sleeping beauties; side by side!

Just to be considerate, you know, I asked Ally if she needed me to drive her back. "Thanks for asking but it's okay," she said. "I've made it home on far worse nights."

Yet, Ally wasn't so perfect after all: she got slightly confused as to the location of a 24-hour Shell gas station. She found it eventually. We then filled up on some Super, which, at around six francs to a liter, was more than three times the price in New York. But even if it were cheaper, it still wouldn't have been proper to let a girl drive me around all night and pay for the gas, too. But Ally wouldn't hear of it. She said she would get reimbursed for it next week.

"That's awfully nice of Charles," I said.

"Bof, don't fool yourself. He just likes to make me work. He is really a big miser, you know—in disguise! I don't even think he carries any money around. I have never ever seen him give anyone a tip. Never! Even for doing a good job."

"Come to think of it, he didn't pay his lunch bill, either; nor last night's supper."

"See, I know it," Ally said with a shrug. "He is lucky he has people who indulge him."

"And you?"

"I always have cash and my checkbook ready—out of necessity! If I am in a car with him, and I don't pay for parking or toll, what am I going to do? Sit around and listen to his operas all day?"

"You are a riot, Ally-ce, you know that?"

"I am always pumping gas for him, too," she added. "I always find the tank empty after he returns. I fill it up and he uses it up. Do you know the song *Running on Empty*? That's me. I wish I had that tape with me right now."

"Great driving tape—as long as there's gas in the car that is. You like Jackson Browne?"

"Jackson Browne, James Brown, James Taylor."

"Not bad. No wonder you feel at home in America."

"Don't worry, Mark. A few more days, you will also feel at home in Paris."

She had a point. With a little imagination, sitting in a car at a gas station was not too different from sitting in a car at the Dairy Barn on a late night in Port Washington, picking up beer and chips for me and Stew and stocking up on milk and sodas for the house. Those were the sober nights, of course. Then there were times when I was so shitfaced I was a threat to humanity. I told Ally of this one time when I had drank so much that I couldn't even get into my car, much less drive it home. So I ended up walking back to the house. When I woke up the next morning and looked out my window, I was like: *Where's my car? I don't see my car on the driveway? Don't tell me I totaled my goddamn car last night?* I went fucking ape-shit and nearly freaked out. Thank god Stew-boy came to the rescue and found out that my Celica was still back at the bar.

Well, that was my first bout with memory loss. Hours of fun and games from the previous night were just wrung out of my brain. It was scary, my first blackout—even scarier than the first time my penis ejaculated! But like playing with yourself, playing drinking games till you became totally trashed was also habit forming—nothing wrong with getting a little brain cell damage every now and then is there? My sperm cells are never much to brag about, but brain cells I have many. I hope.

When we were in high school in Port Washington, Stew-boy and I used to scurry back late at night like bats looking for the cave. Generally speaking, our house was a safe haven. Mrs. Reed, Stew's mom and my guardian, having raised a large family, took everything pretty much in stride. It wasn't that she didn't love her kids or couldn't have cared less about what they were doing at night, not at all. Rather, having been on the final stretch of child rearing, she had pretty much seen it all and had everything in perspective. The house was also big enough so we didn't really disturb her sleep when we came home late. As a matter of fact, there was this one thing that we used to do that was even kind of cool, peculiar as it might have been. What we did was: late at night, after us having crashed through from the back door into the kitchen, we used to always have to sign in—I kid you not—it was like going to work. There was this piece of paper on the kitchen table with everybody's name on it, and you would sign in before going upstairs. Stew-boy and others used to even put down the actual time they came in. It was not a way to punish anyone for being too late or anything, but rather so that she would know not to disturb them the next morning till they've had their eight hours of sleep. What a mom!

The same couldn't be said for some of my friends, though. I remember one particular incident with my buddy Bruce. A bunch of us all went out to see Timberwolf, a Grateful Dead impersonator band. It was a great show. Their *Scarlet-Fire* was as good as the Dead's. So anyway, we drank, tripped on mushrooms then mellowed out at an all-night diner to sober up. When it came time to drive Bruce home, it was already dawn. And as soon as I pulled my car into his driveway, Bruce let out a big "Oh, nooo!" before I even realized what was happening. It was his mother. She was in her robe, sitting on the steps outside the front door, and sobbing as if her kid had died or something. Boy, if ever there was a time I was overwrought with guilt, that was it. I mean, wow! I couldn't go over to Bruce's house for the longest time after that. And that was only guilt by association. Imagine how my friend felt. Boy, them Jewish mothers, they really know how to spring it on you. But I love them, though—by far the funniest people on earth, bar none. Well, some of my grandmother's friends, them *old queens*—I loved them, too. Boy, could they ever put me on the floor! Figuratively, in most cases.

All right, I don't want to get too controversial at the moment, so let me get back to Jewish mothers. I've gotten to know them pretty good—pretty well, and not from watching Woody movies, either. So many of my friends are Jewish that I'm often mistaken—or rather, taken—as a member of their tribe. When Lisa first met me, she thought I was Jewish, too. And I think that was part of the problem. While at times I fit into her ideals of a nice Jewish boy to a tee, other times she came away very disappointed. She never gave up, though. Deep down, I still think she believed that one day perhaps she could turn me around. *How can you convert me into something that I more than already am—even though I'm not?*

We met while we were both tutoring city school kids, Lisa and I. It was a program where graduate students from local universities volunteered their time to help disadvantaged kids with their school work and stuff. At the time, Lisa was still at Columbia, enrolled in their graduate program, in one of the humanities; while I was going for my MBA. Strange as it seems now, me and Lisa hit it off right away and became good friends. Besides being very lovely, she was also a nice girl, as in well brought up and not very rebellious. At her best she was supportive and encouraging—trying to get me to accomplish what she had deemed to be my potential. Of course, her efforts were constantly hampered by my own lackadaisical ambivalence.

One of the things that most attracted me to Lisa, and perhaps even resented her for, was how perceptive she was. "Mark, do you know why you are often mean-spirited and don't relate well to people? It's because you were left unattended growing up and didn't relate well to your parents." She was very interested in my problems, and certainly made me more personable, or at least made me able to *act* more sociable and pleasant. But she also got upset when I didn't listen to her advice as much as she liked. I mean, at times, we were so good together—we got along so unbelievably well, that we should have been a great couple, and were. Then there were other times when, if people over heard us talking, they would have said that we ought to just stop pretending and go our own separate ways. That we also did, after more than two years together. In hindsight, it was much more my fault than hers. I was the psycho. "Drinking your Hyde juice again?" she used to say to me. "Letting off your esteem again?"

Yeah, I do miss her a lot. She was kind and sweet, and most importantly, she really cared about me, far more than I cared for myself, which was probably why I couldn't quite face up to it.

The happiest times we shared were mostly when we went away together. Lisa said I was a much nicer person on the road, much less autocratic and more considerate. We used to go away all the time: Syracuse to see the Orangemen, Charlotteville to visit her friends, Chicago to visit mine, and of course, Boston for the college hockey tournaments. She's a big Ranger fan—blame it on Ron Duguay. I, however, prefer the Islanders—I know, I know—so sue me (How about that goal by Ken Morrow in sudden death, huh?). Now you know why me and Lisa went away to college hockey games. But of all the places we had been to, I believe we both loved San Francisco the best—no major shock there!—the whole Bay area, in fact; and Lisa wasn't even into the Dead. But the deal was: first she goes to the shows with me at the Greek Theater; then *I* sit through a cup of mocha-cino at the Strada, rubbing my right elbow against leftist radicals. When in Berkeley, I guess. Just kidding. Berkeley was cool. Everything around Frisco was frisky. Even the time when we got lost after taking the narrowest little mountain pass that connected Napa to Sonoma. But that rarely happened. I'm a pretty good navigator. I seldom get lost for long if I didn't get too cocky and just stop to ask for directions. The exception, of course, was going to Bolinas. Not only can you *not* find people who will tell you how to get there, but you've got people who intentionally remove the road signs just to keep the day trippers out. *Hippie Tyrants!* Then again, maybe that's where I'll end up living one day.

So anyway, me and Lisa got along so well on the road that I frequently took her along when I visited my mother in Orange County. We had some great times there: holiday concerts at the Performing Arts Center, the annual Festival of Arts in Laguna Beach. And, on the opposite end of family values, there was the Cuckoo's Nest, a Costa Mesa rock club with hot local bands. Hot for me, but too loud for Lisa. She preferred the more subdued places I took her to, like watching bodysurfers timing the sidewaves at the Wedge, or maybe an evening stroll around Balboa Island, then ferry over to the beach to hang out. Lisa also liked to go for a little bite at Ruby's, this burger and ice cream joint at the tip of Balboa pier. I liked it, too. I'd trade my mother's hacienda in one of them notorious Newport enclaves for a cottage on the beach any day.

The same could not be said for my adorable Lisa. She liked my mother's lifestyle. So after a while, our fun and games inevitably became a disaster in disguise. The irony was, Lisa got along so well with my mother and Ira that, when we were all together, it seemed as if it was *I*, who was tagging along *her,* in visiting her parents. I mean, it totally backfired on me, my strategy. I brought her along so I could have an excuse to keep a little distance, you know, to not to have to spend day-in and day-out with the grown-up folks. But boy, was I ever in for a surprise. That Lisa, that darling of a girl Lisa, she ended up going to Sak's and Nieman's with my mother than to Tiajuana or Catalina with me. *C'est la vie*, I guess.

Before you jump to the conclusion that Lisa was just trying to pal pal with my nearest and dearest to make a good impression, let me say this: Lisa and my friends never really got along. She thought they were loafers, gamblers, and rude and crude to her. She liked the yuppish crowd—the ones who already knew how to decorate their two bedroom condos before they've even been approved for a mortgage on a studio. She thought my friends were a bad influence and would drag me down with them; that they were always broke and had borrowed too much money from me and stuff: "You know, Mark, it will be some time before you'll see your money again."

"If ever," I'd answer back in retaliation. She thought that just because I liked them as friends, that I was going to be as irresponsible as well. After a while, her hints of displeasure just got real tiresome. "Look, Lise, they are good people: they love sports, they are funny as hell, and they're into the Dead. Three out of three is pretty damn good if you asked me."

Another big complaint of Lisa's was that I was mean to her, especially compared to the way I treated my friends. Like I'd be real snappy and abrupt in my conversations with her over the phone, but when I talked to my sports buddies, I could get ten times as excited. Hadn't she ever heard of the word "parlay" before for Christ's sake, hadn't she ever heard of a game being a "push!" One time, after she had griped endlessly about me having been away for a whole weekend at a bachelor party, Edwin turned on his electronic keyboard and churned out this rendition of *Feelings* that really got Lisa sore as hell: *"Feelings, nothing more than Lisa's feelings, feeling of unhappiness...."* On and on he went. It was one of those moments where I was damned if I didn't back Lisa, and damned if I didn't at least shed a trickle of laughter. So I did both. In all fairness to Lisa, though, just as I was the most pleasant and likable when we went away together, I could also be the most monstrous in my own surroundings, particularly my own apartment. She said I was too petty toward her there. Like I'd get real *poi-toib-ed* when I see all her pills lying smack on top of the vanity—I'm chemical free now and I'd like to keep it that way! Then she'd practice her own version of water torture on me when she forgot to flip the shower dial *out* of the shower mode; I'd even get irate everytime she inserted a roll of toilet tissues backwards. "Mark," she'd say, "you notice every little thing about your room but not a drip of my running mascara."

Well, running ice cold water down my neck is a pain in the neck, but the running mascara is no big deal. Lots of things in life are no big deal. But I get the sense she was always trying to pin me down. "How could men just go to a bar and drink?" She'd say to me. "Hell, I don't know? How could a girl go to Bloomies and stare at a fucking dress for half an hour?"

I've always been a pretty decent counterpuncher. So when Lisa got frustrated because I was as good or even better an arguer as her, she'd also get depressed, saying I had hurt her feelings and stuff. I didn't mean it, though. Lots of times it was unintentional; like when I would make fun of her tendencies to be somewhat injury prone. I don't know if I was bad luck for her or what, but she was frequently getting hurt. I mean, we could be jogging merrily along in Central Park and, suddenly, she'd step into a little hole and sprain her ankle. And *I* got blamed for it! Or, we could be strolling along at the Third Avenue Street Fair and eating cotton candies when—bingo!—directly in front of us, an old man with a beard just happened to swing his umbrella back our way, right smack into her face. Her pain was further aggravated when, I, not only didn't comfort her, alluded to the martyring of Charles Sumner instead, when he was caned into unconsciousness in the Senate after he had accused a Senator from the South of "taking slavery as his mistress." American history trivia...well, maybe not so trivial. All right, I admit I was *poking* at her a little. But mishaps happened so routinely to her that they lost their severity. Things even happened when she was asleep. One time, I swear to god, she started screaming in the middle of the night—no, not from the delayed effect of my miraculous staying power (I wish!), but rather from a sudden pull of her calf muscle. And if she could do herself harm while remaining perfectly still, just imagine the harm she could do when she was tossing and turning, as it was one other night when she actually fell off my bed and hit the floor. Couldn't believe it—and it was a big bed, too! Of course I busted her chops when it happened. How was I to know at the time that she had just separated her shoulder. Oh brother, was she ever sore at me after that ordeal. In fact, I still feel like a guilty bed-hogger to this day.

It was kind of like that with cards and gifts as well. She liked to shop and buy things, so naturally I got more presents from her and didn't buy her quite as much in return. So she was hurt. But outside of business obligations, I think a person ought to buy a gift only if he or she feels like it; not as a return of favor. Cheap as I am, when I give a gift, or in Lisa's case, when I gave her all those frequent flyer miles, I didn't need anything in return. I mean, that would have ruined the whole purpose of giving. So it was all those little things and more that slowed the relationship to a standstill, if not making it skid downhill. She did *not* help matters any with some of the stunts she'd pulled or tried to pull. Boy, I get...never mind, I'd rather not get into the messy details if I can help it.

In many ways Lisa was kind of like my mother: a master of gentle pressure—but more pressure than gentle—for I felt it. Oh, how I felt it! It was familiar territory, and being such, it had a totally repelling effect on me. See, it's not that, I mean, I cared about her an awful lot; and still do! But somewhere along the way, the intensity subsided. God, how she used to get upset at times when I didn't treat her right. Sure, a part of me desperately apologized and tried to make it up to her. Yet I was never able to give her all my sincerity. Temporarily comforting her was about the best I could do. I was simply not mature enough to take on so much, how should I say it, so much brotherly love and devotion. She said I got weird on her every time she started to think she could trust me. The problem was: I couldn't even trust myself—even now—not so much due to my being a man or anything, but more because...I don't know, maybe I'm just crazy.

I've always been that way. It's always been more fun for me to take in a sentimental movie, to see all the actors get all emotionally charged up and stuff—like watching a rerun of *Casablanca* on television; it's great! But projecting all that romanticism back on myself is no easy task. Especially at home, where I like to be left alone. Where I don't need to be so goddam noble. Save that for the hills of Beantown and San Francisco.

You know, I've been accused of being lots of things by Lisa: from childish and juvenile to unbalanced and unreliable to down right mean and nasty. But never could she stick it to me as an ego*man*iac who would throw away the keys. I know it's not a lot, but at least it's something. A base from which I can start improving. As I mentioned earlier, I don't need to feel that certain macho power trip derived from being the protector of the female sex. In fact, the way I look at it, the more self-reliant the woman the better. Her being able to achieve on her own won't hurt my ego a tiny bit.

One last thing I'd like to talk about before we call it a night. That is this notion that women get depressed when their relationships aren't working. That somehow, they live to *love* while we, men, love to live. That's just as big a crock of cockamamie bullshit as I have ever heard! Everybody gets depressed. You should see how I get depressed. It's just that most men don't openly reveal it to others, that's all. We men just take it in and take it in till one day we finally snap our bananas and go totally bananas.

FOURTEEN

I felt pretty good as I woke up the next day. No hangover or nothing. Just a little cramp in the neck. Although it was late in the morning, it wasn't too bad considering I immediately got up and hit the shower. No question I would have been up earlier if it were a Saturday morning in New York; but if I didn't have to go to the office, or go sailing, or do anything specific, I'd be liable to just linger away in my room forever. You know, put on a Dead tape, take a couple of bong hits, do some school work here and there and so on. After all was unsaid and undone, I would suddenly come to the realization that I had just blown off three hours doing practically nothing. But sometimes you need that; sometimes you really need to just sit on your toilet seat for an hour to constipate... and procrastinate.

On that particular morning, however, I couldn't even see myself blowing off half-an-hour in my room. Yes, it had the charms and delights of a French country house: the antique gaming table in front of the fireplace, the oriental rug in the center, and a roll-top desk on the side and so forth. But due to it being virtually mess and clutter-free, it wasn't nearly as fun-packed as my bedroom at home. And since I had yet to stay there long enough to spread my things all over, or to have had any of my things misplaced, the place was more like a boring hotel room.

There is nothing more frustrating, or rather, addicting, than looking for misplaced items in my apartment—especially when I'm searching for my TV's remote control. By the way, I think that all televisions ought to feature a paging device that could beep the remote control in order to track it down. My unit gets misplaced far too easily: under the pillow, between the sheets, inside the couch, or even in Edwin's room. You name a place and I've found it there. That's one innovation I'd gladly pay a premium for. God, the time it would save me. Why, I could have read *Moby Dick* in the aggregate time I had spent searching for my remote. Anybody out there who is gadgetrily inclined, please give it a shot. It shouldn't be too hard, I don't think. Not to mention the great public service it would provide to male channel-surfing maniacs like me.

Shortly after I showered and brushed my teeth, I went out to the backyard to say hello to Charles, whom I had already spotted earlier from my bedroom window. When I passed the door to Ally's room, which was right off the second floor foyer across from the staircase, I couldn't detect a sound. The door was virtually shut; and no music was blaring out. She must still be sleeping, I thought, that fly-by-night of a Parisienne!

So anyway, I walked downstairs, through the salon, pushed out the french doors that opened onto the terrace, and found Charles just sitting pretty on a low chair with a stack of newspapers on his lap.

"A good morning to you, Uncle Charles."

"Yes, it's a very good morning indeed! Glad to see you are finally up, old boy."

"Up and standing, but dying to be up and sitting."

"Then by all means do sit down. Have some coffee, too, while you are at it."

Charles then told me to gather up another lawn chair and open it up. They were cool chairs; kind of like those Adirondack beach chairs except much longer, so you can stretch out and lounge on them comfortably. Charles said they were ideal for cricket matches. Yeah, so perfect you can take a nap and wake up without having missed a thing. Such is the game of cricket, it never ends. Neither did the bitter aftertaste of my coffee. It was too strong even for me.

"This is a cool terrace," I said, "Sure beats those typical wooden decks in the backyards of suburbia America."

In fact, looking around this backyard, it was hard to imagine that I was in the center of one of the most densely populated cities in the world. The terrace was built across the entire width of the house, with a limestone balustrade wrapped around it, and wide steps in the center that went down into the yard.

"Uncle Charles, this would be a great place for a backyard barbecue. Why, you can probably squeeze in a couple of softball teams onto the terrace alone."

"My dear boy, this is *not* the backyard as it is commonly referred to in America. It is rather known as the garden, and it differs from your suburbia in that the garden is what the most important rooms of the house overlook." Charles then told me to walk through the hedges onto the middle part of the grass near the fountain, and look back toward the house from there. "Now that's the view you ought to take back with you," he said, "More so than the familiar courtyard perspective as you enter from the street."

"*Le jardin*, of course!" I should have known. It's just that my idea of a garden in France was more synonymous with park, like the Jardin du Luxembourg nearby, or the Jardin des Tulleries next to the Place de la Concorde. But Charles was accurate in saying that the house was more dignified when viewed from the garden. Everything about the architecture appeared balanced and geometrical. The simple classical lines gave the house a solid, regal look. I especially liked those balusters on top of the house, which at once hid the roof and created symmetry with the balusters down around the patio—I mean the terrace.

Now, I don't want to give you the impression that Charles's little garden was a miniature version of Versailles. Far from it! In fact, there was an impression of an overall lack of maintenance. The grass in the garden, what little of it remained, looked too long and uneven; the trees and shrubs appeared shabby and uncared for. Such was also the case for the ivy around the walls: they looked much too thin. No outfielder at Wrigley Field would have wanted to chase deep flyballs at full speed if he had known that this was all the protection that awaited him. Don't get me wrong, I'm not trying to belittle the garden, it was most charming, albeit a bit run down; or, in modern home improvement euphemism, it needed a little "tender loving care."

The reason I had expected Charles to demand a perfectly manicured garden was due to my impressions from a visit to his summerhouse in the South of France twelve years ago. Villa Harmonie was not a tiny little villa, but a beautiful house set in a luxurious private park. It had a carpet-like croquet lawn surrounded by flowers and rare plantings, and a greenhouse of ancient bonsai trees. As for the summerhouse itself, it was designed in a style quite opposite of his Paris home's classical layout, with more nooks and crannies than... I can't think of a metaphor now, but there were clusters of little rooms that opened out to the verandas and balconies and patios. Some of which offered the loveliest views of the Mediterranean. On a clear day, you could even see a hint of the Italian coast. Otherwise, you only had to settle for the consolation prize of the tranquil and open sea on one side, and the town of St.-Jean Cap Ferrat on the other. And what a charming little village it was—at once quaint and glamorous—it had the perfect blend of ancient architecture and modern toys, especially during the high season, when all sorts of pleasure boats line up off its quay.

Villa Harmonie was indeed a rarity of a house in an even rarer setting. The only drawback to that property was the lack of a beach-front and its own dock. The house was built on a bluff, resting on solid rocks that jutted straight up from the sea. I remember the day when Charles's footman took me down to the waterside. It was pretty scary as we had to go down and around some slippery rock formations, not unlike the cliffs that the Allied soldiers had to overtake on D-day, except the enemy fire was fired from the fear within, not from the firing lines above.

I had some fine memories of that stay at Villa Harmonie. Not only were the surroundings an eye-opener to a little kid like me; the staff and visitors, too, were eccentric and colorful. There was this one guy there who was friends with both Charles and a lady nearby; and several times a day, when he got bored at the neighbor's house, he would try to find amusement at Harmonie. However, he found the regular walking distance going around the streets to be long and tedious; so to save time, he built, or rather, just hammered together, a wooden overpass and laid it over a deep ditch that separated the two properties. Then, surprise, surprise, he gave the damn thing a name—his own. It was the hilariest!

"Uncle Charles, what's his name again, the guy who named a bridge after himself at Villa Harmonie?"

"It was Pont Nicolas. Ahhh yes, good old Villa Harmonie."

"Why did you ever sell that joint...I mean the villa?"

"An American friend, on hearing I was to spend more time in Corsica, and seeing the exchange rate at ten francs to the dollar, just made me an offer that.... Well, let's just say that she had better things in mind for the house than I did. The villa and its upkeep had grown a bit tiresome, especially considering that I was preparing to retire."

"Is Corsica any better?"

"Life is simpler, at a more agrarian pace. The main town close by, Saint-Florent, an old fishing village, has only a couple of thousand or so permanent residents. I acquired a choice piece of property quite some years ago, with the main house right on the beach; and have subsequently acquired additional acreage extending back to the mountains." Charles then went on and told me of the livestock on the farm, the little vineyard, and the age-old fruit trees and olive groves, not to mention the enchanting scenery.

"Sounds like an idyllic paradise. Guess I should have swung by in the Summer of '85."

"It is still not too late, my boy; especially should you decide to explore career opportunities in Europe."

"Gee, tempting idea. How far is your retreat from civilization?"

"If one needs to go to the mainland, it's less than half-a-day by boat."

"Speedboat, right? Not that yacht of yours with them disco lights?"

"No, no, Mellery took over the yacht when I retired. It is now docked in Sardinia, at the Costa Smeralda Yacht Club. Even more so than Harmonie, the yacht was primarily for business. It was much too big for my own personal use."

It was a big boat all right, over a hundred feet in length. Even though I didn't go cruising when I was down there, I did get a tour of the boat. It was originally built as some sort of patrol boat, but was completely refitted into a modern yacht, with a large party room, and several staterooms all around. Luxurious, certainly. But since I'm getting to be somewhat of a sailboat snob, I don't have dreams of owning a big yacht someday and inviting young girls up to its disco and partying the night away. That's really what many of them do down there. The coastline from Monte Carlo to Cannes is dotted with multi-million dollar yachts, many twice as long as Charles's. They are owned by old tycoons and Arabs who indulge in whatever fantasies and excesses their monies can buy. "Arab sheiks with as many sheep aboard their yachts as girls in bikinis," said a crew from Charles's yacht.

But you know, Arabs aren't the only strange birds. There are those who own big yachts who haven't even the faintest interest in sailing. Another neighbor of Charles's, who had also made a habit of stopping by for dinner, had this castle-like mansion at the end of the Cape. He owned a huge yacht as well, which he kept fully staffed. Every afternoon, he would put on a colorful commodore-like outfit, and head down to his yacht for his fifteen-minute cruise around the Cape. Why so short? Well, all he wanted to do aboard his yacht was to zero in on his property with his binoculars to check out his house and grounds. "I rather fancy the way my estate looks from the sea," he said. "The swimming pool, the tennis court, the gazebo; and I always have my Rolls Royce Phantom straight in front of the fountain, to make it perfectly visible across the sea." Unbelievable, some of the rich. No wonder they needed Charles to manage and invest their money. How did that silly man make his fortune? He was once upon a time a famous international celebrity.

"Uncle Charles, have you been back to Harmonie often?"

"Not nearly as often as others had hoped, though I am expected to pop in for a few days in July, after attending a birthday party in the vicinity." The operative word there, of course, was "expected."

After I had my coffee, I flipped through the Paris *Herald*. The biggest news in Paris, a Korean was appointed musical director of the Bastille Opera. At times, the French idea of *égalité* is truly genuine, though I had hoped that he at least knew some French. Next I turned to the paper's sports section, as I needed to know the baseball scores; especially that of the Mets and Yankees. Reading the *Herald* and tracking the pennant race at home was one of the highlights of my European tour in the summer of '85—waking up each morning in agony or ecstasy. And frequently, after reading about a great game—hometown sickness, home *game* sickness. One time, I was so desperate for news from home that I got some of us to chip in and paid the equivalent of something like fifteen dollars for a thick Sunday New York *Times*, with all the statistics on all the players and everything. Not to mention all the news and stories and ads from the Big Apple. But you don't have to go to such extremes anymore. *USA Today*, the CNN of newspapers, is widely available. And, in a step beyond the *Herald*, it also contains box scores, possibly the single most important invention since baseball itself—for statistics sticklers anyway. However, unlike when I was in grammar school, stats are now used for more than just fun and games. They are a prerequisite to some serious and calculated wagerings.

You know, as much as I am the world's biggest chicken when it comes to bodily harm—I mean, you can't *pay* me enough to stand in front of a charging lion, not even with a rifle in my hands. But put me in a real tense wagering situation, with lots of money on the line, I can be as cool as absolute zero. No sleepless nights there! So while my threshold for physical pain is not even that of a sissy, I'll put my mental threshold up there with the best of them. I mean, I'm ready to call anyone's bluff—just give me the odds! And if my internally-calculated odds compared favorably to the official line, you've got yourself a bet! And that's not just for football or basketball or sports but on anything. Even on whether or not I would someday be cured of my penchant for action.

By far the most captivating action on earth at the time was the democracy movement in China. The French, as a people, were as vociferous as any in giving the totality of support to the students. In spite, or perhaps in view of the fact that they, too, had had their own student uprising in 1968. While I'm not a political activist, when I see democratic forces pitted against a totalitarian state, there is little doubt where my sympathies lie. I hardly even have to look at the issues, which in this case were glorious all the way. Millions of students petitioning the government to rule fairly, not arbitrarily.

For practically the whole month of May, I cheered the students on in front of my television screen. It was electrifying, seeing the images of all those faces on the streets of Peking and hearing their rallying cries at Tien An Men Square; I couldn't help but feel a sense of optimism for their cause. The students all talked of their willingness to die for freedom and democracy. How could they not succeed with such noble aspirations?

"You know, Uncle Charles, this whole series of events has just been absolutely incredible. The Western news media went to China to cover Gorbachev's visit; instead they stumbled onto a revolution. Talk about being in the right place at the right time."

"The right time for the media, but a terribly big headache for the Chinese government."

"Ever in your wildest dreams thought those students could conceivably overthrow the government, with no force of their own save pure drive and determination?"

"In my wildest dreams, yes; but realistically, no." Charles then let out a long sigh, "Yes, communism is indeed in a desperate crisis."

"Do you think there's no turning back? I mean—forget democracy!—the way this thing is brewing up, it'll either result in brutal repression or a long march to anarchy."

"Correct you are! What would you rather see, Mr. Vermont? Order or chaos?"

"I think a people's power type of uprising would be glorious."

"Easy for us to say in the West. Unfortunately, China is still predominantly agrarian, with vast numbers of farmers equally suspicious of Communists and intellectuals alike. To many of them, liberal democracy is just as far-fetched as radical Maoism. Even the students themselves have not thought this one clearly through. A movement of this magnitude requires more than just putting on a good show for the Western media, it needs physical and mental courage—a willingness to put their lives on the line."

"Well, they say they are not afraid to die. I seriously think the students have a chance: they've got that wild card called momentum on their hands."

"My dear boy, this is not a football game. One prerequisite of a willingness to die is desperation. And, like it or not, the students are not as yet in desperate straits. They are still very much seen as a privileged class in China."

"Okay, say you are right. Say the students are not quite prepared to die for democracy, but they can still succeed—'cause in order to die, somebody has to do the killing!"

Charles was silent for a moment; possibly jolted by my somewhat naive optimism. He then took another deep sigh and, in a resigned tone, he spoke: "Young man, throughout history, men who are willing to kill have far outnumbered those who are willing to die."

Boy, did that shut me up good. *I* was now the one at a loss for words. "Can communism…should we...no that's no good. Damn it, why is it that power always end up in the hands of those who don't deserve it? I mean, every single time there is a crisis, we can trace it to a bunch of stupid power-hungry idiots at the top." I was getting real angry, to the point of shouting: "Just what the hell is it about power that nobody wants to give up? Don't they care at all about the eye of history?"

"Yes, history is important," Charles said. "But no man wants to lose while he is still alive."

"I would. I'd be perfectly willing to let it go and take a loss. I'm a good loser, I'm used to losing; which probably explains why I'm not cut out to be a leader."

"You are still young, my boy. Give yourself time."

"I don't think so. I wouldn't want to be a leader. Don't want any leaders anywhere. Period."

"Interesting point of view."

"And now that I'm agitated, I'll go on record and say that wouldn't it be nice to eliminate all that is powerful in this world. To weaken all the power bases to the extent where no man or group can materially influence the course of history."

"An interesting idea. Then again, whoever or whatever it is that would achieve such a feat, that would neutralize all the power bases, would inevitably become the most powerful force *in* history. For in effect, they will have *ended* history as we know it. A rather *powerful* accomplishment, is it not?"

I threw up my hands in disgust. "There's just no way around the power of power, is there?"

"It's hard to say," Charles calmly replied. "In physics, there are laws on the conservation of mass and energy. One imagines that the same may apply to power, as well. One may cut it, slice it, and dice it, but it will never vanish or disappear."

"Then let it at least be cut properly, then," I said grudgingly.

"One possibility would be to simply pass the power down the line. Disperse it—so as to give the people power over their own lives."

"What are we looking at, a circular structure? A triangle or pyramid, perhaps?"

"Just the opposite. We don't want layers of power stacked up like bricks in a pyramid. We want to take away the middle chunks. Remove all those meddlesome subsidiary power centers. Free them up! And where will the excess power go, you ask? Well, most of it could be passed on down to the masses."

"But some still make their way upwards, right? Isn't that still consolidation?"

"I see it more as interaction," Charles countered. "Inevitably, the more power one gives away, the more it reverberates back to oneself.

Indeed, power is, in many ways, a dynamic and fluid process. Give people the power over their own lives and they, in turn, will entrust you with greater powers to rule."

"There's a new one: that only by giving away power can we ever hope to hold on to it."

"Another way of seeing this is to picture a single brilliant light source at one end; and, by way of a prism, that light is dispersed into a spectrum encompassing billions of different wavelengths."

"Wow, nothing like quantum politics! Whatever happened to baby politics back on earth?" I cracked. "Just to clarify things a bit, sir. When you say single power source defracted to form a spectrum of color, that source needn't be a person, right?"

"It could be anything, or a combination of things. Call it the super-ego of humanity if you will—human rights, fairness to thy neighbor, even an economic model."

"And also democracy?"

"Yes, democracy, too; if we could all agree on what it is."

"Don't you think it's a most vital ingredient—democracy?"

Charles didn't answer.

"Not to beat on a dead bush, sir; but there is still another thing I disagree with you on China. That is, given the present total domination by the Communist party, I don't think the desire of the Chinese for democracy is far-fetched at all. In fact, I have a hunch that if the students were to have their way, they could very well design a democratic system that is more benevolent and sincere. Not the selfish and often cynical versions practiced in the West. It would instead be a democracy to promote the goodness, not merely to check the badness."

"I don't want to dampen your optimism, my boy; but human beings are, by nature, quite the opportunist. That is to say, even if the students were to indeed devise a better system of government, it will still need tremendous execution to work on the scale of a billion people. And, absence of self-discipline as a method of enforcement—which requires education as well as technology—there are but two possible outcomes. One, back to the oppression of a tightly centralized military rule; or two, a quick dissipation of the moral high ground as greed and corruption seep in from every feudal corner of its unsustainable empire."

"Are you saying that given enough inducements, the students would inevitably turn corrupt themselves?"

"The dynastic tendencies of the Orientals cannot be underestimated," Charles said with assurance. "My dear fellow, China is a huge country, and democracy tends to works best when it works least—when it works not by national decrees but with the support of local constituencies; meaning the more diverse the population, the less effective the government."

"You don't want it *too* small, though," I said, half in jest, "or you yourself will *be* the government."

"If that day should come, Mark, then you shall find me firmly in the camp of central planners."

I laughed, "Have you no moral backbone left, Uncle Charles? Demo-cratic one moment, and demo-crazy the next!"

Charles nodded lightly as he let out a smile. "Morality and democracy don't always mix, my boy. One must bear in mind that democracy at times is merely a process, not an ideology or a belief unto itself. Comes to that, the citizens of a country or a locality could, theoretically, vote to have their right to vote curtailed—even rescinded!"

"Yeah, but democracy generally has a positive connotation, at least in the West. Even so, has it ever happened, though, people yielding their freedom to a dictatorship?"

"Well, the rise of Napoleon, for one, was the triumph of order over the mass madness of Robespierre. Then there was Germany after the Great War. What the Weimar needed in addition to political freedom was economic aid. On that they received nothing—thereby paving the way for Adolf Hitler."

"Wonder if Adolf is still a popular baby's name in Germany?"

Boy did that remark catch Charles off guard; he got a kick out of it, though, which in turn got me laughing as well. I didn't mean to be a wise ass; it was just my deranged subconscious at work.

"I didn't think such a side of you existed, old chap," Charles said in amazement

"Well, a fair warning to what being born and bred in a democracy can do to us all."

"Yes, indeed. Democracy, O democracy, so easy to preach, so difficult to perfect."

"I continue to sense, sir, that you are tickled, but not to death about it?"

"Sometimes I quiver for democracy, a process that tries to squeeze out a winner at any cost. The way it forces us to choose."

"But, sir, how can you have a democracy without voting?"

"We can't. At least not as yet. Nonetheless, when people vote, it is often at the expense of logic. This may sound a bit reductionist, but if everybody can't agree that 1+1=2, then how can they all agree that 2+2=4? By the same reasoning, if they all agree on the former, then anyone who disputes the validity of the latter should be sent back to school. Yet such is the flaw of democracy: one could conceivably vote for the former yet veto the latter, and still be seen as totally correct!"

"Yeah, infinity+infinity=infinity; but infinity×infinity=infinity^2. That's the problem with voting, I guess, with majority rules often resulting in majority fools. Maybe we ought to have something similar to a jury verdict, where the majority must persuade the dissenters of the final position—otherwise they all get hanged!"

"How so. But first it is necessary to establish a mechanism by which reasoning can be logically and consistently applied."

"If that's not best done under a democracy, then under what?"

"Perhaps a restricted democracy, or even a benevolent dictatorship."

"So you *are* challenging the basis of one-man-one-vote?"

"Not the spirit of it, which is admirable. What I do not like is that despite democracy's namesake, it is still a rather arbitrary practice. Who is eligible to vote? Whole persons, you say? And registered adults over eighteen? Rather easy numbers to work with, are they not? Very tidy in terms of units. But fair representation is not a tidy affair; it is hard work. What makes the age of *eighteen* such a magical number? Why should a parent with dependents have only a single vote?"

"Well, like you said, sir; it's convenient."

"But is it fair?" Charles's voice grew louder and more serious—even bordering on disgust. He was about to shock me once again: "Why should a seventy-year-old man have just as much say about the future as an eighteen-year-old child? What if the old man were to drop dead next year?...Or tomorrow?"

I was speechless; not only out of shock but confusion. Although I understood what Charles was saying, I still found it to be most uncharacteristic of him to belittle himself as such, to make himself so insignificant—if indeed that was his objective—that it's unfair for a man approaching the last years of life to have just as much representation as the rest of us who are still young. Especially an eighteen-year-old with fifty more years of productivity.

"Well, sir," I tried to be consoling, "in many instances, we do not strictly vote for our own agenda, but for the good of the future generations as well."

Still, my remark didn't help. "Then let someone be the proxy for the interests of the young, the babies, and why not even the unborn?"

The unborn? I couldn't believe what I was hearing. Instead of net present value of future cash flows, it's the net present representation of future unborns. Then I thought of something: what of the dead? What if we believe in eternal life, does that mean the dead should be represented too? What the hell! What the heaven! But just when I was ready to let Charles have it, I checked my swing. It was the wrong direction, I did not want the conversation to veer further down that dead-endless path.

"Let me ask you something else, sir. How about the other side of the token. That just as certain topics ought to have equal universal representation, should some other matters not have it? What I mean is, should we, on certain other matters, have weights built into the voting so that some parts of a population will have more say than others?"

"If any at all," Charles responded. "This is partly what I meant by a restrictive democracy. For instance, why should a non-taxpayer, in theory, have as equal a say on government spending as a billionaire?"

"So on issues dealing with spending, or money matters, you don't much favor the notion of one-man-one-vote."

"No, I do not. Certainly not at this moment in time."

"Then what would you like to see, sir, one dollar, one vote?"

"Not so extreme as such. Nonetheless, on issues dealing with expenditures, the taxpayers ought to have the most say, not least the top payers, the top asset holders, and why not even the corporations themselves?"

"Hmmm, that's a new one. I never really thought of it in such light. But in theory, it does address a very basic right: no taxation without representation! I mean, why should the GEs and the Du Ponts pay billions in taxes and have no formal voice. But then again, can we afford to open up the floodgates? Just think of all the complications that would result."

"You have a point there, Mr. Vermont. To calibrate the weights accurately is indeed a monumental task. Nonetheless, if one truly desires to have a society that is purely based on money, then the floodgates must be opened."

"Another interesting question you've just raised. Is that where the world is headed? Money and nothing but money."

"In the near future, yes. Money is, sad to say, the only common pursuit in the world today—the least common denominator as it may be."

"Do you foresee a world in pursuit of more than just money and wealth?"

"Such was the attraction of communism," Charles said in a praising tone. "In some ways, its ideas are still ahead of its time. It states that people shall work according to their abilities. That the goal of work is not for self-enrichment but to benefit the society as a whole."

"That would mean great sacrifices, would it not, to the ones who have to do all the work?"

"My dear boy, why must we look at such things as sacrifices? Why can't we make hard work an elitist idea!"

"I suppose you could, if you have people all doing what they like to do. But who's going to dig the ditches in Cap Ferrat?"

"Unskilled jobs could be filled by the young as a public service, or be made less laborious through advancements in technology, and last but not least, with increased monetary incentives."

"This might be a tough question, sir, but is it possible to have a perfect society?"

"It is not likely. One reason being that we are far from perfect ourselves."

"Are we making progress at all?"

"The world as a whole—not nearly fast enough."

"What's it going to take? I mean, how do you see this road to perfection—as a spreading phenomenon? Or will it be something from over the top, like what you said of a giant light source spotlighting the whole spectrum?"

"I see two components in such a march. One road is the human front, on that I see a gradual spreading of moral principles: that of democracy, freedom, and individual rights. Then there exists the technological front, which is just as critical. However, contrary to the evolutionary bend on the humanistic side, the advancements in technology shall hit us like a bolt of lightning from above."

"What do you think that bolt will be?"

"A breakthrough that could ring in the age of abundance."

"Wouldn't that be nice. Hate to put you on the spot market, sir; but what are the odds of an end to scarcity?"

"A very long shot at the moment. There is much yet to be done on the human front—motivation for one—as we still lack even a basic universal consensus as to what motivates people."

"You know, sir, in a way, that is one of the things I'm trying to answer. I keep...tell me if this is wrong, but shouldn't it be obvious to everyone that the total wealth of a society is best achieved through a combination of higher highs and higher baselines. Meaning, that not only should we create an environment conducive to the new Einsteins—to get them to hit those home runs that might ring in the age of abundance; but simultaneously, while waiting for miracles, we ought to find ways to bring the bottom of the barrel upward; to narrow the disparity."

"You are on rather idealistic grounds, Mark. Allow me to also point out that raising the baseline need not necessarily be mutually exclusive of pushing out the frontier. Indeed, I dare say they are rather complementary. That by reducing poverty, one also increases the pool of potential Einsteins."

"That's it. That's exactly what I mean. It's a win-win proposition. I'm not even an ultra-liberal and I like the sound of it. I know it somewhat contradicts my general belief in the survival of the fittest, but since we can't just cast human beings aside like flies, we might as well figure out a way to help 'em snap out of their poverty."

"Easier said, my boy. What one must first ask oneself is this: whether poverty is an absolute human condition or a relative one."

"Hmmm, that's a toughee. I would say on the physical level, it's relative—as the poor in America are far better off than the poor in

Calcutta. But mentally, I'm trying to think...I guess when it comes to the mental state, the condition is more absolute, since the anguish shared by all who are impoverished is equally great—if not greater for an American due to the income disparities. See, I realize there will always be poverty, but as long as there are people getting out of it, and others dipping into it, it's tolerable. What my conscience can't square with is this multi-generational thing, especially in America, where mobility is one of our greatest trademarks."

"And where, might I ask, would you place the blame? On the welfare system? *The Great Society?* Or perhaps on the lack of family stability?"

"You know, sir, lots of people like to blame single parenthood, as if people choose to be single parents and could, therefore, easily de-choose it and solve all the problems. That's stupid! If anything, I think a family is quite an overrated system of guidance."

"How curious," Charles was a shade amused.

"Yeah, take out the hate and bigotry being discoursed every night at the dining room table, and you'll open the kids up to a more benign conception of the outside world. Which brings me to ask you this: do you think the state should have the right to take kids away from incompetent parents?"

"You are stepping on controversial grounds, my boy, especially in a democratic society. Besides, what makes you think the government can provide so difficult a service as parenting when they have failed on far simpler tasks?"

"At present I don't think that. Yet my gut feeling is: if we apply mass production techniques to social services, including childcare, we should be able to *both* improve the quality *and* cut its cost."

"Ah, but there lies the difficulty. Bringing up a child, unlike manufacturing a product, has a multitude of inherent specifications. Unlike products, the children cannot be conditioned via assembly lines."

"Not even if we start them really early? I mean, surely there's got to be a point where the divergence is minimal, where conditioning need not be so customized."

"My dear boy, there is only one stage in life when everyone is more or less on equal footing, that is the infancy period. Soon after, much will depend on the upbringing."

"So I am the way I am due to the upbringing?"

"Yes—or if you prefer—the complete lack thereof!"

"Ha! And I thought it was all due to my Neanderthal genes."

"Genes might help, but it could also wreak tremendous havoc when the expectations become too great."

"Speaking from personal experience?" I counterpunched. But Charles just shrugged that one aside. "All right, sir. Look, I realize that to give everyone the necessary skills to succeed is an impossibility. But there must be a threshold somewhere. There must be a minimum standard from which to serve as a jumping-off point into the mainstream. Now, I am not saying this minimum requirement is going to enable the have-nots to compete ounce for ounce with the haves; but if we can throw enough mudpies at a kid, some of it is bound to stick to his teeth. And if we do some mental calculus to figure out just where the most efficient providing point is, we can reinforce at that point and start moving toward some sort of an equality equilibrium."

"Correct me if I'm wrong, Mark, but I get the sense that somehow, your belief in equality is too finely calibrated and not purely altruistic."

"Well, like what they say back home: As goes General Motors, so goes the U.S."

"Perhaps it's true. Yet it also seems as though you want to make *equality* down at the bottom a means toward *inequality* at the top."

"Well, sir, I do believe in meritocracy, if that's what you mean. And in a meritocracy, people are ranked, albeit more fairly than they are now. Look, I just want as many people as possible to have a shot at hitting those home runs, which would in turn benefit the society as a whole. And, although I don't believe that every man must be equal, I do believe that greatness can come from all walks of life. America is a proof of that! But if a child is under-fed, under-cared and under-guided, he can't possibly have a chance—even if his IQ is at genius levels. And every time that happens, it's a loss to us all!"

Charles didn't respond right away, just raised his eyebrows. He then leaned his head back and said: "So geniuses you are willing to harness; but the general populace, they may have to yield."

"No, no, no—not yield! But facing limited resources, we have to find a point where we can nudge the largest number over the hump.

Eventually, with the arrival of abundance, anyone who cares to sit back and relax can do so, and live a life of happiness. You said so yourself."

Charles again raised his eyebrows in amazement, which made me kind of skeptical myself: "So what do you think, sir, of these child-ish experiments? Of mass producing tender loving care? Think they are a healthy thing?"

"On the surface, they seem like wonderful gestures. Though I do sense an underlying feeling of frustration and desperation with the problems at hand."

"Yeah, it's pretty radical, I guess. Trying to factory assemble personalities. Big brotherish, too."

"One might say there exists an element of cynical benevolence—a facade of unselfishness that is mere prejudice in disguise. But as you said, it is also economic reality. Food and shelter the system will attempt to provide to all—out of compassion, out of responsibility. But if one wants to live a fulfilling life in addition, then one has to work for it, one has to try for some...home runs."

"You know what this also brings to mind, sir? Those *Utopian Socialists* of the nineteenth century. Guys like Robert Owens, where one great visionary tries to lead the ordinary to a more orderly life. Still recall them from my *Euro*phoric high school days."

"Eh yes, Fourier, Owens, Saint-Simon and the rest—quite an eccentric bunch; did some interesting social experiments, too."

"That they did. You know, one of Fourier's phalanxes in America actually went on for a good number of years."

"Eh yes, *les phalanstères*! They were indeed a *hit* in America."

"Wouldn't mind seeing more of those utopian types of things today," I said. "Except for a couple of friends who are having a ball herbirvoring it up at some meditational community near San Francisco, everyone else is still hobbling along on the rat racetrack."

"I am very much in support of your commune friends," Charles said. "One way to make 'work' an elitist idea is to encourage people to work for work's sake, be it communes, the marketplace, or whatever creative setting one cares to envisage. Personally, I am all for social experimentation. It brings out an element in us that says: don't tell us what to do. That we, as a unit, shall determine whom we shall become."

"What if we yearn for more than interactive relationships? Or, to put it in another way: don't you think we should know ourselves first before we try to get along with the rest?"

Charles was silent. But the grimace on his face reflected the intensity of his thoughts. "In all the fields of human endeavor, there is no field as dangerous, nor potentially as rewarding, as the will to test ourselves—mentally, physically and psychologically."

"Needles and cages?"

"Experiments needn't be confined to laboratories. To test the outer limits of human capacity, we must be willing to put man himself on the line, to take the boundaries as far as they go."

"Is that the ultimate quest, sir, the pursuit of the cutting edge?"

"We both crave it and fear it. We yearn to know the unknown; yet as we approach it, we stop—out of guilt, out of ethics and morality, out of hope that perhaps some day, a perfect guinea pig might come along."

"Will it?"

"No. The only perfect guinea pigs are human beings ourselves."

15 / EDWIN MIGHT HAVE TAUGHT ME HOW TO SHAVE, BUT NORELCO TAUGHT ME HOW TO BE A MAN!

The door to Ally's room was still virtually closed when I went back upstairs. But this time I heard some paper shuffling noise from within so I decided to sneak a peek. It was supposed to have been a quick little peek, till the door squeaked. Then I was left with no choice but to knock on the door and barge in.

Ally was already fully up, sitting by a desk next to her window with a glass of orange juice, appearing as if she had been studying. She had on a pink tank top and floral boxerish shorts—desk and breakfast wear, if you will—clothing that allows you to sit still for hours. Not at all suited, if I might add, for the footloose and dancing free creature from the night before.

"*Salut*, Ally!"

"Mark-uh, good morning! Did you have a niii-ce sleep?"

"*Merveilleux*!" Wonderful, I said. "*Et toi*? You seem to be fairly relaxed and at ease."

"Not really; I've been up all morning studying!"

"Oh yeah?" I was surprised. I thought she was still asleep when I passed her room the first time, on the way down to see Charles. That girl's got some energy all right, more energy than a ton of fire rockets.

Although Ally had no aspirations to become a rocket scientist, there was a specific reason why she was studying that morning. "I would like to ask you something, Mark. How did you do on your Graduate Management Tests?"

"The GMATs? Reasonably well, I suppose; close to 700. I really had to. My GPA wasn't great so I needed a high score to get into the graduate program." It was fortunate I pulled it off, too; especially on the verbal, which I didn't do so hot on in the practice tests. "Ally, have you been sample-testing yourself?"

"Pardon me?"

"You know, scoring yourself on the practice tests."

"Oh, I score about 75% on English and 95% on math."

"That's very good, especially the English score. Just keep doing more practice tests and you'll see your verbals improving."

"But I'm not going to have much time. The test is in two weeks, at L'Université Americaine à Paris."

"Is the test location nearby?"

"Not far, on the other side of the Seventh near Les Invalides."

"In that case, what you should do is, a couple of days beforehand, go to the room where the test will be held, familiarize yourself with the place, perhaps to pick out a seat you like. And, if you have a friend who is also taking the test, bring her along; that'll help you relax. I remember one guy I knew who registered late and had to go to Staten Island early in the morning to take the test. And after the stress of waiting forever for the Ferry crossing, he didn't do so hot." I then told Ally some standard stuff, like get the math over with quickly and turn to the verbal. Of course, to do this, you need to be good in math. Meaning, the marginal time spent on reviewing the math won't get you a significantly better score than if you had invested that time on the verbal parts instead. It's not "legal," I know; but everybody does it, so it's kind of the system's fault. If they don't reward students for finishing early, then they are not calibrating the scores well enough. One other thing I let Ally in on was a somewhat unconventional way to improve her score. It's strictly my own invention, so far as I know; and it's based on the principal of time maximization. See, one of the ways to save time is to simply write the answers down as quickly as you can. How, you ask? Well, instead of filling in the whole answer key like a stupid lotto ticket—which could take a long time—you just stroke a pencil line across the correct answer. It's amazing how many people there are who would just sit there and spend precious, precious seconds darkening up the answer keys. I mean, with six tests and up to thirty-five questions on each, the time you save per question could gain you a couple of extra minutes—enough to improve your score by quite a lot. And don't worry about the answer keys being unreadable, either. The trick is, you go back and darken them up real good during the intermission. Yes, it's cheating if you kept your test booklet open as you continue to answer the questions during the breaks. Shame on you if you stoop to that level. But as far as trying to make your answers more readable, arguments can be made both ways.

I hope what I said was not too controversial. I know it's stepping out of bounds somewhat, though it's not nearly as blatant as some of the other things that go on in the test rooms. Personally, I don't believe in time limits. True, there are some real deadlines in certain professions. But the reason they don't give you enough time is not so much to prepare you for the real world—far from it!—but rather to make easier the task of differentiating everyone's scoring. In a sense, they are right. If two people both get perfect scores, the first one took an hour, and the second one only forty minutes, then the forty minute person has to be seen as the more intelligent of the two, or at least having a better grasp of the material.

While I'm at it, allow me to take this opportunity to defend the multiple-choice-test-format a bit. I believe it's getting a bum rap from all those crybabies who just aren't fast enough on their feet. And head! I don't care what anybody says, the truth of the matter is, life's a bunch of multiple choices. In fact, more than 90% of the questions we face in our lifetime are probably multiple choices: Cowboys or Redskins; SF or LA; overalls or mini-skirts; Hilton or HoJo's; station wagons or pick-up trucks; which Chippendales dancer you want to slide your fins into and so forth. You can go on and on down the line without end. Pretty much the only essay questions in life which we *really* need to think through are career, marriage, kids, and divorce. And plenty of time we'll have to think them over—certainly more time than thirty minutes. Even sex isn't much of an essay question, as many of us would much rather treat it as multiple choice. Boy, would we like to have multiple choices to pick from—Marcia Brady or Laurie Partridge!—though unfortunately for some of us, we'll gladly take whatever we can get. Why, if we treated every damn decision we make in life as an essay question, we would have compiled enough material for an encyclopedia by the time we die. And lord knows we've got plenty of outdated encyclopedias laying around. I know, I'm getting way out of hand again. It's just that...this urge to pontificate like a Frenchman.

Ally was quite pleased that I had passed along some ways to stretch the test rules. I was, too. It's nice to be useful now and then—especially to someone who, by nature, is very much a self-starter. So much so that, sometimes, I almost wished I could be more of help, to give her a little extra boost. She was indeed very bright, verbally and abstractly. You should've seen her there trying to test my deductive reasoning powers.

"Mark, are you ready to find out how intelligent you are?"

"No."

"Too bad. So here is the question: I have four postcards on the table. One has a picture of the *Eiffel Tower*, another has the word "Paris." Third card has a picture of *Santa Monica Beach,* and the fourth card has the word "California." Okay so far?"

"So far so good, Alexandra La Ch'Eiffel."

"*Bon*. Your job now is to prove or disprove my statement: 'If a postcard shows a picture of *Eiffel Tower*, then the hidden side of the card must have the word "Paris." So which cards will you have to turn over to verify my statement."

"I take it that a card can't have pictures on both sides?"

"Correct. Photo on one side; a place name on the other side."

"That's easy. Turn over the *Eiffel Tower* card to make sure the word "Paris" is on the flip side; then turn over the "Paris" card to see if a picture of the *Eiffel Tower* is on the flip side."

Boy did Ally ever have a smirk on her face when she heard that.

"No?"

"Only half-right," she shook her head.

Did I screw up, I wondered. Then all of a sudden I turned as red as Hollywood: "Oh shit, I fucked up!" I banged my head with my fist. "I should have flipped the "California" card instead, to make sure it had a picture of the *Beach*; or rather, to make sure the *Eiffel Tower* hasn't moved to Santa Monica. Very tricky, Ally!"

"Now you are right. Remember my only condition: if the photo is the Eiffel Tower, then it *must* say "Paris." I did not promise you that if you flip the "Paris "card over, you will see the Tower. So you don't have to check that one. Neither do you have to bother with the picture of the beach; that one is also irrelevant."

"I got'ya, I got'ya." Boy was I ever set up, like a studio party on Santa Monica Pier.

"Never underestimate the power of tower," Ally said, tiding in the last vowel as I threw in the towel.

Even though I was shaking my head, it was in a delightful sort of way. I almost felt like giving her a big kiss for being so brilliant.

Ally was also very good with numbers. She showed me this test paper from a statistics test she had taken, with regression and correlation analysis and everything. "I received the highest score in class," she said.

"Bravo," I congratulated her. "You know, Ally, instead of marketing, maybe you ought to take a stab at Operations Research?"

"No way, I ken-not! That area is much too boring for me."

But Ally sure knew how to make up some interesting numbers when she gave me another tricky problem to solve. "You are in a snowmobile. You go south 10, then go east 2, then go west 7,"

"All right, I'm at south 10 and west 5," I said.

"Then go north 5, go east 10, okay so far?"

"I think so. I should be at south 5, and east 5."

"Now go 5 more to the north. Okay, if I say to you that you are back at where you originally started from, where on earth are you?"

"What! I found myself 5 miles east of where I started, not back to the same place. Is that right? Don't say it isn't!"

"Okay let's try again," she said. Then she proceeded to give me even bigger and weirder numbers, like 60 south, 20 west, then 35 east. What's more, the numbers seem to have nothing to do with one another. I had the hardest time just trying to keep up. When I finally got the answer of something like 25 miles east, Ally still said I was only half correct.

I was getting pissed: "Ally, is that the tricky part of the question, that there is no correct answer?"

"Ha-ha-ha!" she threw her hand down on her desk and laughed. She was having a good time making a mockery of me. "Oh, no, there is a definite answer. What you seem to have forgotten, Mark, was the original question, which asks you: after you have traveled all those miles, where on earth *are* you if you still ended up back at the exact place where you started from. I can't believe it, Mark; you told me yesterday you are a good navigator on a boat!"

"Aaaaah, sailing! I seemed to have broken through a barrier of sorts. For instead of trying to decipher a confusing word problem in a text book, my mind had begun to create a picture of myself on an iceboat, sailing off those miles in the morning calm of the Arctic. Moments later, I solved the trick question. "I got it, you are at *le Pole Nord*, the North Pole!"

"About time!" she rolled her eyes.

"Yeah, how easy every thing is after you know the answer. If there are people out there who are as confused as me, let me just quickly explain it. If the North Pole had actually been a flag pole, then in theory, whichever way Santa Claus goes east or west matters not; meaning, if he walked east 2 miles then due north, he'd still end up at the flag; or, if he walked west 2 miles, then north again, he'd also end up at the same flag. I felt embarrassed that I had accused Miss Santa Monica Claus here of not knowing the answer. She only knew it all too well to know that as long as the north and south coordinates zero out, the dizzying circles one makes around the pole are totally irrelevant.

Speaking of dizziness, a symptom which word problems often bring to many people; I, at least for the time being, will try not to add a final complication to this matter—regarding the difference between true north and compass north—which you need to know if you ever want to be a sailor or navigator. But for now, let me just finish up with one final thought, especially for those of you out there who firmly believe in the idea of permanence. In perhaps a thousand years or so, the earth's magnetic field will undergo a reversal—meaning that all the compasses in the world will be pointing south instead of north. Yeah, believe it! Just what sort of chaos will be awaiting all the navigators during the transition period, I only hope I don't live so long to find out. Maybe I'll move to Mars; they don't have magnetic fields there. Getting spaced out again, Vermont—must be missing your weekly fix of Saturday morning cartoons in bed. Time to move back down to earth—you were a captive in Ally's capsule, as it were.

Unlike some other girls her age, you needn't possess a compass to find your way around Ally's bedroom. And, unlike most of the other rooms in Charles's house, you needn't be in possession of a time machine analyzer either, to tell you the age of her furniture. Everything in her room spelled contemporary! No, not the avant-garde-post-modern-futuristic kind, just 1980s blond wood à la IKEA use-it-till-it-breaks contemporary. The sitting area of the room, the part we were in, was sparsely laid out with a desk and chair in front of a window overlooking the courtyard, and some cheap-looking bookcases along the wall. And, you guessed it, a not-so-cheap-looking stereo. Above the stereo was a big movie poster and a small blurred photo of Madonna.

"Where d'ya get this picture of Madonna?"

"She gave a concert in Paris two years ago, we all went to the Hotel Crillon to see her."

"Jesus, I don't even go to the St. Regis to hang out with the Dead."

But Ally didn't solely have famous stars on her walls. She and her friends, too, were well represented, with various photos taken at costume theme parties, vacations, etc.. Two of my favorite pictures were photographs of Ally on a beach. The first one had her in a swimsuit, just out of the water, wet and glistening. The other one was taken on the same beach, wearing shades, but she wasn't wet or anything; instead, she was in a mini-skirt, making a really sexy pose. But the unique thing was, both photos were of the same outfit. It was a bathing suit that actually folded down into a mini-skirt on land. As baseball's Mel Allen likes to say, "Howww'bout that!" One minute she was a baby doll; the next, a femme fatale. And she could pull it off convincingly as both!

As for passing herself off as my favorite rock and roll queen, Ally had to try harder—at least on the musical front—based on the compact disc collection that she showed me. Although she had quite a few of them, they were mostly of the newer pop-rock variety: the George Michaels and the Janet Jacksons, along with some older folks like Blondie, Cyndi Lauper, Rod Stewart and Chicago, as well as a stack of film sound-tracks. Ally told me she had gotten most of those discs from America, where it was much cheaper. Well, at least she didn't spend her hard-earned salary from Charles on those...no, I'm not going to say it; I'm not going to criticize pop music and have millions of American Top 40 fans chasing my head off with flying CDs. If a French girl likes American pop, so be it.

"Mark, do you want to hear a good song?"

"Why not," I said. Actually I wanted to say not really, but I also knew she'd play it anyway. It was a tune from the soundtrack of *Grease*, one of her oldest records. "I was only ten years old when I boat this—it was my first American album."

"And the rest was history!" I said, with Olivia Newton John singing "Tell me more, tell me more" in the background.

Grease was a while back—just before high school, I think. Blame it on John "Night Fever" Travolta for my *dis*going to that movie, though I did see the original Broadway play in sixth grade. Truth be told, my taste in music hasn't been mainstream pop since the early junior high years of Styx, Toto, and Hall & Oates. I have Edwin to thank for that—credit him with getting me into some serious rock and roll at boarding school. I swear to god, in one year, I changed from being one of the millions of teenagers who claimed that "Nobody loves the Beatles more than I do," to the music of the Doors, Floyd, and the Who. I mean, *Quadrophenia* was unlike any other record I had ever heard; Floyd, too, whose spacey sound eventually led me to ELP and Yes. A hell of a record that *Close to the Edge*, till the Dead rolled in with the morning dew.

You know, it's ironic that, after having taped a hundred rock albums from Edwin, who was primarily responsible for turning me into a rock and roller in the first place, I would stab him in the back a couple of years later by getting into the Dead, only the Dead, and nothing but the Dead. Edwin's altruistic intentions sure had gone down the grooves all right, as he not only did *not* convert me into a slave of rock and roll, but I became, instead, a condescending Deadhead monster. Rock and roll, albums, recordings...big deal!... who cares!...strictly for the birds! Edwin likes the Dead, but he's also into sound, and the Dead is just one wall of sound amongst many to him. Lately, not even; as he thinks he's on the verge of inventing some new and underground sound all by himself. Yeah, him and a thousand other bands. Still, every so often, he likes to remind me that if it weren't for his exposing me to classic rock in the first place, I would not have had the necessary preparations to be a Deadhead. Sometimes, being a prophet of the gospels of rock is a thankless job, as in building rocking foundations on clouds with slippery linings.

Although Ally's record collection had bored me somewhat, her bed sure got my attention. No antique leftovers here; instead, it was a big futon mattress on a low frame, with two pillows and a partially covered comforter on top.

I went and sat on her bed to test its firmness. "How do you like sleeping on the futon?" I asked, "Isn't it a bit hard?"

"No, it's super. It's all natural and the best for my back! After I slept on it last summer in California, I was convertibled."

"Converted." I corrected her.

"Yep. It's very popular in California, you know, the fu-tooon."

"In New York, too. You always see them advertised in the *Village Voice*. I guess lots of downtown artists like to sleep on them."

"Do you know what I sometimes use it for? Exercise." That said, Ally proceeded to show me her routine. It was fairly simple: just lying down flat on the futon, arms stretched past her head, and doing leg lifts and arm lifts all at once. But the key was to do it slowly to get the muscles straining. As sexy as Ally's body was at twisting and spinning the night before, she looked a bit silly doing those pseudo-situps, trying to hold her breath and all. Working out just seems so... how should I say it?—so unFrench—such needless exertion! I hate situps as well. They are too exhausting. God damn situps tire me out more than sex! But I laid down on the futon and did a few of those suckers anyway.

"I thought only Americans did these things," I said, gasping.

"But Mark-uh, do you think the French just look good without effort?"

"Well, at least I thought you did."

"Oh, nooo! I have to watch my weight, too. I *don't* want to get cell-u-*leet*."

Ah, yes, that universal fear of fat cells, probably the only fear I needn't be too concerned with for now. I don't have any meaty drumsticks. My bony legs *are* drumsticks. Not very muscular and manly is my body, if you must know.

But Ally's legs were perfect. And she could really spread them, too—I mean in the athletic sense—as she could part them till they have virtually straightened out. Girls can do shit like that; they have far greater flexibility. As for me? Well, I tried. But I couldn't stretch my legs out for beans, just barely got them out to a wide-V, despite Ally's half-sincere and half-mocking way of cheering me on.

"Aw, com'ooon Mark, you can do better than that—push it out a little more!" urged my personal trainer.

"Ally, you like to see people in pain, don't ya?" I said, as I tried to stretch my legs farther apart, inch by inch, with the help of my hands on my knees. Then all of a sudden I lost my balance: my legs flipped straight into the air, my back crashed straight down on her futon. The humiliating fall of bone was complete. Though with the defeat came also a sigh of relief, and an opportunity to finally catch my breath.

Resting my body on Ally's silky comforter and pillow was the one unexpected reward from the ordeal. The mild floral fragrance aroused me. It was especially addictive because it was so elusive—here one moment, gone the next. Yet just when I had given up on the fragrance, it snuck back in and hit me again. It was very sexy, the scent. And for a few fleeting moments, many thoughts raced across my mind. I couldn't help thinking what Ally might have been like between those sheets. What it might be like to be next to her; really, really, close to her. But of course that was just in my head. On the surface, I was totally cool and at ease. No girl is going to arouse me with just her sheets alone. I even got up and undid the mess I'd made, by spreading her thick comforter to all corners of the bed.

"Aye, you don't have to do that!" Ally said.

"No, it's okay, I wanted to." But I also wanted to tease her a bit more: "Hey, Ally, didn't your mother ever tell you to make your bed everyday?"

"My mother is not here," she answered back.

"What about Charles?"

"Bof, he doesn't care—as long as I don't interrupt him when he's working and *don't* ask him for a raise at anytime! But the old maid used to argue with me about cleaning my room. She was always complaining to him and fighting with me. Then she goes out and gets drunk herself on Saturday nights."

"Well, at least it's better than raiding Charles's liquor cabinet."

"Who knows? She probably did that, too. She was such a pain in the ahss."

One thing about Ally, she could get a little bitchy at times, or at least lacking in empathy. I guess she hadn't studied enough psychology to realize that, maybe, just maybe, that old timer was feeling a bit threatened by Ally's youth, vigor and intelligence. Even I was intimidated—quite a lot intimidated. And knowing she had adventures I didn't have and talents I didn't possess made me even look up to her. Like her love of skiing, for instance.

Up against the wall next to the inner doors was a blue and white snowboard. I don't know much about skiing, but enough to know that it ain't easy, especially trying to ski on that little board that Ally's got.

"You're supposed to go down those steep Alpine slopes in this thing?"

"Of course."

"Good grief! How do you possibly stay in balance?"

"Easy, you use your arms," Ally said as she started wobbling her arms around like she was skateboarding. She looked quite comical, bending and gyrating her hips; though I bet she must have looked pretty cool while surfing down the slopes—with a pair of shades on and sporting a colorful outfit. And, unlike other girls in pretty outfits, she probably skied like a tiger, too.

"You are a lucky son-of-a-gun, Ally, you know that—you can go to any vacation spot on earth and have a great time. I mean, not only can you do all the water sports when you are down by the sea, but all the winter sports, as well—when you are up in the mountains."

"Yep. I've always always loved mountains and skiing, and both alwayses very very much."

"Al-leee, there you go again! What kind of English is that, a new form of parallel-skiing-ism?"

"You understand me, don't you?"

"Umm...barely!"

"Then it's okay, non?"

"Oh, it's okay all right. You know me, I like your English. And I also like the fact that you are a snowboard surfing beach bum. Let me ask you this, though: do they allow snowboarders to share the same slope with the normal skiers?"

"In France, yes. Individual pursuits are very sacred here. I don't know about America. You people are more...how do you say it, law-conforming?"

"Law-abiding and less chaotic."

"Exactlee! But in France, you know, anything goes!"

"I noticed. Have car, will drive. Whether there is room on the road or not."

"Yep. Have skis, will ski, whether other people are skiing or not."

Boy, was she a fast learner. She could just about repeat everything you had said and throw it back in your face with double the momentum.

Still, despite her confidence, Ally also had a kinder, gentler side. She was one of the officers of the student government at her university, and she worked very hard to organize ski trips to Tignes and La Plagne for her class. Both trips turned out to have huge turnouts as the council raised some much needed money. Of course it was all for future student events. Not one dime of it went to her personally as she was still very much on a tight budget, with the money from Charles as her only source of income. She even had to sell her...well, when I asked her if she liked snowboarding more than regular skiing, she said she liked shredding so much more that she wound up selling her beloved skis just so she could buy a snowboard. *Comme c'est triste!* How sad I felt when I heard that. If ever was there a time I felt like calling up Rossignol and ordering up a complete set of their top of the line skis for a rush delivery, that was it. Sometimes I can really work up quite a sympathy—in one of those flashes where suddenly I realize there are people out there whom I care about.

16 / THE LITTLE GIRLS OF NEW YORK MIGHT KNOW HOW TO HAIL A TAXI BEFORE THEY'VE LEARNED TO WALK...

That afternoon, I tagged along with Ally to take care of a couple of her errands. It would also be the only time during my visit that I took the Métro. So much for telling my friends that I was in and out of Paris without even seeing its indispensable subway system.

The Paris Métro, as some may know, is far less intimidating than New York's. Its trains are quieter, they run more frequently, and there is an overall feeling of an invitation to ride. The promotional poster in the station said it best: *"Le Métro—Votre deuxième voiture!"* The Métro—It's the perfect second car!

But Ally wasn't in full agreement. "If I have a choice, I drive," she said. "Especially if I'm out late at night. The Métro only runs to one o'clock in the morning; much too early for my needs."

"All the more reason you ought to be nice to Charles so you can drive his car."

"I drive it anyway: whenever he isn't home; whenever he's asleep." Alexandra Lachapelle, forever battling for her right to party!

If there is a single greatness to the subways of New York, it's the speed. When the express trains are doing what they're supposed to do, they are peerless in getting you to places in a hurry. The East Side IRTs, despite the frequent congestion, are still the best bangs for the buck. From Wall Street, they zoom straight Uptown in fifteen minutes. How can you beat that kind of convenience? Taxi drivers in Paris can't even go that fast. Most of the trains in Paris, too, are on the slow side: with station stops not so few and far between. In fact, Ally and I were about to get off at the Victor Hugo station when she told me that if I wanted to go one more stop, she could show me where her school was. No problem, I told her. Unlike the one stop on the A train that takes you from 59th Street to 125th, one stop on the Métro is nothing.

Porte Dauphine is the last stop on the No. 2 line. Porte means "the door," and in this case, one of the doors or entrances to the huge park, the Bois de Boulogne. The plaza in front of it's entrance, the Place de Lattre de Tassigny, is sort of the counterpart to New York's Columbus Circle—a grander, cleaner, and quieter counterpart.

"I must say, Ally, that this is quite a lovely place. Even the subway entrance is beautiful. I couldn't think of a single subway station in New York surrounded by shrubs and hedges; not to mention that funky and twisty metallic frame over the entrance."

"Yes, it is niiice, but-tuh, I rush by here every single day, running late to class." Typical no-big-deal response from Alexandra the Late.

Across the way from the train station is an institutional looking building that could have passed for a smaller version of the Pentagon, had it not been for the words Université Paris IX Dauphine painted in blue. Unlike Mr. Lack-of-School-Spirit Vermont, Ally loved her school: "Dauphine is the best of the ten schools in the Paris University system," she said. "It is the only one where admission is based on test scores. It is where everyone wants to go."

"I thought everyone wanted to attend those Grande Écoles, like the Polytechnique."

"Those are very hard to get into, especially the top business school HEC. So a university is more realistic." Ally then told me about this girl she went to high school with whom she had bumped into recently. "Mathilde was a snobby little girl when we were at the lycée together. When I told her I was to attend Dauphine, she said to me: 'Oh, I don't think I can picture myself going to a city universite.' But do you know what happened? She spent two years trying to study for her Grande École, but she was too stupid to pass the tests. So she ended up in Dauphine anyway. When I saw her last, I had to try extra hard to control myself from laughing at her. She had made fun of me for attending Dauphine years ago; and now, it is me who is two years more advanced than her. Isn't that great?"

"Unbelievable, just astounding! Ally, do you ever *not* get the last laugh?"

"Never! I o-ways get the last laugh."

"Yeah, I figured that much."

"I used to o-ways be able to walk to school, too," she said. "It was very convenient. But that was before I decided to move out of my parents' place."

"Does that mean you used to get to class on time?"

"Yes, I o-ways made it to school on time, but not to the classroom. Oh shit, we have to go! Christine is waiting for me. She's already fet-up with me being late all the time."

"That's right, you were late yesterday, too."

"Don't remind me. Everyday I'm a day late."

Maybe it's only my imagination, but the French aren't nearly as hung-up about time as I am. They just don't seem to take deadlines and appointment times seriously. They seem to have a casualness toward promptness, like Californians.

Don't tell the residents of Avenue Foch that they are California-casual; no-sir-ree! In fact, I don't think there's another street in Paris quite like Foch in its formality. It is straight, wide, and lined with rows of trees—all leading up to the Arc de Triomphe in the yonder. Another feature of Foch is that it's probably got the widest sidewalks in Paris—the Champs-Elysée without the stores and offices and traffic, if you will. Just solid old buildings in impeccable shape, combining the grandeur of Fifth Avenue with the charm of the townhouses right off it.

Halfway up Foch, we turned off to a street where Ally's half-sister Christine had her law office. Ally was dropping off some documents for her friend Renée, whose father wanted some advice on a workman's compensation case. He felt he deserved a larger disability settlement than what he was originally offered.

"Christine should be able to get him more money," Ally said. "She doesn't normally do this type of work, but she's very good."

"So this is more a favor to your friend?"

"Yep. Christine has lots of business. She works like crazy. But since contract is one of her areas, I told my friend maybe she could help."

While waiting for Ally outside, I surveyed the area around Avenue Raymond Poincaré a bit. The scene was certainly consumer driven. Smart little boutiques, jewelers, baby clothiers, and home furnishing stores—including the likes of Laura Ashley. Even the most ideological people in the world can fall in love with consumption. Could've sworn I had seen a Laura Ashley shop on Friday as well, on the way to the movies. Yes, the French could get into that Victorian shit, too. Who knows, give them ten more years and they might even start naming their yuppie babies Ashley, just like their New York counterparts.

A while later, Ally reappeared. As we walked toward the Victor Hugo Métro, Ally suggested that instead of going to Les Halles, where she had to exchange a gift, we could just hang around out here. Seeing there were plenty of interesting little things all around, I agreed.

One major action center that you will inevitably notice in your walks in Paris are the ubiquitous Salon de Coiffeurs. Why are there so many coiffures was the question I put to Ally.

"Pourquoi est-ce-que Paris a tant de coiffeurs?"

"It's a tradition," she said. "Many people start going to hairdressers regularly as early teens. My mother used to go two to three times a week. She used to quote Alexandre to my father and say: one has only one head and one has to live for it!"

"Who is Alexandre?"

"He is the Paul Bocuse of hairstyling."

"Who is Paul Bocuse?"

"You don't know Paul Bocuse? He is very famous—the Pierre Cardin of cooking...now don't tell me you don't—"

"I know, Ally, I know! Everyone knows who ol' Pierre is. His key chains and wallets are only as much a part of New York's sidewalks as frozen spit."

"Huhhhh, Markkuh—you're *hor-riiib-le!*"

"Yeah, but not as horrible as piss vapors."

All kidding aside, though, Ally told me coiffeuring is big business in France, and the best stylists are even pedestaled to national treasure status. "Haute cuisine, haute couture, and haute coiffeur." Yes, even the coiffeurs are classified into groups based on price. How strange, one of the vainest pursuits of humanity is also done in France with a form of regulatory equality. Not only are the grand dames and bourgeoisie allowed coiffeurs, but it is available to all the citizenry. Egalité indeed!

"*Et toi*, Ally? Do you go to a hairdresser?"

"Bof! Who is going to pay for it? All I do is, first, I wash and shampoo, then I turn my hair upside down in front of my fan, brush, style and go. *Voilà c'est tout!* As you like to say, Mark: no-beeg-deel!"

Yeah, wished dear ol' Lisa was like that. My mother used to take her to one of them fancy schmancy spas south of Orange County and spend the whole day there. The plant-oil body massage, the facial treatment and the rest of that herbal-infested crap. No wonder they call it the "New" Age. For if they had told everyone the truth: that it's all age old remedies that you can get in India for practically nothing, then how could they ever justify all the money they are charging? And all the fortune they are making?

As for me, I could, in less than an hour, get my hair cut, my nails chopped, my body showered, shaved, dressed and ready to go. No sweat. No small fortune. And I'm not even a real man. As a matter of fact, I don't even know if I want to be a real man anymore. When I was growing up I did; but now? Save it! What's more, if I should be forced at gun point to choose between being a real big-man-on-campus or a moisturizing lotion-bearing fruitcake, I might even have to think about it. The wrinkles on my forehead might have to think about it; the cracking skin on the balls of my feet might have to think about it.

If you should think about making it to Paris, and succeed, and have some spare time left between your relentless museum hopping and what-not, then do take a stroll through the Sixteenth Arrondisement as me and Ally did that afternoon—particularly around the Place Victor Hugo—where there is an abundance of local color and neighborhood liveliness. The shops in the area are also first class. Many of the finest designers names have branches in the *Seizième*, to serve a predominately Parisian clientele. Perhaps the last thing a regular Parisian wants is to be seen shopping at a Givenchy or a Guy Laroche boutique on the Right Bank and bump their rumps with the foreign tourist set.

However, unlike those tony shops of New York, you don't need a million francs on hand to shop till you stop. There are no stuffy stores that tell you to please ring the door bell for service. In fact, many of the stores in the Sixteenth are a smart shopper's paradise. Top-quality designer fashions are sold in attractive clothing shops at second-hand prices. Ally even had friends who used to check those shops for new arrivals of "pre-owned" designer clothes; many of the outfits virtually new, worn by the rich and famous for a gala or two and then let go.

On one of the rare occasions I felt confident to give a fashion opinion, I said: "Ally, if I were a girl and hated to pay retail? I'd rather pick out a dress that is slightly used for half the price than a new overstocked item that is also on sale at half off. I just don't have the fashion sense to decide whether the new item is being marked down due to bad styling or color or whatever. At least with the used, there is a sense that whoever bought it new felt it was stylish enough to warrant the full retail price for it, you know what I mean?"

"Yes and no," she answered. "Just because someone has money, doesn't mean she will have my taste. So nobody but me will decide what's good for me."

"Nobody except your friends, right?" I teased.

On Rue de la Pompe, across the streets from some of the second-hand shops, is Lycée Jason de Sailly. "This is where my sister will be graduating soon," Ally said.

"They haven't kicked her out yet?"

"Oh, no, this is a city school. It's different."

"Wait a minute, you have a sister still in high school?"

"What do you mean *still*?" Ally gave me a frowning look.

"I...it's like you said: you're already a working girl!"

"But I skipped almost two years, and she is almost ready to graduate from her lycée."

"Oh yeah, right, forgive me, pardon *moi*!" Because Ally seemed to know so much, I sometimes mistake her for being around my age. But she's still quite young; as well as easily distracted, and short-tempered, and quick on the defensive, and this and that. Yet for some strange reason, I didn't mind at all her being her imperfect self.

"So, Ally, I take it your sister isn't quite as smart as you?" I decided I had to make her feel better.

"She studies hard, but she worries too much. 'Oh, Alex, I am worried about taking the Baccalauréat. I fear I am not going to do well on the exams.' 'You must!' I told her. 'You must at least get into Dauphine. Otherwise how can I tell you who the best teachers are!"

"Alexandra Lachapelle, I like the way you think!"

You know that classic line from *The Graduate*, "Plastics!" Well, the magic word that afternoon was rattan! It was rattan galore out on the sidewalk terrace of Dupré, all rattan except for the marble tabletop. Not bad those unrottenable chairs, lighter than plastic and waterproof.

So, on my third day in Paris, I was finally ready to do what many visitors must have done the moment they arrived—to sit at an outdoor café and watch the world of Ally's feet leaping out of her shoes. For those of you who think that Paris smelled more of coffee beans than fresh air, a rare pair of sexy motionless feet resting in a tea salon should add to the odorous mix. After we ordered some teas along with macaroons and *financiers*, I continued to delve into my sudden streak of foot-fetishness.

"More than a few girls have lousy-looking feet," I said. "Just totally bent out of shape."

"My feet are fine," Ally said. "I hardly wear heels."

"That'll do it to you Europeans every time, squashing your feet into those sexy little heels that you could barely even stand in, let alone walk in. Y'all waitin' for Prince Charming to come 'n sweep you off your feet?"

"What about you Americans?" she countered. "You wear your sneakers with business suits. Do you know how ridiculous it looks, especially for men?"

"Well, Ally, you're the one who likes California. A friend of mine in Silicon Valley, forget about it! It's like, shorts and tee-shirts eight days a week!"

"You will never see that in Paris, not in a thousand years."

"Well, Paris is at the other extreme. You guys don't even buy jogging shoes for jogging."

"Why should people have more than one pair of sneakers?"

"If that. Tell me, Alexandra, do any of you French kids attend gym classes in your dress shoes?"

"Aw, com'on. Don't be ridiculous!" Ally detested. "But you know, once I wore my friend's cowboy boots to school, and I got into big trouble with the nuns. That was when I was still at the Couvent. See that church on the left near the intersection, *that* was my old school—Couvent du Sacré Coeur. It is much smaller than the lycée we just passed."

"Is that because they had kicked out all their pupils?"

"Everyone. Especially me!"

"What'y'do that was so bad?"

"Absolutely nothing. They had an official dress code, with uniforms and everything, but I felt like wearing bluejeans. Some other times, I was also late to class. The nuns would then call my parents in, and make me go to school on Wednesday afternoon to do manual labor. Wednesday is when the kids have no school."

"So while your friends went to Wednesday afternoon matinees, you went to detention."

"Exactlee. Those nuns were always picking on me—making me go every Wednesday. Can you believe it? Do you know the movie *Breakfast Club*? I was easily a member for life."

"A lifetime member. Good one, Ally. And I thought you were just a member of the coffee-break club."

"So finally, I was sooo fet-up I just stopped showing up on Wednesdays. That was when they told my parents I had to go. I was too big a disturbance."

"They didn't even want you to wash the ash on Wednesdays, huh?"

"Not any more. But I tried...and tried."

"And you still couldn't get to the church on time! Were your parents angry?"

"Not too much. They are not the religious types."

"Then why'd they send you there?"

"Because you're supposed to get a better education there. But I was getting old enough to go to a lycée. I was even supposed to go to this one around the corner, Jason de Sailly. But it was full, so I went to La Fontaine instead. It was a little far, but still much better than that jail."

"Yeah, we've all gone through our shares of jailhouses while growing up."

"But this one was bad!"

"Ally, I was locked in boarding school in the middle of nowhere for a...well, luckily for me, not very long; but it could have easily been four full years out of my life, my childhood. Edwin, my roommate did it, and look what happened to him. They molded his life irreversibly."

"Is your school just like those portrayed in the movies?"

"Sometimes. But for me it was worse, like going to college without the freedom. In fact, we all got nailed the first week we got there." I went on and told Ally this story of how, one night, Edwin managed to get a group of pupils in our corridor to sneak out after we had gone to bed already. It was supposed to be some sort of a secret circle's initiation dare. So that night, after lights out, we all tip-toed out of the dormitory to a nearby lake. Everyone then dove into the water, took a quick swim, and ran back to our beds. The whole thing couldn't have taken more than fifteen minutes. But apparently, we left enough hints all over that, shortly after, one of the masters came into each of our rooms and pulled us out of bed. My phony snoring didn't help. What he did was, he came right up to my bed, then slowly pulled out one of my arms, and began to suddenly take my pulse. The remarkable wickedness of that sneaky bastard! Naturally, my heart was still pounding like crazy from all the running and swimming moments ago, not to mention I was also scared shitless. Man, that bastard was so good at pulse taking that not a single one of us alluded him; except for Edwin. Luckily for him nobody ratted. He was really a lucky stiff, that Edwin. One other time, I found him in the altar area just before chapel—hammering away on the school organ with "She's a Rainbow." But when the rector came in, he was merely disturbed but not furious: "Kindly get down from there, young man, if you please." For Christ's sake, if it had been any of us, it would've been our heads. But no, not Edwin. Things like that happened to him all the time; he was always getting away with borderline infractions. What I did not realize back then was that his father was on the Board of Trustees of the school, and his family had donated loads and loads of money to them. In fairness, though, Edwin wasn't the kind of guy you wished ill-will upon, even in those days, when we had our share of differences. He had always been exceedingly generous and managed to spread things around. Boy, when I went to the tuck shop with him, it was always "Take whatever candies you want and it's on me." Of course he didn't pay for it, the candylady merely took care of the bill in another way. Fortunately for me, I was not a junk food junkie; otherwise, I would have been enslaved to his every beck and call. In fact, I had always stood up to him. Nearly came to blows, too. The main reason we didn't get along at the outset was because of his loud music playing next door. And that he didn't want to switch rooms with me so I could be at the end of the corridor with at least one quiet wall to lean upon. As a result, I was constantly finding myself in the library, the main reason I did really well in school that term. I was very anti-social as a child; I was such a damn loner it was pathetic. I still am, in many ways; just more socialized and less temperamental. A better actor, too. A *much* better actor. Though I must say my fascination with Paris was genuine, one of boundless enthusiasm.

"You know, Ally, while our conception of a Paris café is one situated on the Left Bank, with old writers sipping espressos and claiming they know Sartre, and older-still waiters bragging that they had *personally* known Camus and Hemingway, this setting is nevertheless just as delightful."

"Of course it is! Me, Sophie and others, we come here for lunch all the time. You are experiencing real Paris here. Closeup, you have people going about their business, and zooming far away, umm...."

"No, wide-angle-ly, Ally; from an extreme long shot, you have the Ally-usive Eiffel Tower looming across the river, the tower which Superman saved from terrorist bombs."

"And rescued Lois Lane."

"Very good, Ally. But then again, if you ever wanted *me* to rescue *you* from the Tower, you'd first have to go up there."

"No, I'm sorry," she laughed mockingly, "*You* would first have to be Superman."

I was trying to bust her chops, she ended up beating mine.

"Alexa, *c'est toi*?" It was a young French girl carrying some fancy shopping bags.

"Eh, Isa, salut! Quel surprise! Comment vas-tu?"

"Ça va. Et toi? I have not seen you in months!"

"Haven't been around the house!" Ally shrugged. She'd just met a friend. and quite a young one at that. Even younger was the little girl who was tagging along.

"Mark, this is Isabelle, a good friend of my sister's, and that's her little sister Charlotte."

"Enchanted to meet you both," I said. "Ally, should I round up a couple more unsuspecting chairs?"

"Don't see why not. Isa, would you like to join us?"

"Okay."

"*Genial*!" Love the way Ally says genial, with her head and lips in full motion.

We made room for the girls then squeezed them in. Charlotte, the younger one, sat next to me. Quite a little darling she was, decked out in an embroidered shirt and skirt. Her hair was short and a bit messy, but she had just the liveliest set of eyes. She kept making faces at me and trying to smell me out from the corner of her eyes. Yet she wasn't shy or anything. She had a bag of candies with her and wasted no time in asking me if I wanted to buy some: *"Voulez-vous acheter un bonbon?"*

"Combien ça coûte?"

"Un franc, monsieur."

"Peut-être après le thé." Maybe later, I told her.

Isabelle and Charlotte came a calling from the same boulevard we had just traversed—la boulevard de Window Shopping. Only they had bought bags full of goodies from the other side of the window glass. Charlotte was already trying on a pair of red canvas sneakers.

"Quelle impatiente!" yelled her older sister, who then told Charlotte that she was going to get them all dirty before she'd even get a chance to wear them. Charlotte just smiled and took a bite from my macaroon.

When it was time for Isabelle to order her food, she told Charlotte she'd get her a hot chocolate and a broiche. But Charlotte didn't want any of that: *"Je voudrais une Glace Etoile."*

"Ooh là là, you already had ice cream yesterday."

"Ça fait rien!" So what, said Charlotte.

Isabelle was rather nice about it, though, and honored her little sister's request. Maybe because me and Ally were sitting there next to them. Meanwhile, the terrace was beginning to crowd up. There was a couple next to us ripping apart the biggest palmier I'd ever seen; *butterflies*, I call them. After that, they began devouring this chocolate mousse-like concoction. The guy told me it was called the *Marquise au Chocolat*. It looked real enticing; and due to the fact that the sisters had already eaten what me and Ally had ordered, more sweets seemed to be in the cards. So when the waiter came around again, I gave him the word: *"Garçon, je vais prendre une... Marquise au Chocolat!"* Charlotte just about flipped when she heard that. She was looking at me with her mouth wide open in disbelief, as if I was competing with her for the title of dessert king. Instinctively, I looked back at her and matched her with an equally wide open mouth, in equally wide amazement. Poor girl, she thought she only had her skinny sister to contend with!

While Charlotte and I were entangled in mutual amusement, Isabelle was engaged in a one-way denouncement. She was telling Ally of all the cramming she had been doing while preparing for the Baccalauréat. "I'm not even going to go out tonight," she said. "Just a little shopping today and maybe a little tennis in the park tomorrow to dispense some frustrations."

The *Baccalauréat*, for those who are unfamiliar, is an all encompassing series of exams that all French high school students must take if they want to get into a university. The two weeks in June are seen as reign of terror weeks for lycéens across France as they prepare for it. The tests are similar to the Achievement Tests we have to take in high school, with students pre-selecting the areas they wanted to concentrate on. The difference being that the French version take days instead of hours, and are therefore much more in-depth and strenuous. For example, the English test, which is becoming extremely popular, which Ally was supposed to help her sister with that weekend. There are three written parts to the English tests, including short answers and a three-hundred-word essay. On top of that, there is a twenty-minute oral exam, on which you will be judged on useful English expressions, clarity of thought, and originality of ideas, as well as your understanding of the culture. Imagine, all that just for a foreign language. For Christ's sake, some of us don't even test English in such depth as a *first* language!

On that day, however, Isabelle was not as concerned about English as she was about the philosophy exams, which was scheduled to be given on the first test date and required lots of writing. "I am stuffed to my neck with philosophers," she said with disgust. "Anybody care to chop my head off my neck and free me from existentialism?"

"To free you from *existence*," Ally corrected her matter-of-factly, with the quiet assurance of an expert. But Ally being Ally, would never let go of an occasion till she has given it her own spin. "For my Bac, I took category C: mathematics and physical sciences; it is the most challenging category. In the more scientific schools like Louis-Le-Grand, almost everyone takes the C category." Then she lowered her voice, turned toward me and said with a smirk on her face: "But in those snobby girl schools like Lübeck or La Tour, that is where Isa goes, most of the girls take either the A or the B category; which is mostly languages and social sciences."

"But Ally, what's wrong with being artistically minded?"

"Nothing is wrong; only that the students who take the C's also score the highest in literature and economics. So selecting A is really a cop-out, my sister is taking the A exam as well."

"Hey Ally, not everyone aspires to be a nuclear physicist; right Charlotte?"

"Ça c'est sûr!" she agreed.

"Which Bac are you going to take, Charlotte, when you grow up? A, B, C, D, or E?"

"ABC, Do-Re-Mi."

Knew I had heard of that melody somewhere, just unable to pinpoint where.

It was a lovely tea time. My Earl Grey was great, Ally's orange pekoe was beau, Isabelle's almond financiers were addicting, and most of all, my Marquise au Chocolat lived up to its looks—an island of dark, orange-flavored chocolate surrounded by a light sea of cream. It was even better than that Pear Charlotte I had at that Left Bank bistro on Friday. *"Dites, Charlotte, vous-savez la Poire Charlotte?"*

"Hah!" That was when Charlotte gave me that big astounded look again, this time with a hand over her shocked and opened mouth.

"C'est delicieux, la Charlotte aux Poire." I continued.

"Meilleur que ma Glace Etoile?" Better than my ice cream, she said.

I thought for a moment and decided to yield. "Nope, nothing can beat your colorful ice cream, dear Charlotte. Your ice cream is the best!" Indeed it was quite impressive, her Glace Etoile, little scoops of ice cream forming a star-like shape. A little more than a scoop but less than pint—Shakespeare!

By the way, when little kids are in a mood for ice cream, you might as well just let them have it. In fact, it's almost un-American to deny the little kids their ice cream—especially during the era of pre-budget and trade deficits Americana, where kids of Main Street, USA would gather up and head for that neighborhood ice cream parlor. You'd take a girl there and buy her a big root beer float or something, sitting in one of them ripped vinyl booths with ripped vinyl seats and a table side juke box to boot. The conversation? Well, just talking about all the different flavors of ice cream at the counter, or that afternoon's baseball game. No problems, no schools, just worry-free bliss. That's life in paradise for ya. I'm starting to get sentimental again, but I get crazy when my mind wanders out there. I'm not even twenty-seven and I'm already missing the good old days. Wait till when I'm fifty-four.

While it appeared doubtful that Ally and Charlotte would ever reach maturity, Isabelle was clearly on her way. *Tres raffiné* in that still pose of hers. Why, she could pass for Charlotte's mother if it weren't for her school-girl looks. Oh, she was a dandy: one leg over the other, one arm folded in front, the other arm supporting a cigarette, her Gauloise. She'd light one up and hold it so far toward the filter end that you'd think it was about to fall off her finger tips. She also had a tendency to rest her cigarette really high and upward—right beside her ear. It was so dangerously close to her hair that one mishap and it'd be liar, liar and hair on fire.

Still, soon as a teenager begins to chirp, her silent refinements are suddenly tossed out the window. In turn, she becomes the very model of a gossipy school girl, yakking away at everything in sight. *Ce type* this, *ce genre* that, a good *folie* here, a bad *folie* there. That was Isabelle all right, as she showed Ally a striped jersey she had just bought.

"*C'est chic!* It would go nicely with your kilt," Ally said, "*mais... trop cher pour moi*!"

"Isn't it a bit too prim and proper as well?" I said.

"Absolutely. *Mon dieux*, can you imagine me in a kilt?" Ally shook her head and laughed. "It looks so ridiculous. My mother wears it sometimes, but it is *definitely* not me." Then Ally leaned close to me again in that ready to dish some dirt mode and said, "Do you want to know what we call Isabelle, with her Marks and Spencer kilt and her Agnès B. jersey, her Chevignon jacket and her Upla school bag?"

"A French teenager?" I said.

"No, we call that style *BCBG.*"

"BCBG? Sounds like a punk-rock club on the Bowery."

"Oh, no, I'm afraid this is completely opposite of punk rock," Ally said. "It stands for *Bon Chic Bon Genre*, it's a style."

"You mean like Jewish American Princesses from Long Island, with their Gucci Gucci Guccis?"

"No, BCBG is less Italian and more English; and American, too, like your preppie kids."

"But Ally, all the preppies I know ain't got no clothes—take Edwin, he doesn't even have socks!" It was now my turn to crack up. Parisiennes! Just when you think being French meant Chanel, St. Laurent, and Christian Dior, out of the hat comes Agnès BCBG, le style country and cosy! Only their beat up loafers aren't so beat up, and old sweaters aren't so old and oversized.

But that was not the end of it. While there weren't many JAPs in Paris, there was a more exclusive BCBG subset which Ally called the NAPS. "It stands for Neuilly, Auteuil, and Passy, the *quartiers* around here. They are very stuck up."

"Are you a NAP, Alexandra?"

"I used to be. Now I share camaraderie with my fellow bankrupt slaves in Saint-Germain."

"Poor Ally, from BCBG to *BEAT*."

"Don't worry, Mark. I'll manage. No complaints." Her eyes were rolling now: "So what if my sister dresses better than me? Although I can't afford Chevignon and Agnès B.; I can still have my 501's and my Gap 'T'."

"That's the spirit. Just like a California girl!"

"Exactlee! But no heavy metal tee-shirts and tattoos. Just lots and lots of 501s. *On n'a jamais trop de Levi's!*"

Yes, we can never have enough Levi's. But I think me and my hyperactive bladder'll take zippers over button flys, thank you very much. You know what else I noticed? Once I knew what to look for on the fashion front, I began spotting hundreds of Bon Chic Bon Genre Nappies all around me: the café crowd, the sidewalkers, the whole scene—everybody had on at least one piece of clothing that was sort of BCBGish, including me. As a matter of fact, the atmosphere in that neighborhood sort of reminded me of the after-school hours in Carnegie Hill, around upper Madison Avenue. Many of the Parisians passing by could just as easily pass for those proper Upper East Side parents: taking their kids home from school, or onward to their music and dance classes, French lessons, etc.. The difference being that those Parisian brats possessed the added toy of Japanese motor scooters. Here's to waltzing down the Avenue Georges Handel in their Yamahas. Banzai!

On the subject of music, Charlotte delighted me by engaging us in a bit of song and dance ourselves; mostly because we didn't know what else to do with ourselves whilst Ally and Isabelle were gossiping away. It all started when Charlotte picked up her sister's teacup with both hands, simultaneously looking at me and taking a sip. From the expression on her face, it was not teaspoon licking good.

"What's the matter, Charlotte, don't like your sister's tea?"

"Tea, I drink, with jam and bread, that will bring us back to doe. Doe a deer a—"

Not losing a beat, I followed right up: *"And when you know the notes to sing, you can sing 'most any-thing."* Boy, did that put Charlotte to a screeching halt. She was stunned, her mouth wide open once again. I wasn't exactly sure if it was due to my not knowing the next verse or that I even knew any words at all. I think it was the latter. She was in disbelief: once more, she had met her match!

Ally and Isabelle turned around. "Oh, *The Sound of Music* again," Isa said almost embarrassingly. "She and her friends just recently got it on video. They have been singing it ever since."

I wasn't sure how cute the little ones in *The Sound of Music* were in real life, but Charlotte was right up there, especially when she began hassling me again to buy something from her.

"Achete une photo?" she said as she pulled out four mug shots of hers taken a bit earlier.

"Combien?" I asked.

"Cinq franc."

"Five Francs? How much did it cost you?"

"Fifteen for four."

What a smart cookie, she stood to make more than a franc's profit from me. "Tell you what, Charlotte: throw in some bonbons and it's a deal."

"Ça marche. You are a very *good* negotiator?"

"Only for things I like." I said in a snap.

The picture I got was a very funny shot of Charlotte and Isabelle squeezed into an instant photo booth. Isabelle was a bit embarrassed at the photo: "Charlotte is so impatient, she bought a vest and she had to put it on to see how it looked on her."

"Oh yeah, where did the vest go?"

"Ask my sister. May I wear it now?"

"Oor-là-là, the price tag is still on it!"

"Eh, alors!" Charlotte pleaded.

Isabelle finally caved in. But not before she swung the bag at Charlotte's chest and told her to put it on herself.

Charlotte then placed the bag on her lap, and opened it up real nice and slow, as if she had no idea as to what's inside. What a precious little child.

Ally was cracking up too, upon seeing the store name on the shopping bag. "Chec-kit out, she boat something from SAP, it is sooo BCBG, that store."

"Charlotte, are you becoming a BCBG girl?" I asked.

She shook her head innocently.

I didn't think so, either. "Why, with that floral vest on, you can almost pass for a hippie, just like me. Simply make a few rips in your skirt and grow your hair real long," I then laid my hand on Charlotte's hair and rubbed it around a bit.

"Do you like my hair?" she asked slowly.

"Yeah-ss."

"But do you like my sister's hair more because it is longer?"

"Not necessarily."

"But look, I can make my hair to be just like hers." Charlotte then took a handful of hair from the top of her head and tied it with an elastic. "*Voilà*!"

It was pretty comical. What Charlotte was trying to do was to copy her sister's trendy hair style of having her hair wrapped in a thick ponytail all the way at the top, then layering it over the rest of her hair. However, Charlotte couldn't quite duplicate the feat.

She had so little hair on top that it stuck straight up—looking like the arrow on a World War I Kaiser helmet. She kept her hair like that as we were walking on the street as well. Though she finally took the rubber band off when I started dribbling my hand on her vertical ponytail to get her to hurry up.

By the way, after we had desserts, Isabelle talked Ally into going to some store further on down in Passy, close to where she and Charlotte lived, where Ally used to live. So Charlotte and I, being powerless followers, just sort of tagged along behind them. We actually fell pretty far behind, mostly due to Charlotte's singing and clowning around.

Instead of using the walkpath, Charlotte had to be right along the curb, on that stretch of stones along the edge of the sidewalk. And, instead of walking, Charlotte was treating that narrow stretch like a balance beam. You should've seen her trying to be like Olga Korbut, with her arms wobbling around like a drunken gymnast. She didn't do any cartwheels or anything, but she did take a good many leaps and turns. Little kids do the darnedest things; there's no doubt about it!

Surplus de Passy, in the heart of the Rue de Passy shopping district, was the shop we wound up in. Busy and crowded and catering to the younger, more price-conscious Parisiennes, it sold an eclectic mix of old and new. The closest resemblance to a store that came to mind would be something similar to the Antique & Unique Boutique down in the Village. Surplus was quite a fun store to shop in, with lots of cloth and lots of jazzy cliq-claques and accessories. They also had some things for moi-men, which came in handy as well. As it turned out, it was the only store in Paris where I bought some stuff for myself.

The first purchase I made was of some tee-shirts with the words "JE SUIS FOUS DE PARIS" written in fancy, artistic calligraphy. Then I picked out some pastelish ties in the pattern of those tri-color French flags, to celebrate the 200th year of the French Revolution. I planned to give one of them to Edwin. Every now and then, he likes to put on a club tie while he's on a boat, and I think the French flag looks just as breezy and colorful as one of them jobs from the Centre Island Yacht Club.

The final batch of merchandise I bought was a bunch of boxer shorts, with at least one going to my secretary Connie as a practically wearable joke. I bought the boxers mostly for their design, which was about as subtle as *Take my knife, please!* Let me explain: instead of flag-waving ties commemorating the Bicentennial of the French Revolution, the designers of those boxer shorts had a more erotic tie in mind. What they did was, they put a print of a guillotine right around the, how do you call it—the opening? The opening slit of the boxer shorts where your prick pops out; where the head of the penis pisses on the heads of the *ancien régime.* I mean, that guillotine was right smack on your hard-on, right where it counts, right where it cuts!

By the time I rejoined Ally, she was in the middle of deciding on a gift for her friend Sophie, whose birthday was to be the day after. It came down to either a wide, silver-buckled belt or a pair of spandex shorts, with them two-toned color trims along the sides to make the thighs look thinner. Ally decided on the shorts; one, they were less costly, and two, they would get Sophie off her ass. Or was it to get some ass off of Sophie? Women are the same the world over. If you have a product that would make them appear thinner, you're guaranteed a fat and happy profit.

Same goes for decorating a woman's body. We were over at the jewelry counter as Ally had her attention focused on a set of funky earrings. They were unusual in that there were silver balls attached to the clips, and attached to the silver balls were a pair of black aeroplanes made from a nerf-like material. Nerf earrings—the stuff I used to play basketball with in my room as a kid while listening to Marv Albert on the radio.

"Do you think they look good on me," Ally asked while looking in a mirror.

"They're all right, I guess, This is the first time I've ever seen them, though."

"Yep, me too. I love earrings."

"They go nicely with your ears," I said, snapping my fingers at one of the aeroplanes and watching it vacillate in the air. Besides having a great nose, Ally has cute little ears, too, especially if you compare them with the big ears of yours truly. But at least I have amazing hearing—a small consolation for taking after Mr. Spock.

It was interesting watching Ally shop. *"C'est vulgaire!"* She said of an outfit she didn't like, the one with them fancy frilly stitchings down around the neck. "And this one over here, with the huge red circles—that's too goofy looking!" Yet rolling off the cuff of her opinionated remarks was that of an educated shopper. I think I've probably told you that she's got quite an eye for detail. She said she wanted to get some plain white tee-shirts, simple enough. But as much as she hoped to buy them from the pre-packaged multi-packs, she did not find their quality to her liking. "They are not thick enough," she said, "You can almost see through them."

"But undershirts aren't supposed to be too tightly woven," I said, not to mention that a little bit of see throughness ain't gonna hurt anyone. "How about in some other colors, then?"

"No, I need them in white, to wear under my jacket. I prefer not to have to pay higher prices, but if they don't have any thick ones in three packs, then I have no choice but to pay more. That is one thing they have in California: quality white tee-shirts that are cheap."

"Hurray for Hollywood! That's because they're all glowed out in neon already, them surfing peons."

"No, you're wrong; most excellently wrong as usual."

Boy, oh boy, the personalities I had to deal with. So what a relief it was when Ally finally found some tee-shirts she liked. They were more expensive and hung on a rack. But it was worth it, she said, as she compared its texture and thickness to the underwear kind. And, rehearsing for a future in marketing, Ally also asked about the percentage of shrinkage. She then took a bunch that seemed large enough to fit her and scrutinized the hell out of them: rejecting some with bad stitching and others for being slightly off white. Why, she was pickier with the simplest, boringest white tee than Coco Chanel was with her knitted suits. If Ally hadn't looked so mesmerizing the way she went about her inspections, I would have been annoyed and embarrassed, like going shopping with a finicky grandmother. Instead, I loved every moment of her dilemma and tribulations.

Our due diligence was suddenly broken up by Isabelle's loud interruption: "Alexa, *regarde*! This is perfect for you."

"Ah, J'adore ça!" Ally said excitedly.

It was a navy varsity-styled baseball jacket with white leathery arms. But I knew she liked it because it had a big letter "A" in front.

"Oh, parfait! C'est combien?"

"Trois cent francs. Cette une excellent occasion!" Only three hundred francs, said Isa, a bargain.

"Oh, non. C'est trop cher." It may be too expensive, Ally said sadly. But she tried it on anyway. A tad long on the sleeves, otherwise just right. She walked over to the mirror, posed a few poses, then laid her hands behind her head and shut her eyes. When the eyes opened moments later, she had made up her mind. "I'm going to *faire une folie*," she said, letting go of her arms and releasing them into the air. In a matter of seconds, the drama was over.

"This jacket is *per*fect," she said. "I have an older red one which I paid only a hundred francs for at a flea market. But it's worn out already. So I think it's time for a new one. This one is in such good condition. I like the dark blue color too, and that letter A in front."

"What does the "A" stand for?"

"For exceptional! Who cares what it was. From now on it stands for Alexandra!" She was happy, I could tell. "So what do you think, Mark, does this meet your approval? I'm relying on your knowledge of athletic style."

"*C'est exceptionnel! Marveilleux! Fantastique! Magnifique! Sensationnel*!" Pretty boastful adjectives for someone who has never owned a varsity team jacket in his life!

Boy that Ally, was she something else or what? After taking her sweet-ass time being as meticulous as hell over some cheap old tee-shirts, she turned around and bought a jacket that cost a lot more in a split impulsive second. She had indeed made a folie, but like all folies, the heart won over the mind; and the wallet too.

"I make too many folies," Ally said. "Last week, I just had to get this *petite robe noire*, a little black dress. It was an unbelievable fit, with the thinnest black strings over the shoulder."

"Well, one folie a week, keeps the bank account at peak." I don't know, it just seemed like a thing to say.

It was almost time to say good-bye to Charlotte and Isa, my two lovely natives from the neighborhood. Charlotte was clearly my favorite. She was still at her tomboy stage, still eager to drag her sister to the playgrounds in the Jardin du Ranelagh. Ally and I were going to take a taxi back because she was late already, otherwise I wouldn't have minded going into the park with them. Ally said

Ranelagh was her favorite little park, too, "Less crowded than the Jardin du Luxembourg we passed yesterday, with almost no tourists and mostly local people."

"You mean it's NAP central, USA?"

"Exactlee! Playing hide and seek from their nannies; *nou-nous*, we call them."

And I thought my childhood of playing home run derby was exciting—the way I could uppercut a curveball!

As Ally and Isa were saying good bye, which as usual took forever, Charlotte took my hand and walked me to the taxi stand. As we waited for a cab, she rattled off her favorite little number from *Annie*, "Tomorrow, tomorrow, I love ya, tomorrow, you're only a day a way." Boy did she sing that one good. Of course, I then had to blab back with "Let the sun shine, let the sun shine in, the sun...." It's from *Hair*, I told her, *my* favorite movie musical.

"I do not know *Hair*."

"Well, it ain't exactly *Annie* or the *Sound of Music*. You're still young, Charlotte. Your proper parents probably aren't ready to let you watch a bunch of naked dancing American hippies just yet. But give it a couple more years."

"Then you will come back in a couple more years?"

"Sure I will; but in the mean time, I'll just say adios amigo!"

"So long, farewell, auf wiedersehn, adieu," Charlotte was up at it again.

"Adios, au revoir, and *auf wiedersehn,"* I sang back à la Lawrence Welk.

Boy, was I going to miss her spontaneity.

...BUT THE LITTLE GIRLS OF PARIS KNOW HOW TO SAY "CHANEL" *BEFORE* THEY EVEN HAVE TEETH!

SEVENTEEN

After getting back to the house, Charles asked me to help him move some boxes around. Heavy cartons, actually, of old manuscripts and letters. The ones he had already gone through were taken out of the library, and the ones still covered in dust were brought out from the card room. Besides being a banker, and indeed throughout his life, Charles has acted as a repository of sorts for other people's correspondence. Some gave their letters and records to Charles because they wished not for their papers to end up as part of a library research collection. There had even been instances where they had asked Charles to compete with the libraries and archives for outstanding material. In most cases, however, there was little need for that. While Charles's circle knew of, and possibly even controlled some of the famous; they themselves weren't celebrities. To Charles, more important than fame was the individual's eccentricity, and the peculiarities of his psychological makeup. Perhaps it was the psychoanalyst in him. Once he had asked me when I was little: "If Uncle Charles could give you one special gift: that of Superman's vision or super duper hearing, which would you choose?" Took me about a second to answer that one. To see naked girls, of course! But now I'm not so sure. For if I'm able hear all the secret dealings going on in this world, I'd be rich enough to *buy* Superman!

"Uncle Charles, to see like Superman or to hear like the Bionic Woman?"

Charles smiled for a moment. He then pointed at me and said: "If I could get into your head and know what you are thinking, then I could conceivably be Super *and* Bionic."

Or be none of the above if animals overrun this planet, like they had overrun that room.

The card room we were in was located next to the salon. As you know, the salon was the formal reception room centered in between the entrance vestibule and the back garden. It was also flanked by the library to the right and the card room through the doors to the left. Quite symmetrical was the whole layout of the house, aided by the fact that all the rooms were relatively large, making them easier to keep track and easier to manage—certainly more manageable than a dark and twisty two-hundred-year-old chateau/museum/warehouse. Unless, that is, if you happened to be looking for a game in the two-hundred-year-old card room.

My first glimpse of that room was not at all fun and games but rather that of an old bedroom. Well, it had a bed, and a huge one at that—fit for a palace in both size and decor. Set against the back wall and facing the garden, it stood almost like a monument, framed by wooden posts and a canopied top. As for the bed's interior, it was covered with an orientalesque patterned bedspread that also served as the upholstery that extended up to the top of the bed. From there, it jutted out to form a tented crown edged in golden shrouds. In addition, attached to the front of the crown, at the highest point of the bed, was a statue-like figure of a child either sleeping or praying. Finally, what made that room really cool was that the whole sleeping area was partitioned off by a curving balustrade divider, about knee-high, that stretched across the width of the room.

"Uncle Charles, how do you get to the bed from where we are?"

"Couldn't see a way in, aye?"

"I guess not. Don't tell me you have to jump over the railing?"

"No, don't jump, Mark! Go closer to the balusters...no, the other way...a couple of steps away from the side wall, you should spot a section that can be pushed in. But do be careful, my boy, just give it a slight lift as you push; don't try to force anything."

"Oh, I see it now." I then crossed over to the bed side, placed my head over the bedspread, and inspected the patterns on the inside of the canopy. I tried to imagine what it would feel like to sleep in such a room. Perhaps that was the purpose of the curtains around the bed: a way to make things a bit more intimate. I was about to play around with the curtains to see how they might open up when I, or rather my nose, sensed a musty odor—strong enough for me to remember the basement of the house in Port Washington; strong enough that I dared not try to pull the curtains for fear of disturbing the century-old accumulations and turning them into a downpour of dust flakes. Another thought that went quickly out the door was to sleep on that giant-sized bed for a second. I feared my weight might overwhelm its fragile two-hundred-year-old frame; a frame made possibly more fragile by its orgy-sized mattress. Oh, what fun those glorious years!

To cleanse up after an orgy, you'd go through a door in the back that led you to what was known as the boudoir. It had a marble sink, mirrors, and even a fireplace—everything except a toilet. I believe the boudoir was an ancient French phenomenon which combined the features of both the dressing room and the make-up room. Or, to be more American about it, the forerunner to those apartment-sized multi-purpose live-in-closets that they built in them hillside developments of Newport Beach. The way Charles explained it, in the era in which his house was built, the Madame's bedroom was often not upstairs in the sleeping quarters but rather on the main floor next to the salon, such as it was in this case. In fact, the room virtually served as an extension to the salon: to play cards, to accommodate larger crowds, or to simply serve as a place to gather up the ladies to gossip, especially after the men had gone into the library to smoke cigars. That was, incidentally, one reason for the balusters: to divide the room into a private area and a public area. In a way, it was consistent with today's bedroom life as well, especially for young people. I mean, we had always invited friends to each other's bedrooms when we were growing up; it was no big deal. Though I also know that in some cultures, the sleeping area is very, very private and strictly verboten to all.

While the bed stood out as the most overwhelming feature of the room, it was far from being the only eye-catcher. There were objects d'art all over. One area in particular, around the vicinity of the bed, whole collections of animals of all sorts were scattered about, many of them quite large in size. They had all belonged to his mother, Charles told me. Let me see: there were Indian elephants, Tang horses, Chinese water buffaloes, and tigers, too—all kinds, from bronze age Chinese tigers to white marbled Siberian ones. And if that weren't enough, tagging along as stand-ins were a slew of cats and dogs, bulls and rams, and so on down the line. There was even an Aztec eagle. Still, that was merely a sample of the full-fledged animals. There were plenty of half-breeds as well, like those half-human, half-beast creatures of Greek mythology.

Well, if the space on the bed portion of the room looked like a miniaturized version of the wild kingdom, the other side of the railing was just as wild and random. Countless pieces of crystals, porcelains and carvings were there on display. No, not exactly on display, more like being spread all over the place; and they, too, had taken on the animal motif. Put it this way: the front part of the room, in its better days, had probably had the ambiance of a Victorian parlor, with all those relics and knic-knacs being displayed in a coherent manner. But now, forget about it! After years of standing still, things just stood there—here, there and everywhere—totally out of order. As a matter of fact, the room hardly even looked like a part of the house; more resembling those cluttered antique shops down the block, with a place for everything but nothing in its place.

The same also held true for the furnishings. For unlike the rest of the house, the furniture and artworks in the card room had not even been arranged to make a favorable impression. They were just kind of stacked up in rows. The pieces themselves were piled so tightly together that you couldn't even get to the curtains, much less open the windows. No wonder the room was so damn dark. Even Charles admitted that the card room had become one of his storage rooms, though he didn't seem the least bothered by it. Mostly they were his mother's things, Charles told me, "Random purchases and gifts. Ines was crazy about animals, so people just brought them over as a matter of course."

"Anything good?"

"I suppose that somewhere in the muddle lie a few one-of-a-kind pieces. But they are more of a roaming variety: a sixteenth-century Indonesian wild boar there, a seventeenth-century Medici horse here."

"Surprised nobody got her a Trojan horse," I said, half jokingly. "Perhaps too big to fit into Ines's Ark, Ines's messy but one-of-a-kind Ark."

"My dear boy, sometimes I truly wonder," Charles shook his head in casual laughter. "We may have to educate you on European sensibilities first, before placing you in a managerial position in business."

"That bad, huh? How long do you think an impetuous New Yorker can last in Europe?"

"If his job is operating a street-corner hot-dog stand, a lifetime!"

"Ha! Now, there's a thought. I could sell hot *dogs* and wild *boars* during the museum hours and, then at night, perhaps a job awaits me at Galerie Charles Martin—cataloging collectibles! Or at least gloriously displaying them in their proper cabinets."

"A waste of time, my boy. Paintings and furniture aside, not many items here are of a prized variety; more a result of a whim than the undertaking of a connoisseur."

"What'a you talking about? You've only got a whole wall of snuff bottles here. That's a pretty serious collection if I do say so myself."

"An accumulation more than a collection," Charles said dismissively. "One voyage to China was all it took to lug back half the total. Traveling the old fashioned way, as it were, with case after case at departure, and trunk upon trunk upon returning."

"And all the while she didn't even lift a finger. Now we know why Ines didn't hesitate when it came to shopping."

"Oh, shop she did, and finds she made a few. Yet overall, Mother did not possess that carefully trained eye required for serious collecting."

"You don't think much of this is real?"

"One can never be sure," Charles said. Then he reached up and grabbed something off a shelf: "Take this Assyrian horse plaque or that gold-leafed Summerian doe, we might be talking as far back as the seventh century BC; but to me, they are of the most doubtful authenticity."

I laughed. I liked the way Charles put it: of the most *doubtful* authenticity. "How come?"

"Because one can't take just anyone's word for it, least of which an irreputable seller's."

"But, sir, even if they aren't genuine, they could still fetch a pretty penny."

"Depending on when the forgeries were made, I suppose." Uncle Charles, ever a man of doubts. Or, to put it another way, everything of his is genuine; everyone else's is all fake!

There could, however, be one other reason, besides mere authenticity, that had made Charles gather up his mother's animals and threw them all into one den—Charles simply was no animal lover.

He said so himself that Friday afternoon as Mellery was raving about his grouse hunts and horse farms: "Frivolous pursuits aside, as time and technology march on, the animals of this world are slowly living out their usefulness." Words of wisdom from Charles the Vegetarian. Yet, in a way, I believe Charles felt even deeper than that. Animals, or to be more precise—pets—are seen as moving inanimate objects, rather than as alive and living companions. If they enhance our lives like furniture, fine. But under no circumstance should they get in the way. To Charles, cruelty to animals is unthinkable. It would be too emotional an act. Simple indifference would suffice.

I like animals. I think they add variety to life on earth. But I don't feel passionate for them or anything. Loved pets when I was a kid, but I was a bit allergic. So I took on goldfish tanks instead—fish in general. Call me and Charles both cold-blooded, but in my view, it is down right selfish to impose animals to a life in the densely populated concrete jungles of New York and Paris.

They are a weird bunch, those animal lovers. Many of them are just the most loving, giving and devoted people on earth; while others took to the animals out of loneliness and selfishness. I guess it's reason enough, though I've never truly understood that need for animal companionship myself. Hell, I'm like the loneliest guy. But when you've got television, who cares! Not to mention all the money you'll save from having nine cats. Man, these animal freaks. They are the ones that either can't, or won't deal with their fellow human beings. Those mentalities are very often quite dangerous. They seek control, blind obedience, and if not content, those sick monsters can be downright cruel. At least Charles was consistent. He despised all living things. No, that wasn't entirely true, but he certainly was more at ease floating on an abstract wavelength than in the midst of your everyday human arena.

Strangely, one of the few times that Charles had not been a restless soul in search of solitude was when he fell for my grandmother. She was still Audrey back then. A lovely young woman with a pad on Rue Jacob, in the same house as Jules, my eventual grandfather. Incidentally, my grandfather, though born in France, had always had an American bent. Some of his childhood years were actually spent in New York. And, if it weren't for the First World War, he might well have remained in the States. My grandfather's family was actually living in New York in the early part of this century. But they returned to France to fight in the Great War. It was supposed to have been a very patriotic war—people fought in it just for the hell it. Thousands of Americans joined up, too; way the hell before we officially entered the fighting in 1917. World War II, however, was a totally different story. People were getting out of Europe en masse, especially foreigners; Audrey, my grandmother, included. Even so, before the exodus had begun, a nice little love story was brewing in Paris: between Charles and Audrey, more Charles than Audrey; more *amore* than lust.

It wasn't long after Audrey moved into the neighborhood that she became a familiar face. So familiar that she soon found herself as Charles's unofficial tutor in English. He was still in high school then, and even though he had already become fluent in German, due in part to the Austrian side of his ancestry, his English was still limited. But Audrey changed all that. She was the one responsible for adding *Gone with the Wind* to Charles's reading list, in addition to his Hegals and Nietzsches. Not quite in their rank was Margaret Mitchell, I'm afraid; but then again, what do Germans know about love anyway, compared to Scarlet and the Italians, that is. So Charles, ever the emotionally passionate—even as a child—was, nonetheless in this case, clearly smitten by my grandmother.

"I still remember the day that Audrey took me to the Brentanos on avenue de l'Opéra and bought me my very own copy of *Gone with the Wind.* She did so reluctantly," Charles said, "knowing full well that I wasn't quite ready for such an undertaking. At the same time, she also didn't want me to be constantly borrowing her copy, which she hadn't yet finished reading."

"That's right, sir. It was a very thick book—over a thousand pages, I believe."

"Ah, but it was marvelous. My thirst for it was so great that I wished I could devour it in one night, just so I could discuss it with Audrey the next day. Of course, I was only deluding myself. When Audrey finished the book before I had even made a dent in it, I was green with envy. I wanted to lock her up in a cage and not have her do anything but read to me—word for word!—until I was as fluent as she."

Indeed it was more than just a book. The signs were everywhere: young Charles was in love, falling hard for his own live Scarlet, before the world had even heard of Vivien Leigh, or anyone else in the running. As far as Charles was concerned, anyone other than Audrey would have been a let down, in spite of her Yankee accent and all. To Charles, tomorrow was more than just another day, especially if he was to show off his English vocabulary to Audrey on the terrace of Café d'Harcourt.

"So what else did the young people do for fun in those pre-rock concert days—besides going to cafés, reading books and going to the cinema?"

"My dear boy, you are referring to Paris here, not a small town in frontier America. This is culture in its fullest bloom. Let's see now, Monday nights would be an Italian or German opera. Tuesday night was always theatre at the Comédie Française, perhaps a Corneille or Beaumarchais."

"What of the Odéon nearby?"

"The Odéon was quite a delight. We went there often, Audrey, Jules and I. There was *Lorenzaccio* by Musset, *Les Compères du Roi Louis* by Fort and so on. Audrey also loved the more musically flavored Opéra-Comique, she had always shown great love for the performing arts."

"Visual arts, too," I said. "She only worked at the Museum for thirty years."

"That she did. Don't know if she had ever told you, but your grandmother had very much looked forward to the art salon exhibitions every year. She attended them all—from the conservative Salon des Beaux Arts to the chaotic and free-for-all of Salon des Indépendants."

"That must've been fun, those exhibits. Did you try to show anything just to impress her?"

"If I could have done so, I would have. But my artistic talents, such as they were, did not quite pass muster. The only performances I had managed to give were of the circular variety. Every season, friends, neighbors and relatives would gather the children and have one Monsieur Nollet train us in performing circus acts. The show got bigger and bigger by the year until it became a much sought after event."

"What were you good at doing? Don't tell me at being a clown because I won't believe you."

"Being a clown was easy. One year we had to learn to juggle, both your grandmother and I."

"What of singing old Frehel tunes?"

"Don't laugh!" Charles said, himself laughing, "Frehel was fabulous."

"Must've been a wonderful time to be in Paris, those years preceding the Second World War."

"Ah...it was marvelous. Audrey was an amazing woman. She had a special kindness about her: generous and giving, not a nasty streak in sight. The day she left for America was one of the saddest days of my life."

"Well, you were still young back then; physically, at least."

"Emotionally, too, at times, my dear friend. As you know, the war with Hitler was fast approaching and, honestly, I didn't think I was ever going to see her again. I had been so miserable that, the night Audrey told me she was leaving, was the first time in my life that I drank for the sake of getting drunk."

Charles was visibly overwrought with emotion. A rare show of sentiment by a man of unwavering neutrality. It was heartwarming to hear Charles speak so fondly of my grandmother. Even felt a tinge of regret that Audrey found out she was pregnant soon after her arrival in New York. Well, I don't mean I was sorry for eventually being born; but you know, on a symbolic level, a romantic level. For it was indeed my grandma more so than my grandpa who had maintained the steady stream of correspondence over the years. She had been very special to Charles, and he to her as well.

Suddenly, things had taken a turn for clarity. For it was not so much a love that dared not speak its name as it was the first love that never really went away.

Like Charles, I, too, remember my most romantic love as clearly as yesterday. It even paralleled Charles's experience in some respect. Her name was Celia, and we met shortly after I had transferred to NYU as a sophomore film student. Although I'd had a few crushes and flings here and there, none of them came close to the degree I fell for Celia.

Celia was a student at one of the sister schools up in New England, though at the time, she was doing a program at NYU, in our School of Arts. Like many other girls from Boston, Celia could drink gin and tell stories better than most of the guys. But being from one of the sister schools, I believe they still call them the "Seven Sisters," she was also highly intelligent.

I was impressed with Celia at our very first encounter. We did a film together. Well, I was just an extra, lending a friend a hand on this relatively elaborate shot. It was a short film about a young gangster who is going prematurely bald. Gino is his name. Even though he deplores violence and has yet to whack anyone, he is nevertheless obsessed with this compulsion to shave other people's hair off—as much as it pains him on the inside. Sometimes, Gino would get so obsessed that, when he is unable to persuade others to let him shave their heads with offers of money and favors, he would force his will upon them. It's a stupid story, *Gino's Revenge*, but it somehow served the spectrum of film school's cinematic objectives pretty well—with every cliché in the book!

The one major outdoor action shot in the film was of a night on the town in a white stretch-limo. The site chosen was a new Mexican restaurant called Caramba that had just opened near Tower Records. I don't know if anyone still remembers, but back in the early 1980s, Lower Broadway was still seedy and deserted. But Caramba changed all that when it became one of the hottest joints around and really ushered in the Mexican craze.

So anyway, our rag tag film crew was setting things up for a shot where the limo comes around the corner and the actors come out of the car and into the restaurant. I was helping out with the lighting and Celia was doing the shooting. Due to the camera being on a low dolly, Celia had her whole body lying flat on the sidewalk pavement as she checked the various angles—all the while showing total disregard for dirtying up her clothes.

After a take, she sensed it was still too dark. "We need more light!" she demanded. When I told her that all we had left was a small hand-gripped spotlight, with neither bulb nor power, she was kind of pissed; but only for a moment, as she soon had the good fortune to find an adapter buried in a separate case, as well as a small quartz bulb. What she did next was, she went over to a waiting taxi and made a deal with the driver (They still spoke wheeling and dealing English back then). "No, mister, we cannot use the sealed beam of your headlight; but if you would kindly let us plug our movie light into your battery, we'll give you five bucks for sticking around." Five dollars went a long way back then so the cabby agreed; and that was the first thing I did for Celia: I held and focused a 200-watt spotlight for her.

You know the old saying that "There are no small parts, only small actors?" Well, I certainly agreed then and there. I was so in awe of Celia and her resourcefulness that I immediately felt privileged to be working with her—regardless of how small a part I played. Then a few days later we became friends, or rather, I befriended her. When I learned that she had been crashing at someone's studio during the week, I naturally offered her my place to crash instead. I even told her she could use it on weekends when she happened to be in the city. My grandpa had passed away not long ago so there was lots of room. To my amazement she accepted; and in doing so, became my first roommate.

I was very happy that Celia took my offer; though I also knew it was just that: roommates and very new friends. We had fun together, Celia and I, especially at the cinema. *Videodrome* was the first movie we saw together. She liked Cronenberg's gory weirdness, and a surprisingly good performance from Blondie. I liked it too, more so than I would have had I seen it on my own. See, that was the magical thing about Celia: she had a personality that could persuade. Of course, I was still young and wide-eyed back then, far more malleable than I am now. But that didn't mean she liked trash and got me to tag along for the ride; not at all, particularly when the subject was the movies. Celia preferred the old classics—from Howard Hawks and Preston Sturges to Tallulah Bankhead and Veronica Lake. Naturally they rubbed off on me as well. She was the one who introduced me to *All About Eve* by the way, which, as great a movie as it was on its own merits, was made even greater by Celia's command of its cutting and clever lines. And boy did she know her grand old movie stars. I mean, everyone is familiar with Betty Davis and Norma Shearer, but she would rattle off the careers of Ida Lupino and Greer Garson, actresses I had never heard of before, but totally first class acts in their own right. If anything,

I was the grape in the "subterranean grapevine," more into a *noir* rerun than a first-run box office smash.

She was quite a bright girl, that Celia. There was this aura of magnetism about her that made me want to follow her everywhere. It was such a pleasure doing things with her, learning from her. Although she was very pretty, you could tell she wasn't the type that was too keen on receiving compliments for being beautiful. She took far more pride in her creative talents, like the way she could see color coming out from everywhere—even out of black and whites! And the way she played the guitar, too, much better than I did at the time. And last but not least, there was her literary bent: not in that elitist show-offish sense, like quoting a bunch of allegorical lines that nobody could understand, but far more down to earth. Why, she could quote from the Bible to Virginia Woolf—both of them Greek to me—and still make them sound as if she was quoting lines from the movies. She made them *that* understandable.

Yeah, good old Celia, I'd be mad if I said I was not in love with her. I'd also be mad if I thought I could just tell her how I felt. For one thing, I didn't even know how to do that. I mean, I knew how to be a face-to-face asshole, had plenty of practice doing that. But a romantic? Plus the fact that Celia just didn't make herself available in a sexual kind of way. Who could blame her. She was three years older and ten years wiser. Not to mention I was no Mel Gibson; nor Sigourney Weaver. Knew I shouldn't have taken her to see *The Year of Living Dangerously*, right after the night we saw *Videodrome*, too.

In many ways, my relationship with Celia resembled that of the movies: very imaginary. I considered myself lucky to be just hanging around her and absorbing her wisdom. I think the relationship we had was the only one conceivable between us. Anything more intimate would have been quickly over. Still, not unlike what happens in the Hollyworld of make-believe, I was certainly free to fantasize about her—nothing she could do about that! And boy, was she constantly on my mind. I don't even think an hour went by without me thinking about her in some way; probably even less than that. Man, did that Celia do a number on me. Even inspired and traumatized me to such a degree that I began writing bad poetry. How unfortunate a trait; the remnants of which're still visible t'is day!

When I wasn't dreaming of Celia, I spent my time observing her every move. She had the most naturally smooth motion of anybody I had ever seen; simply flawless. Like the way she'd make her entrance into our building: soon as she was about to reach the top of the steps, she'd slide her right hand into her pants pocket and, in a split second, pull out the key ring with her fingertips on the exact key needed to open the door, while simultaneously using her left hand to flip back the hood of her parka. Then, in one sweeping motion, she'd shake the snow off her hair a little, aim the key perfectly into the keyhole and lunge right in—no fumbling, no bumbling.

Pretty small act in itself—opening a door; but that was just the prelude to a whole series of things she would do in the apartment. She was unbelievably precise—be it at chopping onions or putting up a movie poster—everything she did seemed effortless. That, in turn, put enormous pressure on the-not-nearly-as-graceful me to *not* foul up.

Instead of being worried, however, I looked forward to the challenges. Although I had given up on ever typing as fast as her, I did learn to make a mean omelet—especially the part near the end when you finish it off by grabbing the panhandle from underneath and gently tipping the pan over the plate until the omelet slides itself off into a perfect shape—just like the way Celia did it! To this day I love to make omelets for people. Another thing that was satisfying to my ego was to walk down the street straight and swift just like her, matching her posture by posture, stride by stride, as if a part of her body became mine; a part of her greatness had passed on down to me.

Besides copying her actions, I imitated her style and mannerisms as well. Like dishing off a blasé remark here and a sarcastic insult there. It was especially fun when I was able to catch her off guard, like when she said or did something stupid—giving her a taste of her own medicine. Every now and then, an insult of mine would get to her, especially when I teased her on her numerical reasoning powers. When that happened, she'd lower her frowning eyebrows and snap her head away from me, in that "I can't believe you said that" kind of look. It was one of my favorite expressions of hers. She looked very beautiful when she did that, with that bob of bouncy reddish hair a bit out of place. You know who she looked like? A younger version of Molly Dodd. Of course Molly wasn't around yet back then, so imagine my surprise when her show appeared on the tubes. It was like déjà vu all over again, or was it me still not over her yet? Either way, it's the only prime time sit-com that I really love to watch; that I make a point of watching.

Loved Celia, too. Idolized her. Like a child looking for the slightest approval from his hero. But unlike a child, I kept my cool in that semester of discontent. No matter how much I wanted her, my facade was totally professional, even bordering on competitive, as if to see who was the more composed, me or her. It was really strange, as if keeping my composure had become a goal in itself; as if just winning her over wasn't all I wanted anymore. In a way it had become a game, and Celia had taken on the characteristics of a puzzle instead of a character in real life. And you know what else was strange? After a while, my lust sort of subsided, but what took its place were fantasies, lots of fantasies, usually of her being the more dominant aggressor: like she'd one day barge into my room, drag me back into her's, then force me to make love to her. Imagine, me in complete submission as her sex slave? As usual, fantasies tend to veer toward the most unlikeliest of outcomes.

It had always been my hope that, if Celia and I could just stay together long enough, things might somehow work themselves out one glorious day down the road. Well, that glorious day of reckoning came all right, but it was not what I wanted to hear. For instead of remaining in New York after graduation, she decided to move west to Los Angeles. Needless to say, I did not take it well. Not at all! God, was it dreadful. I was like, shit, what's going to happen to me? Who's going to watch Letterman with me? Who's going to make me laugh through all those triple-header Mary reruns late into the night? I was so sad I almost cried in front of her. It was more than just missing someone to watch TV with, there was this indescribable emptiness—wondering how I was going to manage without her. A typical reaction from someone still in love, I guess. In fact, Celia's departure had a great deal to do with my deciding to say *sayonara* to film school altogether, to transfer out of the emotional rollercoaster of the School of Arts and into a more single-minded pursuit of a business degree.

Looking back, I'm glad I handled the whole "breakup" in a calm and cool manner. Oh, there were occasional lapses here and there after she was gone, when I felt that urge to see her and confess it all. But I never allowed myself to get to that point. A part of me just couldn't do it, possibly because I knew that even if I were to see her just once, it would have been enough for me to get re-addicted to her, to make me want to see her again and again all over again. That was one of the reasons I stayed away. I didn't see her for the longest time. So in a crazy sense, I still remain that strong, silent type before her, despite my not very much feeling like one on the inside.

Incidentally, an accidental result of that ordeal had been a steady rise in my mental toughness. I soon became convinced that if I could get over Celia, I could get over anybody. And indeed I have. It's kind of liberating—to know that you can just walk away from anybody or anything. At will! But god, that Celia was special. A silent smile comes to my face every time I'm reminded of her. We still keep in touch by the way, but more Christmas and birthday card friends than drinking buddies. I just haven't seen her much, save a couple of times I was out West with Lisa.

Around last Christmas, though, me and Celia did manage to get together. She'd been living in West Hollywood, sharing a bungalow with friends. She was actually delighted to see me. First we got a little high on Thai at a place I know in Nieder Brentwald, then she got me hot on caffeine at a coffee house in Mid-Wilshire. I have to admit that Celia was still rich with ideas and not shy about expressing them; especially when she felt like lashing out and being real critical. The difference being that, in the ensuing years after my sophomore crush, I have also gained my own share of self esteem. Almost as opinionated, too, if I might add. Like when we were talking about how much we both loved this new series on television called "A Year in the Life," and how pissed we both got when it got canceled after a year was up. In her New York days, Celia would have written to the station and complained. But now that she has become a part of the system, she just complains directly to the guys at the network. Same old Celia, only now she's even more of a gossip, far more than me. Man, the things she'd come up with on the secret lives of Hollywood stars. Marlene Dietrich had it right all along, that it *too-k* more than one man to change their names to Hollywood Lillies. Or is it Billys?

Celia's doing great by the way. After starting out in television, she eventually wriggled her way into the feature films. Last I spoke to her, she was about to do a shoot up in the Pacific Northwest, as a production coordinator. She was rather modest about her success: "Just another female production coordinator on a low budget feature," she said. Nonsense. What with a few more films under her belt, she ought to be ready to handle the job of production manager. *If* that is what she really wants to do. For I get the feeling that deep down she knows she could create. She's certainly talented enough. In fact, during her periods of "downtime" over the years, she has gained some acting experience; as well as having had her agent put several screenplays in circulation. "Stored in bytes and waiting for a bite!" I kidded her. Then I told her that if she should land a large enough an acting role, one that really makes the final cut, then she'd have a foot in three doors already. With odds like that, the ends are likely to be happy ones.

You know, as much as I love New York, I must be fair and say that if you want to break into the pictures, you really do have to move out West, and that includes acting. I know you can mail your tapes in and so forth, but nobody really looks at that shit. They just get piled up next to some casting executive's office, in videotape hell! And why not? Why should they bother with you when they've got hundreds of candidates right up the freeway; hundreds who could get to the studios at a moment's notice. So you really do have to be there or be square—even though there is no there there! I mean, let's face it, most of the parts being offered don't require a heck of a lot of acting. Anybody with a little imagination can do it! Even me. So what's so special about some stuck-up New Yorker who needs his daily fix of at least four cab rides a day? Besides, how are you going to screw the producer from twenty-five hundred miles out east—with phone sex?

EIGHTEEN

Dinner that night was at the Maison Poisone; an old, almost decrepit-looking building situated between the Louvre and Les Halles. Poisone was a cavernous place, with somewhat of a strange layout. There was a large sunken dining room, seen as you entered from the street, with only a screen of oriental panels separating you from the activities inside. An imposing feature of the room was its vaulted ceiling with exposed beams. They extended quite a way up, particularly in the center. Another thing that was a bit odd was the arrangement of the tables. On the left side of the dining room, they were mostly of the small variety; but dominating the right side of the room was a single banquet-sized table in the process of being set up. That was pretty much it, except for a couple more long and narrow cafeteria-ish tables placed against the back wall, which were an eyesore all the way as they lacked even basic table skirting. Clearly, at least in terms of furnishings and decor, Maison Poisone was a far cry from the polished, de grand luxe styled interior of the Restaurant Vignon on Friday. The lone, elaborate exception being the chandeliers. They looked as though they were huge floral arrangements. Everything from the hangings on down was wrapped in flowers. Even the light bulbs.

We took our seats near the center under one of the chandeliers. As Charles sipped his mineral water, he looked around a bit and nodded to the other guests. He seemed especially friendly to a party of three sitting at a curved banquette in the left corner: an old couple, older than Charles, and a beautiful middle-aged woman in a fancy blue dress. Charles was very suave, passing them a kiss with his fingers. The younger of the two ladies was so thrilled it seemed to have sent ripples up her ruffles.

The service staff was dressed elaborately as well—in red. They looked like young horseguards in full uniform. One of them came over to Charles and said that they would begin serving momentarily, even though a large party was still waiting for some fashionably late people to show up. He also passed on to Charles that there had been some last minute menu changes but, hopefully, there would be enough food for all.

"What happens when there's not enough to go around?" I asked.

"We shall then have to learn to starve," Charles replied, "just like the animals in the wild."

"But, sir, isn't the main reason we evolved into modern man in the first place—I mean, unlike many animals, we no longer spend most of our waking hours in search of food."

"On the contrary, my dear boy. We spend more time at it, much more. One reason we made great progress as a species was due in part to our desire to revolutionize food gathering. We wanted not only to think about food when hungry, but to fantasize about eating when we're not. Day and night; consciously *and* unconsciously. That was how we progressed; and, eventually, found ways to store and preserve food for tomorrow."

"You said progressed instead of evolved. You don't believe in evolution?"

"I didn't realize I was making a distinction. However, now that you've brought it up, let's talk about it. The way I see it, evolution, at times, connotes chance or randomness. For all we know, the chameleon might have originally been a deformed reptile, but that deformity had given it the means to survive; whereas the regular uncamouflaged chameleons were soon picked off by the eagles and became extinct."

"So nature evolved just as much by eliminating the perfect and worthy as by creating the deformed and unworthy?"

"Oh, I'm quite sure it has created more worthiness—leaving the human race out of it for now," Charles laughed, "the jury on that still being out. But what if we take flowers? Once upon a time, the earth consisted merely of plants. Then, as soon as it became apparent that the dinosaurs were eating up the plant supply, *flowered* plants came into being, using their color as shield. The change, though innocent, was devastating in its logic. Surely their 'intention' was to survive, not to blossom into something for human beings to enjoy million of years later."

"Man and bees alike," I added. "And what of progress?"

"Progress signifies a force of will, an intentional effort to speed up the change or destiny. Unlike biological evolution, progress involves failure, and lots of it. To seek progress, an extra step is required: a more mental step—one of *want* more than that of natural need."

"In other words: greed rather than need."

"Agreed!"

"Agreed indeed, as now we can start the feed."

The first course was a turtle soup with saffron. Wonderful soup, with not a strand of red hair out of place.

After the soup, we were served Madeira. "There was Madeira in the soup," Charles said. "So now we wash it down with the real thing." Shouldn't be to anyone's surprise that I detected no Madeira in no soup, but then again, it did seem to have some rational rationale to it. Still, I couldn't help but feel that this was going to be one of those long, irrational, and intoxicating evenings.

To keep our appetites going, we were served eggs. Not the eggs which many Americans start the day with, Charles told me, but grand cuisine eggs; which meant poached, then molded with minced bacon and baked. The thing that really gave it the elegance, though, was a single piece of oyster on top and a single bed of artichoke on the bottom. And, for the finishing touch, a light cream sauce over the whole dish. Nothing like programmabled eggs and bacon à la française, I suppose.

The course that followed the egg dish was fish and it was a dandy. Truly had to be seen to be believed! The servers brought out this silvery salmon the size of a shark. That damn thing was so big it could've had me for dinner. The salmon was placed on a cart, with one person doing the slicing and the other one adding a green sauce. It is rare to see a salmon of such size today—simply too big to come from a hatchery. Someone must have gotten lucky and caught it near the Arctic.

The fish was accompanied by a white Bordeaux. Never knew they even made egg whites down in egg yoke country. But I didn't have an opportunity to ask Charles about it, as he was in the midst of espousing his views on war and destruction. His contention: while war in theory was inevitable, the waging of full-scaled wars struck him as an act of utter insanity and stupidity. "One should *never* wage a war that might be one's last," he said, "as in a nuclear war of assured mutual destruction. Secondly, one should never go into a war one war at a time. Always prepare for the aftermath, including the prospect of defeat!"

"Interesting idea, sir: one war at a time. Come to think of it, rarely has history ever had wars which began and ended with a single go-around. Even after the most crushing of defeats, the losers still managed to seek vengeance years on down the road. Could that help explain why a war is one of the most illogical acts of all time?"

"Not to the parties which stand to profit from it," Charles said. "However, when one wages a war against an enemy that is far weaker in strength and number, then *even* if the end result were triumphant, it bespeaks of failure. Indeed, to have to resort to any full-scale fighting at all—against a puny opponent—signifies grave incompetence on both sides of the fight."

"That would leave your choice of wars to only those that are closely contested, where you need everything to go perfectly in order to win, which, undoubtedly, makes luck a crucial variable; and you should never depend on luck to win a war!"

"Well, there you have it, old boy—the paradox of warfare."

"Yeah, no war should be fought where instead it could be bought!"

"Amusing," Charles said, "Unless, of course, it is the killing and destruction that man is seeking."

"What do you think of SDI, or *Star Wars*?"

"Beautiful idea if it can be perfected quickly and secretly. Otherwise, the Americans run the danger of facing a pre-emptive nuclear attack. A better way would be to share the technology with the Russians; although not without its own risks, the consequences are far less destructive."

"Does all this say anything about human nature? The fact that we are able to bring about destruction far more readily than we can bring about rebuilding? I mean, why does it always seem like it would take years to build something, and then, within seconds, it could burn to the ground. You know what? I don't think I'm asking this properly. I guess what I'm trying to say is: shouldn't it be true, at least in theory, for construction to be just as easy as *de*struction? That technology ought to go both ways at about the same pace? And I don't mean only for bombs and warfare, but for anything. Take that Valdez oil tanker in Alaska: despite my endless devotion to the sea, that accidental oil spill brought out a terrible dilemma. Like, wouldn't it be nice if we could counteract the millions of gallons of oil leakage as quickly as the short time it took to spill it? That there ought to be some sort of an antidote—an environmental injection, an environmental tetanus shot, for lack of a better word—something that costs far less than all those inefficient manual laborers who are trying to, literally, *scoop* up the mess?"

Charles sensed I was a little perturbed. It was, after all, as long a question as I had ever asked. "I concur," he said. "To spend billions on the clean up is ludicrous. It would be wiser to view the incident as a sacrifice and pour the funds into the research for a chemical neutralizer; into advancements in the treatment of future catastrophes."

"What about my point on reconstruction?"

"As to your concern over the pace of construction being far slower than the speed of destruction, I don't have an answer."

Another first. Charles Martin silenced at last by an amateur. Only for so long, though. "It is, nonetheless, an interesting question; one which we might be able to approach from a philosophical point of view. That is: if something is so easily repaired, or so easily made anew, then wouldn't it be seen as not so terribly irreplaceable? Surely we would not be guarding it with our lives. Then again, take water—it is worthless in a rain forest, but worth its weight in gold in the desert."

"So it comes down to economics after all, with time and supply determining how precious a thing it actually is."

"Very good of you to mention preciousness. In general, we regard what is precious as those things which we have worked hard for. If we can rebuild a building as quickly as we can tear it down, then we may not value it as much. To put it another way, the act of destruction will not be seen in so horrible a light."

"What about the less tangible things? Like intelligence, or ideas or—"

"Yes. The intangibles may also be defined according to their relative preciousness," Charles said. "If you, a college graduate, have figured out a way to handicap the college basketball finals, I would certainly be impressed; though not so overwhelmed as to be reverential, as I know full well there is much more original thought from where it came."

"Thank you very much, sir. I'll try my best for an encore."

"However, if a child from a tribe in New Guinea had invented algebra all on his own, then wouldn't you say that he could be more precious than you and me? We may even go a step further and say: if I folded some papers up and made a paper doll out of it, it'd be worthless; crush it or rip it apart as you like. On the other hand, if a monkey had acquired such a skill, and went on to create origami figures of beauty and substance, then wouldn't you say that those pieces of paper would become collector's items?"

"Collector's items? Why, they'd be nothing short of museum-able masterpieces!"

"Cheers!"

"Cheers to you, sir!"

So, back to the rich food, a far more personal form of war and destruction. I had the pleasure of tasting sweetbread for the first time. It was the entrée dish; or, to make it less confusing, the fourth course. Sweetbread is called *ris de veau* in French. Braised in crayfish broth with a mushroom puree, the taste was instantly addicting. Supposedly, sweetbread is a learned taste. I guess I must've been a fast learner then. You know, sometimes you really do have to hand it to the English language. Take the word sweetbread: it is neither sweet nor bread, though it sure has flavor. And, in the hope of not deterring anyone from trying it, I'm not going to mention just which part of the calf it is. If you are really interested, you can always look it up.

I will, however, bring up the question which I asked of Charles since it's not so easy to look that one up. "Uncle Charles, let's square out the nomenclature of entrées once and for all. Why is it called entrées, first of all, if it is not the first course? And why do Americans take the word to mean the main dish when it is merely appetizer-ish in portion?"

"Originally," Charles said, "in traditional banquets, there was another course called the remove, or *relevé*, which immediately followed the fish. Due to modern dietary concerns, the fish—salmon in this case—became the *relevé*; but officially, one removed the remove by entering with an entrée. That was the original meaning."

"Makes perfect sense." I lied, as if what we were eating was in complete accordance with modern dietary concerns.

"Now, as to the American use of entrées," Charles tried to clarify, "I can only surmise that perhaps it is due to the entrée being the last course of the first service, as it is the case here. So, after a little sorbet to clear the pallet, we will be starting the second service."

"How nice to know," I shook my head. "How nice for my stomach to make more room for food."

"Not to worry, my dear fellow. We haven't eaten all that much. So long as we keep to a nice slow pace—unlike some of the others who are here tonight—we can go at it all night, as we indeed shall!"

What Charles was referring to as *others* was this long banquet table that hogged the whole other half of the dining room—oh, about a free-throw's distance away from us. The eighteen people seated at the big table were devouring up the food as if it were their last supper. Let me just backtrack a bit to better explain this phenomenon. When Charles and I started our dinner, that bunch hadn't even entered the main dining room. Yet, from the sound of the off-key piano playing and the off-color singing from beyond the walls, you could tell there was a boisterous crowd somewhere, ready to filter in as soon as the service staff was done arranging their table. See, while Charles and I were being served the first few courses, the same dishes and then some were also being put on that banquet table across the way, on top of warmers and then covered. The dishes were all placed quite symmetrically, on and between a large silver candelabra, a bronze vessel, and a flower basket. Soon after everything was set, the hostess led her procession in from an adjoining salon. A footman in full dress then seated the hostess in an even fuller dress as her whole entourage followed. It was certainly *not* the Gashouse Gang, as many of the ladies were decked out in Marie Antoinettesque gowns, and gentlemen's outfits varied anywhere from David Copperfield to Marquis de Lafayette. Then, after that group had been seated, the servers took their respective positions and, in seconds, lifted up the covers to all the dishes. Next came all the "ooh"s and "ah"s and the "oh là là"s as a photographer snapped a bunch of pictures from the various angles. The table did look great, I must admit—fishheads and all!—with so much color and variety that it looked like the garden of eating. And eat they did. Shortly after the graceful preliminaries were over, the scene quickly turned into a gastronomic free-for-all, as if the deadly sin of gluttony was alive and well and living in sin. It was truly every man for himself: like a bunch of crazy kids at a birthday party. Charles noticed my amused amazement: "I see you are in unusually high spirits this evening."

"Unusual, aye? Didn't I tell you I travel back in time to dine, every *single* night."

"Now that you mention it, I seem to recall—if I'm not mistaken—that it was back to the days of the ice age, with nothing in your 'ice box' save a case of Budweiser."

"Hey, let it be known that a bottle of beer can go a long way in staving off starvation."

"Naturally. So can a field of grass."

"Nahhh...I'd rather chew on coca leaves," I said. "You know something, Uncle Charles? I used to want to be a Boy Scout when I was growing up, not so much for honor and team spirit, but just so I could learn to survive. Like being dropped into the middle of nowhere and still being able to make some tree-bark soup, or hunt down animals and cook 'em up for food 'n stuff. Just like the way the caveman had done it thousands of years ago."

"What happened, my boy?"

"I couldn't see myself cutting up a deer or a pig and then having to cook it. I mean, what if I didn't clean them properly and ate...well, what if I ate its asshole by accident—I'm getting nauseous just thinking about it. What finally did me in was this one time when I was over at a friend's house, and saw his mother kill a real live chicken with a knife cut right under the throat. Then she bent back its neck and drained its blood; but even after that, the headless chicken was still flopping around endlessly in a new pool of blood."

"Did you have any difficulty eating that chicken afterwards?"

"No."

"All right then."

"But I was still too young to make a connection between killing and eating. All that shrieking and struggling left so permanent an imprint that, to this day, I only fish. Opening up a fish and cleaning it is about as far as I go, and even *that* is rare. But since fish don't make no noise when you cut them up, it's a more sanitizing kill."

"If a way can be found to silence all the screams," Charles said, "then the world would indeed be a more manageable place."

"Though just as dangerous."

"If not more so," Charles stressed. "The Nazis tried to apply such a method of killing and were terribly successful. Once the individual is cleared of personal responsibility, then killing becomes a breeze."

"So by removing the *M* out of murder, they've reduced their guilt to that of killing inanimate objects."

"Trivial, inanimate objects."

"Think the Holocaust will ever happen again?"

"I'm not ruling it out." Charles said. "Rest assured, however, that it will appear to be completely justified by the killers and their backers," Charles added. "Still more, it might even be seen as an act of kindness, or survival, rather than an act of cruelty."

"But don't you think that because news spread so instantaneously today, it will be difficult to carry on atrocities for years and years without the knowledge of the outside world?"

"My dear boy, the killings are not going to take years, perhaps not even months."

"You know, sir, to this day, I'm still confounded that a great people like the Germans could allow a Hitler to have such power over them."

"Ahh, but it was precisely due to Germany being a greatly under-utilized nation. Otherwise, Hitler would have remained a mad, fame-seeking showman on the fringe. And, like other madmen before him, he was no chess player but a mere gambler; a gambler who, with luck and some brilliant help, had developed an aura of invincibility. A gambler who felt he could not only silence the five million people that died, but the soldiers and guards and everyone else in between. Five million is a great number to hide in any human statistic."

"Was it worse that Hitler tried to hide the killings? That he knew it to be a crime against humanity?"

"Yes. One reason history will never forgive him is that Hitler knew the act to be murder. Yet to him at the time, the consequences weren't alarming. If the Allies had been more forceful in their threats, particularly after they had begun their bombing runs, millions might have been saved."

"So the severity of the crime was not made clear to the criminal."

"The sad truth is, the Final Solution elicited far less opposition from the Allies than today's apartheid in South Africa. So the free world, by not laying out the strong repercussions, must also share some blame. We should openly acknowledge that just as such cruelty by the Nazis was inconceivable, so was our own selfishness in those years."

"Is that the reason why, today, there are constant reminders in the media about the Holocaust?"

"You see, Mark, in some respects, the tragedy of the Holocaust was more than in the act itself, but in the retrospective introspection that followed. That is: how could we civilized Europeans do something so monstrous? And how could still more freedom-loving people have tolerated such atrocities? This was not an act of five hundred years ago but of less than fifty; it happened in our liberal, progressive lifetime. It took us down a notch by showing how a part of us is still terribly barbaric, terribly uncivilized. This is not some unknown island tribe we are talking about—practicing its ancient nomadic rituals. This is Western Europe, hours away from France. Such is what makes this episode all the more shameful; and all the harder to digest."

Well, it's nine o'clock on a Saturday, but the old man wasn't having no tonic and gin. Instead, it was ducks—roasted wild ducks—parading down the aisles on serving carts with the pomp and pageantry of a royal rollercade.

Even Charles was surprised at the presentation: "I thought we were going to have pheasants. Apparently, something spectacular has come along at the last moment."

"What is that big shining corkscrew looking thing next to the duck?"

"That's the duck press, used for making the sauce. As for the ducks, we begin with wild birds set aside to age. The point at which they are at maximum ripeness is when they are just about ready to decompose."

"Sort of like an aged Omaha steak."

"But far dearer in supply, my dear fellow."

Charles, ever so careful to avoid comparisons between classic French cuisine and American cowboy food. As much as I love to rave about the highest heights of haute cuisine, most of me is still a democratic epicurean, or should I say diner-cratic. "Uncle Charles,"

I tried to keep a straight face, "the duck press that the juices are oozing out of, could that be used to mash potatoes, too?"

"Heavens, no!" Charles was shocked I could even say such a thing. "Have you lost your senses, my boy? Does this place look like a roadside coffee shop to you?"

"No, of course not. I was just so mesmerized by the gadget's movements that...well, I thought perhaps I could bring one back as a souvenir." It was indeed a wonderful gadget. You put the carcass of the duck in through the top along with a cognac-based mixture, and out comes the juice below. One of the assistants would then strain the liquid through a couple of times and pour it over the duck as it was still being cooked. What an unbelievable flavor, that duck sauce, light years away from the duck sauce at my Chinese takeout. As for the fillets of duck themselves? Sensational! A cross between that of a Peking duck and the flavors of what people might refer to as "gamey"—whatever the hell that means.

"Superb dish," I said to Charles. "Simply palate-boggling!" And, of course, the wine. A 1979 Burgundy from one of the Domaines of Romanée-Conti. We talked about the *Bourgogne*, of how it compared to the Bordeaux. "The Burgundy wins: through finesse," Charles said. "It is not as festive as the best Bordeaux, but to its loyalists, it rests at the top of connoisseurship."

"But which is a better wine?"

"There are less great vintages in Burgundy due to it being farther north and more susceptible to bad weather. But that only makes them even more prized. The older Romanée-Conti have practically vanished from the market. Not surprising when one considers that it consists of less than five acres."

"That's it? Five acres? Why, a busy artist could probably paint five acres in a lifetime."

"One does not judge works of art by the yard, my boy; but you have the idea. That is why every time one gets an opportunity to sample a great old vintage, such as the '59 La Tache I had last week, one seldom plays it cool."

"How about a '79?"

"Still a moment to be treasured."

In this state of heightened drama, I impersonated Charles like an understudy to a star and took a deep slow sip of my own. I forced myself to concentrate on the wine, weighing it on my tongue as my mind worked superfast to seal its flavor to memory. Seconds later, I declared it a masterpiece. "Mmmm...what a mouth-filling sip of aromatic delicacy."

"You learn quickly, Mark."

"I have a good teacher." I returned the compliment. If the good teacher only knew how long a way I still have to go. My sudden pretense of sophistication could not quite bring me to openly reveal my dilettante upbringing: that my favorite Burgundy up until then was the Chambolle-Musigny—because I loved the way it sounded.

And what, you say, is the sound of truffles being shaved right on to a plate of foie gras? Well, it isn't quite the tingling sound of cutting fine powder from a big rock of cocaine; *but*, similar to it, the appreciation is also one that requires acquiring. Truffles, you see, despite being as legal a substance as water, are worth their weight in heavy water. Once you are aware of their rarity, the next time you see someone shaving them, especially onto a slice of pâté de foie gras, a Pavlovian classical conditioning of the human kind takes over. One more slice, you say to yourself, hoping the server would shave away all traces of stemless shrooms from the room.

Badly as we humans desire those black balls, Pavlov's dogs love them more. Charles told me that in the mountainous Perigord region every season, dogs and pigs become fungus hunters. The only rule of thumb to finding truffles is to remember that they can turn up anywhere, in any form. They usually appear as about the size of a cherry tomato, but occasions when dogs are being attacked by killer tomatoes are not unheard of. Louis the XIV used to attack those killer truffle tomatoes as well—at a clip of a pound a day.

As for the pâté de foie gras, to say that it merely melts in your mouth does *not* quite do it justice. A more appropriate descrption would be to say that when accompanied by a Château d'Yquem, you have created a combination as seductive as love and sex. Rich, sweet Sauternes grapes of the noblest ancestry, spoiled rotten in the growing season, were left to spoil and rot at harvest time, to produce a wine with a flavor that hugs the silky texture of the foie gras, and pampers the crunchy flakes of the truffles. It is a menage à trois of the highest order—truly the climax of gastronomic promiscuity!

"Here's to nothingness!" I raised my glass.

"Here, here. When the bells are tolling with food and laughter, there is nothing better than to simply drift along in worry-free bliss."

"But once you wake up from the sips of good spirits to the dips of reality, you have no choice but to lay down the laws of life and death."

"Are you equating philosophical treatise with sobriety, my boy?"

"All's I know is, when the good spirits wear off, you find yourself in the middle of a deep void, and isn't that how thinking first originated? From people who were in the midst of idleness. And, like what you said earlier about food, if every Early Man had to hunt day and night just to survive, then those who preferred to sit on their lazy asses and think away wouldn't have evolved anywhere. But as it turned out, some of our ancestors did manage to come up with surplus time, which enabled them to *pensé* away and pray. Furthermore, isn't it also true that since France has always had a relative abundance of food, it inevitably originated a class of mind-roamers."

"About that there can be no argument," Charles smiled. "Yes, I very much like the sound of that. Do keep it coming, will you?"

"That's all I'm afraid; just trying to put in my two francs' worth."

"There are, nonetheless, some additional connections between creativity and idleness. One being that although spare time is a prerequisite for creative learning, it is essential that inner conflicts exist as well: conflicts that are unbearable yet refuse to go away."

"Yeah, a desperate attempt to remain idle and *not* go back to the farm." I quickly added. "Speaking of creativity, sir; remember Thursday night when you and Luke were wondering if ever one day there'd be a robot that could drive us from the airport to his hotel? Well, he said it's unlikely to happen in our lifetime, and you said you weren't so sure—which one of you is right?"

"Who do you think?"

"I have to side with him, sir. There are certain tasks that a machine's going to have some difficulty doing: like spotting a traffic sign down the road or avoiding a man jaywalking."

"I'll grant you that. But why should robots have to drive next to human beings in the first place."

"Because a road is a road is a road."

"Even so, why can't we in the future build roads for robotic cars only, with their own system of sensors and directional guidance."

"Too expensive, sir."

"We don't know that. True, to drive a car on the road along with humans may not be an easy task, but my point is: why must robots drive up to Pike's Peak in circles when they're able to go up straight. There exist many ways of getting from A to B."

"To B from A; or, to A from B."

"You'd be an interesting machine someday, Vermont."

"To B and not from B, that is the question—Shakespeare!"

"About what one might expect from poetic machinery, I suppose."

"Thank you very much. So where were we? Was I trying to be coy? All right, so you are saying is that if robots could walk through concrete like Superman, then why must they take the long way home like us humans and walk around the block? No pun intended."

"None at all. Neither is the shortest distance between two points a mirror!"

I totally blanked out for a second after that remark—didn't know *what* he was talking about. "I'm going to let you have that one, sir, but what I'm saying is still this: that robots, despite having all those abilities that we humans lack, can still not duplicate everything we do—meaning—making a specific set of decisions that would enable them to go around the block. It's just too hard. So it's a tie; and ties go to the incumbent—the humans."

Charles took a long pause and cleared his throat. I wasn't sure if it was out of impatience or just stunned at my unreasonableness. He began calmly once again: "Supposing we had a dog that could sniff its way from the airport to the hotel. Now, is there a reason why we humans must mimic such a way to go from A to B, even if we could, which we bloody well couldn't?"

"Of course we can't. Our sense of smell is far inferior to that of the bloodhounds."

"All right, then. So having established that we cannot possibly smell our way from A to B, does it also imply, then, that dogs are superior to humans?"

"Most certainly not!"

"Then why should the robots have to *drive* to prove *their* superiority when we humans needn't *sniff* to prove *ours*?"

"Well, we are not dogs, sir, but superior beings. We've built highways specifically for the purpose of getting from A to B and everywhere else in between."

"But from the point of view of the robot, does it not strike them that the man-made motorways are slow and tedious? Just as we see the dog's way of sniffing as primitive, slow and tedious.

"Hmmm, I'm starting to see your drift; though there is still this disturbing nag about it. I'm...."

"Perhaps this will help. I am not saying that robots are necessarily superior. Nonetheless, to infer they are *inferior* merely because they can't replicate certain human acts is premature. Moreover, many of the things they can't do aren't so much down to their fault as down to our inability to teach them or to program them properly."

"Well, sir, how about languages then? Why can't they learn English or French and talk back to us in human ways."

Charles laughed. "What makes English so good that a machine would want to mimic it? Surely there are easier and more efficient ways for machines to communicate than having to learn, for instance, all that 'polite' talk that is so built into our languages."

"Star Trek, the second Mudd episode: 'Then there is a word in your language which we find untranslatable: *please*!'"

Of course I was the first and only one to laugh. But no matter. It was yet another example of Charles's quirkiness among the intelligentsia. The methods by which he used to dismiss his contemporaries had been so unprecedented that people could not quite rebut him. He wraps a philosophical overcoat over every overtone. Even if the others had been right in the details, they would still be overruled and overridden overall!

Undeterred, I launched a final assault: "Sir, while it's true that machines will one day be capable of matching man's productive skills; or, more precisely, his physical abilities. Can we ever expect to transfer to them emotional duties as well? Like understanding, or guidance?"

"Why in heaven's name would we want to?" Charles said. "Next thing you'll want to know is: can we get a child to love a robot instead of a real person."

"Now that would be interesting to see," I said. "As a matter of fact, I'll have you know that the cartoons on TV were the best babysitters *I*'d ever had."

"And look what has become of you."

"Thank you very much, once again!"

"In all seriousness, Vermont, we are dealing with machine and human interaction here—a daunting task considering that billions of human beings have yet to learn to interact amongst themselves."

"So you don't think a machine can ever give emotional comfort and advice?"

"Emotion has so many facets to it. A machine of tommorrow might grasp a couple, but it would be impossible to get them all."

"Why not?"

"Because it won't understand contradictions," Charles responded in that gentle, professorial tone. "Take for instance the feelings of hate, which we touched on earlier. Do we hate something because it doesn't do what we want? Or do we hate something because we don't like what it does? They are rather subtle distinctions to a machine, but plain and obvious to human beings. In one case, the objective is to destroy the hated object; whereas in the other, it is to salvage it."

"Gee, you're right! One is hating the enemy, the other is saving a friendship."

"Or, it could contain elements of both: to destroy parts of something, and rescue the remainder."

"Hmm, interesting point; complex, too. For if we had to invent a new word for every subtle distinction, we would need a dictionary many times longer than the present. And if you ask most people, they'll tell you we've got enough words as is."

"Quite so. Even if the computer could store all the distinctions, it is still at best a reflexive translator, just an illusion of intelligence. Then again, the computer has only existed for a generation. While man, after thousands of years, is still at the early stage of understanding how the mind truly works."

"Well, from Newton to Einstein was what...about three hundred years? So if we begin the mental revolution with Freud, then we ought to be about a hundred years in by now."

"As I said this morning, it shouldn't take too long to achieve the next breakthrough. However, the final piece of the puzzle is still impossibly elusive."

"Any idea on what the equation might look like?"

"I haven't the slightest. But I will tell you one thing that might offer some hope. It is that despite all the contradictions found in human nature, we indeed do strive to be logical creatures. For one thing, we don't purposely do anything against our wish; that underlying all our actions and inactions are motives; meaning, whichever action we undertake, at the moment of the act itself—that split instant before we act—we clearly do deem it to be the most justifiable thing we can do; otherwise, we would not be doing it."

"Even when someone is about to kill somebody?"

"For at least those milliseconds before one pulls the trigger, the answer is yes. This is true whether it is killing someone, or rolling a million-dollar roll of dice, or whatever. One decides to act because a majority of one's brain cells tells one to go ahead. Even when one's state of mind is that of nothingness, it still *isn't* one of unintended randomness. Of course, this is not to say that one fully realizes the consequences of all of one's actions or that one wouldn't regret the things one had done soon after. But those issues are irrelevant. They only mean that the previous decisions might have been based on erroneous judgments; they do not change the fact that at such and such a point in time, one was doing what one *most* wanted to do. So there it is: not much, mostly just common sense, but I think it's a start."

"I love it! It's brilliant in its simplicity. Actually, what you said did help solve a lot if you look at it from a parameter point of view. It knocks random aimlessness right out of the equation. Kind of like less than zero or greater than zero, it immediately nullifies half the field. Wonder if I may borrow that one for the opening statement of my forecasting thesis; or whatever it is I might write someday."

"It is yours for the taking."

"Then let that be the first basic truth then. All we need now is for someone to carry on writing—to carry on perspiring—after an inspiring 'Call me Ishmael' like opening. What is the French counterpart, by the way?"

"'*Longtemps, Je me suis couché de bonne heure...,'* Marcel Proust, *A La Recherche Du Temps Perdu;* Recapturing Lost Time."

"Aw, man! Hope this equation isn't as long as that one."

"Be it in prose or quadratic or differential or gravitational, it will likely be very long."

"Hey, how does an existential equation sound? $E=MC^2$, part II: $\text{Existentiality}=\text{Mortality}\times\text{Cost}^2$." I had to laugh at that one. It was so ridiculous it made sense. Nothing like reducing human nature to a tiny equation.

Charles was pleased as well. "Mankind from a distant view is nothing but a formula. Like food, it might come in all shapes and sizes and forms; but no matter the appearance, it all breaks down into a few essential chemicals."

"A fuel by any other name, Shakespeare!"

"You are improving, Vermont," Charles smiled. "Yes. Survival! That's all eating is meant to be. Nothing more, nothing less."

"You of all people, Uncle Charles," I shook my head. "To expect you of all people to be saying such a thing—and right in middle of a Parisian feast of a lifetime."

The dinner was about ready to enter the third service—the one après the roast. It was a good thing that I hadn't eaten anything all day except for my afternoon tea with Ally and her friends. Even so, it's amazing how your appetite can suddenly expand when you are eating for more than just eating's sake. When the word appetite signifies a desire rather than a condition.

The break in the proceedings was also table-hopping time. Actually, there was schmoozing going around ever since that banquet group got seated. Periodically, you'd see minglers of all sorts taking their turns working the room, some stopped at our table on the way to the big one, others said hello on the way back—just like they do in Hollywood.

We began a new round of grazing with rounds of cheese. No, not all round: some were cylindrical, others pyrimidical and still others disc-like in shape. Charles had the Roquefort again, the same cheese he'd had at lunch on Friday. The less monotonous me asked for something less legendary which the server had at his disposal. But after he offered me a cheese from the North that looked like shit and smelled almost as bad, I decided to mellow out the flavor just a tad.

"Give him something milder, perhaps a Tomme from Savoie," Charles suggested.

"From the Savoie, we have Roblochon."

"That'll be fine," Charles said.

"May I also recommend the very special Saint-Marcellin," added the server.

"In that case give him a little of both," Charles told him. I was at first slightly embarrassed. I think you are supposed to get just one piece of cheese on a plate. Then again, the dinner was getting more and more informal, and if Charles didn't give a fig, I didn't give a shit!

"Wonderful cheese," I said after a bite. "Tastes like a homemade cake; creamy and nutty, but not too runny."

"Lots of care goes into the making of a fine cheese, not unlike that of a fine wine."

"But do cheeses have all those, um, technicalities built in 'em, like they do with wines?"

"No. A bottle of wine is a more elevated art form—truly a miracle from above—the drink of gods, if you will. Cheese, on the other hand, is on a cloud below—"

"How low? 'bout the height of god's smelly feet?"

Charles gave a little crackle: "You *are* doing well tonight, Vermont. Don't stop on my account."

"Sorry about that. So you were telling me about cheese's more humble status."

"Well, cheese has always been more earthly—a product of ordinary farmers. It gives them pride and independence when they can age some old milk and transform it into something quite grand. Take the Saint-Marcellin: during the day it could be sitting quietly at an old farm near Vienne; but that night it could end up being the cheese course chez *Point*."

"Chez Point? Wow! Rubbing penicillium on the rich and famous. Hey, that's pretty cool! But do you think the mass producers will eventually drive out all those mom and pop outfits?"

"They already have. Yet handmade cheese will never go away—if only due to its superior taste."

"But taste isn't set in stone, Uncle Charles. You get a kid who grows up with pasteurized cheese—or better yet, plastic-wrapped American singles—then that, in time, will become his standard."

"Yes, as we can plainly see," Charles laughed. "To some extent I'll grant you that. Unlike many other goods where the only difference in quality is perceived by a logo or a brand name, there is a marked difference in cheeses. Therefore, so long as the price of the handmade is within reason, it will survive."

In order to properly accompany the cheeses that have been around for hundreds of years, we moved to a vineyard just as ancient. The chateau was Ausone, the vintage, 1975, and not for nothing was the size—an Imperiale—so big only one bottle was needed to serve all the tables. I was told it was a special order and possibly even the last Imperiale of that vintage in existence. Here was another souvenir that would look great in my living room. Unopened, it would also be the most costly. The chateau just didn't bottle many in large sizes—it didn't make much wine. Period. While some might compare the Ausone to Cheval Blanc, its much larger neighbor; Charles preferred to see it as more of an alternative to the Petrus, the elitist of all Bordeaux just up the road in Pomerol. They are both tiny in size, and have been passed down the generations with hundreds of years of tradition. Small is often beautiful, especially in the era of big, corporate-owned chateaux.

I felt a certain anticipation drinking the Ausone. But how do I go about getting completely soaked into the experience—especially when it's someone without much experience in the first place. Well, Charles advised that I should try to seek out both the sublime and the assertive—the nuances of balance and complexity. Meaning, to train yourself to feel all the great powers at work in the wine: some acting in harmony, others rivaling for your attention. Keeping in mind that first and foremost, this is your own personal experience; that as much as you ought to be kind and respectful of others, you mustn't treat their word as definitive and final. Remember the wine the way *you* want to remember it. Then and only then can you be on your way to mastering it like an expert. And through it all, you must show effort. It is no accident that the great wines are also memorable. They work hard to permeate themselves permanently into your senses. But they *can't* do all the work by themselves. You have to be willing to weigh it in your mouth a second or two longer—to gauge the uniqueness of its character, and balance it with the complexity of its finish. And, as long as you concentrate, you should soon muster enough confidence to form an independent impression; even retain it for your memory.

That said, I was determined to reach out for that something unattainable. I took a big bite out of the cheese, then married it with a couple of sips of wine. After that, I just waited. Waited and waited:

looked up at the towering floral chandeliers and waited; looked across at the towering hairdos of the women at the banquet and waited. Yes, of all the wine and cheese parties in all the towns in all the world that evening, I could very well be at one of the best. Then why was my head fighting for a chance to get the hell away from all this crap, to wander out into the wilderness? There I was, a shepherd in the Alps, possibly high noon. I was totally alone, no one even within my echo's edge, not a living being except for a couple of dogs and my sheep. Heaps of sheep, grazing up a storm. Unhurriedly, I ripped open my brown bag and drew out a baguette, then I cut up a thick chunk of Alpine cheese and laid it on the bread. Finally, a little oil and vinegar on a bed of shredded lettuce. I had no idea where the lettuce came from—perhaps from that morning's supply mule; and that was my dinner. But it was like a dinner in misty heaven, washed down with a whole bottle of intense, ruby red wine. It was a wine still crackling with the body of a twenty-year-young fighter. It was a wine of courage, independence, and destiny. Nothing ever tasted so reassuring. I was sitting on the edge of the cliff without fear. Absorbing the exalted Alpine cleavage with the deepest of my breaths, marveling at the even higher peaks across the way. Yes, that was where my route would lead up to in the days ahead.

Me? Afraid of laying in the bed of nature and dying? Impossible! Moi? A case of vertigo? Im-po-seeb-le! I was a man tied to his mountain peaks, living a life of simplicity, while down below in the Valley of the Kings, ladies in statue-esque hairdos were charming their way into the pants of men in funny dresses. Those gentle ladies and fair gentlemen—resplendent in their two-hundred-year-old costumes. I shouldn't be in the same room with them! I was not the shepherd but the odd sheep out, in a land where feudalism was still in vogue. Just listen to them talk, like Marie Antoinette mouthpieces in Pompadourie hairpieces...

"Oh, the poor, cannot afford the chateaubriand? Then let them eat sauce!"

"No, it is not true. Did she really trade in two handsome thirty-year-old playboys for an ugly sixty-year-old billionaire."

"Yes, too hard to make *that* much money—far better to marry it!"

"If you only knew the way she *conned* him into marriage. She's really a peasant, you know; lived in a clay hut and never saw shoes!"

"How shocking this must be. I thought he would *never* marry his mistress."

"Anything for you, my sweet Princess: no request too big, no request too small."

"Oh, of course not. The real reason the Countess won't remarry is so she can keep her title."

"How pitiful! That minor starlet now wants to play major aristocrat, trying to inject hundreds of years of ancestry *intravenously*."

"Grand Duke XYZ, he had just spent a night at a Left Bank hotel with someone a third his age."

"Let us not forget Princess SOS. She is a royal bastard—an accident of an *orgy*!"

"Oh that old tramp. She claims to have beautiful skin; but I will have you know that there is a thirty-year difference between her face and her neck."

"Agreed! What she claims to be her age, just as her paintings, is nothing but one big lie."

"What a parvenu! She wants to climb the social ladder faster than her husband can climb on his mistress."

"What fools! One needs more than money, dear, to penetrate this world."

"Yes, even more money!"

There you have it: aristocrats of dubious lineage, parvenues of questionable taste, all grandiosely gathered for a night to pass themselves off as direct descendants from the royalties of the past.

"May I present Mr. Mark Vermont!" It was Charles and a lady in blue walking toward me. "And Mark, may I present the Baroness of Sartois." I stood up to greet her. As I was about to casually shake her hand, I realized the right thing to do was to give her a *baisemain*, a hand kiss. But it was too late, so I took a bow and, in my nervousness, blurted out something totally stupid like "Enchanted to meet you... your royal baroness-ness." God, it was awful and ever so wrong! Well, guess that's what happens when there's only a split second: You either end up too casual or way overdone. She was a nice lady though; lots of class and lovely, too. Especially when she flashed that friendly smile. Unlike those mocking birds at the big table, she was not snotty at all, just graciously exhibiting her aristocratic air.

"Isn't this just the most lavishing dinner?" she said to me.

"You better believe it."

"Ooh, and the ambiance—I feel as if I'm embracing the brush strokes of a Fragonard." The Baroness certainly had imagination. "Monsieur Martin, if you do see the chef, would you kindly give him my highest compliments for such an extraordinary display of his talents."

"Yeah, thank the chef for me, too; sir."

"Now, now, it is far too early for that. I still have yet to taste his sweets."

"What remarkable metabolism," the Baroness said of Charles. "How he ever manages to eat so much and stay so trim is beyond us all."

"The secret is to eat well, chere Baronne," Charles said slyly. "This way, one will not be easily distracted by American junk food."

"Heyyyy!" I woke up. "Tell that to Henry the Eighth!" I cracked. I'll have you know that this Frito's and Raisinets lover is not so bad on the gut front himself.

Shortly after, Charles got his Montmorency pudding. The Baroness then picked a couple of fruits from a chock-full of fruits display, and the unaristocratic I made the server work by asking for Crêpes Flambées. The show was worth it. Just like the duck, the crepes were prepared next to the table with the flaming of the liqueurs providing some extra razzmatazz.

"Mmm...it smells divine," the Baroness said as she watched me take a bite.

"And the taste...just delightful, delectable, delicious, and de-lovely as you."

"My, my, Monsieur Martin, you have quite a disciple on your hands."

"You're too kind, chere Baronne," Charles said with a grin.

As I sat and watched the Baroness share a bite with us, I must say I was star-struck. She had this elegant, graceful aura about her; a silky and sexy bare-shouldered dress didn't hurt either, it brought out the shine of her chunky sapphire necklace. But she was more than enough of a beauty in her own right—too young to be my mother and too old to be my sister; kind of like a tweener, though quite a lovely tweener at that. Shades of Carole Lombard without so much blond. Acted like her too, chatty with an edge of silliness. "So tell me, dear boy, have you been enjoying Monsieur Martin's wit and wisdom for the past two days?"

"Immensely," I said. "And you, Baroness?"

"Oh, he never ceases to astound me. He speaks of such nice things one wonders how he ever got to write such horrors down."

Charles just smiled. "The role of the speaker is to please; the role of the writer is to offend."

"Not so from what I've been hearing, sir. The speakers at that big table have been viciously at it all night."

"Monsieur Martin can be cruel, too; can't you dear?"

"Never unintentionally!"

"Are you sure?" the Baroness sharpened her voice. "I thought the way you treated your newest neighbor was rather harsh."

"Don't tell me Uncle Charles is still brushing off newcomers like he brushes off dust?"

"I'm afraid so. A foreign tycoon who moved in last year—week after week, his wife made a habit of having their butler deliver her dinner invitations, along with some of the most inappropriate gifts. Charles didn't know whether to laugh or cry."

"She was a frightful bore," Charles said. "With an empty bag for imagination and totally devoid of wit."

"Not from what I have heard, Monsieur Martin. I have been told they are quite an amusing couple. Charles, darling, can you keep a secret?"

"Most certainly. I shall allow the Baronne to spread her secrets at her own leisurely pace."

"Oh, good. Now, rumor has it that this foreigner has a fleet of vintage sports cars, and he plans to build an underground garage, dear—right through your courtyard!"

"Why, that pompous fool!" Man, did Charles look agitated for a second. The Baroness was right, he didn't know whether to laugh or cry.

"And that's not all," said the Baroness. "They have been hoping that perhaps Monsieur Martin could pick up part of the cost."

That got him. "Those buffoons! What revolting idiots they are!"

"I see what you mean, Baroness."

"Oh, you have no idea," she smiled.

Then Charles got up. "Would you excuse me for a moment? I'm going to go and bring your mother over here so that we can all have coffee together"

"Oh, that would be charming," said the Baroness. "But please tell her it is your idea." Then the Baroness turned to me, "He likes to put words in other people's mouths."

"How do they taste?"

"Embarrassing. Especially when they come in the form of a surprise attack. What's worse, he strikes in such odd ways that one tends to think the wounds are self-inflicted. But I have finally had my revenge. I knew my little *secret* about the underground tunnel garage would irritate him irretrievably."

"You're pretty clever yourself, Baroness."

"One does what one can," she sighed. "Even a bit too clever for my own good at times. Take last night, after dancing, we played bridge. The Mellerys against Charles and myself. But after Catherine Mellery and I had both scored some crucial wins, I made the suggestion that perhaps the ladies ought to team up and take the men on."

"I take it you shouldn't've said it."

"Oh, dear. I backed the great, the one and only Charles Martin into a corner, sure enough. 'Women,' he said, 'give them half a chance and they'll want to take us for all we've got!'"

"That's our Charles."

"Men! What beasts they are!" the Baroness continued, with a hint of revulsion and an air of rebellion. "No different from any other animals, those *men* creatures, don't you think?"

"Oh...absolutely," I concurred. "Just ask the women that raised them."

"*And* the women who tolerate them. 'Don't underestimate the female sex,' I said to Charles last night. 'Despite our lesser physical strength, we didn't thrive for thousands of years by being stupid. On the contrary, we are the most precious entity the world has ever known.'" The Baroness spoke without betraying any conceit. "'More than anything,' I continued, 'it is the women of this species that have distinguished ourselves from the rest of the creatures. It is *we* who possess the emotional qualities that make humans what they are: beauty, charity, breeding, grace, intuition...'"

"What's the matter, Baroness?"

"I should *not* have said intuition. It gave Charles the weapon he was waiting for. 'Ahhh, a woman's intuition, you say? A curious thing isn't it—certainly most unique to your gender.' Then he looked at me with those devilish eyes of his and said, 'but isn't it true, chere Baronne, that her intuition was ever so sharpened by that constant subconscious desire to guess the date of her period!'"

Boy, was I in stitches after that remark. It was disgusting. Period. At least to most men. But maybe, just *maybe*, those periodic practices do make perfect that fine art of intuitive prediction.

"Well, Baroness, boys will be boys; but girls, like it or not, do grow up," I said, still shaking my head with laughter. "While Charles gave you credit for women's uniqueness, he somehow still managed to sneak in a low blow. Look on the bright side, though: at least I now know why my mother's intuition got better and better as I was growing up; and then, all of a sudden, it flattened out after her menopause. Sorry Mom."

"My dear boy, if only life were as predictable as a period; sometimes, I wish Charles could rather be more so as well."

"But you do adore him anyway?"

"He is the joy of my life," said the Baroness. "The rest just bore me to pieces. I bore myself too. Alas, I can't leave myself, so there isn't much I can do, is there?"

"No, I'm afraid not," I said. "Yeah, I like Charles, too. He is like a walking encyclopedia. He could answer any question I have; food...history...life!"

"My dearest boy, what is food but a bridge through the history of life."

"Nicely put, chere Baronne—like a bridge over your perfumed waters."

The mamas and papas of the Baroness arrived. He was a Count, she, a Countess. They looked it, too, in the sense that they both seemed up there in age—certainly more so than Charles—more frail and not as steady as she goes. Charles was truly a most vigorous man, with more vitality than both of them combined.

This time around, though, I greeted the guests properly. I think. I stood up, took the Countess's hand, then bent down and gave her an air hand kiss. After that, I shook the Count's hand as I took a little bow.

Charles sat them down between him, with the Countess closer to me. How eerie I felt, like a trashy paperback from the new world sandwiched between the bookcovers of some *ancien régime* library —with titles as long as their ancestry.

"You have your uncle's eyes," the Countess said to me.

"Yup, eye, ear and throat. Though I must admit he has the ears of far more beautiful women."

"Monsieur Martin, your nephew brings you much honor," said the Countess.

A faint smirk appeared on Charles's face. "Give him time, my dear Comtess, give him time."

Yeah, give me time is right. In fact, me being so inferior to my tablemates had freed me from worrying about the proprieties. "I must say, Madame la Comtess, that it was timely of you to come to our table just now. Why, a little longer, I would have fallen madly in love with your daughter."

"Oh you poor dear, that would be tragic."

"I know it. A lifetime of nothing but pain and heartbreaks."

The Count was amused, too: "Look on the bright side of suffering, young man; it might start you on your way of becoming a great artist."

"Naaahh, a life of poverty and ear cutting self-torture is *not* my idea of a good time. Plus the fact that I don't even believe much in posterity. You know what, maybe I'll just be a jewel thief instead—stealing fabulous jewels from the rich and famous and returning them to their rightful, original owners."

That worked up the Baroness. "Oh, what a lovely boy," she said, touching me on the head.

"Speaking of jewels," the Countess said to Charles. "I wonder who is going to be the lucky one this year?"

"We'll find out soon enough. I promised Madame Mellery that we'd wait for her this year, provided she gets here soon."

"That would depend on the Monsieur," said the Count. "If he is winning well at the Club, we may never get to see him."

"Oh, let it be me to win it again," the Baroness said to Charles. "I was just getting used to it around my neck."

"It will be the luck of the draw," Charles said. "Besides, you wouldn't want to leave your mother out now, would you?"

"She has won it already."

"I was the first winner," the Countess said proudly, "exactly twenty years ago."

"Sorry to hear you have to give it up," I said to the Baroness. "You look ravishing with those jewels on." I wanted to have a closer look at it, that sapphire necklace laced with diamonds. But I didn't want to embarrass the Baroness by getting *too* close to her cleavage. "That center sapphire is the largest I've ever seen."

"It is over one hundred carats," the Baroness said. Then she whispered softly towards me, "115.3 carats, to be exact."

"Wow! And all those diamonds to boot—just brilliant!" Though I wasn't sure how brilliant it was of Charles to circulate a priceless piece of jewelry, year in and year out. "Uncle Charles, a necklace of such extravagance, what if something should happen to it?"

"It has survived wars upon wars, and countless revolutions. No doubt it will be around for some time to come."

Charles, sometimes his naïveté knows no bounds.

Well, the moment we had been waiting for had arrived. The last course—the dessert—the final pièce de résistance. It was called the *croquemouche*—two of them, actually. From a distance, they looked like two little Christmas trees, standing side by side at the gate of heaven. A closer examination revealed hundreds of angelic pastry balls, placed in a circle and stacked all the way up to the tree top.

It was impressive. I mean they were *it*. I know I might have inadvertently exaggerated in the past, about food and otherwise. But there can be no exaggerations about this dessert. It was just a colossal feat. "I must confess," I said, "For a person who doesn't even know the difference between baking soda and baking powder, this has been quite an evening of baking-out."

"The chef will sleep well tonight," Charles said, "seeing how everyone is devouring his food."

"Isn't it sad, though," added the Countess, "to see all this beauty disappear in minutes?"

"Such is the irony of a culinary masterpiece," Charles said. "The more we break it down, the more ingrained we are of its delights."

"Yup, an irony pill a day keeps the rust at bay."

"Why, Charles, he is a poet, too; just like you." The Baroness had been nothing short of surprises all night.

"That was very clever, my boy."

"Thank you, sir. Poetry in s-looow motion if you will—a direct result of eating too many cream puffs."

"Yes indeed," Charles nodded, "Comes to that, Mark here is quite cerebral in his own right. Did you know, Monsieur le Comte, that this boy here is one of the brightest young crossword puzzle solvers in America. A semi-finalist in the American Crossword Puzzle Tournament for the past two years."

What? I literally flipped when I heard that. My coffee nearly flipped out of its cup, my dessert nearly flipped out of my mouth. Certainly I was in shock, as it totally blew me away. How could he say such a thing? I thought. I don't care for crosswords at all. It's a big waste of time—a very inefficient way of gaining knowledge. But how do I get out of this mess? I couldn't say Charles was wrong. That would have totally embarrassed him in front of his guests. Then it dawned on me: perhaps Charles was intentionally trying to put me on the spot. Shit! Why couldn't he have said that I was a finalist at the World Series of Poker? Or a world class sailor? I could have easily bullshited my way through those subjects and told them everything they wanted to know. Dammit! I didn't even have any crossword puzzle friends to draw upon. Think Vermont! Think!! Well, about the only ones I know who liked crosswords are the people who wore glasses in the subway and people who sit next to me in airplanes. It's a start, at least.

"Yeah, I like doing crossword puzzles. It keeps me busy on the subway everyday, helps to keep out the rudeness; or rather, to make me part of the rudeness. The puzzle is also wonderful in airplanes. It forces me to concentrate, a way to block out the sound of babies crying."

"It's very addicting," I continued, "I would get out the New York Times puzzle every Saturday night and struggle with it. It used to drive my girlfriend crazy. In fact, I think that was why she left me. She used to say to me: 'Mark, if you had understood the meaning of love half as well as you could twist its letters around, I might well have stayed.'"

They all laughed, the four of them. I thought it was funny, too—which gave me some desperately needed confidence.

"Yeah, I must admit that solving crosswords can become quite an obsession. When I see a word, oh...say POST, I would soon be seeing double vision, sometimes triple vision. You know, STOP, TOPS, POTS, or even MOTS. It drives all the lemon melons crazy."

"Have you always been this way?" The Countess asked.

"Yeah, my grandmother, may she rest in peace, she used to work on the crosswords while she cooked." That was true. Come to think of it, she had a dictionary, too. "The main reason I got into doing puzzles was because I had a really boring childhood." That was also true. "When I was a child, we had an old television set that was always in...um...that never moved down from the attic, yet its picture was always moving downwards. So my choices were narrowed to either reading or listening to the radio." That was an outright lie! "But I didn't feel like reading all the time. It went too fast, page after page. So to counter that, I opted for the slower pace of doing a puzzle. It is the *perfect* thing for you if you're looking to kill a couple of hours. You know: Napoleon, P- -N-I-S."

It was now the Count's turn. "Charming," he growled.

Oh, god. I couldn't believe what was happening. I was actually on a roll. "Yeah, it's very masochistic of me to undertake such a hobby. I was fortunate that I got better and better at it with time. Rarely do I even solve whole puzzles anymore. I just look at the definitions. That way, I can do puzzles almost as fast as I read 'em." Man, was I winging it! But I couldn't stop just yet; I needed to seal it with one more lie. I got one. "You know, Countess, what's even more exciting than reading and solving puzzles is what I've been working on lately—a computer program that could automatically generate its own puzzle. All's I do is, well, first off I set up the guidelines—a database that consists of a plethora of esoterica—you know, the obscure novelists, the lost languages, the rare minerals, the chemical compounds and so on; then bingo, out comes the final product."

"What about the questions?"

Whoops. Forgot about them questions. Can't generate those automatically, can I? "No, the clues are far too great an art form to be done by machines. It's the soul of the puzzle; it's where you show your style. When I write the clues, I try to be fair and equate a hard answer with an easy clue. Say if I want to use OK TEDI; no, that's no good. Say if it calls for the word SEPIK, I'll just say it's the Amazon of New Guinea. But if the answer is PARIS, the perhaps a cleverer definition could be in store—say...SEWER, or is it SEWERS?"

Everyone liked that one, which was a great relief. Whew! That was a close call. So close I felt I needed a cigarette, and I didn't even smoke.

Charles, though, had a better idea. After the ladies had moved on to another table, he picked out two Havanas. A big one for him, a smaller one for me. The wooden matches, however, came in one size only—thick and long. After Charles guillotined the head, he put the cigar in his mouth and rotated it around and around till he got an even light.

"A peculiar smokiness it has," I said.

"Quite. The breath of god, it's been known."

Breath of god! Jesus Habana Cristo, that Charles was being dramatic again. "So inhaling a fine cigar brings us closer to god?"

"Never inhale, my dear boy. Just breathe."

Like drinking a fine wine, the pageantry before the lighting of the cigar is almost a ritual in itself. I was instructed to hold the cigar between the thumb and index finger, inspect the cigar band and the color of its wrapping, then roll it around a bit to feel the suppleness of its body and smell the totality of its aroma. Then and only then do you proceed to moisten its head a little and make an incision with the cutter. "A proper incision is crucial to a good smoke," Charles said. "Too big a cut will not only make the cigar too bitter, but too heated at the head."

Lighting the cigar, unlike the lighting of a cigarette, is very much a personal affair. Traditionalists even like to warm the whole cigar with the flames a bit—more out of habit than necessity as the sealing gum is now odorless. "Don't be too concerned about the temperature of the cigar wrapper," Charles said. "What indeed matters is the temperature of the smoke."

I smoked a medium-strength Corona while Charles, the aficionado of wine and smoky spirits, went for the maximum flavor of a double Corona, a fatter and longer version that rivaled the biggest Mont Blanc pen.

As I smoked, Charles reminded me not to puff too fast—one per minute, perhaps, and spend the rest of the time deliberating over the mysterious glow of the blue smoke. One other thing regarding etiquette: you definitely smoke your own cigar. No passing around the cigar like you do a joint.

"What of the ashes?"

"The ash? Be natural. It is not a contest; neither is it something one tips off after each draw."

With my stomach sounding like the early stages of a volcano, I felt the passing out of Havanas could very well detonate its fate. The match shall light up the cigar and the cigar shall, in turn, light up the bomb in my belly; or so I thought. Miraculously, though, that cigar was most pleasant: not only did it not implode in any suicide mission, it gave off the opposite effect—a mouthful of cool, soothing mellowness.

Charles was savoring the aroma as well. "A good cigar elevates one into a different plane, a higher state of consciousness. It sets one off on the road to calm one's soul."

"And calm, sir, is one state we much long for in this tumultuous day and age. Perhaps that's why gangsters like cigars so much. Then again, how do you explain Groucho Marx? Or better yet, French philosophers?"

"Gangsters exist in every walk of life!"

Wow! Never had Charles been in higher form.

"And pranksters," I added. I was smoking a Havana, too—my maiden voyage. But in order to catch up to Winston Churchill, who was reputed to have smoked over three hundred thousand of those suckers, I needed to more than just hurry up—I needed to also be rich as hell; or at least have lots of generous cigar-donating friends. It was at that time that I thought of a great question to ask Charles, but I waited for a while so as not to abruptly interrupt him in the midst of his smoky contemplation.

"If you were to host the ultimate dinner party, Uncle Charles, who would you select from history as your guests? No Sir Winston nor de Gaulle, since you had known them personally."

"A small intimate party, I take it."

"Oh yeah, just one table. But smaller than the table across the way. Eight to ten people tops."

"Well, Napoleon would have to be on the list, and Charlemagne, perhaps."

"Um…one to a country, if you please."

"All right, then. We'll invite Napoleon, Alexander the Great and Julius Caesar, then perhaps Ericson the Viking and Genghis Khan to eat all the food; and, to balance it out with some minds—oh, let's keep it simple and not too obscure—we'll invite Aristotle of ancient Greece, Da Vinci of Florence, and Lord Shakespeare of England."

"No women in the honor roll?"

"Coco Chanel is still *very* much alive while Cleopatra wouldn't come *out* of there alive."

"Ha! And Maggie Thatcher might just out-*man* any man alive!"

"Yes, indeed. As for an American presence, Morgan and Carnegie are probably too busy. And Thomas Jefferson, you ask? Well, he might become so preoccupied in his negotiations with Napoleon on the Louisiana Purchase that he'd *completely* ruin the party."

I burst out laughing loudly again. Loud enough that others in the room must have heard me. But I didn't care. "Hey, that's a great one, sir," I said. "Either that or Jefferson would have been so appalled at all the tyrants and warlords present that he'd have walked out before the first course."

"War is hell; and the warriors hell's angels."

"How was your own war experience?"

"Mechanical much of the way. Youngbloods all, we were virtually machine-like in the way we took orders. Just as well, I suppose, considering we had on our hands one of the earliest computers."

"Even back then?"

"Well, a rather primitive version, with glass tubes all about. And a monster it was. Bigger than a room yet slower than a tank—used primarily to assist British Military Intelligence to crack enemy codes."

"But weren't you also a spy in Germany?"

"Primarily during the early stages of the war, trying to persuade German industrialists to turn against the Nazis. Old family acquaintances…at the time."

"Were you successful?"

"No."

"Still friends after the war?"

Charles didn't answer right away. "It took very many years," he finally said. "One reason I remained in England for so long after the war was my reluctance to deal with matters at home."

"What was it that Sadat once said, that the enemy of my enemy is my friend? Is the reverse true as well, that the enemy of um..., I don't know, what is the converse?"

"I think what you wanted to know was: whether a friend of the enemy is automatically one's enemy."

"Took the words right out of my cigar!"

Charles again was slow to respond. "It was agonizing: loyalty to an individual pitted against the loyalty to a cause. But during the war against Hitler, any friend of mine who identified with my number one enemy also became my enemy. It was painful, yet very simple."

"When, if ever, should you make an exception?"

"Legitimate question. I'd like to say that one would make an exception if he or she were the only friend one had in the world."

"Hmm, that's an interesting angle. Pretty deep, too. So what you are saying is that if you have a bunch of enemies, and only one friend, then you tend to value your friendship, even though he sided with the enemy."

"The marginal need for a single friend is greater than the marginal desire for additional enemies."

"By the same token, sir, if you have too many friends already, then you might feel a greater incremental need *for* an enemy."

Charles laughed. "As you can see, my friend, the choices are endless."

"What if you are neither friend nor foe? Are you still relevant?"

"Ah yes—the billions of nameless, faceless bodies that walk the planet—human beings all, but as indifferent to each other as they are to me."

"It's a way to prevent our brains from overloading, I guess. Unfortunately, as I am in Paris for only a weekend, I must face whatever the onslaught of new faces that come my way—overloading my schedule as it may."

"Up to you, my boy. Unlike most of us here who are up in age, and limited to pretty much one place a night; you are, however, free to roam. Of course, should you care to return, the chances are that we'll still be here."

"I can see. I can see. The strolling violinists are straining to fade out, but a swinging new brass section is set to fade in."

"Where will you be fading into, after you fade out of here?"

"What's further on the agenda? Oh...probably either the Zigzag again or this big disco nearby called La Casbah. Makes no difference to me. They might as well have named it La Casbah *blanka*."

"I am shocked, *shocked* that gambling is going on in here!"

"Your winnings, sir."

"Oh. Thank you very much."

"Hey, that was great. You know, sir, if only I didn't revere Casablanca so much, I'd do a sequel to it. What, with the last line being 'Louis, I think this is the beginning of a beautiful friendship,' Casablanca is tailor-made for a sequel. We could even call it *Play it again, Rick.*"

"Will it be in black-and-white or color?" Charles asked.

"Uh, boy. You know, I would probably lean toward color if the scenes were mostly night shots. Color brightens the darkness, providing an added dimension to that moody black-and-white feel. Not to mention it would give me a chance to do some fancy footwork on my lighting techniques. Picture this:

*"Headlights...that is all he could keep his head'n eyes on as he lines up outside Casbah Blanca. Not the headlights on all those northbound trains, but more the lights that shine through those cool Sahara rains...*no, strike that—*the lights that shine through those hot Parisienne legs. Yes, the sight of headlights beaming straight at a row of mini-skirts and their accompanying columns of legs. My, those lean, bright, shapely lines of flesh—there's nothing in the world quite like them. Ahhh, those warm legs of love: when they know how to spread them, they can rock any Casbah known to man; otherwise, they are merely an extension of their slinky, steel-heeled shoes—all tangled up with no place to go....*"

NINETEEN

"Get me a scotch, would'ya? On the rocks, si vous plaît."

"That will be thirty francs, monsieur."

"That's all? Then make it a double then; it'll still be less than a drink at the stupid Casbah."

"You were over there?"

"Over and out! Well, way it goes, one in one out. He's in, and *I'm* out!"

"Bad news, monsieur?"

"The pits. But don't worry, I'll pay ya. They play and I pay!"

He tries to resist again and again, but still he can't repel the onslaught. Hundreds of sounds thunder by, thousands of flashes lightning past. The more he tries to forget, the more tenaciously the images stick. *Head to head, hip to hip; crotch to crotch, lip to lip!* It's as if he's looking at instant replay—over and over. *Scum! Slut! Saluad!! Salope!!!*

His breathing is heavy, his mind crisscrossing left and right, his mouth foaming with profanities. They are mostly directed at the two butt-holes, but partly at himself as well. *How did you fool yourself into thinking she was up there for the picking? Who do you think you are to just drop in like that and have her drop everything just for you? Where the hell is the cool, self-touted analyst from afar? Or are you only in session when the breakdown is remote and apart?*

He is in total confusion. Logical reasoning has evaded him; coherent thoughts can't penetrate his brain. He feels incapacitated—unable to direct the traffic flow within his body. Still he keeps at it, in an all-out effort to regain his rational self, his old sense of balance. He knows he needs to have some quality time alone to think, to get over his depression. Yet, he also feels a need to tell someone, to air it out to others and have them in on his misery.

La Belle Aurore flashs across the neon marquee. Reminiscent of an old sailor's dive in Vieux Marseille. Smokey and slippery and smelly, with sods of squalor all safe and sound. *Drink up, mate, your kind of place, just dip yourself into a nice bottle, then sail through that sea of whisky to give your problems a cleansing soak.*

How could you not have anticipated this? Why did you blindfold yourself with a veil of touchy sentiment. It was nice while your fantasy lasted; but this is real time, and real time means real losers, whether you like it or not. Start facing up to the fact that you are not the next James Bond, but a wimp of a limb passing for a man.

The drinks offer little help. Again and again, he finds himself in great despair—desolate and alone as an ancient ruin.

You've got to get a hold of yourself, damn it! This is no time to be freaking out. Yet it isn't easy. The more he tells himself to hold it in, the more his mind races farther out—with every thought in the scrapbook. Nevertheless he holds, hard as it is; harder than a rusty nail pulling away from a pile of magnets.

Raging and fit to kill, he feels like lashing out at the slightest provocation. He is so inflamed with fury that he could go up against someone twice his size. He wants to take that sucker outside, kick him right in the balls—that two-timing womanizing fuck! *Who the hell does he think he is? Just taking what he wants right in front of my eyes!*

"He challenged me, Mom. He lured Allison away *not* with his charm, but with his new Trans Am—and he challenged me to take her back!"

"You do not even have a license yet, for goodness' sake."

"But she's my girlfriend, Mom. Mine!"

"That is still no reason to dueling it out in a drag race. Have you totally lost your senses? Now, Mark, I have arranged for Dr. Stein to contact you tomorrow morning. I want you to talk to him, to listen carefully to what he has to say, and I will call you again as—"

"Dr. Frankenstein can go to hell!"

"I am not going to give you any pills, Mark. I think you—"

"Why not, Doc? Why can't you just give me some V's like every other doctor in this town."

"Because I do not think your problem warrants it."

"Look, Doc, instead of placing me on a couch, just give me some strong vitamins, you know—stellerzines or navadols or whatever—and I'll be all set. *You'll* be all set!"

"Tell me, boy, are you still hearing voices from time to time?"

"Yeah. Yours, doc. Hey, doc, why can't you be my friend for

once and not my mother's hired keeper? Why can't you be more like that nice helpful shrink in *Ordinary People*?"

"This is not the movies, Mark. I am trained to diagnose neurotic tendencies, manic depression, and various personality disorders. *Not* trained as an actor!"

"Why do you always say that! How many times do I have to tell you that there's absolutely nothing wrong with me. I'm calm as a doorknob and mellow as a sheep!"

She pops out in front of him, looks into his eyes, and blows smoke right into his face.

"Hello there."

"Hi, my name is French, Sylvie French."

"My name is Vermont, James Vermont. Do you know where I might find Miss Galore, Miss P. Galore."

"Right here."

"I must be dreaming. All right, Miss French Pussycat. By the way, how many other delicious names do you have…?"

A line here, a line there. Line by line, it becomes an exchange; exchange after exchange, it is classified as conversation, and sip by sip....

"Hey, bartender, get me another scotch, please? What'll you have, Miss French? Care to have a scotch? Or would you prefer some vodka…or gin perhaps?"

"Yes, gin and some sing is fine."

"How about a gin with some *Sling*?"

"It's O.K. But I would also like to sing to you."

"Oh, no, no, no, Sylvie. You've done enough singing for the night. You see, I'd much rather *sin* for you. On second thought, there's nothing wrong with some gin and some sing is there?"

"No."

"Great, then let's commit some sinful music together."

"O.K..."

...and sip by sip, her hand is resting on his.

"I don't want to get too personal, Sylvie; but how do you make yourself so entertaining day in and day out?"

"The hopes of finding someone young and adorable such as you."

"You are embarrassing me, Sylvie. What's it like, though, with a much older man?"

"Poooh, quite often they are fat and clumsy. But every once in a while, it is wonderful—like making love to a long lost uncle."

"You know, Miss Sylvia French Kiss, you're so seasoned that you're making me feel gauche. Shall we say in about half an hour, in front of Hotel Claude. It shouldn't be too hard for me to go snag some cash...."

"Mark, this is Madame Paulette. She is going to bring you upstairs and have someone take care of you. Don't worry, she won't bite."

"Are you coming too, Grandpa?"

"Oh, no. I will be at the café next door, with people my own age. Besides, this is Uncle Charles's birthday gift to you."

"Seriously?"

"Yes. But don't tell him I told you this when we go see him next week. It is supposed to be a secret."

"Grandpa, you're just like Dad; not very good at keeping secrets, are you?"

"Oh, you'll be surprised, kiddo, you'll be surprised."

"Where is Boogainville, Dad?"

"In the South Pacific."

"Is that where the boogeyman thinks up all those names for the hurricanes?"

"Don't believe everything Uncle Charles tells you."

"But it's farther than Kinshasa, isn't it, Dad?"

"They are both far away, son, though I think the South Pacific is even farther from New York."

"But, Dad, why do you always have to go to such far out places like the South Pacific and Africa?"

"Because those places are filled with mineral deposits. Copper for one; and tin—lots and lots of tin."

"Like the tin they make out of tinfoil?"

"The other way around, son."

"Oh yeah, right. Hey, Dad, if people really want to get closer to heaven, why don't they all live up in the mountains?"

"But how can they guard their minerals beneath the earth if they lived all the way up there?"

"Gee, never thought of it that way."

"Listen, kid, don't you worry about a thing. I will be back in a jiffy. And after I return, we will head out to the field and get you to chase down some flyballs."

"Sounds great. Hey, Dad, can we go to Knicks games, too?"

"You bet'ya! Knicks, Rangers, Islanders, whatever you like."

"All right! I can't wait, Dad."

"Neither can I. Now how about helping your father load his stuff into the trunk."

"Sure thing, Dad...as long as you let me back your car out of the garage."

"But your foot can't even reach the pedals yet."

"Sure I can, Dad; I did it last time, 'member?"

"Okay, Mark, but only out the driveway; no more."

"It's a deal! Thanks, Dad!"

"So, you are from Morocco. Do you speak French as well as Arabic?"

"Naturally."

"No, I meant as *good* as Arabic."

"Naturally."

"I'd love to go visit Africa someday. I've heard lots about it. My dad used to go there a lot. And in social studies at school, we used to learn the North African countries by remembering the word MALE. Know what it stands for?"

"I don't know...Man?"

"Nope. It's Morocco, Algeria, Libya, and Egypt, from west going east. Pretty neat, huh?"

"You forgot Tunisia."

"Whoops. Forgot about them Tunisian camel jockeys. But anyway, Morocco must be awfully nice, I see it all the time in the old movies. Hitchcock, I believe, 'Marrakesh, sounds like a drink' That was from *The Man Who Knew Too Much*."

"The *MALE* Who Knew Too Much."

"Oh, you *are* a doll. By the way, do forgive my manners, as we really ought to talk more about you. You seem...to be fairly at home here?"

"I am at home everywhere. When I am in Spain, people think I am Spanish. When I am in Greece, I pass for a Greek."

"A Greek goddess, no less. And when you are in Turkey... whoops, I almost did it again. You know what it is? It's your dark wavy hair and big alluring eyes. So where would you eventually like to settle down?"

"Here in Paris."

"Would you marry a Frenchman?"

"No!"

"Good for you. They are the biggest dickheads on this planet! Better dead than Fren'd!"

All you frogs can just go to hell! If you think I'm going to put my bank card right back in there just for you, you're out of your fucking mind! They sneak up on him. One of them knocks him against a hidden door while the other one rips the money out of his hand. It all happens so fast that he barely has time to be scared. He tries to give one punk the elbow but his arm is locked. Then suddenly he sees another chance when the skinny one is about to go for his wallet. With all his might, he inches his head back, then snaps it forward and gives the guy the biggest head butt of his life. From the sharp screams, it sounds as if he got him good, but not before he is slammed against the glass door for the second time—steel handle and all. He's being mugged. The bloody pain—it shot up through his bones and right into his head. It is excruciating, as if somebody has just threw hot peppers in his eyes.

The brawl seems to have awakened him, but that has only made him miserable again. *Go ahead, go spread your legs for that moron, see if I care. No tears on my pillow. Go kiss up to his sambucas blowjobs, see if I care. Up your throat with a rubber and a blow! He's nothing more than another Hollywood wannabe, that slimy swine! That swine that took my swan; that shark that took my marlin.*

He's crazy about her: she is the rage of Paris and the rave of his life. *Why? damn it! Why? Of all the quiches and souffles in all of Paris, her eggs have to come acracking into my bowl.* He wishes he had never known of such a rotten egg, but it is too late now. *Of all the crepe makers and grape pickers, she would have to show up as my grave digger. Ah, hell, go with him! Be one of his sycophantic cohorts, see if I care. Or is it sycophantic cowhores. You and your co-whores, stinking it up together like fart and asshole hair!*

One of the best evenings of his life has turned in all but a few seconds into an act of betrayal. And the wheel of misfortune keeps clicking away, all the way to bankruptcy and ruin, right in front of his bloody eyes. Literally. *Didn't even have enough left to buy a towel from Vanna to wipe off my bloody cut. Oh Vanna, dear Vanna, I can forever bow, to the way you tap that vowel.*

"Mark, I have just spoken to your mother. She will be here soon to take you home. Starting tomorrow, and everyday following that for the remainder of the month, you will be reporting to detention. You have done a menacing act to your fellow classmates, Mark, as well as bringing irreparable damage to the classrooms in the left wing."

"What irreparable damage? It was just a short, Mrs. O'Granny, I mean O'Grady. It was just two sticks of tin foil from my Juicy Fruit. I had no idea that the sparks were about to fly."

"You haven't an idea on many things, have you Mark? Including the fact that you are doing poorly in Science."

"Now that's not so, Mrs. O'Grady. I'm half way through that darn book already while the goody-goodies are still in the early experiments. No other science teacher makes you answer so many stupid questions on experiments. Why can't you just do an experiment and move on to new ones?"

"Precisely because you have to show understanding before moving on. If you have a problem with your teacher, there are other courses of action you can take. You were lucky nobody was hurt from the electric shock."

"Who's going to get hurt from a little thing like that?"

"Look at me, Mark. Your mother will be here soon to pick you up. I want you to take the rest of the day off. But you must stop this craziness at once if you want to move on to the ninth grade."

"Well, Doc, one more, that's it, that's all the bullets I have."

"Your mother is worried that one day a bigger bullet shell might explode, with somebody ending up getting hurt."

"What does she know, Doc. It was just noise, harmless noise from some antique shells."

"That is precisely what makes them dangerous, and why you must not go around hammering at them—especially when other kids are in the vicinity!"

"Aye, Doc, what can I say. We just wanted to see if our pin worked, to see if it was sharp enough, that's all. We didn't expect the bullet to pop so loud as to wake up the neighborhood."

"Hey, Doc, where's the couch? How can I possibly reach into myself if I don't even have a couch to lie on...?

"You're getting paid all that money and you can't even provide me with a couch...?

"What'a you mean I'm not paying for the couch? I'm certainly not paying for you...!

"Oh, get with it, Doc, the only reason I'm here is because visits to a couch in a whorehouse are not covered in the plan. But if they only knew, right? If they only know where all the *real* whores are!"

And the Jacque-ass himself, pardon my French! Fucking guy, trying to pass Zigzag for high-tech when everyone knows it's a cheap old disco-tech; all brashy and trashy like the whores it attracts.

Go with him, bitch, go with him! I need you like I need a hole in the head. He is filled with anger, the bottled-up kind. The kind that refuses to subside no matter how he tries to cap it. The kind that renders him incapable of controlling the situation at hand. Worst of all, it is the kind that can pop at the slightest fizzle; the kind that can make someone smash up the furniture—the kind that can wreck a house!

Lots of people in the Sahara room. Blue faces, red faces. Shoulders flashing in orange, bodies flashing in white. Sustaining them all were the legs, lots and lots of legs, all leaping out of their flesh in a flash.

Then he sees them. Amidst the flashiest purple haze they appear. But instead of walking directly towards them, he screeches to a halt. Instead of positioning himself squarely at their disposal, he slashes across sideways behind a column. Whether his actions are reflexively induced, he does not know. All he knows is that he has to both hide and see. But the longer he is standing there taking it in, the more he becomes incapacitated—as if he were pinned to an invisible wall of pins—sticking him with painful reminders with every false move.

The only thing faster than his heartbeat is the rate of their bodies beating together. What bodies? More like one body and four legs—with a tail stuck in the middle—rubbing and grinding as if there's no tomorrow. The sight of the bitch's hair, sweeping over the dance floor like a beaver possessed. The sight of her come-and-take-me body, sunk way down yet floating in air. And then there is the fink, his arms—tangling her up like a snake. His tongue, flicking and slithering as it rolls his lips.

He is not sure what's more embarrassing: to see her flagrantly flaunting it all; or for her to catch him seeing her flaunting it all. *I won't have it. I'm going to step in there and break it up, to put an end to that charade...Wait a minute, not so fast. Quit knocking yourself out over that frogging bitch, she ain't worth it...More important to stand my ground, keep my pride...Fuck your pride, what of your sanity?*

And on and on it goes: no, yes, yes, no, back and forth, forth then back. *You asked for it, didn't you? You said you wanted to witness human nature and its plight first hand, observing it in the thickest—well, you got it! But little did you know that the shoe is on the other foot now—for you yourself have become a participant. Caught between a rock and a block, you have to make the biggest 'to be or not to be' decision of your life. So what's it going to be, your face or your heart?*

He knows he has to snap out of this dilemma, even if he has to shout and scream his way out of it. But his voice box pretty much ignores his plea, as does the megahertz of high-frequency waves blasting out of the speakers. When he finally concedes to give her room, he does so more out of a fear of what he might do in a moment of uncontrollable rage than for any other reason. *Gotta get outta here, gotta take a hike, gotta take a moment to think it through. Stay calm, calm and composed be it, kid. Get a hold of yourself, then get a hold of the exit sign.*

Pretty soon it is unmistakably clear. Step by step, he begins his retreat. He would not let himself have the satisfaction of witnessing a confrontation. He is slowly pulling himself away from the scene. Walking away from it all. It is one thing to watch others fight in a battle, but to watch himself fight a civil war between his body and soul is counterproductive. He would not let his own eyes have that kind of a field day. Why has god only given him a photographic memory of things he would love to forget? They are all there—shelved in his cerebral stacks, ready for instant recall. More than ready. They constantly want to force their way through by breaking out. It is as if there is a battle being waged inside the brain, his will to forget versus their determination to live on. It is a battle all right, right down to those infinitesimal cells. The cells that care not how these shock waves might effect his condition overall. Their only job is their single-minded pursuit of being used—like the millions of sperm racing for the egg—each wanting to be the cell that gets fertilized into his mind—permanently!—whether it destroys his sanity or not. *Well, I won't let them. No bacteria is going to feast on the remains of this host.*

He tries reaching back to the far reaches of his consciousness, hoping for a new burst of concentration to steady himself. It doesn't happen. He still feels trapped and confused—held in limbo by an interconnected set of magnets. On one end is the magnet at the exit, trying to pull him out. The other magnetic force is on the dance floor, equally exerting itself to lure him back in. The end result: he is kept within the confines, not being let off with ease. The opposing forces have been so locked in battle that, despite his retreat, he finds himself actually walking backwards, at times virtually at a standstill, desperately wanting that one last peak. The voyeur's obsession for visual excitement; the masochist's yearning to be on the fringe of pain.

No! No fucking visuals! I'm going to go out into the night to find my own. He fires neurons from his head to his toes. Slowly, his feet turn around. As he stands facing the exit, he gives his legs their final marching orders. Forward and out! This time with no coming back.

Go with him, you little slut. See how far you're gonna get. Think that chunk of meat of his could give you a good stuffing, aye? Well, go ahead then. You can crawl and brawl with him all night, see if I care? Perhaps he might even offer you a drink after your headlining dance fever performance. How does a vodka and pussy juice sound to you? Freshly squeezed and screwed!

Have it your way, bitch. Think you're hot shit, don't you? Well, think again. You are but just another alley cat, nothing special! A cat in the alley ready to be collected and injected. Better yet, microwaved! Ever see a gut pop? Well, it ain't cat stew I'll tell you that much. Probably be closer to whoremeat for all I know. Trying to piss me off, huh? Well, that's all right, better the devil you know than the devil that blows.

Fuck'em, fuck'em all! Everyone in Paris can go to hell—this god damn city of assholes and asskissers, don't need this crap. Have it your way all you fucking French shitheads, all turds with a toad up your ass. You are all nothing but a bunch of anti-American frog-legged sissies, jealous of our world wide cultural domination and deserve to be fried to a crisp.

There is no big deal about you. You can't cook, you can't draw, you can't even dance ballet like my grandmother. All you know is how to flaunt your temper and boss everyone around. What's so hard about that? You are just like the rest of them in his fan club; probably laid on a surfboard for him in Malibu last summer for all

I know, for some screwy surf and turf. That's right, you ain't fooling me one bit. You are just another birdbrained Californicating airhead, swarming to that crotch-grabbing scum like birds swarm to shit. Go ahead, go rub your goddamn crotch against his. But next time, let's see if you can at least rub it in to some decent music instead, rather than that technoficial house garbage. Or maybe you won't. After all, what's more appropriate than garbage music in and two low-life garbage cans out!

The only sound louder than the pounding of the pavement is the pounding of his heartbeat. Heartbeat filled with hate. So much so that he can't get her out of his system, as if it is far better to think of her with hate than to not think of her at all. How could she do this to him? He knows how dangerously tempting that Eurotrash playboy can be. Still, if only she didn't have to be such a slut. *Fucking outfit she had on! That skimpy little black number barely even covered her ass. Just let it all hang out, why don't you—front and center! That's right, you are the 'pea' and he's the 'cock'! And what the hell did she wear for me? A pair of resown jeans passing off as a skirt. The nerve of her, trying to brag about her patched up rags. Nice try but you don't deceive me one bit you little brat, spending all your money on beach houses and cowboy boots, and now you complain that you're so god damn broke. Oh, you'll live you conniving bitch, your kind always do and always will. Just keep doing what you do best, just keep wearing those froggy frocks and keep dancing limb to limb with that pimp of pimps.*

He does not feel too well. There is a stinging headache on his left side, extending all the way down to his gut, like something is being slowly wiped away inside. Intermittent stomach-lining wipers! Soon after he begins to cough like mad, as if a fly has gotten into his throat. He is coughing so hard that it's inducing flashes of heat; his face, blushing and burning with an itchless itch.

A tiny pimple-like bump appears near the top of his forehead. When he presses it, it gives his face an irritating jolt. The whole left side of his head is not faring well. A slight pinch on his cheeks is all it takes to get that numbing, swelling feel. Each time he swallows, a ticklish sensation travels right up into his left ear, causing great discomfort. *Oh my ears, ringing deafly, worse than being next to a church bell. I must be sick...depressed...drunk...delirious...or perhaps all of the above. I need to calm down, dammit; right now! There's La Belle Aurore, go in and mellow out for a second. I'm cutting my losses. Gotta cut my losses. Can't go back to face her and get an even bigger slap in the face. Better just settle into my old self again. No tunnel of love is going to stir you up anymore. Fucking Paris, it actually conned everyone into believing it's the city of love; nice try but it's not!*

The more he thinks about it, the deeper his delusions go, layering one lie on top of another until he decides she is all his. Then, a splash of cold blood wakes him back to the realities. The realization of how stupid and false his pretensions are; how easily everything falls apart; and how rapidly he can descend into the sea of despair.

"Mrs. Vermont, I'm afraid Mark has crossed the line irretrievably this time. We can not have this sort of behavior surfacing again and again each time he feels some uninhibited urge."

"For chrissakes, Mrs. O'Grady, I didn't streak naked around the cafeteria. I...well, I...I just—"

"You just created a gross disturbance that interfered with the last two periods of classes. What on earth were you thinking of?"

"Look, Mrs. O'Grady, I drank too much liquid at lunch, so I had no choice but to let it all hang out."

"Did it ever strike you that you could have asked the hall monitor for a pass?"

"Look, Mrs. O'Grady, Mrs. O'Wise One, I didn't want to do it at first, but the pot grew and grew till it became...well, there was an awful lot of money at stake—enough to last me a good month at Friendly's. Enough for me to buy a whole year's supply of Girl Scout Cookies from Sondra."

"Mark, there is no excuse whatsoever for exposing your private parts to the whole school!"

"What exposing? All's I did was taking a piss into the water fountain, barely even pulled my jeans down—what's so big deal about that? Have you ever pissed into the bathtub, Mrs. O'Grady? They've only been doing that since the days of Julius Caesar for chrissake. And, as I've already told you, I'll clean and disinfect the whole area right after school...right after detention, every last drop of it!"

"It is not going to be a detention this time, Mark. I'm afraid you will have to take a suspension."

"Now that's not fair! If you know anything, Mrs. O'Grady, you'll know it's not all my fault. Just ask my mother, why don't you? She'll fill you in on why the hell I'm so screwed up. Just ask her, Mrs. O'Grady!"

"Mr. Mark Vermont, I know you're not misguided, *you* know you're not misguided, but why do you have to make the whole school think you are? I realize there might be problems at home, on that you have my sympathies. Nonetheless, I simply cannot allow the school to be an outlet for your continual transgressions."

"What the hell is the meaning of transgressions? Look, Mrs. O'Grady, if you're trying to get me out'a here, it won't work. I ain't goin' t' no military academy in the boonies. I can discipline myself just fine, thank you very much."

Aw, man, I hate this world. I hate every godforsaken inch of this germ and war-fed world. Double to you gutless frogs! So idiotic you can't even tell your assholes from your gun barrels. Have you forgotten Railcar No. 2419—yeah, that's right—and the Krauts got the last licks, too, what do you think of that? By the way, your Allies forgot to tell you something: never have so few done so little yet took credit for doing so much! That's right, you bunch of cowards, always did need Americans to do your dirty work for you! Well, this Yank is getting the fuck outta here, out of this frog-infested marshland you pass for a city—first plane out, dammit! Tomorrow! Tonight!!

"Thank you for calling..., the fastest...in the world. For super fast service, if you have a touch-tone phone, please press one, now. For flight arrivals and departures, press one; for..., press two, for..., press three, for..., press four..."

"Bang!"

1-8-0-0-5-5-5-8-4-3-3

"Thank you for calling..., the world's—

"Beep."

"You've just pressed zero. Please remain on the line. An operator will be with you momentarily."

"Hey, customer service, why is the sound level of commercials on your cable system so much louder than the programs themselves?

"Don't you tell me to buy a better TV set. *You* buy me a TV set! You buy me a set with automatic volume control...

"Get your boss on the line right now, you ignoramuse...Why? 'Cause I'm suing you for noise pollution, that's why.

"No, I'm not canceling my cable service. I'm not giving up my rights to sports televison just for you. It's the only piece of sanity I have left for chrissakes."

You've got to be in control, dammit. Don't let this crazy world get to you. Come out of this like you've climbed out of other pits. You can handle it, pal. Ain't no shit's pits piled so high that you can't climb over!

"You must be strong, son; for your sake, for my sake, for everyone's sake."

"I will, Dad. I promise. I'm not going to show no weakness to nobody, not even to myself."

"Hey, Dad, can we ride the bus once more to South Ferry? And this time, we'll take a new longer route I'd just discovered. Look, I've got it all figured out right here, right on this map. First we do a crosstown; then after we transfer, we'll go *all* the way down the West Side. But on the way back, we'll do the East, through Chinatown and the U.N. It'll be great, Dad, it's a good half a day!"

"Perhaps I should have gotten you comics and picture books instead. Certainly not transit maps."

"Nah, drawings ain't no fun, Dad."

"Hey, Dad, how come it's trick or treat? Shouldn't it be the other way around? Shouldn't it be *treat* or *trick*?"

"Well, first there is...Sounds better the other way, son."

"Oh yeah, right."

"Two balls, two strikes; two on, two out; score is tied at two two, in the bottom of second in the second of two. Boy, the deuces are wild, Dad!"

"Hey Mark, try not to think about cards all the time, will ya!"

"All right, Dad; I'll think about you instead. You and me, sailing the seven seas."

"I love you, kid."

"Luv you too, Dad."

"Okay, Mark, have you got the tails all attached?"

"Yes, sir."

“Remember what I said earlier: you draw on the string like so, with a slight jerking motion. But first we need to launch the kite.”

“We got enough wind, Dad?”

“We’ll see in a second. Now, go upwind to the edge of the outfield and stretch the line tight. I’ll be here at homeplate holding the kite. When I release it, I want you to reel it in fast. If that still doesn’t work, place the reel on the ground and pull in the line hand-over-hand.”

“It’ll work, dad, ’cause I’m *superfast*!”

“Hey Dad, Geronimo! Geronimo, Dad!

“Geronimo to you too, kid. Ready to launch our little water rocket again?”

“Yeah, and this time I wanna do the pumping.”

“You got it. Only try it now with a little less water; that way, the bottle becomes lighter, thus easier to take off.”

“Could I change the angles, too, Dad?”

“No problem. Just don’t aim it straight up or it’ll land on top of your head.”

“Gottcha.”

“Okay, you ready now? Start pumping! One Mi’ssippi, two Mi’ssippi....”

“Wow, look at it go, Dad, that one really took off! This is great!”

“Now pay attention, Mark. To avoid getting caught in irons and possibly even capsizing, don’t allow the boat to run out of inertia, especially in strong wind. So lets try coming about once more.”

“I’m ready for action this time, Dad. I’ll just let the boat drift a little with the sails luffing and then—*Boom*!”

“That’a boy. Okaaay...*Ready about*! Now *hard to lee*!”

“Wow, what a spin by the tackmeister! Check out the sails, Dad!”

Suddenly he hears something. Sounds like bottles and cans rolling on the ground. He hurries up to the intersection, turns a corner, and sees the bowling pin. There she is, only steps away and closing. So close she nearly stumbles as she comes up to him, bumping him on the chest. He immediately smells it, her alcoholic breath. Yet he also sees a gentle, carefree smile on her face. Before he can say anything, she already has her arms around him. Yet his eyes are looking beyond her, focusing directly at the two little punks that are steadily approaching. One of them throws a soda can at her. Another having thrown a battery that landed just short. To him, it is obvious what is happening: they are hoping for her to tire out; like trailing a mare in heat, waiting for the right moment to snatch her up. *No way, fric and frac, not if I can help it!* Despite him being still in pain, plenty of courage still remains. He even wished they were the two punks who tried to roll him at the cash machine, but he is glad they are younger and smaller, just the same. *You two I'm not worried about,* he says to himself. He feels almost like a seasoned veteran now, with blood still seeping out of his forehead to prove it! He holds her steady as they pass him by, one on the left, one on the right. There is eye contact, lots of eye contact. *Now beat it, you douche bags, she's under my protection now. That's right, I ain't gonna hurt ya, I'm just gonna bash your brains in.* If he could see his own face, he would know that he has never looked tougher. Miraculously, the standoff works. The pursuers decide not to make the first move. They begin walking away, looking back every other step or so until they finally fade into the darkness.

"Are you all right, me'moiselle? Can I get you anything? Need somebody to take you home?"

She doesn't say anything, but from the way she kisses him, he knows she is thankful.

He checks her into a hotel, settles her down, then proceeds to draw her a bath. He tries to clean himself up a little as well. First getting out of his dirty suit and smelly shirt, then sinking his head into the basin. He is kneeling next to the tub and testing its waters when she comes into the bathroom. This time, instead of staring past her at the punks, he can't keep his eyes off her. The firm legs, the tanned shoulders; and the dents and swells under that tightly towel-wrapped body. That and the inviting expression on her face hook him. Slowly she begins to walk toward him, and this time there is no stumbling as she stops a few inches away. He looks up at her, dazed by her beauty, amazed that only a towel is separating them both. A blink of the eye later, she loses the towel. He is now eye level to eye level with the iris of her belly. She bends over and reaches past him, lifting one corner of the towel and dipping it into the tub. She then lowers her body to squat down in front of him. Although she is naked, he can't look at her glowing skin, her pubic hair—he can't look anywhere except into her eyes. It is indeed a moment of tenderness rather than lust, a moment of telepathy rather than sound. An instant later, her towel blocks his vision of her body once again; though this time, the towel is not meant for covering up her nakedness, but as an act of kindness. With one hand on the towel and the other hand holding his head, she carefully begins to clean up his cut. The way she softly taps the wet end on his forehead, delicately massaging the redness around his wound.

Without warning he starts to cry. Tears of joy out of one eye, tears of sorrow out of the other. He tries to dry the tears with the towel dangling before his eyes, but the outpour is too substantial, augmented by the drops of steamy vapor condensing down his head. She is sitting between his legs now, her thighs around his waist. She smells like some male designer's perfume; he smells like a male sprayed with designer gin. It begins as a staring contest. She staring at him with her fiery eyes, he staring up her nose and down her breasts. The eyes of her breasts—erect and looking at him with unhurried expectations. They move closer, close enough that their bodies touch in a hundred places. The smoothness of her skin, wrapping him up like a warm satin sheet. He kisses her, and this time all of her. The teeth that only hours ago were armed to the teeth with anger are now biting at every part of her figure. The hands that not long ago were pinned to a doorway in pain are now running all over her body like flame. She begins to let herself go, begging him with her eyes; pleading him to please her again and again. He responds in kind, licking her body instead of licking his wounds. There they remain on the tiled bathroom floor, rolling ecstatically over one another...slipping, sliding, and splashing until finally his warmth intermingles with hers; until they are both joyfully warmed by the soothing lubricating sea of their overflowing tub.

As he goes out later to get some coffee and croissants, he feels a tremendous high overcoming him. A high seldom experienced in daily life. When one gets the right high, one feels an inner satisfaction—regardless of how strangely the strangers might perceive of him. Regardless of whether strangers are stopping him to shake his hand. There is nothing quite like that perfect high; that feeling of time well spent. Those fleeting moments on the highway to royal highness—even if one is just asking for some french coffee and french donuts, meaningless acts to everyone else, yet one knows those moments are far from boring. A good high is never boring. It triggers a certain exuberance, a certain freedom...complete unburdened freedom.

He finds her in the tub when he returns. She has fallen asleep to the sound of the drippity drips. "Hey, Céline, wake up. Look what I got ya, café au lait et pain du chocolat. You like?"

"Yes. Yes, I do. I like lots of things, but there are three things I like the most: love, love, and love."

"Wowww, and I like you, you and nothing but you."

"Oh, that's so nice. The water's so nice. It is so nice and relaxing I can stay here forever and ever."

"Well, you sure looked relaxed when I came in. In fact, if I'm not mistaken, I'd say you were smiling in your sleep."

"I had a wonderful dream. I dreamt of being friends with all of mankind—one man at a time."

"My hero, my lovely heroine."

"Oh, by the way, Céline, should you want to stay in Paris for another night, just tell the lady down at the desk. Everything's all been arranged."

"Thank you! You are beautiful. Paris is beautiful. It is where I always dream about...so many people, so many things. Sometimes, when I open my eyes in the morning, if I do not see a beautiful boy lying next to me, I feel like closing my eyes and going back to my dreams, where all my fantasies come true."

"Dar-ling, that is certainly the stuff of dreams—Shakespeare. 'She's got high hopes, she's got high hopes, she's got high Eiffel Tower in the—sky hopes.'"

"You sing very nice."

"Thaaanks. You wanna hear another?"

"Oh, yes!"

"Umm...how 'bout this one:

You had a dream, well, I had one too,
I know mine's best 'cause it was of you.
Come, sweetheart, tell me, now is the time,
You Tell Me Your Dream, I'll Tell You Mine."

If there is ever a dream he would love to realize, it would be of himself in a parallel life as a man of adventure—as one who scours the war-torn regions of the earth for rescue and relief missions. In the process, he falls in love with a passionate yet unselfish woman. She is attracted by the hope he brings, he by her tenderness, her beauty, and her fierce determination to survive. Through her he learns courage, caring, bravery in the face of adversity, and love. A love that combines mutual dependability and responsibility. A love that conveys to him that, for the first time in his life, someone is counting on him; that he can ill-afford to screw up; for what they are playing is the ultimate game, the game of life and death.

For one fleeting moment with Céline, he sees himself as that hero, that savior. The man that would breathe new life in her. She moved him, she loved him, and perhaps most of all, she desperately needed him.

"Mark, have we peaked, too, you and I?"

"No, Lisa; we haven't even climaxed yet. My prick is still looking down at the basement, with nowhere to go but up."

"Why do you always have to be so corny?"

"Why do *you* always have to ask stupid questions?"

"Well, *I* think it's a legitimate question. Just as you like to dump stocks once they've peaked, you like to dump people the same way, don't you? Throwing them by the wayside once they have peaked to your satisfaction."

"Oh come off it, Lise. I've always had nothing but the utmost praise for your qualities."

"News to me, Mark. Everyday you find ways to belittle me."

"For godssakes, Lisa, that was just between us two. Have I ever insulted or degraded you in front of other women? Of course not! You've always been nothing but the best."

"Sure, Mark. Only your compliments aren't even worth the papers they are written on."

"I can accept that; but only if they were gold-leafed papers!"

"Ouuu, I hate you!"

"Get with it, Lisa. It shouldn't take you thirty minutes to put on a stupid jogging outfit—for a ten minute jog, no less. So let's strive for a little drive next time, shall we? Like at least thirty minutes of jogging, and at *most* ten minutes getting dressed?"

"What's the matter, Mark, can't stand the thought of missing the first inning of a double header?"

"No, but if we bump into one of your gossipy friends from the West Side, I'll never hear the end of your yakity-yak."

"Your mother was right, Mark. You are always trying to make yourself out to be so darn sanctimonious. But you know what, Mr.

Holier-than-Thou? You're full of hypocrisy—constantly contradicting yourself. So much so that you can't even see it."

"That makes a hell of a lot of sense, what you just said."

"It's true and you know it. How many times have I seen you trying to play dumb in front of people—especially my friends—just so you can be anti-social. And then there were other times when you just totally make up things and act like an expert on topics you know *nothing* about!"

"Boy, that really hurts, Lisa, coming from you."

"It is not just from me, Mark. Everyone knows it! Like the way you constantly trash California in front of your friends in New York; but you and I both know that you're out there *all* the time. You're just too embarrassed to admit that going out there is one of your greatest latent desires."

"Yeah, and my greatest *blatant* desire is to suck the cockpit of a Ferrari. Get a grip, Lisa. You don't even know how to accuse anyone anymore. That was just about as sheer and total as baloney can get."

"Is it? Just count it up, Mark. You spend more time with your friends on the West Coast than you do with my friends on the West Side!"

"Ohhh, so now we know what this is all about. Now we are finally getting somewhere—to the source of it all—your conspicuous, and consuming, sports club sidekicks."

"You put down conspicuous consumption, Mr. Self-righteous. But anyone who really knows you *knows* that you're just too cheap to spend any money on anyone. You're just jealous, Mark—jealous of those who are better than you."

"Hey, wait a minute now, let's get something straight for a sec. First of all, nobody you know is better than me. Second of all, I don't get jealous. So there!"

"See what I mean, Mark. You get so seriously uptight every time you feel threatened. And cynical! The truth is, you are extremely spiteful. Once you develop a grudge against somebody; then, regardless of how successful they happen to be, they still can't escape your condescending ridicule. Instead, they can always count on you to constantly find faults in them. Looking for ways to take them down a peg, to make them undeserving. Why can't you give a little credit where credit is due? Why are you always filled with such animosity and negativity toward other people!"

"Why? Well, let me ask you this: why do *you* have to make them out to be some sort of a god's miracle on earth? Take that hot shot real estate guy you're in love with, is it really a big deal to dump a building or two on the Japs? Like those suckers really know what the hell they are buying. And while I'm at it, does it really do the movie going public any good to keep steering investors' money into a bunch of pre-packaged second rate films. A chunk of the gross came back to his wife, by the way, in the form of another mink coat—another sorely needed possession for those Southern California winters!"

"You're a riot, Mark. If you had given me as much as a raincoat, I'd die a happy woman!"

"Well, don't wait up! In fact, keep putting that cute little ass of yours on Mr. Furrier's furry laps and he's bound to make you dry and happy; better yet, warm and wet!"

"Mark, you're insane!"

"So I hear you went out of your way to see Celia the other day. What's the big idea, Lisa? Not quite a field trip from a writer's workshop, is it? Or are those the things they teach you to do: how to snoop and scoop!"

"What's it to you, Mark? I needed some assistance and I called on her."

"Well, ask somebody else! You have no business calling on her and digging into her life. She's off-limits, Lisa; she wants nothing to do with you."

"How do you know *what* she wants? Who died to make you the authority. On second thought, why are you so concerned about her all of a sudden, or is it something else in disguise."

"Fair warning, Lisa. You're *not* in her league, not by a long shot. So leave her out of it. You want to get back at me and my friends, fine; but leave her out of it!"

"It behooves me to say, Mark, that not only is she—"

"It behooves you to say what? Anyone who uses words like 'it be-hoooo-ves me to say' hasn't got a damn thing to say!"

"Oh, that's so typical of you, Mark. When there's nothing left to say, just think of the worst way to say it."

"You've got it backwards, pal. When *you* have nothing to say, you *con* someone else into saying it for you. Well, *that* is gonna stop. I swear to god, Lisa, lay off Celia and lay off now. Go pick on someone else. You can go prod my mother for all you want, I couldn't care less. Better yet, as I have long since taken myself out of her will, why don't you see if you can ease yourself into it—in fact, tell her I insist!"

"Have you no shame, Mark Vermont—bribing me with someone else's money. Only this time I'm out here on my own volition. So I'll do what I please and see who I please."

"Whom, Miss Marina del Rey, see *whom* you please. Who's been teaching you writing in that colony of yours, Mickey Mouse? Doing a great job, too, I might add."

"Anything is better than being overdosed by your brand of morality."

"I see. Well, don't say you haven't been warned, Lisa, for if I find you writing anything about Celia, there's going to be hell to pay!"

"Good-bye, Mark. And next time, don't call me so early in the morning."

"Not if you keep...Hey, don't you hang up on me!"

Go ahead, Lisa, stay out there and don't come back. All of you, just get the hell out of my life. You can all rot in Hollywood, for all I care. Be like Celia and Ira, hang around the fringes and beg for scraps. Yeah, real fun that Hollywood—wigs on skates and dykes on bikes. And they all bite!

"Okay Mark, I'm going to show you how to lay out the interactive imaging graphics. Remember what I said: perspective, perspective, perspective. Grasp the mathematics of perspective. Then *rewrite* it!"

"What of the colors, Luke? And the special effects?"

"No problem. Say we have a picture to manipulate. We first compress it and transpose it onto its image matrix coordinates; then, to give it a spacial, three-dimensional feel, we integrate the images through our workstations with my AI expert system software. From it, we can pinpoint any part of the image for mixing and multiplying. Or, we can use the system to mimic the movements of virtually anything. Just think, every possible image is theoretically at our disposal. We just weave it in, so to speak, and make the subject spring to life."

"What of the different angles of shots, Luke? For instance, a reverse angle interplay?"

"With our machine's 3-D processor, you can exercise pixel to pixel control over the movement of any objects being filmed. Correct that, being created. Even if you desired a movement that is not in the database, you can still finesse it out of the system using a manual imagery override."

"That's great, Luke. Kind of like a graphic spreadsheet with a custom data set. But what about background enhancements?"

"Still working on it. This particular chip we're developing will eventually allow someone to paste on as many layers of detail onto a plate as he wants, without sacrificing the quality of the original master image. Everything is digitized, with error-free transfer from model to reality, enabling the individual designers to just add sound and—wham!—he has manufactured a video that is more life-like than 70 millimeters of Panavison itself."

"Wow, that's great, Luke! Of all the Silicon Valley chips and silicon-coated tits, this is the greatest thing that has happened since Charlie Chaplin. Why, in the years to come, making movies will no longer be a multi-million dollar chore anymore. It'll be as easy as writing a book, with one or two people having total control of the content. Screw the movie stars and their agents and producers. We can manufacture our own superstars and sex symbols, and make them better than any person alive. Not to mention the fact that they'll never get old! Boy, I can see it now, right around the horizon: the day we render those million-dollar actors obsolete. The day I tell the sixty-million-dollar-man to go take a hike. Christ, Luke, we did it. We've destroyed Hollywood. From now on, films will truly be a test of imagination and creativity, not one relying on the egos of box office stars. For not only can we do any million-dollar block-buster scene we can think of, but we can do it in less time, and at fractions of the cost. You know what this means, Luke? It means *Good bye, Hollywood*! Filmmakers around the world unite! You have nothing to lose but those greedy studio racketeers. Pretty soon, instead of stars of Hollywood looking down at planet Earth, it will be the other way around. It will be ordinary earthlings manufacturing their own Hollywoods. Wow, Luke, this is great! Power at last to the people. I told you we'd show'em."

It is the wee hours now, almost the edge of dawn. Noiseless, crowdless, with only the flashing of neons to remind him of what once was. Ah, those tireless lights, like night's shining armour, glowing bright and right. He only wishes that some of their endless energy could pass on down to him. His whole body, feeble and lacking strength. His mind, drained of all its vigor. He plants himself across a park bench, so tired he can't even swing a bat at his eyelid; little less at an intruder.

"Hey you, mind moving over? This here is *my* bench."

"Look buster, I ain't moving for *nobody*. Besides, I got here first!"

"Then can I have your raincoat?"

"No!" He said loudly, his arm clutching his raincoat.

"Guess I'll just use the grass as my mattress."

"I've got a better idea: why don't you go and get lost. You know what, go find yourself some hay instead, just like them Roman Legionnaires used to do. Or are you too lazy a bum to know the difference?"

"I will have you know, young man, that I was once a soldier myself, in the Légionnaire Étrangere. Shortly after I got chased out of Sicily."

"What do you want, a medal? A medal for a bum who can't even sniff out the nearest flophouse?"

"My friend, I do not sniff, I drink; and medals I have had many. Including a Croix du Combattant in the North African theater."

"Yeah, that and a token'll get you a bench to sleep on. Quick—who made the trains run on time?"

"The TGV?"

"No, it was Mussolini, stupid. *Il Duce*! He made the trains run on time! And you call yourself a soldier. All right, second chance: quick—where's the headquarters of the French Foreign Legion?"

"In Algeria."

"Where in Algeria, and don't tell me Algiers."

"No, no. It was at Sidi-bel-Abbes, outside Oran."

"Well, till I check it on a map, I'll take your word for it. Now wait a minute, when was that, the 1950s?"

"Yes."

"But that was when you frogs were getting your ass smashed in Vietnam—at Diem Bien Phu. The hell were you doing in Africa?"

"I was a new recruit, saw my first actions in Morocco."

"No shit. Well, don't just stand there, old man. If you cannot afford the neighborhood flophouse, then amuse me with a story or two if you want your stupid bench back."

"Let me see now, the most magical place was Marrakech. Calm as its snowy mountains by day, chaotic as its blazing souks by night. Fortunately, since we were there as the guests of the Pasha, the great El Glaoui, we were safe from the natives. The same could not be said for Fez. It was hostile territory when we took it over, with surprise after surprise. For every wrong step one takes inside their medina, one increases the risk of getting lost. And once lost, one will never be found, certainly not by the natives. Such was the extent of their animosity."

"Why did the Arabs hate your guts so much."

"Fez was where the Sultan had lived before he was driven out by a coup. He wanted independence, while the Pasha of Marrakech, who had ousted him, was aligned with the French. Naturally, the exiled Sultan's people in Fez did not look upon their occupation force with favor. One day, on the way back from a bakery, I took a detour to avoid the foul smells of a tannery. I was walking and walking, then all of a sudden, something dropped straight down from above and hooked me right around my neck. You know what it was?"

"What?"

"It was a giant snake."

"Hahahaha... Holy shit, you and Cleopatra, both. Was it a cobra?"

"If it were a cobra, I would have been a dead man!"

"So that was their method of ambush. Certainly faster than the Vietcongs with their booby traps."

"Morocco was not Vietnam; however, when the riots broke out in Casablanca, the whole Arab slum became a trap. The only way to counter them was with force, and force we used. From tanks and machine guns on the ground to tear gas sprayed from the aeroplanes. Even so, it was hard to crush the revolutionaries. We had to resort to the *ratissage*—a house-by-house search for fanatics—if one wished to call those tin-can huts of theirs houses. Such was the poverty of those *bidonvilles*—right in view of the Casablanca skyline. Little wonder that every set of eyes we saw could have passed for the eyes of a terrorist."

"Well, that's what you get when you *colons* exploit the natives to the hilt."

"Let me tell you something, boy. No man, not even a white man, deserved to be killed with his body mutilated and his penis stuck in his mouth."

"Uhuh. Oh, man! God, that must've been awful. What barbarians!"

"The white man was not without blame, my friend. They tortured more than their share of Algerian nationalists during its civil war.

That was another rough operation, chasing the FLN out of Algiers. I got shot in the leg while at it—been walking around with a limp ever since."

"I'm terribly sorry to hear that. You have the right to be bitter, just like our Vietnam vets."

"Look, I am no politician, certainly no saint. But I knew the end was near when the generals attempted a putsch in 1961, against de Gaulle of all people. I was a mercenary and I didn't even feel like fighting. Needless to say, the half million regular troops stationed in Algeria didn't even leave their barracks."

"See, old man, you should've stayed in Morocco, in Casablanca—unloading tear gas tanks from Lisbon, hanging out at the airport hangar, enjoy a snake-meat fillet and chase it down with some Vichy water. And every so often, round up the usual suspect. Now, *that* is a life. *Ça, c'est la vie*!"

"If that is so, my friend, then let us make our way down there."

"Us? No, not us. My love will always be here, in Paris. I need to get her back. I *have* to get her back!"

"She will come back to you. You look like a generous man. Parisian girls love a generous man. *Everybody* loves a generous man!"

"Yeah, I wish. Look...um, look, old man, since the sleeping arrangement at this *hangar* don't quite mount to a hill of beans, here's my raincoat for you to sleep on. Good luck, old man!"

"Oh, merci monsieur. Merci beaucoup. Vous êtes très galant. I think this is the beginning of a beautiful friendship...hey, where you going, boy?...between me and my new raincoat."

Why me? Why now? What am I doing here? What the hell am I trying to prove? Hours ago, he barely would have admitted to the depth of his feelings for her. Yet, suddenly, he senses a change. He can no longer stand the thought of losing her—least of all to that undeserving worm. He is going to win her back if it takes him all his days. He is too enthralled by her vitality; too engulfed by her vivacity; too encaptured and enraptured by her exuberance to let her just slip away.

He is feeling possessive again. Yes, she is the water of his life; yet how easily she could heat up into the vapors of steaming hell—or chill into the freeze of icy death. *Nobody is going to fuck me from under and get away with it. Nobody! She's mine, the reason*

I'm still in Paris. If I find her screwing around, she's going to get the breadth of my wrath.

He gets out of his bed and slowly motions out to the hall. He comes to a door, the door to her bedroom. Luckily, it is half open. He holds his breath, stretches his ears inside, and waits. *Can't hear a damn thing. What now? Back track, or onward and forward?* Neither. He opts to get down on all fours instead, trying to tip-toe and tip-finger his way in. *Is she there? Hush hush now! Keep to the walls...take to the corner.... Dammit! There's another set of doors.* Much to his dismay, the inner doors are going to be a much tighter squeeze. One of the panels is nearly shut, the other one barely open. He tries to push them out a little. They squeak. *Damn, those frigging froggy doors! Just when you need them to be open and clear! What now, god dammit? Let me at least try to hear something for Christ's sake!* He sticks his head and nose into the gap. The scent is there—the same spicy scent he inhaled that morning. But it's too quiet, not even a single hiss. *C'mon, dammit! Can't she snore a little for crying out loud! She's got to snore. Such a loud mouth volunteer during the day just can't be so dead and silent at night.* He peers in again, this time sticking his neck out. Again the results are inconclusive. The bedspread appears to be half flat and half piled, with what seems to be a lump in the middle though no definitive body. No movement, no tossing no turning, not even a ruffle of the sheets. *Should I go for it? To see and be seen once and for all? No, better not, still not too late to backtrack. Let's chill out and wait till tomorrow. Tomorrow, I'll get you all! No, not tomorrow...it can't be tomorrow ...it already is tomorrow. The suspense is killing me now!* A sense of urgency seizes him; and courage. He does not even bother with crawling. Instead, he bursts through the door and takes a diving plunge, right onto her bed.

Silence....

He is blank...numb...empty...and as dead as the dead. The leap of hope has become a freefall into despair. The search for one body turns out to be pillows upon pillows. *Sissy pillows!* He begins pounding at them, out of unvented anger, out of self-loathing and hatred. "Where is she? *Where* is she!"

Suddenly, a light turns on. "Mark, are you all right? Did you need anything?" Standing in front of him is Alexandra, in her underwear, with a glass of fruit juice in her hand.

He is speechless—stunned!—as he turns his head around. He watches in silence as she glides over to the other side of the bed. She places her juice on her night table and lowers herself onto the bed. She is sitting about half way up and facing him, leaning on her right elbow. She gazes down toward his head. "Are you all right, Mark?" she says in a soft and endearing tone, "You look owful! What happened to you? I was *so* worried."

"Oh, Alexandra, I was worried, too." He brings his right arm around and hugs her left hip: "Thank god you're home, Alexandra. I'm so sorry. I'm sorry for everything. I'm sorry you had to find me like this. It's just that...oh, god, I missed you so much. I—"

"Shhh, I missed you, too, *mon petit*." she says, as she cuddles his head against her chest. Then, with one hand massaging his hair and the other hand massaging into his tears, she looks down at his face and smiles. It is a tender, loving smile; one a mother would give to her child, a babysitter to the baby. Moments later, she slowly lowers her head and kisses him goodnight.

EPILOGUE

"Mesdames et messieurs, notre atterrissage est prevu dans dix minutes à Paris Charles de Gaulle...."

"Pardon, monsieur, c'est votre papier?"

"Oh, merci. Merci beaucoup, madame. Vous êtes très gentile. It must've slipped out of my hand as I dozed off."

I must have read this letter a thousand times in the past seven months, each time with the hopes of finding something new, only to end up as clueless as after the first. Perhaps Mellery was right, that there was nothing between the lines.

Paris,
13 July 1989

Dearest Mark,

It is with the fondest memories that I say goodbye. From this day on, I should very much like you to act on my behalf, including the setting up and running of a charitable trust, to which all my assets will be transferred. Thomas Mellery will furnish you with the details and will be there to assist you in any way he can.

My dear Mark, I know it is all quite sudden—this favour I am asking of you. Yet you must not feel daunted or overwhelmed by the task. Rather, look upon it as a challenge. Believe me when I say that, in no time at all, most of the work shall be within the realm of your capabilities.

Just a reminder: accept nothing and trust no one at face value; especially those who claim I promised them such and such. I have done no such thing.

Well, then, take good care of yourself and others; exercise your best judgment; and do put the moneys to some good use.

Fondest love,
Charles

P.S. Please make every effort to discourage others from trying to look for me. Tell them I am dead if you need to. I shall not be found; I will not be coming back.
Live happily and meaningfully... C.M.

It is now February, 1990. Merely seven weeks into the final decade, but already seven months after Charles disappeared—vanished into the dimensions of space and time. The details are still very sketchy, almost nonexistent. On the morning of July 13th, he got up and went out, just like any other day. Only he never returned. When he became a no-show at the opening night festivities of the new Bastille Opera, several friends inquired as to his whereabouts. Ally didn't know; nobody knew. That weekend, I flew to London and saw Mellery. He gave me Charles's letter.

For the remainder of the year, things were mostly on a holding pattern. I waited, sometimes anxiously, other times half-heartedly, for Charles's just as abrupt return. Nothing ever came of it. Not one minutiae of his existence, rumors or otherwise, had blown within our reach. I was somewhat surprised at the completeness of the blackout, though not too surprised that Charles did not return. Still, I felt that the months spent waiting up for him were right and honorable: to make one last call before we proceeded.

So, since the beginning of this year, my life, too, has undertaken some radical changes. I'm based in London now, serving as Warren's representative on a new venture in alliance with Mellery's merchant bank. We hope to launch a potentially lucrative service that combines the features of management consulting and mergers & acquisitions. I'm really excited about it. Nervous, too, from the pressures and the challenges. In fact, I've been so busy with work that I haven't even had the time to be homesick. I didn't even watch the Super Bowl! One reason is due to my weekends being spent in Paris, to mind personal concerns.

It took a bit getting used to at first, this dramatic change of scenery; me being such a winter person and all—winter traveler on top of that. But I think I'm starting to get the hang of it. Every Monday, I'm up and out before dawn, arriving in London two hours later, only one hour if you take in the time difference, which isn't so bad. Then, for four long days, I work predominately out of our office in the West End, though I spend some time in the City as well, where Mellery is headquartered. Then just last week, I found a way to cut the pricey hotel rooms of Mayfair in half by taking a bedroom at a club in nearby St. James, a twenty-minute walk to Berkeley Square, where our office is. Also last week, Ally and Olivia came up to visit for a couple of days, so I remained at the hotel. Next week, though, will be twin-bedded week. But as the club also throws in a fine English breakfast, I can hardly complain. So hopefully, at least on the London front, things'll start to normalize.

As for Paris, I'm afraid the work has barely begun. My first priority is to get the house in order. It has seen tremendous neglect over the years, from a leaking roof to a flooding cellar. Not wanting to overload Ally's schedule too much—she hopes to become a brand manager for a cosmetic company—I have enlisted her friend Olivia into the service as well. Olivia is experienced in cataloging, a skill which I sorely needed in the process of storing and upkeeping of the things in the house.

Besides the main rooms, there are also tons of items in the attic—in even more disarray. I get intimidated just thinking about it; so I try not to, or as Ally advises, "Just Do It!" Well, soon as the weather warms up, I will. I'm going to have a contractor come in and work on the exterior of the house. Once upon a time, it was stone and marble. Now, the exterior stone work is either coated with coats and coats of gray paint, or contains areas that have cracked or been damaged due to water and weather.

As for the interior, it is undergoing renovation as we speak. I have set out to convert the two floors of the kitchen wing into the residential quarters. As soon as the second floor of the wing is renovated and divided into rooms, Ally, Olivia and I will all move there; leaving the main house as a work in progress, a very slow work in progress, as major overhauls are required to bring it out of its antiquated state. It's all going to keep everyone pretty busy. The rotten floors in the attic will be replaced; A new fire and security system will be installed throughout to safeguard the art and the furniture. And backing it all up will be a whole new electrical system, capable of handling Ally's phone calls and climate controls alike.

Why, you might wonder, am I so predominately occupied with the many aspects of physical alterations? Well, for one thing, being a newcomer and all, I am still flowing with adrenaline, still psyched enough to get things rolling. I only know what complacency is all too well. A second, and perhaps more important reason that I'm dealing with the physical aspects first, is that I'm still quite baffled by Charles's...I don't know, such pie-in-the-sky requests. Just what was it he was expecting from me, if anything? No doubt he has left behind a vast amount of wealth. Why, his paper assets alone are enough to contribute to many worthy causes for lifetimes. But personal fortunes, no matter how great, are small potatoes when used in the context of direct aid to the world. Just look at how the Berlin Wall had collapsed—the whole of Eastern Europe, in fact—as all of us watched in disbelief. Such unforeseen pace of change; and just as evident, a sudden new set of realities. The realities of much needed Western aid and investment to promote and protect those changes. The cost of reconstruction is to be in the tens of billions; beyond the resources of any one man, any one country.

So how best to spend the money? There are several fronts being explored at the moment, including a think-tank type organization, perhaps to be called the Paris Institute, that would fund research projects world wide and in all fields. Personally, I do not favor, nor do I feel Charles would want, another version of the Nobel Prize. He is far too low-key a man. If we do end up giving out awards and prizes, they ought to have less elements of honorary after-the-fact recognition, and more elements of a tiered, merit-based arrangement where, as a way to encourage younger talents to strive toward their potential, the funding could flow for many years, perhaps even for a lifetime.

Just as we want to honor progress, we ought to also support those who speak out against the evils of man; those who expose the lies and hypocrisies around the world. For their voice is often the loneliest of all.

Still, before I jump ahead into a new arena, I need to first do some backtracking: to revisit the life and livelihood of the man behind it all, to get a better sense of who he is and what he isn't; as ultimately, it is his legacy the organization must uphold, not what is deemed to be my or anyone else's own personal views and politics.

Far easier to say than to define, I'm afraid. Charles's nature is a hard one to pin down. At times he was full of life, other times completely self-enclosed: in his circle, in his house, in his own head.

Everywhere I walk in this cold and drafty house, I am reminded of his presence. And so overpowering his presence was—walking up and down the staircase, collecting thoughts in the dining room, enjoying a cigar in the library—everywhere and everytime, he stood tall and mighty.

So why did he decide to leave us? What were the motivating and underlying factors that pushed him out, if pushed at all? While I should refrain from speculation, I would not at all be surprised if there were many forces at work. Charles was never a man to do something for one reason and one reason alone. His prolific career attested to that. Perhaps he had detected a loop hole in the face of time, where a set of circumstances all intersected at some center core; where, faced with such ingredients, the reasons for him to go had become so overwhelming that he had to go for it—even just for poetic reasons. Sort of like the Halley's comet, things just converged in a once-in-a-lifetime offering. So Charles Martin, after a lifetime of being everywhere at once, decided not to be in anyplace at all.

Although my encounter with him had been brief, I am confident enough to say that I don't think there's another man as misunderstood, as prone to prejudgment by others as Charles Martin. Might there have been a tortured soul underneath all that confidence? Was he overwhelmed by contemporary society, or was he simply answering to a higher calling? Or worse, could he, despite his veneer of absoluteness and certainty, be filled with doubt, insecurity, or perhaps even sinisterness?

What was it that Winston Churchill once said, about something that is a "mystery wrapped in an enigma?" Well, I get the feeling that Charles went even beyond that. He was a man of extreme and divided loyalties; an ardent traditionalist wrapped around a post-modernist soul. And last but not least, at the core of all the mystery and enigma, lay a man of brutal honesty and bare simplicity.

I was able to get a glimpse of such qualities on that Sunday in May, in one of the final talks we had, shortly before I was to be homeward bound. I caught up with him as he was doing some writing in a tiny chapel at the side of the house.

"Composing Sunday Evensongs or don't like to use the library?"

"Conceivably both. I often write in the chapel—preferring its sparse, uncluttered feel. Nothing to distract me here."

"Except god, of course. You do believe in god, I gather?"

"On a symbolic level, naturally. Just not so much in a religious sense."

"Separate god from religion, sir, and you're left with…umm... dogs. Or are animals not quite a part of god's given world?"

"What makes us humans so much a part of it?"

"We have a soul, sir; and according to certain religions, possibly more than one!"

"And god, inevitably, must have a soul?"

"I guess soul," I cracked. "I mean, I'd like to think that we are at least not worshipping a...a non-entity."

Charles paused for a moment, a while, a quite a long while, idly sitting there and gathering his thoughts. Some people have a way of exuding the best of their powers even as they pose in what seem to be the simplest of positions. Charles was one of them; sitting with that lean and erect posture, focusing with those all-knowing eyes.

"My dear fellow, visualize if you will a picture of the planet Earth in space. Then imagine yourself moving away from it—traveling at lightning speed—for billions of light years, through other solar systems, galaxies, constellations—ad infinitum!"

"You mean looking back at earth in a continuous wide angle, for zillions 'n zillions of years."

"Good enough. Now my question to you is: what do you expect to find at the edge of the universe, if an edge should even exist?"

"Don't know. Don't suppose anyone knows; or, rather, it's open season to anyone's guess."

"Very well. Suppose one speculates the edge of the universe to be a skin-like layer, the skin of god, if you will, and 'wrapped' within it—the whole of universe. And, if I might add, a very young god at that, still growing and expanding for light years at a time. Of course all this is rather more a metaphorical picture than an actual one, as the mathematical details are sure to be more complex, touching on areas such as hyperspherical geometry and multi-dimensionality. But for the moment, and for argument's sake, what do you suppose are the instincts and impulses of our universe."

"I don't know. I'm not even sure where to begin. To tell you the truth, sir, I'm a little freaked by it all. Are you implying that we are living inside some living thing? I don't believe I've ever heard astronomers describing the universe in such a way."

"Nonetheless, would it be safe to say, if such a super-entity were to exist, if god itself were in fact that super-entity, then such a god would not place so highly on his priorities a tiny spec within himself known to us as Earth?"

"If at all," I shrugged. "We'd be lucky if he even notices our solar system, or the Milky Way."

"Very well. Let us turn around and reverse the situation. Let us imagine a single-celled organism living inside a body—your body. And a couple of molecules from that cell, call them a couple of hydrogens if you like, decide to leave the host cell to scout for additional oxygens. So off they go, passing billions and billions of their fellow cells, light years in their relative time, till they eventually reach the surface of your skin and come out as sweat. *Now* my question becomes: should you, as a multi-cellular being, be in any way impressed by such a feat?"

I was more impressed by the question than anything else. And perplexed. I had to think for a while, of hydrogen bombs pouring out of the pores on my skin. "Theoretically, yes, I suppose, as I'd be quite impressed by how far my sweat had traveled. But of course, Einstein also said that it would be wonderful when a beautiful theory also turns out to be true. And therefore, realistically, I have to say no. How can I possibly be aware of the existence of a couple of sweat molecules? I mean, who am I to bestow anything upon them? However, I am beginning to get a handle on what you are trying to say: that the cells in this case are just like the earth in the previous example—an extremely small part of the whole. And the hydrogen leaving its cell can be seen as a spaceship taking off and leaving the earth behind, going where no man has gone before. But still, what does it all mean on a symbolic level? That we are all blood, sweat and tears?"

"You may think that if you wish. What I'm trying to do here is to present the notion of relative size. That despite you being the super-entity to your cells, you have only limited power over them, and by inference, our god has little power over us."

"What if god decides to self-destruct? He could blow us all up!"

"*Even* if it chose to self-destruct!" Charles raised his voice a notch. "The factors to bear in mind are the various levels of time at work. We mustn't thrust *our* time frame on to the universal scale. Who knows, one blink of god's eye may indeed be a lifetime here on earth, and the natural death of our host may, in all likelihood, take an eternity to effect us all—millions of years, perhaps!"

"That's pretty interesting, the multiple dimensions of time. That what's instantaneous there isn't as instantaneous over here. And if in fact the history of mankind is all but a few flickers in god's eyes, then there's not a damn thing that the gods can do *even* if they wanted to. Not a *damn* thing! We're free and clear!"

"The implications of free and clear go both ways, my boy," Charles said. "It also makes *us* just as irrelevant to the heaven above."

"Now you're getting me worried. Making me feel belittled. And confused. Thought we were the king of the hill for a second. But if what you said were true, then we'd be lucky if we could just remain the king of the *ant* hill. Perhaps not even that!"

Charles nodded, "Ounce for ounce, ants are as socialized as any creature on earth."

"Don't give them too much credit, sir," I blurted out. "Or they might just get the hint and take you up on it. And believe me, nobody likes the idea of our planet being covered by ants—knee-deep in ant jelly!"

"Quite. Consider then, if you will, the scenario whereby I, myself, have somehow transformed into an ant. I live in your house, and see you as a god of sorts. Would that do anything to you? Would you, in any way, feel all the more powerful by being able to dominate a hill of ants?"

"The answer is no, right? That we, as humans, despite being worshipped by ants, have our own agenda. Just as our god is into his own schtik."

"Not only are we not interested in being the arbiters to their antsy rivalries, we couldn't pull it off even if we wanted to. First, we can hardly tell the rivals apart. Second, even if we wished to take sides out of amusement—say some children out playing in the garden: trapping them, burying them and stepping on them—we still can't kill them all."

"Especially with the wrong type of shoes," I interjected.

"Yes, indeed! Efficiency and thoroughness are not always combinable."

"Hey, that's pretty powerful; and in a peculiar way, mighty controversial as well. Because if our god saw us merely as ants, then he wouldn't be able to take sides even if he wanted to." I was glowing with spaciness, Dante-esque spaciness. "Sir, yet another question still remain. It might sound stupid, but, when we reproduce, we provide contact; the physical universe, on the other hand, surely they can't just meet and—boom!—make babies."

"How do we know that for sure?" Charles said. "What might be known as regeneration to the physical universe could very well be a phenomenon totally incomprehensible to us. Frankly, who is to say that the outer edge of our god is the be all and end all? How do we know that our god is not in a battle with millions of others just like him. A battle of immortals, if you like."

"Wow, all this is blowing me away. You're asking us to...I mean, you are *only* asking us to change every rule in the book. The billions of people who think they are god's children won't like it. Neither will the scientific big-wigs, all those cosmologists who think that there is nothing beyond our universe, that they are inching their way into the black holes of total truth, the origins of everything."

"It is not a question of one field replacing another," Charles said. "Each has its own objectives and therefore, its own pace. Whereas one approach emphasizes the generation of big ideas, another approach requires fundamental discipline and verification, as in the building of a skyscraper from the bottom up. Indeed, the building has been ongoing; the progress of astrophysicists in recent years has been nothing short of miraculous. As technology improves, there will undoubtedly be greater discoveries, with greater precision. This can already be seen from the research being done into the theories of chaos, and the theories of complexity. They are all quite ambitious, and all rightfully commendable."

"But...Is there a 'but' coming up somewhere?"

Charles laughed. "But to what extent do fundamental theories explain and reflect the everyday realities here on earth?"

"I don't know. Though I'd like to think that cosmology, and micro-cosmology, for not knowing a better word, is...well, it's probably more applicable than most other obscure academic pursuits."

"It makes no difference," Charles said. "It is my belief that we shall never know the truth of the universe *until* we have found the truth within ourselves."

"Hmmm, that's rather humanistic of you, sir. I thought, if anything, you'd be more of a naturalist, more geared toward the natural order of things in space."

"What greater good will come of it if we are unable to take what we have observed and translate it into applications. Look around, all the best discoveries have had that connection: electro-magnetism, the speed of light, DNA, to name just a few."

"Well, give cosmology some time, sir. It's only in the early stages. Hopefully, one day down the road, they can drag something down from high above that is both definitive and useful, like discovering god for example."

Once again Charles laughed. "You know, I once gave a lecture, in my more 'freewheeling' days, titled 'God and Imagination'. I walked into the lecture hall and said, 'God exists. Yet it only exists in ways which we cannot possibly imagine. As soon as we are able to imagine it, it no longer qualifies as our god.' After those statements, I walked out. Needless to say, it was the shortest lecture I had ever given."

"Short but not forgotten," I added. "That was a good one, sir—sealed nice and tight—with notta way out of it. That once we know our god, it's no longer worth our knowing. No, wait a minute, it's a step beyond that, isn't it? Not just knowing but imagining."

"Quite right, my boy. There are lots of things we don't know, and don't understand. What I was emphasizing were things which we can't possibly even *imagine* ourselves knowing—a small but clear distinction."

"Now you're getting me way off course. I mean, speculating on aliens is about as far as I go. Even *that* is highly speculative—like, I don't even believe in UFO's."

"Yet suppose aliens exist. Suppose one day an extraterrestrial comes down from the sky and visits our planet. How do you think it will go about assessing us?"

"Depends on whether it's a friend or foe, sir. And, whether it feels totally alien to us, or sees a connection somewhere. Now, as far as the intellectual front is concerned, namely, what type of principles the alien might hold, or the reasoning skills it might possess, I have not the foggiest. Or rather, let's all hope that it doesn't get its kicks from eating us all up!"

"I must disagree with you, Mark" Charles said. "This fear of some monster-like being coming down to earth to destroy us all is ludicrous. No, I do not doubt the existence of other life forms. Indeed, some of the entities may very well be more advanced than ourselves. Nonetheless, my contention is: we human beings, besides possessing the basic survival instincts of the lower life forms, will soon possess reasoning powers comparable to any creature in existence, including those that appear to be far more advanced than ourselves."

"I'm lost. What's your point, sir? That we are lowlife and superior beings all at once? What are we, middle-class citizens? Like, just moments ago, you said our lives are inconsequential. The earth is inconsequential! Now you turn around and say we can tangle with the best of them, the best the universe has to offer. It all seems a bit paradoxical, almost a contradiction." Without sounding too self-congratulatory, I think I was getting good at talking to Charles. Starting to get a hang of him, of his tendencies to maneuver arguments to his own liking, to tilt facts to his favor. Or so I thought.

Charles took a breather and pondered for a while. Perhaps looking for a simpler way to convey his ideas, one within my understanding. Not that the language he had been using was academic jargon. In fact, I would have to say that throughout my visit, both his analysis and vocabulary, despite their occasional spaciness, have on the whole been the stuff that a twenty-something American with an undergraduate degree in the New York *Times* and a graduate degree in *Wall Street Journal* was more or less able to grasp.

"Very good of you to mention middle-class," he began. "It is not everyday that I would categorize human beings as such, as signs of superiority are so overwhelmingly in evidence. Yet, we need no more than to go back to the beginnings of modern man to see how far we have come. Homo Sapiens, mind you, have never possessed natural abilities on a par with the animal kingdom. Take the hearing of dolphins, the eyesight of cats, or the sense of smell of pigs; they are all far and above that of man. Any man. Neither are we anywhere near the fastest or strongest, nor are we the most populated for that matter. Even today, the number of birds and bees in this world far outnumber that of humans beings."

"Ants, bees, and cicadas, the ABC's; not to mention the birds and the bees."

"You are thinking, my boy," Charles smiled, "But you have also disrupted my thoughts. So where were we?" Charles truly had lost his place, I don't believe he had ever done that before, with me. I mean, I know *I* was confused and barely improvising along, but I didn't think I was able to confuse him in any way.

"Ah, yes. I believe I was trying to single out some animals with superhuman capabilities," Charles said.

"Well, terrapins, too, sir," I interrupted him again. "Stationary as they are, they do in fact have quite a long life span." I tried to say something just for the hell of it. "Turtles that go into soups in general. Especially compared to the average life span of Early Man," I was really just saying anything that came to mind, "Perhaps it was due to our mental activities that we have steadily increased our life expectancy."

That seemed to have ignited a torch. Charles was no longer just idling along but taking charge. "But how *did* the mental state of man and his ancestors develop?" he said. "I believe it is partly due to humanity having to compensate for the lack of a singularly dominant natural ability. The way our various senses have been set up forces the brain to intervene at critical junctures: to give boost to situations where the individual senses, when acting alone, could not have possibly reached the threshold of action they would have in their combined aggregate. Just as well, in situations where our individual senses offer conflicting reports, the brain again intercedes: to mediate and delegate amongst the interested parties. So in light of it all, an expandable brain was the only possible way for us to survive as a species. For indeed it has been the cumulative and coordinating tendencies of our multi-functional brain that has allowed us to overcome the superior skills of other creatures; to overcome the weakness of our own physique. Don't you see, by being the jack of all trades, we have learned to not rely *solely* on a single area of strength. Whereas the animals have allowed one or two of their fortes to become so predominant as to crowd out or even replace the other senses; thanks to brain power, none of *our* senses have deteriorated much, and that has enabled us to incorporate them all into the total scheme of being alive."

"Wow! So the caveman was practicing the first portfolio theories before he even saw a wooden nickel."

"A distinct possibility. Moreover, you, by making the middle class analogy, have further reinforced my thinking. That is, any extra-terrestrial that makes it down to earth, or merely journeys into space for that matter, must possess the types of skills and aptitudes that are similar to our own. They, too, shall not be so blessed with all the physical and natural abilities relative to their world. They, too, would have had to scramble and rely on their brainpower to overcome various shortcomings to climb the hierarchy of *their* home planet."

"So your take on alien visitors, sir, is that they are well-rounded, rational beings?"

Charles did not respond directly. "Allow me to simply say this: with the nearest galaxy being a million light years away—a million light years!—it is doubtful that we will ever encounter any being from outer space. That is not to say, however, that they don't exist. Indeed with billions of planets out and about, the mathematics of probability should practically guarantee the existence of alien life; of friends and foes alike, come to that. And, because they exist somewhere, it is in our duty and obligation to ponder and speculate on their character and behavior. My take is: the alien species which are trying to seek us out are *not* the evil, one-track minded monsters of science fiction. Primitive monsters simply lack the wherewithal to go into space in the first place."

I must say that Charles did somehow have a knack for finding the most peculiar angles to defend his theories. For that was about as provocative a thought as any I had heard from him: that space cadets are actually Joe Blows, our middle class-cousins rather than superior beings. Still, as much as I ought to be reassured, I found it hard to believe that aliens could so resemble our own nature. It just seemed so statistically improbable. I mean, our industrial revolution is all but a couple of hundred years old. So whomever we do come in contact with is likely to have marched much further on down the time-line than we have, and therefore, far superior in all ways. I told Charles that for us to comprehend such advanced extraterrestrial beings is like bringing a Medieval monk into the world of today. There's no telling how lost he'd be.

"Not so," Charles said emphatically. "As long as the underlying principles of the space travelers are reasoning based; by that I mean a truly advanced being would know that there exist those who are inferior, who speak a different language. And it is the superior beings' obligation to communicate: to convey and explain themselves to the lower forms."

"You are forgetting one thing, sir. That is, are we advanced enough to understand'em?"

"We are getting there," Charles said. "Despite us still being thousands of years away from our true potential; we may, in the next century, master much of the mental conflicts and ethical dilemmas that we face today. Once we reach that stage, we stand a good chance of cracking all the alien forms of reasoning known in our universe."

"You don't have any definite time projections?"

"I'm afraid it's up to the people. *They* will have to decide the time frame for bringing the thought process up to par with modern realities. For just as political reform follows economic progress, so will technological progress follow mental awareness. As a matter of fact, it is my belief that phase one of the technological revolution is all but over. That is, until our thought process can take a new giant leap, we shall more or less remain in a state of incremental fine-tuning."

"Fine-tuning?"

"Yes. While most modern prophets will continue to predict exponential accelerations in technology, my position is guarded. If the mind is not liberated, technology—even the future of biotech and nanotech—will not be speeding fast forward. Only if we are clear as to what we want and where we stand, can technology then be unleashed to provide it. When such a time does come, it will usher in the second great revolution—one that begins from within. Just as our creations and re-creations of the physical world have so vastly transformed the surface of the earth, so will our understanding of ourselves transform life into more than just living, but an act essential to the *continuing* evolution of our species."

"So until we really evolve mentally, we won't be able to comprehend the higher forms of intelligence?"

"Higher *and* lower. The more we understand ourselves, the more we understand others. Mind you, with every new breakthrough comes the good and the bad, winners as well as losers. Perhaps some fear that with all the advances in science, we'll become too technical. That the life of the 'good old days' will be no more. Perhaps we do not wish it to be upon us all so soon. Perhaps we want to remain living as human beings for as long as we possibly can."

"I'm not sure if I should be scared or sad. I mean, well, isn't it funny that if what you said is true, then the faster we live, the faster we get there. But then what? Like, if we squeeze thousands of years of evolution into a few hundred, then might we not get bored the rest of the way?"

"You are assuming there is a fixed potential out there that, once reached, the game is over; that we can no longer go any further. Yes and no to that. As I mentioned earlier in regard to complexity and chaos, I believe they are mostly subset phenomenas within a multi-leveled hierarchy. For instance, one must be very careful when looking for a perfect unifying equation between the stock market crashes and violent weather patterns. Indeed, it is still my belief that underlying everything is order rather than chaos. It shall be something simple and beautiful, something that comes around in a full circle. That one way or another, the most complex theories of life would re-emerge at the other end as basic truths. That the core of reasoning, just like the laws of the physical world, is universal and accessible to all."

"That's very enlightening, sir. And reassuring. Especially if we can prove it. Can we prove it?"

"Not yet. But we can make a start. Let us take a simple idea—how about idea itself?—the thought process. Now, we all know that a thought can be derived from past thoughts, present observations, and future hopes. Yet what is not so readily apparent to many of us is that the mind has a unique ability to transcend space. Thought, in its purest form, is faster than any physical phenomenon in existence.

True, it takes the sunlight six seconds or so to reach the earth; but in only a split second, the mind can wander from the earth to the sun and back again. True, the galaxy of Andromeda is a million light years away; but once again, our brainwaves can propel us there and back in an instant. Sure, the skeptics will say that it isn't real. But sometimes, the bottom line of reality is to provide a medium to build further realities—similar to a catalyst in a much larger reaction."

"So in the mental sense, you truly believe that we have just as much potential as any *ET* that descends to earth."

"Absolutely. We have within our reach a simple yet extremely powerful energy known as the "speed of thought"—far and away the fastest thing in the universe!"

"Wow, so it's kinda like, less is more...more or less."

That Charles was something else. He was constantly able to push the crucial factors into a corner, then unburden them in such a way as to make his conclusions the only natural progression. And doing it all with the simplest ideas. He certainly lifted my spirit to a higher level. I actually visualized my thought waves shooting through the depth of space—toward infinity. Of course that was just for a fleeting moment, until the brakes of reality set in, the reality that most of us can't concentrate for shit!

"Uncle Charles, you've said some good things here, certain attributes of ours which are god's equal. But what about the bad? What are we doing now that is the most illogical?"

No answer. Either it was too easy a question, or too hard to answer.

"Is it violence and destruction? Hate and worship? Perhaps greed, or just the fact that we want something for nothing."

"You have said it well," Charles said. "In a nutshell, we are still all too human."

"But you just said it's good to be human; that it's good to try and try again."

"In the individual sense, yes; but in the aggregate, it is at times wasteful. By not knowing where we stand, we time and again contradict our own behavior, our own ethics. Did you know that we are the only species that lie to ourselves."

"So when we stop lying to ourselves, the truth will come out?"

"It is my hope that, the more we modernize, the more ways there are to look for the truth. Of course, the liars will become more clever as well, playing on our fears and prolonging their hold on the weak for as long as they can."

"So it might get worse before it gets any better?"

"I am afraid so."

"But just what *is* the truth?"

"Mankind has pondered that for thousands of years. No constant has yet been found."

"Is it the survival of the fittest? Supply and demand? Or is it more Freudian: along the lines of the id, ego and superego?"

Charles just sat there, with a hand on his chin, eyes staring at a head of Jesus in the front of the room, the sole remains of a broken crucifix that predated the French Revolution.

"Are you familiar with Russian roulette?" Charles calmly asked.

"Yup."

"How much would I have to pay you to get you to pull the trigger?"

"One bullet in six?"

"If you like."

"Gee, I don't know. Depends on how badly I needed the money."

"What about a beggar on the street, how much do you think *he* would do it for?"

"I don't know."

"Do you think the price tag would be less than yours?"

"Probably, yes," I said, though I did find myself rubbing my forehead and feeling a bit uneasy with the answer.

"Take a starving child from the Third World, do you think the mother would take a million dollars to end the child's life?"

"No...yes...I mean, I don't know. She might decide to give up her own life for a million."

"Do you think anyone would offer her a million?"

"No."

"How about a hundred thousand? Ten thousand?...Do I hear a thousand?"

"I don't know." I had no idea what Charles was leading to, if anything at all.

"Is it fair to say, then, that one tends to put a higher price on one's *own* head than others might?"

"I guess so."

"But why are they different? *Should* they be different? What does it all say about human life? Or, to go a step further, how should one go about deriving such a price tag, if there is to be one at all?"

"Wow, this is some radical stuff, sir. I can't begin to fathom the difficulties."

"What is so difficult?" Charles said nonchalantly. "You think of a number, I think of a number. If we differ, we try to narrow the difference."

"Yeah, but there are so many variables, some of them unknown."

"Then allow me to ask you this: what would you rather see, an earthquake that destroys billions in property but few lives? Or a neutron bomb that kills thousands yet leaves intact the properties?"

"I'm not sure what to say. I'll tell you this, though: I wouldn't be *completely* honest with myself if I said I would take the earthquake over the bomb any day of the week. I mean, I know that property can be rebuilt, and lives not; but if I have to toil for the rest of my lifetime just to do the rebuilding, then wouldn't I have indirectly sacrificed my own life, my own hopes, for a stranger? Well, I don't know if I can do that. Certainly I wouldn't want that to be forced upon me by society."

"No need to feel guilty, my dear fellow," Charles's tone became more gentle. "Many people feel the way you do, but are unable to bring themselves to admit it. The fact is, in some parts of the world, life is cheap. To view every life as equally sacred is nothing but self-deceit. So the longer we go on deceiving ourselves, the greater the problems will become, until one day, calamity strikes—when humanity's ugliest sides begin to dominate our conscience."

"Not long ago, there was a case of a little kid with leukemia that needed a hundred thou for a bone-marrow transplant. He died when the funds raised were still twenty thousand dollars short. Twenty lousy thousand bucks."

"You should be aware, Mark, that one hundred thousand dollars can go toward the saving of many lives in other parts of the world."

"So is that the ultimate step, to face our own existence?"

"I believe so. Life must not be taken for granted. Not only should we live as if we had to *earn* it, but we should be prepared to make sacrifices. There must be a willingness, on one hand, to give oneself up for the good of others; and a willingness on the other to spread the wealth for the good of all."

"What if sacrificing draws a low turnout?"

"Then it becomes darker and bloodier—resulting in either the disintegration of populations or the disintegration of wealth."

"Lovely prospects both. Any way to not fall into those extremes?"

"Through prevention and reaction," Charles said. "Plainly, we can't prevent everything, as unfortunate events are bound to occur.

Just as plainly, we can't simply react to everything as it happens, that would project weakness and a lack of resolve."

"Still, where do we draw the line? How do we walk that tightrope between moral bankruptcy and financial ruin?"

"The most efficient way is to walk a straight line: helping those who can help themselves. In reality, however, we tend to waver back and forth. One day we are theoretical logicians, the next day we are moral theologians. Of course, the nature of things being as they are, we frequently end up failing on both counts; aggravating the situation to its worst possible scenario."

"So, ideally, when we go out on a limb for humanity, we ought to only go out just enough to satisfy our own needs and wants."

"Ideally, my boy, we ought to do everything we possibly can. But realistically, if a problem goes beyond a certain critical mass, we have to either accept the new realities, or apply force to keep the status quo; to exercise self-preservation."

"Say if the problem before us is over-population, how would you go about solving it?"

"One option is to make some passive adjustments. We could live in smaller quarters, exercise more sharing, and eat a lighter diet. Believe it or not, there are surprising benefits to all of those changes. On the active side, one thing we could do is to continue to build upwards. Why live in a one-story house when the technology is there for mile-high skyscrapers—to live, work, shop, *and* play in!"

"Hey, artificial reality; a virtual model of reality. Lock yourself in a simulated stimulation room in the sky and experience the vast empty space like you've never experienced it before. But where do we get the raw materials for Skyscraper & Company? Can we *de*freeze Siberia? Or flood the Sahara for arable land?"

Charles shook his head and sighed. "Global-warming or a new ice-age, two sure-fire ways to solve the population problem." Then he leaned back, and crossed his arms and legs: "Not to sound flip about it, but over-population, to some, is a misnomer. A condition which they believe will never *ever* happen."

"Sure it will. With all the advancements in medicine, we are sure to live longer and longer. And in denser and denser surroundings."

"I'll grant you that. Nonetheless, density is a relative term; while the earth, at this moment at least, is *not* a shrinking planet."

"I don't get it."

"The only way to *over*-populate is if we go on living forever. As long as people *die*, as long as there *is* death, as long as we remain *mortals*, we can *never* over-populate."

I had the strangest, strangest feeling upon hearing that. So strange I didn't even know how to respond to it. I just sat there, picking my nose. All I could think of was that Star Trek episode where Kirk was alone in a mock Enterprise. And there were these pounding noises from outside the ship which turned out to be the sound of heartbeats from an over-populated planet. But Charles said that that can never happen. That we would have killed each other long before reaching that stage. It was the eeriest feeling. A minute ago it was between life or property. Now, the issues have become density or death.

"Uncle Charles, is a doomsday, all hell's breaking loose kind of predicament the only way to get people to see the light?"

"No, but it's the quickest. And, the riskiest. It says that the only way to rescue humanity is to *humiliate* it first!"

"Wow, that's heavy. Is that the view of an optimist or pessimist?"

"It is the view of someone who says that if we don't all stand up and leap at once, the earth will remain in it's orbit as is." After that quip, Charles's voice turned more sombre. "Allow me to present two concepts: deduction and perception. Briefly, deduction entails the gathering of facts: the weighing of options following the weighing of costs and probabilities. If we don't know the numbers, or disagree on their accuracy, then perception kicks in. The guidelines of which are dependent upon the values of a particular society. If a society views all life as sacred, then it ought to act in ways to promote that belief. Over-*populate* as it may. However, if a society sets mobility and individualism high on the alter, then there could be an alternative set of rules which best reflect such sentiments."

"So it's sort of a scientific democracy in action, based on the balancing of a shared set of principles."

"But it could only work and survive if we are all informed properly and act in a responsible fashion. And lastly—transcending it all—honesty, honesty, and more honesty!"

"That's asking a lot."

"The day we learn how to honestly draw the line, and become able to convince others of the fairness of the line as drawn, will be the day we finally put an end to the counter-productive debates and move singularly into the third millennium."

Uncle Charles, wherever you are, may you find what you are looking for.

ACKNOWLEDGMENTS

My deepest gratitude to Geraldine, without whom this would have been a piece of...garbage.

Much appreciation to Elysha Lenkin, Susan Perlbachs, and Elizabeth Sivers—thanks for keeping me in line!

To Babette, Christine, Florence, Sabine, Valérie, Mathieu, Sébastien and Vincent: *mille merci!* To Catherine Yates and Gordon MacIntosh from across the Channel, *Than'kew*!

Heartfelt thanks to Celeste Harrington, Edgar Bilan, Tom Campbell, and Michael White for their invaluable assistance and guidance.

Thank you all: Deborah, Kim, Michelle, Wendy, Emil, Phil, Rob, Scott, and Stewart. (Can get a *renewal* on my license to steal?)

To Nancy Boensch, my editor and Lloyd Yaneau, my direditor: next time, let's break *all* the rules!

Lastly, this goes out to darling Mother dear and Superdad: Paris is the midpoint between LA and SA!

RON CHURCHILL has, for most of his life, considered himself a New Yorker; though in recent years, he has been splitting his time (and personality) between the left and right hemispheres.

To stay in touch with his friends, the author, from time to time, jots down his thoughts in a newsletter. Naturally, he considers his readers (and critics) close to his heart as well. To be placed on the list, please write to the author at:

Box 899, New York, NY 10023-0899